# CHARLES III AND THE REVIVAL OF SPAIN

## Anthony H. Hull
University of Massachusetts

UNIVERSITY
PRESS OF
AMERICA

## SOURCES AND ACKNOWLEDGMENTS

Two archival funds in Spain provide the basis
for the present work -- the Archivo Histórico
Nacional, Madrid, and the Archivo (General) de
Simancas, Valladolid.  Visits to these funds were
made a few years ago, when a large collection of
microfilm was assembled, then enlarged to regular
size.  Since the handwriting of the period can be
difficult to decipher, much of the material has had
to be transcribed by professional orthographers.  In
both funds, research was confined mostly to folios of
the secretaryship of State (*Estado*).  These folios are
ranged in bundles or *legajos*, arranged by numbers; and
where Charles' letters to Tanucci of Naples are concerned, they are in books or *libros*, arranged by numbers,
and located in the Archivo de Simancas.

Also consulted, in the 1970's, was the Public Record Office, Chancery Lane, London, with its valuable
fund of State and Foreign Office papers, which throw
much light on Anglo-Spanish relations of the eighteenth
century, including the Stanhope-Keene papers.  Also
visited was the Division of Manuscripts at the Library
of Congress, Washington, D.C. where there is an interesting collection of photostatic material taken from the
Archivo General de Indias, Seville, relating among other
things to Spanish relations with Russia.

Further details on these sources can be found in
the bibliography of the present work.

My grateful acknowledgements extend to many people
in the preparation of this book.  Two Spanish scholars
-- Sr. Luis Sánchez Belda, director of the Archivo His-
torico Nacional, Madrid, and Sr. Ricardo Magdaleno Redondo, director of the Archivo de Simancas, Valladolid
-- made me more than welcome in Spain through the labyri-
nths of the nation's rich archival resources.  Signore
Raffaello Causa, superintendent of museums and works of
art in Campania, Italy, was kind enough to furnish me
with much rare data on Queen Maria Amalia of Naples.
Among others may be mentioned Mrs. Antonetta Prigmore
from Mexico, whose invaluable assistance made many a
dull-looking Spanish document come to life; South American specialist John R. Fisher of the University of
Liverpool, England, who leads one of the most advanced

iii

Hispanic history programs in the English-speaking world; Mr. William Wells, keeper of the renowned Burrell Collection near Glasgow, Scotland, who gave me much useful information on Neapolitan artists; and Canon de Zulueta,S.J., who filled me in on the religious aspects of the period. Here in Boston, Massachusetts, the staff of the Kress Library of Business and Economics, Harvard Graduate School of Business Administration, ministered to my every request on economic history; as has also Professor Aaron Jacobs on the faculty of Boston State College. A distinguished language scholar on the faculty of this same college is Dr. John Staulo, who gave me his time unsparingly, and without whose vital help I might well have foundered in foggy patches of Italian print dating from the eighteenth century.

To conclude on a personal note, Dr. Alfred Barnaby Thomas (retired), former professor of Latin American history at the University of Alabama, great teacher and among the foremost scholars in this field, inspired me with the idea of writing this book in the first place. My family -- wife Elizabeth, son Mark, daughter Vivian, and mother Mrs. K. Ormsby Wells -- have made most valuable suggestions to text or photographs. Indeed without all their help and encouragement, this book would not have been written at all.

A.H.
December 1979
Sherborn, Massachusetts

## ILLUSTRATIONS

The writer wishes to express his indebtedness for the courtesy of the following institutions and publishers in allowing the following illustrations to be reproduced.

Charles III, by Anton Mengs       frontispiece
(Museo del Prado, Madrid)

Charles aged eight, by       page 6
Jean Ranc (Museo del Prado)

Charles and Maria Amalia,       page 47
fragment of an imagined family
ensemble, by Louis Michel Van Loo
(Museo del Prado)

The Palace of Caserta (Soprinten-       page 65
denza per i Beni Artistici e
Storici della Campania)

Marchese Tanucci, engraving after       page 82
an unknown artist (Soprintendenza
alle Gallerie della Campania, Museo
di Santo Martino, Naples)

Maria Amalia, by Francesco Liani       page 96
(Soprintendenza alle Gallerie della
Campania, Museo di Capodimonte, Naples)

Conde de Campomanes, artist unknown       page 172
(courtesy of el Fondo de Cultura
Económica, Mexico City)

Conde de Aranda, artist unknown       page 244
(courtesy of el Fondo de Cultura
Económica, Mexico City)

Conde de Floridablanca, engraving       page 276
after Goya (courtesy of el Fondo de
Cultura Económica, Mexico City)

The Royal Palace, Madrid       page 291
(courtesy of Thames and Hudson, London
and Chanticleer Press, New York)

Charles III, by Francisco Goya       page 315
(Ayuntamiento de Madrid)

v

# CONTENTS

SOURCES AND ACKNOWLEDGMENTS                iii

ILLUSTRATIONS                                v

INTRODUCTION                                ix

PROLOGUE                                     1

1  SPANISH BACKGROUND                        7

2  TRIUMPHANT PRINCE OF ITALY               20

3  FAVORED KING OF NAPLES                   48

4  TENSIONS IN THE TWO SICILIES             66

5  STEPS TOWARD CASTILE                     83

6  TROUBLED KING OF SPAIN                   97

7  THE FALL OF THE JESUITS                 124

8  LAND AND THE ENLIGHTENMENT             147

9  STATECRAFT AND REARMAMENT              173

10 CHARLES III AND THE INDIES             196

11 CRISES AND CONSOLIDATION               221

12 THE SHOWDOWN WITH ENGLAND              245

13 FURTHER HORIZONS                       277

14 THE FINAL YEARS                        292

15 VALEDICTION TO A KING                  306

FOOTNOTES TO THE CHAPTERS                 316

BIBLIOGRAPHY                              364

APPENDICES AND MAPS                       381

INDEX                                     390

ABOUT THE AUTHOR                          402

# INTRODUCTION

Of all the enlightened kings in the eighteenth century, Charles III of Spain, perhaps, is the least written about. Yet his importance is all-pervasive. His country was undergoing a remarkable recovery after the war of Spanish Succession, and it was no accident that the powers of Europe did their best to accomodate his parents' wishes that Charles as a young prince, born in 1716, be given an honored place. Thus he became potential heir to Tuscany and actual Duke of Parma. Spain's invasion of Naples and Sicily dispelled any doubts about his country's revived strength, and Charles settled down here to be the best sovereign in modern history Naples ever had.

It is ironic that Spain's victory should have helped to dim his once-famous name, for Naples in the eighteenth century has been singularly passed over by the historian; and as the same rather applies to Spain as well, Charles has been left out on both counts. Moreover, as we look back at the Europe of those times, too often is overlooked the predominant part of the New World as it then existed -- the Spanish America culled in large degree from Mediterranean civilization.

This very diversity helps to explain why Charles is such a neglected figure to begin with. Every inch a Spaniard, he spoke fluent Italian and French, and married a German princess from Saxony, Maria Amalia. As Charles VII of the Two Sicilies and IV in Naples, he left this kingdom in 1759 to become Charles III of Spain, where he now achieved real power. Bereft of his wife whom he was to mourn for the rest of his reign, he devoted himself with zeal to reforming the Western world's largest empire. Yet beyond this point there are difficulties both for himself as well as the writer. Charles certainly helped American Patriots separate from the British empire, for example, but in doing so he was faced with the possibility that the same could happen with his own. A valiant and determined monarch is thus pitted against the tides of history; and here his passion for routine as well as drastic reform -- his passion for trivia and the grand at the same time -- makes him at once an absorbing larger-than-life figure in coming to grips with the enormous tasks confronting

him. But from the writer's standpoint there has to
be some compression on to a smaller canvas so as to
include, within the limitations of space, equally important features of Spain's revival which arose simultaneously on the national scene.

How then should we judge Charles? and what has
been the criteria in selecting his deeds for judgment?
In attempting to meet these questions, due emphasis
has been given to his decisive effects in solving
bitter conflicts -- in the rivalry of classes, of regions, of competing economic forces. Here Charles is
given high marks. Whether in Naples, Spain or Spanish America, he frequently appears after many crises
as the triumphant symbol of popular unity; and this
was largely due to his infectiously moral qualities,
his firmness of purpose,which enforced efficient government on his many disparate kingdoms. In this he
was helped by the currents of enlightenment; for it
was still an age when politics and scholarship blen-
ded (unlike our own middle-class democracies), while
the power of the nobles was slowly merging with that
of the merchants, leaving feudal structures increasingly moribund. In an age of transition -- away from
feudal capitalism towards smaller mercantile capitalism -- it was perhaps this very resolution of conflict in conditions of extensive upheaval wherein
lies his strongest claim to greatness. In a word, he
made absolute monarchy work absolutely. The man has
been judged in the context of his own pre-revolutionary times and has not been found wanting.

In imparting new life to the bureaucracy and
institutions he inherited, in choosing ministers from
wider sections of society, in making government serve
the people including the very poor, Charles emerges
by any standards as an important monarch, helping to
shape the age in which he lived. He truly personifies
the reform spirit of his times. And in bringing into
focus all the contrasting features of Spain over two
hundred years ago, he left this Spain intact, albeit
for a short time only, as a decidedly great power in
Europe and the world.

CHARLES III BY ANTON MENGS

## SOME OF CHARLES' RELATIVES

| | |
|---|---|
| Louis XIV | Charles' Bourbon great grand-father |
| Philip, Duke of Anjou (Philip V of Spain) | his father |
| Isabella Farnese of Parma | his mother |
| Ferdinand VI of Spain | his half-brother |
| Philip, Duke of Parma (Don Philip) | his brother |
| Luis, Cardinal-Archbishop of Toledo | his brother |
| María Ana of Portugal | his favorite sister |
| Philippe Elizabeth, Princess of Beaujolais | his child bride (marriage not consummated) |
| Augustus III of Poland | his father-in-law |
| Maria Amalia of Saxony | his wife |
| Carlos, Prince of Asturias (Charles IV of Spain) | his son & heir |
| Ferdinand IV of Naples | his son |
| Gabriel Antonio | his favorite son |
| María Josefa Cármela | his daughter |
| María Luisa Antonia of Tuscany | his daughter (wife to Arch-duke Leopold, later Emperor) |
| María Luisa of Parma | his daughter-in-law (wife to the Prince of Asturias) |
| Maria Carolina of Naples | his daughter-in-law (wife to Ferdinand IV of Naples) |

See also the genealogical tree at Appendix I

## PROLOGUE

Spain, greatest power in the world during the sixteenth and early seventeenth centuries, had become a sorry sight by Louis XIV's time. Her Hapsburg rulers were increasingly effete, the last of them being Charles II, called *el Hechizado* (the Bewitched) by his own subjects. When he died childless in 1700, Europe was plunged into an international conflict known as the war of Spanish Succession. Here two rival dynasties -- Hapsburg and Bourbon -- strove for mastery over Spain's vast dominions, which included much of Italy, the southern Netherlands, the vast patrimony of the Indies, and the Pacific ocean as far as the Philippines.

The war in question centered on a French Bourbon prince, Philip Duke of Anjou and grandson of the resplendent Louis XIV, to whom both Charles the Bewitched as well as Louis XIV himself had bequeathed their dominions in their wills, thus making possible an eventual union of the Spanish and French crowns. No one had minded the Spanish king making Philip his heir -- that was his privilege -- but the action of Louis in doing the same thing portended the emergence of a superpower dominated by France. This the other countries of Europe refused to allow. They had thus gone to war, opposing Philip and supporting the Austrian Hapsburg prince, Archduke Charles, younger son of the Holy Roman Emperor Leopold, as rival claimant to the Spanish throne. This grand alliance against Louis XIV and his Bourbon protégé Philip included Austria, England, the Netherlands, Portugal, Brandenburg, some smaller German states, and eventually Savoy. Apart from France and the Spanish dominions, only Bavaria supported the Bourbon cause. Philip of Anjou seemed hopelessly outmatched by his rival.

The great victories of the Duke of Marlborough and Prince Eugene of Savoy certainly forestalled French attempts to capture Vienna. In Spain, however, it was a different story. In the central and southern regions there was disenchantment with the Spanish Hapsburgs of the past for undermining Castilian prosperity, and here pro-Bourbon feeling

1

was strong. It is true there was a widespread peasants' revolt in Aragon, Valencia, and Catalonia against French soldiery and feudal overlords; but in an even wider sense a whole range of foreign marauding armies -- Austrian, British, and Dutch, and creating a dangerous situation for an intervening side in any civil war -- hurt the Hapsburg cause more in the long run.[1] There was a growing national feeling that Philip with his capable young wife, María Luisa of Savoy, was preferable to any other foreigner; and though Catholics of both sides would handsomely plunder the churches, it was a double crime when committed by English or Dutch Protestants. Two great victories -- Almansa and Villaviciosa in 1707 and 1710 respectively -- turned the tide in favor of the Bourbons. When shortly afterward the Duke of Marlborough fell from power in London, and the Archduke Charles himself succeeded to the Hapsburg throne in Vienna, the latter's cause in Spain was doomed. With both sides exhausted, the way was clear for the treaty of Utrecht, signed in April 1713.

The Anglo-Austrian team and its allies drove a hard bargain at the peace conference. Philip was recognized by most of the powers as Philip V of Spain, but his throne could never be united with that of France. England received Gibraltar from Spain (captured in 1704), as well as Minorca; and by a concession known as the *Asiento* was entitled to import black slaves into Spanish America for thirty years, and to send one ship a year to the annual trade fair at Porto Bello in Panama. England moreover won recognition from France of its claim to the eastern maritime part of Canada, besides recognition of its Protestant monarchs. Austria meanwhile was busily grabbing the lion's share of Spain's possessions in Europe. These included the southern Netherlands -- henceforth termed Austrian instead of Spanish -- and much of Italy besides, from Milan to Naples, as provided by the treaty of Rastadt the following year; and by 1720, with Savoy given permanent possession of Sardinia, Hapsburg Austria was in firm control of Sicily as well as Naples.

The humiliating peace terms of Utrecht not unnaturally fanned the flames of discontent in Spain. As Philip alternated between intense activity and fits of melancholia, chafing all the while at the Emperor's refusal to fully recognize him, a number of Frenchmen and Italians were busy trying to awaken the country and bring about something of a national recovery. One such person was Anne Marie de la Tremouille, widow of the Duke of Bracciano, whom the Spaniards called Princesa de los Ursinos. Hailing from Paris with much experience in Rome, she had played an important part in arranging Philip's marriage with María Luisa, and the early years of the eighteenth century saw her with Louis XIV's blessing as chief lady-in-waiting at the Spanish court. Her political wisdom considerably influenced the royal couple and she was a great asset to the Bourbon cause. Working in close concert with a number of Frenchmen, Michel Amelot and Jean Orry among them, she succeeded in getting serious reforms under way, and was still the undisputed matriarch of the realm at the time of the treaty of Utrecht.

María Luisa died in February 1714. Princesa de los Ursinos now arranged a second marriage for Philip with the object of gaining as much ascendancy over the new queen as the first one; but in this she badly miscalculated. The new queen in fact was soon to bring about her downfall. Isabel Farnese, born in Naples, 1692, as granddaughter of Duke Ranuccio II and brought up in Parma, was to turn out the most remarkable consort in Spanish history.[2] For forcefulness of will, singularity of purpose, and duplicity in politics she must surely rank among the truly formidable women of the eighteenth century. Of lively disposition, with expressive blue eyes set in a face spoilt by pock-marks but saved by a defiantly large mouth and chin which bespoke her imperious nature, she had a drive and intelligence which made her the real ruler of Spain -- a trend of affairs made easier by her husband's recurring bouts of melancholia. There is little doubt she imparted bright qualities to her offspring, as much as Philip imparted more sober ones, but her maternal possessiveness and dynastic ambitions somewhat narrowed her horizon

in the true statesmanlike sense. Nonetheless
she contributed much to the recovery of Spain,
successfully exploited Spanish nationalism to
her own advantage, and in the same proportion was
as unscrupulous in getting rid of people who stood .
in her way.

One of the ministers she chose was Giulio
Alberoni, whose enthusiastic references to his
sovereign mistress as "that buxom Lombard" considerably overlooked the treachery which lay beneath.
Born in Piacenza the son of a gardener, educated
by Jesuits and subsequently a cardinal, Alberoni
served on the Duke of Vendôme's staff before
visiting Spain in 1711 as an agent of the Duke of
Parma. Here he established a close rapport with
Princesa de los Ursinos. It was largely upon his
suggestion to her that Philip married Isabel
Farnese by proxy at Parma in September 1714; and
the Princess duly met Isabel near Guadalajara in
December of that year. But she was more than
meeting her match. The new Italian queen shared
lively tales with Alberoni, and she soon gave him
her close confidence. Together they schemed
against their common benefactor and the fallen
matriarch Ursinos, found herself banished to Italy.
With minister Jean Orry and others also dismissed
by 1715, the way was now clear for Alberoni and
his queen to enjoy the fruits of power.

But Alberoni's turn was next. For five years
he continued the excellent work of his predecessors
in putting administration and finances on a sound
footing and rearming the country, especially its
navy; but where foreign policy was concerned, his
efforts were, disastrous. He soon fell victim to
the purely dynastic interests of his royal patrons,
who did not hesitate to discard him when things
went wrong; and this occured in the following way.

In 1715 Louis XIV died and was succeeded as
head of state by the Duke of Orleans. As Regent
of France he was entrusted with the care and
education of the deceased king's great grandson,
Louis XV. Philip V of Spain, meanwhile, was bent
on claiming the French throne upon the expected
death of young Louis XV, while Isabel was bent

4

on claiming Italian thrones for her male offspring at the expense of the Austrians. It was not surprising that such policies aroused the antagonism of Europe. Alberoni in fact soon found himself pitted against France, Austria, and England, not to mention the Netherlands and Savoy. The seizure of the Spanish inquisitor in Milan by the Austrians in 1717 forced the issue before Alberoni was truly ready; and although he had the brief satisfaction of seeing Sardinia and Sicily overrun by Spanish troops, the odds were against ultimate success. England and France swiftly guaranteed each other's dynasty, and they subsequently attacked the coast of Spain itself. With a strong British fleet buttressing the Austrians in Italy, moreover, and decisively defeating the renascent Spanish navy off Sicily, Alberoni's hopes were dashed. The result was the treaty of The Hague in February 1720, imposed by the victorious powers. Having already formed a Quadruple Alliance to include the Dutch, they forcefully insisted on Alberoni's dismissal: and the cardinal was whisked out of Spain without Isabel lifting a finger to help him. The downfall he had wreaked on others thus came full circle, though he lived many years as a papal legate before his death in Piacenza thirty-two years later.

By the treaty's terms, Spanish forces had to evacuate Sardinia and Sicily which now passed respectively to Savoy and Austria, with Philip re-nouncing his claims to the French throne. The Hapsburg empire thus became paramount in all of southern Italy. But though Spain's new baptism of fire ended in defeat, in a sense it was rather the beginning of a victory, namely, recognition by Europe that Spain counted once more among its councils, and that anxious to upset the treaty of Utrecht she could be bought off by some degree of appeasement. Thus Austria at last recognized the Bourbons in Spain, while one of the treaty's clauses stipulated that the firstborn of Philip and Isabel could become heir to the duchies of Parma, Piacenza, as well as Tuscany, in the event of no male heirs succeeding to these former fiefdoms of the Holy Roman Empire. Isabel in particular had come one step nearer to her objective of

5

installing her sons on Italian thrones.  The
country's ambitions also included winning back
Gibraltar and Minorca from England and preventing
foreigners from intruding into Spanish America,
for which purpose it was essential to become
economically stronger at home.

All of these aims involved a young prince
from the day of his birth, and they concerned him
intimately for the rest of his life.  His name was
Don Carlos, firstborn of Philip and Isabel, the
future Duke of Parma, King of Naples, and finally
King of Spain -- the Charles III who was[3] to do so
much to restore his country's greatness.

Charles aged eight, by Jean Ranc

# CHAPTER ONE

## SPANISH BACKGROUND

Charles was born in the old Alcázar palace of Madrid during the early morning hours on January 20, 1716.[1] His mother, Isabel Farnese of Parma, was the first queen in many a year to play a decisive role in Spanish affairs, while his father Philip V, an able if erratic Frenchman and only recently widowed, welcomed the glowing companionship of his new wife. Philip had won his position in his adopted country after many trials of endurance, and now he could afford to relax in unchallenged splendor. Both of them were to bring benefits to Spain, whose prestige had recently sunk to a low ebb; indeed their differing backgrounds, Italian and French, were fortunate for the country in producing Charles, whose destiny it was to carry out reforms with even greater effect.

The regal infant was small and ugly; but his parents were delighted by his birth, the father because his strong wife relieved his inherent neurosis by giving him an addition to the family, the mother beause here was her firstborn who could challenge her husband's earlier offspring. He was thus an object of special favor from the start. Though none could have guessed how bright was to be his star, at least through his veins ran the blood of his ancestors Louis XIV and María Teresa (daughter of Philip IV of Spain); while his maternal grandmother was Dorothea Sophia of Neuburg, now living in Parma and with whom Isabel kept in close touch.[2]

It was a Neuburg relative, María Ana, widow of the last Spanish Hapsburg, together with the Farnese Duke of Parma, who were named godparents at Charles' christening. This took place in the monastery of San Jeronimo, Madrid, at which Cardinal de Borja, Patriarch of the Indies, proudly officiated. Returned to the Alcázar, the infant was assigned the usual multitude of nurses, washerwomen, and palace staff, all of whom received strict instructions to give the child the greatest possible care. Isabel was taking no chances. Though his survival was unsure, the fates were to smile upon this delicate charge who as time went on was destined to draw ever closer to the Spanish throne. His half-brothers in fact -- Felipe, Luis, and Fernando, sons by Philip's first wife María Luisa -- each showed signs of ailing; and as their line declined, the Farnese offspring grew steadily in importance, and Isabel did not hide her elation at her own fertility.

In all came six surviving children.[3] The infanta María Ana was born in 1718. Charles was especially fond of her, calling her by the nickname of dear 'Marianina'. And there was Felipe, born two years later, to become one day the duke of Parma, with whose existence Charles was also very pleased because here was a real brother who could offset the condescending attitude shown him by his half-brothers, Fernando in particular. Relations here never grew very friendly, for Charles to these senior princes was always the intruder, favored by their bossy stepmother; and as will be shown later, Fernando was to give full vent to his feelings by confining Isabel to a palatial prison soon after he was in power.

Charles spent much of his early youth at Valsaín, a favorite resort of his father in the Sierra de Guadarrama region. Nearby at La Granja, Philip commissioned the building of the great palace of San Ildefonso, its gardens laid out in the grand manner; and though on a smaller scale than Versailles it counted among the most sumptuous of its kind in Europe. Other places which Charles was soon to learn about included the famed Escorial of San Lorenzo lying to the north of Madrid, and Aranjuez lying to the south. In the capital itself, the most familiar to Charles was the old Alcázar, his birthplace; but he also knew the Buen Retiro (built by Conde de Olivares in 1632 and destroyed in the French invasion of 1808), besides the smaller Casa de Villa and Casa de Garnica, the latter near the present Opera House. The court rotated its visits to these places according to season -- too long a stay in one residence was irksome to the royal couple -- but this did not mean that the children automatically shared this privilege. Denied the luxury of frequent change, they languished for long periods in the airless atmosphere of the hugh granite buildings, often isolated from one

another to prevent their catching disease and
tending to suffer from precisely the opposite.
Smallpox was the most feared one, but tuberculosis,
vaguely defined as 'fevers' inflicted a heavy toll;
and in the Buen Retiro where the elder Felipe was
confined, it was probably tuberculosis that carried
him off as a young man in 1722.

On this account the parents took special pre-
cautions with the children who remained. Though
Charles' diminutive physique reflected his under-
weight as an infant, this concealed a wiry, hardy,
constitution and he was soon to show keenness for
outdoor life. With Marquesa de Monte Hermoso on
hand as his governess meanwhile, it was the Frenchman
Joseph Arnaud who was given the task of his formal
education. Already at Valsaín Charles had penned
his first letters to his parents at the age of four.
In his capacity as writing-master, Arnaud ensured
that the young prince shaped his capital letters correctly, insisting that the developing cursive script
be given the right slant along the carefully-ruled
paper. Father Ignacio Laubrusel, his religious tutor,
instructed him in the sacred history of the church,
and he was soon taught secular chronology, geography,
as well as military tactics using wooden soldiers.

In the early 1720's his parents ordered that
the prince be handed over to an exclusively male staff.
His new tutors included Francisco de Aguirre (Monte
Hermoso's son), while Francesco Buoncore became his
chief physician and who remained with him for many
years. He was given an entourage of sixteen gentlemen-
in-waiting; but their strict rules of etiquette were
irksome to him, not to mention the stiff lessons he
received at the hands of yet another tutor, the Duke
of San Pedro, and he felt most at home when he could
talk freely with his sisters, brothers, or domestics.
With these he spoke unsullied Spanish, albeit with
a Madrid accent; but out of deference he would
address his father in French on formal occasions.
His mother had taught him Italian as well, which he
later understood in its many dialects -- Florentine,
Lombard, and Neapolitan. Charles in fact developed
a good grasp of languages, and his feeling for
the apt phrase was later to go down well in the

cosmopolitan atmosphere of eighteenth-century
Europe.  Yet perhaps his love of being left alone
with his thoughts explains why this boy of tender
years could so obediently pose for his portrait, his
French painter Jean Ranc working with painstaking
care upon the graceful figure, the princely sleeves
as one hand rested upon a learned book of botany,
the other holding up two jasmin flowers with delicate
poise, a parrot nodding its approval in the corner.[4]

Now hearing matins in the palace chapel of the
Alcázar or watching the Corpus Christi procession
from his candled balcony, the sky aflame with fireworks
from the courtyard of the Casa de Villa, Charles
grew accustomed to the slow-moving cycle of events.
Yet he missed his parents whenever he was alone at
the capital or at Valsaín.  He was thrilled on the
great occasion when he would hear his father give
prayers of thanks for the safe arrival of the Spanish
treasure fleet from America.  Comprising about a
dozen vessels, this huge cargo would contain bullion
worth ten million pesos or more, as well as products
of all shapes and sizes -- fruits, grain, cocoa,
sugar, indigo, herbs, balsam, cotton, tobacco,
tusks, leather, brazil-wood, filigree and copper.
Of the vast bullion which included precious stones,
the royal one-fifth or *quinto real* went to the king, and
thus there was rejoicing.[5]  But perhaps the first
inkling that this exterior world was breaking into
his childhood came in 1721 when at the delicate age
of five, shortly after attending the saint's-day
festivities of his sister María Ana in the Escorial,
Charles was informed that she was to be given special
respect as the future 'most Christian Queen'.  In
other words, she was to become the consort of Louis
XV, engagement to whom resulted from the treaty of
The Hague.  With the French envoy solemnly decorated
with the order of the Golden Fleece, it seemed to
Charles as if the adult world was deliberately scheming to take away his most cherished sister.

But this was only the beginning.  Other marriages were in the making.  Early in 1722 his half-
brother Luis, an ailing boy of fourteen, took as his
bride the thirteen-year old Louise Elizabeth (Princess
of Montpensier), daughter of Philip, Duke of
Orleans and Regent of France.  Whatever emotions

he now felt, Charles was soon told.his turn was next. His bride-to-be was Philippe Elizabeth (Princess of Beaujolais) who was yet another of the Regent's daughters; and having duly arrived in Spain by January 1723 she was formally presented to Charles the following month. A girl aged nine, his senior by two years, she seemed a poor substitute for his cherished sister, and did he but know it his lack of warm feeling typified in minuscule form the lack of cordiality recurring between the French and Spanish courts. The new princesses, it was hoped, would bring harmony between the two nations, but this hope was forlorn. Though the Regent of France and Philip V of Spain had arranged these matches, there was always the ambition on the latter's part that he might soon inherit the French throne in the default of heirs (Louis XV was not expected to live), in which event Philip could vacate the Spanish kingdom, leaving it to an heir of his own. It was an ambition heightened by the traditional contempt with which a Bourbon regarded a member of the Orleans branch of the family. The Regent's wife, moreover, was none other than Françoise Marie de Blois, daughter of Madame de Montespan who had been Louis XIV's mistress. In the view of Philip and his court, such lapses of decorum were amply reflected in the dissolute behavior of young Louise Elizabeth, and Spaniards with their tight rules of etiquette were shocked when she appeared half-naked on the Buen Retiro stairs or masqueraded with her friends as robbers invading the palace grounds.

The fall of the Regent himself in 1723 gave Philip some hope to his French ambitions; but these were countered when Louis XV was declared of age by the new government under the Duke of Bourbon. The Spanish government moreover was having problems of its own. Philip increasingly relapsed into bouts of neurosis, and his habit of eating voluminously made questions of state extremely difficult to resolve. In the palace at La Granja his neurosis became paranoic when objects and notions became inverted in his mind at strange intervals. Thus

the sun he regarded as the moon and vice versa, so
that the court had to retire at daybreak with
curtains drawn and candles lit -- a farce which
lasted until dusk, when the court would then rise
by the light of the moon.  In this insane topsy-
turvy world, Philip made matters worse by displaying
an acute religious mania.  Casting off his robes of
state, he had his son Luis, Prince of Asturias
(rough equivalent of the British title Prince of
Wales denoting heir-apparent to the throne), made
ready for the heavy task.  Luis duly assumed the
reins of government early in 1724 following his
father's abdication, and speculation arose, never
totally proved, that Philip was putting all this on
and arranging this transfer of power in the hope of
gaining the French throne upon the expected death of
Louis XV.  Whatever the facts, things turned out
differently.  Louis XV survived, while Luis died in
August of this year, thus creating the conditions
for Philip's return to the Spanish throne. This was
formally proclaimed in the fall of 1724 by the
council of Castile, the king's chief executive
authority, with Fernando as the new heir conferred
the title of Prince of Asturias.  It was a trying
time especially for Isabel, whose shrewish ways were
scarcely tamed by pregnancy and other royal events;
while she had to be constantly at the beck and call
of both Philip and the state.

What Charles thought of all this is impossible
to say; but the upheavals in his family's affairs
certainly had a happy ending, namely, the return of
his favorite sister María Ana from France.  Louise
Elizabeth, now a widowed princess at the age of
fifteen, had so disgusted the Spanish by her conduct
that even the French envoy, Marshal de Tessé, found
it difficult to defend her.  Inevitably Franco-
Spanish relations worsened, and it was the Duke of
Bourbon who brought matters to a head.  Perceiving
Philip's French ambitions and anxious to secure a
royal heir as soon as possible, he had the seven-
year old María Ana returned to Spain while Louis XV,
already in his teens and understandably impatient,
became engaged to a more mature bride from Poland.
Though María Ana brought back a considerable sum
as a gift from her ex-suitor at Versailles, the

Spanish court was furious, and Philip responded by
having both the Orleans princesses, Louise and
Philippe, returned to France. Meanwhile Charles was
overjoyed that his beloved sister was with him
again.

But soon the threat of another bride hung over
him like the sword of Damocles. The moment was ripe
for any opportunist to exploit this rift in Franco-
Spanish relations; and such a man was Baron Jan
Willem Ripperdá, of Levantine origin, who as former
envoy of the Netherlands in Spain had been made director of a cloth factory by Alberoni before quickly
rising in the royal favor. A clever financier with
many contacts in Europe, he had juggled with Spanish
currency and revalued its gold, ostensibly to stop
specie leaving the country.[6] In the realm of diplomacy his bid for posterity was to try to forge a
Spanish-Austrian alliance against England and France.
He proposed to Philip V and the Hapsburg Emperor
that the young Charles and his brother Felipe marry
the Emperor's daughters -- a ploy that he marred by
exaggerating to both monarchs that each was in favor
of these proposals. The secret treaty of Vienna in
April 1725 which climaxed these overtures came
eventually to nothing, beyond a futile foray with
England and France. Ripperdá's gamble had failed to
come off and he was dismissed the following year.
Escaping from prison in Segovia, he reached Portugal,
then England and Holland, his extradition demanded
by governments everywhere as a man in possession of
too many secrets. Ripperdá finished his colorful
days in Morocco where he became the chief minister,
scheming to the end as the favorite of the Sultan's
wife, his principles as mercurial as his religion.

Once again the young Charles had escaped the
yoke of future matrimony -- this time with Maria
Theresa of Austria, one of the Emperor's daughters
whom Ripperdá had marked down for him. There was
little chance in any case for a close Spanish-
Austrian rapprochement. Memories of the war of
Spanish Succession when the present Emperor Charles VI
had been vying with Philip to win his throne, were
still too bitter on both sides. Indeed it seemed
as if Spain's ambitions in Italy at Austrian expense

were receding further than ever, and that Philip and Isabel were getting nowhere in their common plan to upset past treaties unfavorable to their country. It was true that Charles had been recognized as heir to Tuscany by the treaty of The Hague, in the event of no male heirs; and four years later in 1724, its childless Archduke, John Gaston (Giovanni Gastone), last of the Medici, formally confirmed Charles' investiture rights with Austrian support. Gaston, however, was proving stubbornly desirous to continue living. This same treaty had also made Charles heir to Parma; but here its new duke, Antonio Farnese (Isabel's brother), took a young bride shortly after his accession in 1727 in the person of Enrichetta Modena of the distinguished house of d'Este. This seemed to portend a dynasty which would block the chances for Charles, and any promise of fertility on Enrichetta's part would certainly draw scant congratulations from her sister-in-law in Madrid. Though Isabel could not know it however, luck was to desert Enrichetta in the years ahead, and the treaty of The Hague did ultimately contain true pointers to the prince's destiny.

Charles meanwhile, now approaching his teens, was studious, meditative, and obedient. He was physically alert, and he gave such a good showing at the many hunts approved by his father that he was soon allowed to attend the court season at the Pardo palace in the northern suburbs of the capital, or Philip's favorite resort of San Ildefonso. Most pleasing to Charles personally, as he watched the bullfights at the Plaza Mayor in Madrid or went through the stations of the cross, was the thought of the renewed companionship with his favorite sister María Ana, lately returned from France. No more dull days with Philippe Elizabeth in the Buen Retiro, or thoughts of death when Luis lay dying in the Casa de Garnica. He was glad to be free and unattached. But now a cruel wrench was to take María Ana away from him once more, this time from his childhood permanently. For in 1728 she was betrothed to Prince Joseph of Brazil, heir to the Portuguese throne, at the same time as Fernando the

Spanish heir was to marry the daughter of King
John of Portugal.

To sanctify the occasion, the Spanish court
in January 1729 moved to Badajoz in Extremadura to
meet the Portuguese party which arrived at Elvas.
Now in his thirteenth year, Charles was impatient
to travel and he was taken along with his father.
Half way across the bridge spanning the Caya river
where a canopy had been raised for the occasion,
Philip V and John V embraced each other as they
prepared to hand over their respective daughters.
Charles bade farewell to María Ana, consort-to-be
of the fourteen-year old Joseph, whom he was not
to see again for close on fifty years. From the
Portuguese side Barbara of Braganza, a girl of
eighteen and two years older than Fernando, was
now to be honored as the new Princess of Asturias
and the future queen of Spain. As promisingly
robust as Isabel herself, she was yet destined not
to have any children, and the barrenness of the
couple was to have important consequences for
Charles, who was thereby to move closer to the
Spanish throne. As he sailed along the Guadalquivir river in a gondola towards Seville,
little could he guess the true significance of the
ceremonies he had just witnessed. Indeed all
these events -- the Italian arrangements, the
death of Luis, and now the Portuguese marriage
were combining to mark the day when Charles would
return in triumph to his native country as its
king.

Though by education he was still unprepared
for such a destiny -- his grounding in the written
word hardly extended beyond his fondness for books
and keeping a printing-press -- he did love the
diligence of simple manual work, and this helped
him to shape his thoughts constructively. As the
youth grew more conscious of his station in life,
he became inquisitive about the meaning of monarchy
and the path it ought to follow. On more than one
occasion he showed pique whenever his countrymen's
faults were criticized. He once read some highly
unflattering comments about Spaniards made by the

German friar, Johann Zahn. These had been quoted in the second volume of the *Teatro crítico universal* by that illustrious Benedictine, Jeronimo Feijóo. Spainards according to Zahn, who was comparing them with other peoples in Europe, were "unsightly and slow-witted, dull in attire, austere yet fussy at table, devils for beauty, talkative but secretive, versed in theology and religion yet deceitful, ostentatious in bearing arms, domineering over wives and domestics, and though generous in death, extremely susceptible to all kinds of disease while alive".[7] Charles was furious and demanded that these comments be immediately expunged from the book and burnt. It was an understandably youthful outburst, which Feijóo handled by letting him know through his tutor Aguirre that Zahn's comments only showed how inaccurate he really was. But the prince's sense of outrage, it was noted afterwards, was not matched by his general expression and he soon recovered his composure.

Feijóo's motive in coming to Madrid in the first place during 1728 was to get on the right side of the Bourbons. He knew full well there would be objections if any comments unfavorable to Spain appeared in his writings. Yet a fruitful result of his visit was to get to know the prince, then a boy of twelve, with whom a lifelong cordiality was established. As one of the great thinkers of the eighteenth century, this erudite monk from Galicia may be regarded as the pioneer of the Spanish enlightenment; and his emphasis on the need for promoting experimental science, amassing weight of evidence in determining truth, and purging the church of superstitious practice through rational doubt had some effect on Charles' view of monarchy. It was the role of kings, after all, to fulfill the state's covenant with the church as much as God's covenant with man. Essentially conservative, both men shared a patriotic love of Spain and a desire to see their country catch up intellecually with the rest of Europe. Noting that Prince Charles aimed to be called 'The Wise', Feijóo was to dedicate the fourth volume of his *Teatro* to him in November 1730, and likewise the fifth volume of his *Cartas eruditas y curiosas* completed nearly thirty years

later.  Here he recalled the brief interview he
had with Charles back in 1728, who had done so
much to help him realize his high ideals.[8]  Yet beneath all the flattery lay a deep sincerity which
was mutually felt between prince and subject.

Much of Charles' patriotism stemmed from his
enigmatic father, who vacillating between action
and lassitude at least had exciting tales to tell
about his wartime experiences, and the son sought
to cast himself in his father's image.  As for his
mother -- the capricious 'termagant of Spain' --
she continued to display a spirited drive in
matters of state, so that in a peculiar way the
very contradictions in the royal couple fitted
them to the national scene, bringing welcome color
to the life of society.  As they typified a newer
mode of monarchy inherited from France, so they
promoted in Charles' person the idea of the perfect
prince.  In a cultural sense too they wrought
effect upon the son, as they strove to evoke a
less stultifying climate in which both lords and
learned men could thrive in the latest eighteenth-
century manner; and they can be credited with the
founding of the National Library in Madrid, the
royal Academy of History, a Seminary of Nobles,
and a host of societies and schools.  Philip's
overfondness for palaces was complemented by his
love of music -- his patronage of the singer Carlo
Broschi (Farinelli) is a case in point, with whom
daughter-in-law Barbara was to sing duets --
though where Charles was concerned, the noise of
the chase was far more his idea of harmony.  Yet
father and son had much in common.  Traditional in
religion, Philip retained as his confessor such a
figure as Guillermo Clarke, Jesuit rector of the
Scottish College in Madrid.[9]  At the same time he
encouraged his son's friendship with Feijóo,
anticipating the age when Spanish scholarship was
to give ground to more secular approaches.

Whatever Philip's faults, the crown did
advance in prestige during his reign, and it
recovered many seignorial rights forfeited in days
gone by.  For Philip's aim was to centralize the

monarchy and make it strong. To this end the
influence of the grandees was curbed at cabinet
level, especially among pro-Hapsburg sympathizers
in the war of Succession, and it was now the important
council of Castile, surviving government reorganization,
which became a rallying-ground for the new Bourbon
nobility.[10] In other aspects of reorganization,
intendants based on French models were given sweeping
powers over the provinces. Here traditional semi-
autonomous privileges such as those in Aragon and
Valencia were removed in 1707, the laws being largely
incorporated into those of Castile. The number of
regional courts of litigation known as *audiencias* was
increased from the twelve then existing, and many
of them were now under a captain-general appointed
by the crown. This appointive principle extended
down the line of command, down to crown agents and
even mayors of cities, unless any of these could
qualify as truly feudal patrimonies. In an age of
elitism, patronage, and sale of office, Philip's government could only rely on the new bureaucracy to
enforce its will, but a compensating advantage in
exchange for all the privileges given its officials
was a greater loyalty and efficiency in enforcing the
laws.

While attempts to standardize taxes were
largely unavailing because of the resistance of
vested interests, some headway was made in the more
prosperous parts of Spain -- in the Basque lands,
Aragon, Catalonia and Valencia.[11] In the latter
province, for example, a single comprehensive tax
instead of multiple sales taxes helped to increase
textile looms sevenfold in the early 1720's, as
extra revenue was garnered. To help poorer Castile,
by contrast, royal factories were started with government funds. Elsewhere, protective duties for new
industries, reduction of internal customs barriers,
and the curbing of corruption at the ports created
the conditions for some stability in Philip's reign,
which lasted beyond his lifetime.

Aiding him in these tasks were able men like
Bergyck and Macanaz before Isabel and her Italian
faction took power in 1715, but the work of reform

continued thereafter. Foremost was the Italian-born Galician José Patiño, who after serving in Catalonia was promoted to intendant-general of the navy and president of the Board of Trade in Seville. Subsequently state treasurer as well as secretary of the Indies, he ended up by becoming Philip's chief minister. Between 1715 and his death in 1736, national revenues increased from 140 million reales to over 200 million (those from the Indies climbing from about 30 million annually), all of which was a considerable gain, though weakened by the proverbial increase in public expenditures. These grew from 250 million reales to nearly 340 over the same period, leaving Patiño with an irritating deficit which would not have been so great if Philip's extravagance and wars had not intervened.[12] Architect, like Alberoni, of his country's revived naval power, Patiño planned the successful Spanish capture of Oran in 1732 and played no small part in organizing the invasion of Italy the following year.

Philip's world was contradictory in character -- immense in its diversity, restless but tradition-bound, rich and poor at the same time. Institutions were still sound, even if slow-moving. But with growing political strength, Spain could at least show to Europe that she was no longer so decadent as other powers were wont to believe, and whose charges of backwardness often flung at her were sometimes made to cover up their own. True, Spain's prowess in diplomatic affairs was rather running ahead of her economic capacity to maintain a superpower role; but the nation was going through a period which, though not another golden century, at least showed promise of becoming a silver one. Perhaps the young Charles had already divined the truth about his country, that Spain was striving to reverse her decline and now scarcely behind some other great powers of the day. She still had a huge empire and a sizeable army and fleet to defend it. Unknown to Philip and Isabel, their greatest gift to this empire was probably Charles himself, but not before he had crossed many waters first.

# CHAPTER TWO

## TRIUMPHANT PRINCE OF ITALY

In the summer of 1731, Charles was told the
exciting news that he was going to Parma in Italy
as its new duke.  His feelings were tinged with
apprehension.  But there was the consoling thought
that his mother came from Parma, forging a link
with his future realm.  Ironically, it was precisely
his mother who was to cause many of his troubles,
involving him directly with the wars of Polish and
Austrian Successions which were soon to engulf the
continent.

Lengthy rounds of discussion brought about
this move.  Isabel's ambition on behalf of her two
sons, Charles and Felipe, had been straining the
diplomacy of Europe to avoid a war.  Her aim was
to secure Parma for Charles, along with Tuscany,
leaving to the younger Felipe whatever ducal
fiefdoms she could carve out for him by fair means
or foul.  But with a useless war against England
and France to face since 1727, besides the coolness
of the Austrian Emperor to Spanish pretensions in
Italy, the odds seemed against success.  Yet Sir
Robert Walpole, the British prime minister, and
Cardinal André de Fleury, his opposite number in
France, were both peace-loving men and disposed to
amicable bargaining.  By the treaty of Seville,
signed in November 1729 between England, France,
the Netherlands, and Spain, Charles was recognized
as heir to the duchies of Parma and Piacenza, as
well as Tuscany, in exchange for Spain giving up
her claim on the other parties, including Gibraltar.[1]
Now it only remained for Austria to agree and the
matter could be clinched once and for all.

On January 20, 1731, Charles's fifteenth birthday, news was given to the hushed court at Seville
that Isabel's brother Antonio Farnese had died,
leaving the ducal throne of Parma vacant.  Despite
all the grief, this was a stroke of fortune, for
here was a breach in the wall of Italy, and Austrian

acceptance was now more urgent than ever.  The
Spanish envoy to Vienna, the (second) Duke of
Berwick and Liria, had audiences with Emperor
Charles VI, in which he was reinforced by British,
French, and Dutch support.  England had little
objection to Spanish claims in Italy because of
the accord at Seville; France, reluctant to face a
rival Bourbon branch in Italy, at least had a new
Dauphin in 1729 which weakened Philip V's claims
to the French throne; while the Netherlands were
anxious for Anglo-French support in ending the
Austrian-backed Ostend company which threatened
Dutch interests.

Faced by this concerted force, the Emperor
could now bargain for his main objective -- recognition of the Pragmatic Sanction, that is, the
eventual succession to the Hapsburg throne of his
daughter Maria Theresa in the event of no male
heir, and to the exclusion of any other prince who
might divide the patrimony of the Hapsburgs.  Most
of the interested powers were willing to accept
the idea of a female sovereign.  Accordingly a
(second) treaty of Vienna was signed in 1731
between Austria, England, the Netherlands, and
Spain.  By its terms, in exchange for acceptance
of the Pragmatic Sanction, the Emperor agreed to:
1) terminate any marriage alliance with Spain,
thereby pleasing the English and French who did
not want to see the balance of power possibly
disturbed; 2) abolish the Ostend company, which
pleased the Dutch; and 3) recognize Charles not
only as Duke of Parma and Piacenza, but also as
heir to Tuscany.  A subsequent secret clause
stipulated that unless the Grand Duke of Tuscany,
John Gaston, consented within two months to the
introduction of Spanish troops there, then the
Emperor would not oppose what Spain and England
had agreed to -- i.e., intervene by force to make
Tuscany a virtual Spanish dependency.[2]  The major
parties thus had good cause to be satisfied for
the time being.

One exception was the unlucky Duchess of Parma,
whom her late husband had apparently left pregnant.

Enrichetta, Isabel's widowed sister-in-law and
now abandoned by the powers of Europe, could not
produce the rumored heir to the Duchy, which suggests
fabrication in order to preserve her position.
Her natural resentment of the treaty grew even
more at being excluded from the governing council
which was to administer Parma until Charles'
arrival. Isabel had little regard for mere sisters-
in-law when it came to securing an inheritance for
her firstborn son. To make matters worse, Enrichetta
was shunned by her own mother-in-law, Dorothea of
Neuburg, dowager duchess and ad interim regent of
the realm, for whom was now reserved the place of
honor at the council. This distinguished matriarch --
Isabel's mother and Charles' grandmother -- was to
play an important part in preparing Parma for the
prince's arrival. As for John Gaston, childless
Grand Duke of Tuscany and last of the Medici, he
was too old to care very much what was going on
around him so long as he was left alone; and he
agreed at Florence to recognize Charles as heir
to his dominions -- a fact which José Patiño, Isabel's
chief minister, joyfully reported to the queen at
Seville.

By October 1731, preparations for Charles'
journey were completed. These included the provision of escorts, and a considerable baggage-
train containing the prince's huge chests of money
and personal effects. Taking a sorrowful leave of
his family at which Philip V presented him with a
gift of Louis XIV's sword, Charles set out from
Seville; and proceeding by way of Villarobledo,
Almansa, and Valencia reached Barcelona towards
the end of November.[3] Here he was greeted by the
captain-general of the region, Marqués de Verbom,
to the thunder of traditional cannon. After a
grand reception in which he inspected the historic
fort of Montjuich, and urged to hasten through
being delayed already by too many hunting-bouts
arranged in his honor, he was soon at the French
frontier. Following the coast he reached Antibes,
the port of embarkation for Leghorn, where he
found time to send word of thanks to Louis XV for
providing troops from the Queen Marie Lesczinski

regiment.

The Spanish government, meanwhile, anxious
to hasten the evacuation of Parma and Tuscany by
Austrian troops, had ordered the occupation of
Leghorn in advance of Charles' arrival, with the
aid of a British squadron. Traditional enemies as
Spain and England were, the two countries were
pursuing the unusual course of acting together at
this time in implementing the treaty of Vienna --
Spain in order to secure British naval support for
her dynastic aims in Italy, England in order to
win Spanish acceptance of her possession of Gibraltar
and new trade foothold in the Indies which had
been provided by the Asiento privilege of 1713.
Of England's new status in these fields, we shall
hear a great deal more later.

At this stage, Charles was fairly Anglophile
in outlook. He well remembered talking with
Benjamin Keene, British envoy in Seville, though
Charles' knowledge about England was limited. It
was Feijóo with his monumental *Teatro crítico universal*
who first informed the Spanish reading public of
the experimental methods English thinkers were
advancing, but this made little impact on him at
the time. Charles, however, was not alone in his
ignorance. English books read in Europe were
often in bad French translation -- 'English thought
through a French pen' as Feijóo put it -- while
Voltaire's genuine accounts of his British experience
were barely yet in print. The reverse of course
was true in regard to knowledge about Spain, where
the works of Martín Sarmiento, for example, along
with Feijóo's own, were scarcely read outside the
peninsula.[4] Charles, then, was a prince whose
education was about on the same level as any
other's, and was only vaguely aware of England's
growing importance.

Yet the naval help he was now receiving and
his own quest for orderly enlightened government
instilled in him at least a respect for this
country. He probably had fond memories of the few
Britons he had met in Madrid, notably the Jesuits

23

from the Scottish College, with perhaps a handful
of veterans from the war of Spanish Succession.
To him there were two Englands -- one of peace and
friendship under Walpole on behalf of a Protestant
Hanoverian dynasty, the other also wooing Spanish
friendship on behalf of the Old Pretender, James
Francis Stuart, who had been dispossessed of his
rightful Catholic heritage through the overthrow of
his father, King James II in 1688.  This contradiction -- a Protestant England of growing commerce
and a Catholic one of dynastic legitimacy and intrigue -- must have seemed curious to Charles, who
no doubt thought that in God's good time the country
would revert to its former Stuart rulers.  It was a
contradiction that was well reflected in the visit
he had made to the battlefield of Almansa during his
recent journey across Spain.  Here he would remember
being told as a boy not to hate the English because
so many brave Jacobite supporters had sided with the
Bourbon cause, bravest of whom was James II's
natural son, the Duke of Berwick, victor of Almansa
itself.  And by a strange turn of fate, it was the
Old Pretender's son, Charles Edward Stuart -- the
ill-fated Bonnie Prince Charlie -- who was to be by
his side at the siege of Gaeta during Spain's coming
invasion of Naples.

At Antibes, meanwhile, on December 22, 1731,
Charles stepped aboard the little vessel belonging
to a Spanish fleet of twenty-five ships, reinforced
by a British escorting squadron.  He was accompanied
by his tutor and majordomo, Conde de Santisteban,
and his Franciscan confessor, Father José Bolaños,
both indispensable aides in the treacherous waters
of the Ligurian sea.  Spanish ships in the Mediterranean were usually of the small three-masted type
known as xebecs, while galley-ships were still
employed as pilots, though their use was fast declining in the eighteenth century.  But the young
prince was thinking little of naval techniques on
this occasion.  At this point in time, before the
war of Austrian Succession was to fashion in him
an anti-English feeling, it was with the commanding
grace of a royal traveller about to assume his rule
over an Italian duchy that he viewed the sea

24

before him, unaware of the irony whereby the British men-of-war that today were his friends, tomorrow would become his greatest enemies.

The journey took five days. Despite the rough passage and the seasickness that went with it, Charles lacked no lustre as he stepped ashore at Leghorn, his Lyons velvet jacket decorated with the emblem of the Golden Fleece, his heron-plumed hat adorned by a white diamond, Louis XIV's sword dangling at his side. Here he was greeted by the governor and by Tuscany's chief minister, Marchese di Renuncini. Entering the city as heir-apparent to the Grand Duke with an escort of Batavian guards, Charles then attended a *Te Deum* Mass in the cathedral celebrated by the archbishop of Pisa. Banquets, fireworks, and equestrian games commenced on December 29, with many nations taking part as the people rejoiced in the streets festooned with garlands. Soon came news from his grandmother Dorothea and the Spanish envoy to Tuscany that both Parma and Piacenza were ready for his entry into these duchies, and that Austrian troops there had already withdrawn to Milan.

Such news pleased Isabel Farnese immensely, whose joy that the Austrians had departed was ecclipsed by regret that the same had not happened to the Grand Duke himself. It was common knowledge that for some years he had been suffering from a spreading inflammation of the skin, exacerbated by his favorite pastime of debauchery, but the disease never seemed to bring on death. Charles however, was looking forward to meeting the Grand Duke and viewing the rich Renaissance treasures of Florence. Moving northwards from Leghorn and crossing the Arno river which links Florence with the Ligurian coast, he reached Pisa by February 1732. Here his three-week visit was unfortunately marred through his having caught smallpox at Leghorn, which briefly left its mark on his face and scalp. No one was concerned about this, since 'the pox' was quite common in both its syphilitic and non-syphilitic forms; and the Grand Duke, attuned by experience to assaults on the skin, was shortly to give consoling advice on the subject to his young host and heir.  Appropriately, it was in his stuffy bedchamber at the ducal palace in Florence where John Gaston first met the young prince after his tiring journey up the Arno river from Pisa, and they spent an hour of friendly conversation.

This fifteenth-century Pitti palace where Charles now stayed as a guest of John Gaston and his aging sister, Anna Maria, in the summer of 1732, was an ornate structure of gilded stonework, elaborate cornices, and magnificent patios leading to an interior garden.  All of this impressed the Spanish prince as much as its priceless collection of paintings, including Titian's *Portrait of an Unknown Man*.  Combining artistic curiosity with a social grace at the many ceremonies and banquets he attended, Charles seems to have genuinely won over both Gaston and his more reluctant sister.  After the traditional oath of allegiance had been given the Duke in the Palazzo Vechi square on June 24, 1732, by the assembled Tuscan notables, Gaston appeared on the balcony of the Pitti palace, his body infirm but with an easy mind and conscience, and gladly hailed Charles as his heir.  Even Anna warmed a bit to the intruding prince as she gracefully presented him with a pair of Florentine daggers made of gold.

Charles' arrival in Parma in October 1732 was accompanied by festivities similar to those he had experienced in Leghorn, Pisa, and Florence. The huge dome in Parma cathedral painted by Coreggio loomed above him, just as it had done at his mother's proxy wedding.  He had indeed been told back in Spain of the many treasures in the Farnese domains; now all these lay before him.  Of particular interest was the ducal palace of Colorno, the Farnese summer residence a few miles north of Parma.  This miniature Versailles embellished by Boni with its cobble-stone driveways, its fountains and theatre, challenged any preference he had for the things of Castile or Andalusia, for he commented in a letter to his parents that it was better than the (still unfinished) palace of San Ildefonso.[5]  By the end of the month he was in his other ducal realm of Piacenza, about forty-four miles northwest of Parma, having skirted the

dangerous waterfalls which plunge into the Po.
Here as in Parma he was acclaimed by a citizenry
of modest means, and by the poor, whose fatalistic
acceptance of feudalism was lightened by all the
festivities and a resplendent scenery that curved
back into the horizon of the Po valley. For the
next year, Charles alternated between Parma, Colorno, and Piacenza, hunting and fishing during his
many leisure hours, and in his more studious moments,
reading the books recommended by Feijóo and his
tutors.[6] Increasingly he would attend the sessions
of the ministerial council which met about three
times a week presided over by his grandmother, until
at last, rather belatedly in his seventeenth year,
he received the reins of governing from Dorothea
herself.

Charles' idyllic reign in the duchies, however,
was soon to be cut short by the war of Polish
Succession. Frederick Augustus II, elector of
Saxony and king of Poland, died in 1733 which led to
two claimants contending for the Polish throne. One
claimant was Stanislaus Lesczinski (father-in-law to
Louis XV of France), whose election with French
support was opposed by pro-Russian and pro-Austrian
factions among the deputies. These favored a rival
claimant, Augustus, the new elector of Saxony
and son of the deceased king of Poland, charging
that the election was a violation of unanimous
voting traditional in the Polish diet. In this they
were supported by Russian and Austrian troops. With
Russians threatening the Polish capital and Austrians
mobilizing in Silesia, the French in retaliation
massed along the Rhine. The war soon began in
earnest. In order to redress the imbalance of
forces, Louis XV asked for the support of Philip V
of Spain and Charles Emmanuel of Savoy, and it was
at this point that the French king hit upon the
ingenuous idea of opening a second front in Naples
for the Spaniards to eject the Austrians from this
region.

A modest duke of Parma converted into a
grander king of Naples had a great appeal for
Charles' parents, especially Isabel, who now had

an ideal chance to wreck the peace of Utrecht and attack the Austrian enemy in Italy. Philip on his part agreed to endorse Louis' claims in Lorraine and those of Charles Emmanuel in Lombardy.[7] A result of these overtures was the first Family Compact between France and Spain, signed in the Escorial on November 7, 1733. Here only two weeks before, Philip had written his son a letter appointing him titular commander of all Spanish forces being assembled for the invasion of Naples.[8] But its paternal tone scarcely hid the fact that Charles who was not yet eighteen and still under the guidance of his personal adviser Santisteban totally lacked the necessary experience to drive out the Austrians from southern Italy -- a major undertaking by any standards -- and that José de Albornoz, Conde de Montemar, in reality was to be the general in command of the operation. Nonetheless the youth conducted himself well during its highly successful execution. Armed with sword and pistol as he consulted on horseback with his staff, he soon cut a competent figure; and his ability to work well with men older than himself, his camaraderie with the troops, and skill in bringing up fresh forces from Parma confirmed this impression.

As for Montemar who came from Seville, he had served in the war of Spanish Succession, and in the successful attack on Oran, and besides considerable ability in his own right had the good fortune to be supported by minister Patiño. Now chief of staff at the age of sixty-three, Montemar was posted to Parma early in 1734, where he worked effectively with Charles, proceeding thence south of Florence to plan the invasion of Naples. This was to be made along the Apennine mountains in conjunction with Conde de Clavijo, who was in charge of naval operations down the coast. By the spring of 1734, Charles and Montemar led an impressive army of 16,000 infantry and 5,000 cavalry composed of Spaniards and Italians, well-equipped down

28

to the last saddle-horse, musket, and tent as it advanced across Umbria in the Papal States. Pope Clement XII, more sympathetic to the Hapsburgs, was gradually won over by being granted compensation for his lapsed feudal rights in Parma, thanks to the diplomacy of Cardinals Belluga and Acquaviva, envoys to the Quirinal on behalf of Spain and Naples respectively.

A high morale prevailed in Montemar's army. Its soldiers were not merely keen to recover Naples which before 1713 had belonged to Spain for two centuries; they also experienced a phenomenon rare in the annals of Spanish military history -- they were paid on time -- and this together with a good recruiting and supply system reflected Patiño's organizing competence. With some justification, moreover, the Spanish army appeared to be coming in as liberators, freeing Naples from the hated tax levies imposed by the Austrians. On the Hapsburg side, viceroy Guillo Visconti had as his commander-in-chief the celebrated Otto Traun; but his ablest general in this context was probably Giovanni Caraffa, whose advice if taken might have considerably delayed the Spanish advance when he proposed keeping together the disposable force some 25,000 strong in one concentrated area instead of dispersing it to garrison the wide network of forts such as Pescara, Capua, Gaeta, and Sant' Elmo, which Traun insisted on doing. Their numbers, moreover, were continually reduced through desertions by forced draftees and roaming bands of mercenaries, whose conduct often damaged the Hapsburg cause.[9]

All went well for the Spanish invaders from the start. Bypassing Rome, Montemar stormed through Valmontone, Cassino, and other towns as Charles in the rear followed the course of the Tiber. By April 1734, they had already joined forces at Aversa outside Naples, cutting off Traun who had fallen back to a defensive position at Gaeta, some eighty miles to the north. The three coastal forts protecting the capital city meanwhile -- Sant' Elmo, Nuovo, and Uovo -- soon fell

within a month as Clavijo, having captured the
islands of Ischia and Procida, landed troops in
the bay close by. When vicerory Visconti ordered
the abandonment of Naples and fled to Campania,
Charles was left free to proclaim Conte di Charni
as governor of the conquered region; and the[10]
prince entered Naples in triumph on May 10.

The older generation who remembered the last
days of Spanish rule did not view the regime with
too much enthusiasm, but they certainly disliked
that of the Austrians. Increased taxes and a
variety of abuses within the feudal system, from
arbitrary tribunal justice to confiscation of
property, were high prices to pay for membership
in the Hapsburg empire, whose capital at Vienna
was simply too far away to make reforms effective.
Thus many Neapolitans of all classes had joined
the invading forces, anxious as they were to play
a more national role in the fortunes of their
country.

But the Austrians and their sympathizers were
not yet out of the fight. Gaeta and Capua were
still in their hands, besides parts of Campania,
Apulia, and the island of Sicily. Bad news
moreover came from the Rhine where the (first)
Duke of Berwick commanding a French army had been
killed in action. In a renewed attempt to redeem
their position in the Two Sicilies, the Austrians
planned to send reinforcements across the Adriatic
sea. By seizing the strait of Otranto through
Apulia, a strong counter-attack was to be launched
against Montemar's army from the heel of Italy.

Realizing the serious situation, Montemar
with the able Duke of Castropignano hastened
with 12,000 men eastwards across the width of the
kingdom. Positioning his forces along the Adriatic
coast he was now prepared to confront the 10,000-
man army which the Austrians had landed at the port
of Bari. The Hapsburg commanders -- the princes
of Belmonte and Strongoli -- decided to move to
Bitonto which was judged to be a strong position
on account of its castle walls and ditches, and
here the two sides met. Like the Normans at the battle

30

of Hastings, Montemar tried the trick of feigning
retreat in order to entice the enemy forwards;
but failing with this ruse he had no option but
to launch a frontal assault, and this succeeded
admirably.  On May 25, 1734, Montemar won the
decisive battle of Bitonto.  The Austrian collapse
was due to the superior skill of the Spanish
general and to the low morale of the Hapsburg
troops who were often pressed into service and
only too prone to desert or surrender.  The
latter suffered a thousand casualties, three
times greater than Spanish losses, with General
Radetsky (in charge of infantry) and Pignatelli
di Santo Vincenzo (in charge of cavalry) both
captured.  Some twenty-three Hapsburg standards
were then assembled and sent off to San Ildefonso,
Montemar himself being made Duke of Bitonto, and
a monument was proudly erected on the battle-site
to commemorate the victory.

With the campaign in the east over, Austrian
fortresses in the west fell like dominoes.
Montemar joined his young sovereign at the siege
of Gaeta, and this surrendered in August.  It was
here, incidentally, that Charles stood next to
another prince of the same name, Charles Edward
Stuart, the fourteen-year old pretender to the
British throne, with whom a warm friendship had
developed.  After the siege aboard the galley
that was taking them back to Naples, the Scottish
prince dropped his cap into the sea.  The sailors
were about to rescue it when Charles, feeling
very much the conqueror of Naples, jokingly
commented that as it was floating towards England
where its owner would soon retrieve it, he would
do the same so that he might also have something
to retrieve; and as a gesture of sympathy he
promptly threw his own cap into the sea amid
general shouts of 'To England' on the part of the
crew.[11]  His youthful elation was certainly
justified.  By November, when Capua with its
5000-man garrison on the Volturno river was
surrendered by Traun to Charni and Marsillac, the
conquest of Naples was over except for a few
pockets of resistance.

31

"A liberated kingdom will be yours," Isabel
had urged upon her son, "Go forth and conquer...
the fairest crown in Italy awaits you." [12]  With
these words ringing in his ears, Charles now
prepared for his ceremonial accession in Naples.
He formally entered the city in December, ensconced
in gilded coach bound for the palace, this time
not as a conquering prince but as one who has
already conquered.  Masses in the cathedral of San
Gennaro (patron saint of Naples whose blood
liquefies in the famous glass vial), keys of the
city handed over in submission, gold and silver
pieces distributed as royal bounty -- these were
the traditional acts by which a ruler was acclaimed,
as Charles had experienced when he first entered
the city.  Now ascending an improvised throne
flanked by a canopy of red brocade, by cornucopiae
and tapestries woven in all parts of Italy, he
received the oath of allegiance from his nobles.
These included Sicilian deputies from the senate
at Palermo, many of whom as grandees of Spain
well understood the Castilian language used on
formal occasions. [13]

Dulling the glitter of victory, alas, came
news from Spain that the old Alcázar palace in
Madrid, the place where he was born, had been
burnt down that Christmas Eve of 1734, in which
priceless paintings by El Greco, Velázquez, and
Reubens had been irretrievably lost. [14]  Then a
fall from his horse nearly cost him his life
while on a hunting trip in Avellino province,
Campania, when he plunged into the Ariano river
which had considerably swollen from the winter
rains.  As if reminded that immortal victory
cannot save one from the frailty of existence,
Charles while taking refuge in a wood near Rossano
in Calabria during a storm reportedly made himself
godfather to a peasant woman's newborn son who
was to be given his name and brought up handsomely --
a story reinforcing the legends already associated
with the conquering prince.

Sicily's turn was next to garnish his fame.
It was not his first visit to the island, for he
had been here the previous autumn with the
ambitious Prince Bartolomo Corsini, when Montemar

32

proclaimed him Lord of the Two Sicilies before
leaving for northern Italy. No one, incidentally,
could doubt the latter general's great services to
Spain. Thanks to his efforts, nearly one half of
the entire peninsula of Italy had been conquered
by his arms -- no mean feat by any standards --
and indeed he can be regarded as one of the
foremost generals of the eighteenth century,
ranking alongside Saxe or Traun.

After Montemar's departure, only Messina,
Syracuse, and Trapani, lying at the three corners
of the Sicilian triangle, had remained in Austrian
hands; but in the spring and summer of 1735 these
bastions fell one by one. Messina was surrendered
in March by Lobkowitz (who was to play for higher
stakes in the next war), and Charles entered the
city in triumph. Here he was drawn along in a
gilded barge with beautiful girls singing -- all of
which rather piqued Prince Ruffo who had hoped his
royal guest would liberally take advantage of
these delightful feminine charms.

The mood was one of festive solemnity as
Charles, having received soon after the formal
capitulation of Palermo, historic capital of the
two kingdoms, prepared for his coronation. On
July 3, 1735, he was duly proclaimed Charles VII
King of the Two Sicilies in Palermo cathedral.
Now on the throne, with hand resting on the gospel,
he swore to uphold the rights of the people, city,
and parliament, the latter representing nobles,
church, and members of the royal domains. The
assembled notables then took the oath of allegiance.
The ceremony recalled the bygone days of Alfonso V
of Aragon, reminding all that Sicily had inter-
mittently been Spanish since the year 1295. The
historic crown of the Two Sicilies with its
casque of Byzantine gold inlaid with precious
stones symbolized that a mission had been accomplished with resplendent success; and to celebrate
the occasion, gold and silver medals with the
inscription *Fausto coronationis anno* were distributed
in the streets.[15] All this fired the excitement
of the people who were feeling a new sense of
identity and protection.

A government was swiftly set up in Naples to replace the viceregal structure of Hapsburg rule, with a corps of ambassadors which was soon accepted at foreign courts. The new regime was an accomplished fact, but many hurdles lay ahead before it could enjoy peace and consolidation. Elsewhere, the war of Polish Succession slowly ground to a halt. A preliminary treaty of October 5, 1735, was signed in Vienna recognizing the Bourbon conquest, and this was ratified three years later on November 18.

There was a price to be paid for the Spanish victory in Italy. By its terms, Charles' new lands of Naples and Sicily, including the so-called Presidii states in Tuscany and Elba, could never be united to the Spanish crown, being secundogeniture holdings only.[16] Charles moreover had to surrender Parma and Piacenza to Austria, as well as his claims on Tuscany. Here the archducal throne on becoming vacant in 1737 through John Gaston's final demise, had passed to Francis Stephen, Duke of Lorraine and husband of the Hapsburg heiress, Maria Thersa. Austrian influence thus revived in Tuscany. As for Stanislaus Lesczinski, he was given Lorraine in exchange for losing Poland, whose king was now Augustus III. Elsewhere, Charles Emmanuel of Savoy got bits of Piedmont, with Austria keeping Lombardy and Milan. The Pragmatic Sanction was confirmed, moreover, whereby the Hapsburg inheritance would pass to the Emperor's daughter, Maria Theresa. It was a game of dynastic diplomacy pleasing nearly everyone, whose neat compensations obscured the years of haggling which preceded them.

An example of this can be seen in Charles' relations with the Pope. Desirous of receiving papal recognition of his conquest of Naples, he promptly sent to Pope Clement XII on St. Peter's Eve the customary tribute of a white horse known as the *Chinea*, together with a sum of 6,000 ducats. This was a traditional act of homage dating from the time of Ferdinand of Aragon and expressing that the kingdom was a papal fiefdom. With the Austrians countering by rival offerings, and with bitter memories still

alive through local fighting having taken place
between Bourbon and Papal forces in the late war,
recognition was not easily obtained. As Charles
was to find out later in Spain, he always seemed
to encounter an obstacle in the person of the
Pope, who proved stubborn in yielding the
slightest ground. But the combined efforts of
diplomats on behalf of Naples finally brought
success, when on May 12, 1737, Pope Clement
formally recognized Charles' regime.[17] Consoled
by the feudal trappings of the homage ceremonies
and by the return of prisoners of war, Clement
issued a Bull of Investiture as a 'free gratuity'
whereby Naples was given to Charles in exchange
for the Emperor's 'voluntary' renunciation of
Naples to the Pope; and for good measure he agreed
to bestow a red hat upon Charles' younger brother
Don Luis, shortly to be known as the Cardinal-
Infante of Spain and archbishop of Toledo. The
following year, as we have seen, the Emperor
fully recognized Charles' position in the Two
Sicilies.

The conquest had shown the feasibility of the
Family Compact -- brainchild of Louis XV --
whereby France and Spain together would not
provoke the intervention of England if they
attacked Austria. Though this was to be belied
by events in the next war, it was a moment of restored glory for Spain who had proved that she was
indeed capable of a major military effort, and that
in defeating the Hapsburgs she had won a substantial degree of parity with the great power of
Austria. Charles himself shared a little of this
glory, and was certainly the pride of both his
parents who had received highly favorable reports
on his conduct from Montemar, Santisteban, and
others.

Hardly had Europe settled down to peace,
however, when England and Spain showed themselves
in their true colors and began fighting. Their
maritime conflict in America was a prelude to a
larger one at home -- the war of Austrian Succession -- and here Charles to his dismay was
soon embroiled.

This maritime conflict is especially important to examine since he was one day to inherit
the Spanish throne with its huge patrimony of
the Indies. In essence the conflict was simple:
Spain had been given all the Indies (except for
the coast of Brazil) by the Pope in 1494 -- a
grant based on Columbus' historic discovery of the
continent. Foreigners therefore must be kept out.
In the seventeenth century buccaneers of all shades
had frequently cut Spain's communications with
the Caribbean, whence they harried the coast of
Central America. But in the eighteenth century,
the role of villain in Spanish eyes fell to the
British. For some time they had been advancing
down the Atlantic coast, taking over Jamaica and
intruding into Honduras, besides aiding and
abetting the Portuguese below Brazil. Their
vision of empire, based on trade and settlement,
clashed with the Spanish view of territorial
monopoly based on historic precedence. With the
original grant of power by the Pope in obvious
abeyance as Protestant Britain grew in strength,
the Spanish government was obliged to come to
terms; and the Asiento privilege it accorded at
the treaty of Utrecht in 1713 gave England a modest
trade foothold in Spanish America.

The word 'Asiento' literally means contract,
in this instance the right to import Negro slaves
into the Indies for a specified time, which before 1713 Spain had granted to individuals. The
treaty of Utrecht on March 26, 1713, gave this
right essentially to the South Sea company, which
received a thirty-year monopoly to send 4,800
black slaves annually to Spanish America, chiefly
to Cartagena in present-day Colombia. England
could also send an annual trade ship of 500 tons
maximum to Porto Bello in Panama. But the high
hopes of British merchants that they could acquire
some of the bullion which Spanish America produced,
of which the ill-fated South Sea Bubble was an
example, were thwarted by sporadic wars, contraband, and high taxes. An annual levy of 34,000
pounds, moreover, was imposed on the first
4,000 slaves, many of whom never reached the
Indies at all; and the company's mounting frustration was not assuaged till 1750, when by a new

treaty with Spain, England received compensation
to the tune of 100,000 pounds.[18]   It was all
an evil business where slavery was concerned,
and everyone's hands were tainted in one way
or another.

Despite the sincerity of England's prime
minister, Sir Robert Walpole, in respecting
the Asiento's terms, British public opinion
was focusing on another issue -- the right to move
into Spanish-claimed areas.  When in 1733 the colony
of Georgia was founded in violation of previous agreements, Spain was incensed; and the borderland war
which had been going on in this disputed Florida
region took a more serious turn.[19]   Spain moreover
upheld the right of search in her territorial
waters of the West Indies -- to snuff out smuggling
was a formidable task for any navy -- but this claim
clashed with the British view of free navigation.
Though Walpole temporarily patched things up by the
convention of El Pardo on January 14, 1739, pressure
from British merchants continued to mount.  Spain
had been fortifying the Caribbean sea-lanes against
both smugglers and the English, in which her coast-
guard captains severely punished those unfortunate
enough to fall into their hands; and the story of
smuggler Jenkins displaying his severed ear in London
which had been cut off in such an incident eight years
previously, was enough to launch the famous war
which bears his name.  Thanks largely to the past
reforms of Patino, this 'War of Jenkins' Ear' that
began in October 1739 went not at all badly for
Spain.

It is true that Admiral Edward Vernon seized
Porto Bello and that Commodore Lord George Anson
with his sweeping voyage in the Pacific eluded
capture by José Pizarro, Spanish commander in
these waters; but all this was offset by failures
elsewhere.  Vernon and General Thomas Wentworth led
a combined Anglo-American assault force of 12,000
men against the important stronghold of Cartagena
(Colombia) in 1740, for which Laurence Washington,
brother of George Washington, recruited the colonial
militia; but the whole expedition was a disaster

thanks to the skillful defense put up by the Spanish viceroy, Sebastián de Eslava. Wentworth met with a similar reverse in trying to take Santiago in Cuba; while to the north on the mainland of Florida, British forces under James Oglethorpe were foiled in an earlier attempt to take the Spanish town of St. Augustine.

The fighting now merged with the war of Austrian Succession. This began in 1740 when Frederick the Great of Prussia suddenly seized the rich Austrian province of Silesia. This unpredictable monarch then blackmailed the new Hapsburg sovereign, Maria Theresa, by threatening to withdraw recognition of her in favor of another prince (i.e., revoke his adhesion to the Pragmatic Sanction), unless she agreed to his retention of the province. Maria Theresa refused, but Frederick wasn't bluffing. The beautiful Empress beseeching aid against her wicked assailant and seeking to protect her husband lost in reverie among his wine cellars and coin and butterfly collections -- the favorite patrimony of Francis Stephen -- must have had great appeal to her subjects. Their patriotism for her cause was further aroused when Frederick's hand was strengthened by the anti-Hapsburg pact of Nymphenburg (1741) between France, Spain, Bavaria and Saxony. This was followed by a direct alliance with the Prussian king, and the fighting soon expanded.

Isabel would stop at nothing to regain the Farnese land of Parma, lost to Austria in the last war, along with any other ducal plum ripe for the picking, for her younger son Felipe, whom we may now call Don Philip. Charles supported his mother's policy, fully realizing that his small state, however enlightened, would sooner or later have to fight for its existence among the quarrelsome powers of Europe. But he desperately tried to avoid a head-on conflict. England, still at war with Spain,

38

meanwhile came to Maria Theresa's rescue.  It was thus Prussia and France versus Austria and England in Germany, France and Spain versus Austria in Italy, and Spain and France versus England everywhere else.

Philip and Isabel sent glowing accounts of the war to Charles; and unenthusiastic as he was, he could not avoid helping his brother Don Philip in his attempts to carve out Italian duchies.[20]  By 1742 he sent reinforcements to Montemar's Spanish army in Tuscany, where an English squadron lurked ominously off the coast.  In Lombardy, Charles Emmanuel of Savoy, Spain's former ally, now joined forces with the Austrians under Count Lobkowitz in a successful drive against Bourbon positions; and Montemar, the aging victor of Bitonto, found himself bottled up on the Adriatic coast.  He was shortly replaced as commander of Spanish forces by Juan Bautista, Conde de Gages, an equally able soldier of Flemish origin who had taken part in the Spanish invasion of Naples.[21]

Gages now moved to Viterbo near the Tiber river where he met Cardinal Acquaviva, Neapolitan envoy to the Quirinal.  Toasts were exchanged in the name of Charles and his queen, Maria Amalia (discussed in the next chapter), whose birthday had just been celebrated in Rome.  But more than birthdays was discussed.  Designed to complement this Spanish presence in the Papal States was a 12,000-man army under the Duke of Castropignano, who had taken command near Rimini on the Adriatic.  In this way a mobile defense strategy protecting Naples could be laid across the width of Italy, helping Castropignano on the one side or Gages on the other, depending on the thrust of the enemy.

The war in northern Italy, meanwhile, was mounting in intensity as Don Philip in conjunction with his commander, Marqués de la Mina, launched an attack on Savoy-Sardinia from the Po valley and Piedmont.  The danger to Naples grew with every passing month, and the people began to suffer.

Though Charles had not declared hostilities,
it was only a question of time before his
kingdom, to the delight of the Sardinians,
would face the threat of Austrian armies on one
side, and English naval guns on the other.
Making matters worse that summer of 1742 was
a severe outbreak of the plague which ravaged
Messina and Reggio, while  earthquake tremors
rocked the city of Naples.

The Austrians indeed were contemplating
an invasion; and things took a serious turn
on August 15, when their British ally in the
person of Commodore Martin appeared in the
bay of Naples with thirteen ships and in a
remarkable display of gunboat diplomacy delivered an ultimatum through the British
consul, Edward Allen, that unless the government withdrew its forces from central Italy
and adopt neutrality, he would order the
bombardment of the city.  The people of
Naples were in a panic as they cowered in the
churches not knowing which to fear most -- earthquakes or the English.  Their chief hope was Charles
himself, who as commander of his troops was
cheered along the route to Fort Il Carmine.
A cabinet meeting was hastily convened at
which the moderate minister Montealegre proposed
yielding to the British demands on the grounds
that the local garrison of three thousand
soldiers was totally inadequate to maintain
order in the event of pro-Austrian demonstrations.[22]
Martin himself only heightened the tension as he
held out his pocketwatch before the British
consul, naming the time when the ultimatum
would expire that very Sunday evening, and
counting aloud the remaining hours and minutes.
Charles was not amused by the incident, and
his already anti-British sentiment was to
grow with the passage of time.  But the sting
was taken out of Martin's demands inasmuch
as Charles ordered withdrawals of troops
from Castropignano's army upon learning that
Savoy had reverted to neutrality for awhile;
and thus partially satisfied, Martin weighed
anchor, to the great relief of the nation.[23]

Charles meanwhile was waging an uphill
fight to convince the world of his own neutrality. When by September 1743 at the treaty
of Worms, Savoy once again joined Austria,
Charles received news from his parents of a
new Family Compact between Spain and France.[24]
Since this implicated Naples in the common
front against Austria, the die was indeed cast.
But it is difficult to see how Charles as a
junior and obedient member of the Bourbon
fold could possibly have escaped from his
predicament.

His forces exposed to enemy attack, Charles
now braced himself to face the wrath of
Maria Theresa, who nursing her wounds received
at the hand of Prussia was poised to strike
and settle old scores with her Bourbon enemies
in Italy. As a softening-up process, her
government promised to preserve the privileges of
the nobility in Naples, and as a sop to the
populace, to keep low the price of food. To
counter this, treason tribunals arrested pro-
Austrian sympathizers. The majority, however,
supported Charles' regime. But it was a trial
of endurance as more plagues and earthquakes
added to the general gloom. Hundreds were
stricken, and prisoners were employed to bury
the dead. The years 1742 to 1744 were indeed
critical times for Charles and his people.

The Austrian army which had assembled
at Trieste now advanced under Prince Lobkowitz
in the spring of 1744 for an attack on Naples.
In a race against time, Castropignano fell
back from Umbria to join Charles' forces, as
did Gages through the Papal States. and in
this they were successful.[25] As commander-in-
chief of Bourbon forces in southern Italy,
Charles at last faced responsibilities all
his own, establishing his headquarters at
Castel di Sangro as the two rival forces faced
each other in the Abruzzi e Molise region.
His army including that of Gages and Castropignano

41

numbered about 38,000 men with several thousand
cavalry; Lobkowitz'army numbered about 35,000
men including eight thousand cavalry.  Behind
the Neapolitan forces came the supply and baggage
trains consisting of bronze field guns mounted
on clumsy ox-carts, 12-inch mortars, boxes
of shells, spare muskets, rifled carbines, gunpowder,
and cordage, along with mules bearing cases of flour,
corn, rice and other foodstuffs.  It was a good
effort, and the soldiers comprised many a veteran
who had fought for Spain in previous Italian
or North African campaigns.  But despite considerable Spanish aid to Naples, Charles' command
was often handicapped by contradictory orders
from Madrid, where it was said in jest that
Isabel capriciously directed the war from her
own boudoir.  The fact was that neither side had
any military master-plan.  It was a campaign
distinguished for daring and impulsively brilliant
tactics rather than by consistent strategy.
Lobkowitz was told to take Naples any way he
could; Charles was to resist the attempt.  The
latter's army had good and patriotic officers,
but it still lacked a militia or any sophis-
ticated training, as by tradition it had been
dependent on the nobles, who like the Hapsburgs
had hitherto levied recruitment by force.

Despite Charles' generally unimpressive
appearance -- the unkempt visage, the bulbous
nose with a sense for the chase considerably
stronger than his ear for music, the narrow
shoulders, the threadbare clothes he so often
wore as an escape from etiquette -- he certainly
could look like a commander when he wanted to,
as on this occasion.  His features in fact
masked a lithe agility in a man not five feet
six inches tall, his bright-blue eyes glowing
beneath his fur cap and inspiring confidence
in all who came in contact with him.  Sound
in body and mind though his mind was not an
intellectual one, Charles the proverbial huntsman and marksman was very much a prince of his
times.  Yet while he was personally brave and
capable, having won his spurs in the conquest

of the kingdom, the military life did not come foremost in his nature.  He was not another Frederick
the Great.  The army, however, was lucky enough to
have him as their leader, just as Charles was lucky
to have Gages and Castropignano by his side at this
critical hour.  Successfully concealing his fears
as he mounted his fine charger at the head of Italian
and Swiss guards, twenty-two regiments of infantry
including dragoons and grenadiers, innumerable
squadrons of cavalry, and Spanish reserve troops,
he rapped firm orders in his Spanish-accented Italian.
An interesting comparison this was to make with his
friend Charles Stuart, captivating Scotland in 1745
as he issued orders in poor English with a Polish
accent, and heading a motley array of Highlanders
towards a far more tragic end.[26]

Unable to dislodge Charles' army along the
Tronto river in central Italy, Lobkowitz repaired
to Rome for an attack on Naples further west via
Valmontone -- a shifted plan of operation soon
ferreted out by the wily Cardinal Acquaviva.  This
information gave Charles time to hasten his army
likewise westward towards Valmontone; but a heavy
rainstorm forced him to divert its march and swing
around upon Velletri, about twenty miles southeast
of Rome.  With Lobkowitz also advancing upon
Velletri, it was here that both sides dug in for
the decisive engagement.

Lying on high ground, Velletri became the focal
point of Neapolitan defenses where the fate of a
kingdom was at stake.  Indeed the battle fought here
became the climax of the war in southern Italy.
Charles' left flank guarded Porta Romana, the
central gateway to the city, while his right flank
occupied Monte Artemisio, taken by Gages, which lay
about four miles to the north west.  Lobkowitz
meanwhile was in possession of Monte Spino, perilously close to Gages' position.  The uncanny silence
was suddenly broken when a surprise attack on the
city of Velletri was launched by the Austrians.  On
the night of August 10, 1744, with British ships
stationed along the coast, six thousand men led by
Brown and Novati swooped upon the city from the
direction of the Tyrrhenian sea, overpowering the

guard, breaching the walls, and wreaking havoc on
the defenses within. The Spanish forces were
driven back after a stubborn fight, in the course
of which perished the commander of a crack Irish
contingent, Colonel Daniel Macdonald -- an irony
indeed, seeing that his enemy Maximilian Brown
was of Irish origin himself. Others such as the
Duke of Atri, the Bruzi family, and Conte di Mariani
were fatally wounded or suffered grievous loss to
property; and the fallen lie buried to this day
close by the church of Santo Giovanni.

Early next morning, while fighting was still
going on thanks to the Irish brigade's brave resistance, Charles was awakened in the Ginetti palace
by Marqués de Villafuerte and told the devastating
news. The King wasted no time in flinging on some
clothes, jumping out of the window into the gardens,
and finding his way to the camp at Fort Cappuchini,
guided thereto by the nightflares of the warring
sides. Here he met the Duke of Modena and the
French ambassador, both in a state of panic; but
keeping his nerve, he summoned Castropignano to an
emergency meeting. Something had to be done and
done quickly. Castropignano on the left flank was
to rally his troops for a counter-attack against
Brown's men in the city, while Gages on the right
flank was to try to recapture Monte Artemisio which
had just been taken by Lobkowitz.

With Charles himself in the center directing both flanks, there is little doubt that this
bold plan of action saved his army from complete
destruction. Heartened by this initiative, Castropignano and his men managed to fight their way to
the city, where the Austrian attackers now became
the besieged. The tables were indeed turned, especially when Gages on the right flank succeeded
in storming Monte Artemisio a second time. Much
hand-to-hand fighting ensued until the afternoon
of August 11, by which time Lobkowitz, after a
final attempt to rally his forces, was decisively
defeated. He managed to avoid capture however,
and skillfully extricated much of his army which
he led back across the Papal States.

Charles' attack is best described in his own

words to his parents: "... At last we advanced
toward the enemy positions. The left flank which
included a brigade of Walloons was under poor Comte
de Beaufort, Castropignano, and Don Placido di
Sangro, as I followed in the rear for a short distance... Suddenly an attack was made on our left
flank against two Dragoon regiments of the Flemish
Brigade as we entered the city. But I immediately...
gave the orders to advance and we drove them back
on all sides. General Novati and officers of every
rank were taken prisoner, besides over eight hundred
soldiers who fortunately were not massacred. It
seems the enemy lost three thousand all told, including General Dolan who they say broke his neck falling
down a ravine, with General Brown and the Duke of
Andreassi seriously wounded. On our side we lost
poor Comte de Beaufort who died this night from his
wounds, Mariani who has already been taken away from
his sickbed, besides Colonel Daniel Macdonald.
Indeed our losses have been high, though thank God
not so high as the enemy's. I cannot praise my
officers and men highly enough, including Conde de
Gages in charge of my right flank, Castropignano in
charge of my left, and the Brigade of Spanish Guards
who ably passed on my orders from the center. In
the advance on the right flank, I commend the soldiers
of the Veii Brigade... and of the Albano regiments,
who performed fine feats of bravery as they pursued the enemy along the mountain passes... The whole
engagement here lasted from dawn till after two in
the afternoon, when we never ceased to shell the
enemy... which had been going on for the past two
days... " [27]

With supplies from Barcelona now pouring into
Gaeta and with Lobkowitz in full retreat across the
Tiber, hotly pursued by Gages who was on his way to
help Don Philip in the north, the Spanish-Neapolitan
armies were clearly masters of the situation. His
prestige high, Charles entered Rome incognito where
he was cordially received by Pope Benedict XIV. The
Pontiff seemed more favorably disposed than the previous
one to appreciate that the Spanish-protected
kingdom of Naples provided a convenient counterweight
to Austrian influence, and they chatted amiably for
some time in the sala di cafe, discussing politcs

45

and paintings. Taking his leave and joining the coach provided him by his loyal churchman, Cardinal Acquaviva, Charles set out for Gaeta where his wife and friends eagerly awaited him.

Elsewhere, the war of Austrian Succession dragged on for another four years. Genoa joined the Bourbon cause in 1745, when Don Philip and Gages together launched a successful offensive; but a strong counter-attack by Austria and Savoy led to the recapture of Genoa, as well as Milan and Parma. It was not until two years later, after the people of Genoa themselves had risen up against the Hapsburgs, that French and Spanish forces recovered the initiative, from Piedmont to Provence. With all sides exhausted, however, the way was clear for the peace of Aix-la-Chapelle, signed on October 18, 1748.

By its terms, the Pragmatic Sanction was upheld, i.e., Maria Theresa was recognized as sovereign of her dominions, her husband Francis having become titular Emperor since 1745. But though she recovered the Austrian Netherlands, she had to cede bits of territory elsewhere. Thus Frederick the Great kept Silesia, much to her annoyance, Charles Emmanuel of Savoy received part of Milan, while Don Philip received the duchies of Parma, Piacenza, and Guastalla. These last-named lands were granted as secundogeniture holdings of the Spanish Bourbons in Italy, thus adding to the one already achieved for Charles in Naples. As for France and England, they returned each other's conquests. For once it was a fairly simple treaty, in which only Prussia and Spain won anything substantial, and Isabel and Don Philip had good cause for rejoicing.

Velletri had been a great victory for the Bourbon family in Italy. It meant the salvation and independence of Naples, and this was fully appreciated by the soldiers who had fought in the campaign. They had won their war because of higher morale, a more appealing cause, good leadership, and help from Spain. Not the least of these factors, and uniting them all, was Charles himself. He had proved more than a match for his Austrian adversary, this time in his own right, and the enemy were not to attack Naples again in his lifetime. But the victor of Velletri knew that such glory was evanescent, that it formed a small part of the enlightenment he envisaged for his subjects. At home the task of reforms had barely begun. The age called for internal consolidation, not the vanity of conquest; and the domestic side of his reign is next examined.

Charles and Maria Amalia, fragment of an imagined family ensemble, by Louis Michel Van Loo.

CHAPTER THREE

FAVORED KING OF NAPLES

Two levels of treatment pertain to Charles'
reign in Naples. The first deals mainly with his
personal popularity and need to found a dynasty;
the second, of a more fundamental nature, deals
with the severe social and economic problems confronting him, and this is taken up in the following
chapter.

From the outset the young prince imparted a
Spanish tone to the conquered kingdom; but he more
than received its influence in return, with all the
atmosphere of this southern region. Frequenting
the theatre with his newly-invested grandees, hunting
in the Bovino woods, fishing on the island of Procida --
such activities were expected of him, but the applause
which greeted him en route was genuine enough. The
almsgiving ceremonies and carnivals, the public banquets
replete with the wines of Ischia or Capri, linked
him personally with those who cheered in the streets;
and though there would have been festivities whether
Charles was there or not -- this was the very fabric
of Neapolitian life -- his presence became a focal-
point for popular attention and gave more meaning to
all the ceremonial enactments. His pleasant manner
may have masked a feeling of insecurity and over-
dependence on his parents, but to his subjects he
had made his mark as a princely warrior, and this
was enough for Neapolitans.

Though the kingdom of the Two Sicilies was
virtually a satellite of Spain, at least the new
regime was a change from the tax-levying propen-
sities of the Austrians, and the reign in a personal sense was to prove highly successful. Charles'
popularity stemmed from the honest public image he
presented. He preferred to redress injustice than
revolutionize the state, a task incompatible
at this stage with the traditional character of its
people. That they were generally more pro-Bourbon

than pro-Hapsburg was not necessarily because they preferred Spain to Austria but because they now had an actual king in their midst who imparted an aura from the immediacy of a throne.  Too many viceroys for so long had stood between, obscuring the image of a sovereign, so that when Charles came upon them like a liberator, it was the reality of a liberator they were applauding.  Here was a prince with something for everyone, sure of support from the strong men of Spain yet free enough to reflect a national pride for noble and citizen alike.  It was a new state of affairs, so new indeed that decades later Neapolitian lawyers, hand-in-glove with the establishment, were still arguing whether a sovereign could really be a legitimate authority for curtailing the feudalism they represented.

The kingdom with its population of about four million was certainly backward by the standards of the time.  The city of Naples, like Palermo in Sicily, was a bustling administrative and commercial center -- the hub of the nation with a floating population of some 300,000 -- but it had only tenuous links with the fourteen provinces, where a humble, if in some cases relatively contented, poor were at the mercy of a strong local nobility.  The way of life everywhere was almost medieval.  In the capital, princes rubbed shoulders with pickpockets, *lazzaroni* craftsmen with beggars, pilgrims with hawkers and pilferers, while prostitutes were so numerous that to seal them all off would have taken up most of the city.  Yet religious devotions made up for distinctions in profession, and the cult of San Gennaro in Naples was as unifying among all classes as the cult of Santa Rosalia was in Palermo.  The mob identified itself with the city just as the city identified itself with the sovereign, and in a curious way class antagonism was absent.  In common with other pre-industrial societies, it was for the sovereign to ensure his people's livelihood and keep the cost of living down.  Alternatively, he could contract others for this purpose among the nobles, churchmen, and rich merchants, and who in the process had to pay substantially for the privilege.  If any ruler failed to do these things, the people would resort to force until he did.  Though riots did occur in

Charles' reign, they were directed neither at monarchy nor at Charles' person. It was his good fortune to remain a popular figure. And in an age when slums and street-markets adjoined private palaces, he even acquired local habits of speech.

Facilitating his role was the quality of his own character. Gentle but astute, his instincts were refined, not brutalized, by the tenor of the age. Formalistic in habit and religion -- at other times free and unconventional -- he could be a man of meditation and a man of action, but his natural prejudices rarely bordered on vindictiveness and never on violence. If his insight into human nature became sharpened by experience, this was not at the expense of his own descent into lust or passion; nor was extravagant living ever part of his style. Moral in his private life, judicious in his choice of men, he learnt fast how to use the advice of others, and by his knack of putting them at ease would often extract the maximum of confidence in exchange. This was not to dupe or dominate, but rather to get everyone working for the common good -- and the glory of his Bourbon family. Yet he could be forgiving, and would defend his ministers to the hilt once he had made up his mind to place his trust in them. It was said that he liked old faces just as he liked old clothes. His chamberlain the Duke of Losada, for example, he retained for many years, invariably consoling him in his pique when he lost at card games; while Marchese di Fogliani, dismissed from office in 1755, was at Charles' insistence appointed viceroy of Sicily in compensation. It was a loyalty that well paid off, for his subordinates at least knew where they stood. Respect for the monarchy stood high, and personal treachery against him was extremely rare.

Upon his accession Charles had sworn to abide by traditions of government, receiving in exchange an oath of loyalty from the nobles. Those who supported his cause were amply rewarded.[1] In Spanish viceregal times there had been a supreme council, backed by a so-called collateral college. These were converted into a royal council of state (*real camera di Santa Chiara*) which now met about twice a week in Naples city. Dominated by Spaniards, it consisted of a

chief concillor (assisted by an intendant-general),
and this at first was Santisteban, his chief adviser. In addition were four state secretaries,
later promoted to ministers in varying combinations
of portfolio, each of whom had equal voting rights
in the council. These were José del Campillo
(treasury), Gaetano Brancone (church affairs and
morals), Conte di Charni (defense), and Bernardo
Tanucci (justice). Where Sicily was concerned,
its supreme governing panel was presided over by
a noble state councillor, with representatives from
both portions of the kingdom and functioning in
close concert with the viceroy, parliament, and
senate at Palermo.

Chief councillor Santisteban, now a duke and
steward of the royal household, sternly preserved
Spanish influence at the court; but his condescending attitude to Charles and his young bride
whom he appeared to treat as his wards annoyed them
both, and in 1738 he was dismissed and packed off
to Spain with a pension. His place was taken by
intendant-general José de Montealegre, an old
Spanish friend of Ripperdá, and a conscientious,
if cautious, administrator. But it was justice
minister Bernardo Tanucci who was destined to make
the deepest impression on the kingdom. The ablest
and most forceful personality in the council,
Tanucci more than anyone helped shape Charles' views
about reforming the state, and he wielded a lifetime of influence upon his sovereign.

Born in 1698 at Stia di Casentino in Tuscany,
he was destined for a legal career at an early age.
Receiving his degree in public law from the University of Pisa, he soon acquired a reputation as a
skilled lawyer in various courts of justice. Taking
Spain's side against Austria's claim to investiture
rights in Siena, Tuscany, he earned the gratitude
of Philip V and Charles' attention in Parma. As
auditor to the Spanish army, he became Charles'
adviser and confidant during the invasion of Naples.
Thereafter Santisteban was instructed to confirm
his appointment as secretary of justice when the
government was first set up at Aversa. Later as

steward of the royal household in charge of foreign affairs, he was made chief councillor, then secretary of state in 1755. Tanucci was now in a position of great power to push his reforms, for which purpose he downgraded ministers to their former status as secretaries to make them more subordinate to his central authority.

In the course of Charles' reign, the great Tuscan statesman in whom alternated contrasts of petty malignancy and expansive benevolence -- depending on the person he was dealing with -- did much to check abuses in the courts and to curb the power of the nobles. Various attempts were made to increase the royal revenues through a fairer taxation; and to mitigate hardships on the peasants, the price of corn, for example was fixed in times of depression or disaster. The chaotic system of laws and competing jurisdictions, moreover, was modified by some measure of standardization. Neither did the church escape the sweep of his attacks. One of his early briefs had been his defense of royal claims over the church, of which as a fledgling Jansenist he was critical to the point of anti-clericalism. In this suit, he argued that the power of the state was above ecclesiastical immunity privileges such as granting asylum to refugees from justice.[2] On many occasions thereafter he challenged the church's other immunities, from certain tax-exemptions to separate jurisdiction, over the objections of its conservative spokesmen. It might seem surprising from all this that Charles as basically a conservative himself generally upheld such reforms; but he did so for the contribution they made to his own cause of regalism, and endorsed a concordat signed with Pope Benedict XIV in 1741 which reflected many of Tanucci's ideas.[3] After Charles left Naples for Spain in 1759, he kept in close touch with his minister who continued his drastic reforms for the nation. Their mutual correspondence lasted till 1782, filling scores of volumes and showing how both men did their utmost to keep Naples within the Spanish orbit; and to this end Tanucci was to give a lifetime of loyal service.

The confidence Charles placed in him as
his 'secular confessor' -- some would say Mephisto-
pholes -- touched on more personal matters in those
early years, such as the need for a consort. His
parents were fully supportive of his attempts to win
respectability abroad, for a strengthened Naples
would strengthen their position in the same proportion.
But what about his own position?  Despite the consolidation he was achieving, the fact remained that bachel-
orhood could not ensure the continuity of his throne,
and that sooner or later this question would have to
be faced.  Establishing a dynasty would make it more
difficult for a power such as Austria to dislodge
him from his kingdom, and Charles became one of the
most eligible princes in Europe.

The absence of a bride did not bother him at
first.  Parents were responsible for a selection,
and the happy day of choice would surely in due
course arrive.  Obedience to his parents to whom he
owed his throne meant obedience to the hierarchical
order of church and state alike, in which as a good
reforming Catholic and a good eighteenth-century
optimist, he equally believed.  Obedience was a submission of the will, encumbent upon everyone, imposing obligations on kings and cardinals no less than
on the humblest water-seller in the streets or the
meanest scribe.  It was unquestioning in its simpli-
city, hence stripped of doubt which he later suspected
was beginning to permeate the thoughts of some other
kings and philosophers of his day.  It was for Charles,
then, an act of filial duty to do what he was told,
and to marry without parental consent was unthinkable.

But the trouble was that initiative from this
direction was not forthcoming.  His parents were
reluctant to advance the cause of any definite candidate, for they wanted to make sure that the final
choice would bring diplomatic advantage to Spain and
not jeopardize the House of Bourbon's Italian holdings.
The longer they delayed in the matter, the  more impatient Charles became.  Chaste as he was in private
life, rejecting the offers of free love among the beautiful ladies of his own court, he was human enough to
want to get married, important enough to need a dynasty.
His situation began to bother him more than any other

53

affair of state, as increasingly his parents seemed
cruelly to be absent from the scene of his confusion.
The triumphant prince of battlefield and the chase
was now a prisoner of his own perfections.  He wished
his mother were here to advise him; with her blessing,
any choice would surely turn out to be successful.
But the lead he expected from her never came.  Even
when left to his own devices in suggesting a spouse
there always seemed to be a snag.

There were the Elizabeth sisters, Princess of
Beaujolais and the widowed Princess of Montpensier,
two of the many daughters of Philip Duke of Orleans,
both of whom, it is recalled, had been in Madrid during
the previous decade; but Charles was the last person
to want to get involved with either woman after so many
unfortunate experiences.  There were other French
princesses as possible candidates, for by 1737 Louis XV
had twin daughters ten years old, Marie Louise and Marie
Henriette, both of whom according to the Spanish ambassador, Marqués de la Mina, were inordinately fond
of Charles.  But their extreme youth, Spanish wounded
pride in the past, and French reluctance to satisfy
Philip V's interest as a rival Bourbon nullified any
chances for a union.

Marriage with a Protestant princess, such as the
daughter of George II of England or of Frederick
William of Prussia (the 'Sergeant-King') was equally
unlikely.  Religious differences aside, England and
Spain were drifting towards their maritime war, while
Prussia on her part was hardly to gain very much
through ties with a fledgling state like Naples.  In
the latter respect the Neapolitan envoy to Spain,
Conde de Fuenclara, had held unsuccessful talks on
the subject with the Prussian envoy in Madrid; and when
the ambitious Fuenclara turned on the charm at the
court of Vienna to seek help, it was obvious that
the Emperor himself was just as cool as the king of
Prussia to any similar idea.[4]

Marriage with a Hapsburg daughter such as
Maria Theresa, which had been a pet idea of Ripperdá,
proved highly unworkable.  Not only were the opposite
heads of families, Philip V and Charles VI, still

alive to remember their old enmity in the war of
Spanish Succession, but an Austrian-Neapolitan marriage in Vienna's view would mean an extension of
Spanish influence in Italy at Austria's expense.
There was of course Charlotte of Lorraine, sister
of the Francis who subsequently married the future
Empress, Maria Theresa. Charlotte's smallpox was not
necessarily an impediment to marriage, though hardly
pleasing to Charles' imagination since he himself had
recently suffered from the same disease. There was
the added difficulty that in the event of a war between Naples and Austria -- a possibility that could
not be ruled out and which later came true --
Charlotte would be loath to support such a war while
her own brother was husband of the heiress to the
Hapsburg throne. The problem of finding a bride was
proving more difficult than ever.

In face of so many objections, the young king
grew more impatient. "Please make your mind up for
time is getting on," is the sense expressed in more
than one of his letters. On May 10, 1737, Vesuvius
erupted, and judging from the anxious tone of his
writing it would seem that this disturbance of
nature was affecting his own, driving him almost to
desperation.[5] The names of possible brides were finally whittled down to three, last of whom was Maria
Amalia Warburg, daughter of Frederick Augustus the
king of Poland and of the Archduchess Maria Josepha
of Austria. There were serious objections to this
candidate. Frederick Augustus was the same Augustus
III of the House of Saxony, who now ruled Poland as
the arch-enemy of Stanislaus Lesczinski, on whose
behalf France and Spain had taken up arms during the
war of Polish Succession. Furthermore there was
Maria Amalia's extreme youth to consider since she
was barely yet thirteen; and Charles above all wanted
a bride who could breed well for the House of Bourbon
and thus vindicate his parent's trust in his choice.

Despite these objections, it was Maria Amalia
who won his final decision. Beauty is in the eye
of the beholder, and beauty, in Charles' view, was
concomitant with fertility. Descriptions of her
visage, height and buxomness were all indicative

of good breeding-stock, and Conde de Fuenclara's reports to this effect removed any doubts that may have lingered in the King's mind. That his parents were being won over, however slowly at first, was evidenced by Charles' letters to his father in August 1737, in which he urged parental blessing and promised that as soon as he had settled down after his marriage, he would present his fond benefactors with a host of worthy grandchildren.[6] Fears for the bride's prematurity, moreover, were soon dispelled by Fuenclara and his colleagues as they reported the personal satisfaction of the Dowager Empress Amalia (the girl's maternal grandmother) with the proposed marriage. Being only thirteen, it was observed, was nothing out of the ordinary, for María Luisa of Savoy was the same age when she married Philip V, and despite her youth had brought forth a pleasing progeny; nor did similar tender years prevent María Ana, the princess of Brazil, from giving proof of her fecundity when she married Joseph. The important matter at the moment was to finalize the date for the marriage treaty and the exchange of nuptials.[7]

The Spanish secretary of State, Sebastián de la Cuadra, kept fully in touch with Fuenclara and the Neapolitan court, and there is little doubt of the former's role in clinching the matter at Madrid. On October 31, 1737 in Vienna, Fuenclara negotiated a tentative marriage treaty through Augustus III's Polish envoy, Jan Baptiste Bolza. By January 1738, Sebastián de la Cuadra informed Fuenclara that, subject to His Catholic Majesty's consent to the expenses for a royal court in Naples, a confessor of the Polish king's choosing could accompany the new queen for one year, when she was to be taught Italian and the customs of her adopted country.[8] The letter shows that Philip and Isabel -- the mother in particular -- were taking no chances in allowing their son too much liberty, and would do their utmost to allow even less to their daughter-in-law. But they had obviously warmed to the idea of her impending presence in Naples.

The glad day arrived on April 11, when with the blessing of Pope Clement XII the tentative marriage treaty of the previous October was ratified by a final contract. There was to be a dowry of 90,000 German florins, the interest on which was to be transferred to Charles if he outlived his bride. If Maria Amalia outlived her husband, her regency over Naples and absolute guardianship over her children were to be guaranteed, reinforced by a yearly allowance of 150,000 ducats. If no issue survived the demise of both parties, then Augustus III as father of the bride could succeed to the Neapolitan throne. The latter provision was more to please Augustus than anything else, for such a situation if it ever arose would most likely be fought out on the battlefield in a new dynastic war. Maria Amalia meanwhile was to receive an annual allowance equivalent to 50,000 Spanish crowns for her household expenses, along with a nuptial gift of 50,000 ducats.

It was Fuenclara who arranged her move from Dresden to Naples -- a journey of nearly 700 miles which was to take about a month beginning in mid-May. The nuptials having been celebrated by proxy in Dresden cathedral on May 9, 1738, attended by the papal nuncio and several Saxon and Polish bishops, Maria Amalia was festively entertained in Dresden palace, and thereafter was accompanied by Augustus through Bohemia and Austria as far as the Italian frontier. Taking leave of her father, she then travelled through Venice and the Papal States, reaching Portello by June on the frontier with Naples.

Throughout the preceding weeks Charles had been working meticulously with Tanucci and Brancone to prepare for her reception in the homeland, successfully concealing his anxiety as he washed the feet of the poor in the traditional ceremony during Holy Week. As prayers were offered in all the churches for the bride's safe arrival, Charles at last came to Portello to receive her on that eventful day of June 19, 1738. A garlanded wooden cottage replete with canopied divans, damask, and palmtrees provided the colorful setting. Upon first meeting the King, the young bride prepared to kneel before him as an act of homage, but he took the girl in his arms and put her in the coach bound for Fondi and Gaeta. Here they could spend their evenings together in private, addressing one another in the common language of French, before their official reception in Naples a fortnight later.

The couple were already in the city incognito a short while before the reception, which was set for July 2. On this day, the glittering state coach drawn by eight horses clattered along Reale Studii street past St. Dominic's church, where the square in front had been decorated for the occasion. Charles' statue surrounded by fountains looked across at the procession, flanked by arches bearing allegorical symbols and inscriptions. The coach trundled along streets draped with tapestries as Maria Amalia's brother watched the pair go by, then approached the palace through triumphal portals. The crowds all cheered. It was a happy day especially for Fuenclara, who saw his efforts crowned by the celebrations and handsome rewards as well.

A few days later to affirm his strengthened position, Charles created the knighthood order of San Gennaro. Here he invested sixty initiates with the traditional cloak of membership. The insignia included a cross bordered by four lilies with an image of a bishop's stole and mitre, and under its Grand Master the order soon became a measuring-rod of loyalty to the new regime. Pro-Spanish nobles were naturally given preference since they had been his powerful allies in the conquest; and many of them were already grandees of Spain. Pro-Austrian nobles incidentally, who were strong in remoter feudal regions, were also placated, for to do otherwise would only invite trouble. Santisteban had appointed over a hundred as gentlemen-in-waiting, many of them given golden keys admitting them to every part of the palace. It was a prudent move, for it won their loyalty while weakening their hold over their fiefdoms. Unknown to both noble factions, it was Charles' policy to curb their privileges and power -- a task requiring great tact and skill in which Tanucci was to play an important part.

It was fortunate for Tanucci that he knew how to handle the young queen, for she soon proved herself adept at undermining those she disapproved of -- Santisteban being a case in point. A girl of fourteen when she arrived, she was soon made to feel at home, and a portrait of her by Giovanni delle Piane

(Molinaretto) sent to Madrid was reciprocated by handsome jewels given by her parents-in-law.[9] Fair-complexioned, she was of good stature, a shade taller than her husband, and moved gracefully with child-like ease; but her Germanic dignity and fine taste for decoration masked a temper which worsened as she grew into a woman. Her many confinements aggravated her mood, when she was known to slap the elbows of her attendants -- a mood well concealed in Francesco Liani's fine portrait of her, regally mounted on splendid charger. Yet husband and wife loved each other dearly. Their characters were compatible. His level-headed management of her affairs and her intelli-gent response in a strange enchanting world, their mutual fidelity and constant companionship, lent some basis to the paradox that a couple can exist in idyllic happiness even when one of the partners is somewhat temperamental. Indeed the first years of their marri-age were probably their happiest, certainly the happiest in Charles' long and troubled life.

Their honeymoon was spent at Portici near Vesuvius, about four miles east of Naples, where the treasures of Herculaneum were later to be kept. Frequent trips were made to such nearby places as Capodimonte, where the fig-pecker birds would gather in the autumn season, or to Castellammare on the coast further south, where Charles would go shooting after quails. Back in the city, they would frequent the opera (to Charles' patient boredom), while over Tanucci's objections Maria Amalia would often attend the ministerial council meetings.

An idea of the couple is given by Sir James Gray, the British ambassador reporting to London in the 1750's: "The King of Naples is of a very reserved tem-per; a great master of dissimulation, he has an habitual smile on his face, contracted by a constant attention to conceal his thoughts; has a good understanding and a surprising memory, as his father had; is unread and un-learned, but retains an exact knowledge of all that has passed within his own observation, and is capable of entering into the most minute detail. He is in many things his own Minister, passing several hours every day alone in his cabinet... and is so positive and obstinate that he is seldom induced to alter his res-olutions... The Queen is haughty, fond of power, has

violent and quick passions, and in this, the reverse
of the King, that she always discovers by her count-
enance the impressions things make on her mind. She
has a great influence over the King who is very fond
of her, and by her assiduity and complaisance is capable of biasing him, and even sometimes of making him
change a resolution he has taken..." [10]

But sometimes the King could stick to his point.
On one occasion, Maria Amalia severely scolded the
Prince of Espacaforno, a chamberlain and master of
ceremonies, for accidentally spilling some sauce
on her plate at a banquet given in honour of her pre-
nancy. Concealing his wounded pride, the prince
hastily withdrew from the dining-room. Charles asked
him where he was going, to which he replied with
great presence of mind that he was only leaving to
put on his fulldress uniform for the coming ceremony. This did not fool his questioner for a moment,
who commenting that the prince was indeed a wise diplomat promptly rebuked his wife with the remark,
"There, see what you've done!" [11]

Through all the vexations of her confinements,
however, Charles had to learn supreme patience where
awaiting children was concerned; but in the end he
was amply rewarded. Thirteen were born from 1740
onwards, eight of them surviving into adolescence.
Amalia herself was to die of pleurisy three years
after the birth of her last child. Insanitary conditions took their usual toll, contributing to the
pox, fevers and other rampant diseases of the age.
Hygiene and medical science still had far to go, and
even Charles, who regarded all doctors as downright
charlatans, did not prohibit, though he disapproved of,
a highly unreliable vaccine against smallpox when it
was later introduced.

Charles' favorite daughter María Isabel (name-
sake of their deceased firstborn) had seen the light
of day in 1743, only to die herself at the age of
six. The slightly-deformed but surviving María
Josefa Carmela emerged the following year, while
María Luisa Antonia, born in 1745 lived to become
engaged to Leopold, Archduke of Tuscany. None of

them was quite the favorite that María 'Isabelita'
had tragically been, but at least two of them were
to grow into adulthood, which was perhaps the greatest
gift of all in those uncertain times. In respect of
male heirs, discussed in a later chapter, the Queen at
last responded, producing with regular precision between
1747 and 1757, though some of the products were rather
disappointing. In all she gave birth to six surviving
sons. She had thus done good work in presenting
Charles with a total of eight children, including the
two princesses, and none could fault her achievement.

As if seeking to express the growing solidity of
his rule, Charles developed an early passion for
building. Symmetry and form appealed to him more than
music or social etiquette. When the first big opera
house in Naples was opened in November 1737, named
San Carlos in his honour, it was rumored that he chose
the royal box which acoustically was furthest from the
music on the stage. Connected to a palace, the theatre
was an impressive achievement designed by Giovanni
Medrano and built by Angelo Carasole -- the latter, incidentally, being jailed for embezzlement afterwards.
Its front facade was graced by Ionic columns, while its
marble balustrade, its allegorical figures in richly-
embossed relief reflected its Renaissance style. Huge
mirrors in the foyer caught the interior candles in a
flood of light, adding charm to the many operas which
were considered among the best performed in Europe.

Other embellishments included the reconstructed
Castel Nuovo and the Arch of Aragon; but it was in
the realm of palace construction, along with excavation, sculpture, pottery and design where Charles could
lay his best claim to be a royal patron of the arts.
Naples lent itself to such a climate, for its ancient
Greek settlements of Herculaneum and Pompeii had experienced the great eruption of Mount Vesuvius in
79 A.D., when these two cities with all their treasures
were buried in volcanic ash. Charles took the view
that excavation of these sites as well as construction
nearby would serve to commemorate their natural trag-
edies and leave man's mark for future posterity; and
so the villa at Portici on the bay of Naples and the
nearby palace at Capodimonte were the result, climaxed
by the great masterpiece of Caserta.

The villa at Portici was a favorite resort of
Maria Amalia. It held many treasures from Herculaneum which lay buried at the northwest foot of
Vesuvius. Excavations here had started some years
before, when workmen digging a well stumbled upon a
vault that turned out to be the remains of a theatre
buried underground; but general indifference, wars,
and sporadic earthquakes postponed any action till
1738. In this year, after the towns of Sarno,
Avellino, and others had been damaged by quakes, an
engineer discovered more of Herculaneum while in-
specting a canal near the Sarno river, and excavations
began in earnest. A deep hollow revealed tiers of
an amphitheatre complete with walls, statues, and
the ashen remains of man. Galley-slaves, their chains
struck off, joined the ranks of the ancient dead as
they unearthed one of the most exciting finds since
Roman days.[12] Statues of Apollo, Diana, Venus, Mercury
and Minerva, of youths celebrating the Greek feast of
the goddess Demeter, along with rolls of papyri soon
filled the vaults of Portici, to the delight of the
King and Queen. Wandering among the volcanic ruins,
Charles reportedly quipped that were Vesuvius to erupt
in the future, then archeologists would have the
pleasure of excavating them all over again. The
discovery of Pompeii in 1750 and of the temples at
Paestum in the gulf of Salerno two years later encouraged the neo-classicism in art advanced by the
German scholar Johann Winkelmann, and of which many
of Charles' commissioned works were fitting examples.

The palace at Capodimonte, begun in 1738, reflected the earlier neo-classicism of Medrano, and
was on a bigger scale than Portici; but having a
weak foundation it was never completely finished.
Capodimonte is best remembered for its pottery and
china factory. Its products were intended to complement those of Dresden -- the Dresden of Saxony
where Maria Amalia came from and whose knowledge of
porcelain contributed a great deal to the process
of refinement. She had hit upon the idea of purchasing models of Dresden china in order to study the
techniques of manufacture, and the china clay or
kaolin from Fascaldo (near Catanzaro in Calabria)

provided the raw material for production.  An old
building close by, known as the Guardia Maggiore,
was the chosen place for the factory.  Here as at
Portici, the royal couple felt closest to home,
bound as they were by ties of mutual interest.  Amalia
would advise the ceramic experts on the use of poli-
chrome reminiscent of her youth in Saxony, and would
often chat with Maria Caselli, painter in her own
right and wife of Giovanni Caselli, director of the
Capodimonte workshops.

The royal couple were indeed fond of the de-
corative arts -- their patronage of Vincenzo Re with
his scenes of palace life and festive landscapes is
but one example -- and Charles founded an academy of
design as well as a tapestry factory.13  Neither were
other kinds of craft neglected.  Many individuals received royal grants to fashion such refinements as
white leather goods and glass mirrors, though plans
for a crystal glass factory were never fully realized
until after Charles got to Spain.14  In other respects,
the Bourbon-Farnese museum became one of the most
priceless in Europe, providing sources for study in
archeology, history, and the sciences, and foreshadowing the foundation of the Herculaneum and
Pompeii Academy a few years later.

Charles' finest building was the palace at
Caseta.  Desiring to copy what his forebears had done
at Versailles and San Ildefonso, Charles was advised
by architects to build on more solid ground than at
Portici or Capodimonte, where there were risks from
volcanic eruptions and enemy attacks by sea.  The
site thus chosen was on the plain of Caserta, which
lies about fourteen miles inland from Naples.  The
early settlement of Casa-Erta had been founded by
the Lombards, and a few people still lived among the
ruins.  The groundwork was laid in 1751, though it was
not till 1773 that the palace was completely finished.
Problems were encountered in getting the best men for
the job.  Carasole who had constructed the San Carolos
theatre was still under sentence for embezzlement,
so the King sent for Luigi Vanvitelli, a Neapolitan
living in Rome and one of the finest architects in
Italy.  Vanvitelli and an able engineer named

Francesco Sabbatini, who was later to accompany
Charles to Spain, made the palace potentially one of
most impressive in Europe.  The five-floored structure,
800 feet long and 135 feet high, contained many apart-
ments where guests would witness the magnificent
arches and Doric columns hewn from Sicilian marble
which supported the inner facade.  Gazing back at
them was the imperious figure of the king himself,
mounted on horseback in bronze and set in a recess
between the front cornices.  A circular foyer topped
by a dome gave on to stairways leading to the upper
floors divided by galleries, while to the rear were
four interior courts complete with a chapel.  The
whole ensemble with its carved inlaid woodwork, its
stucco and glass, its sculpture and mural paintings
represented the works of many distinguished artists
and typified the mood of an eighteenth-century Italy
striving to find meaning in grandiose but gracious
form. [15]

The adjacent courtyards gave on to ornate gardens with a sweep of box-hedge stretching back towards the horizon in neatly-planned diagonals.  Nearby was a theatre of alabaster columns like a Roman
temple, which contained forty gilded seats laid out
in a semi-circle.  Elsewhere the gardens were adorned
with obelisks, statues, and marble steps where copious
fountains splashed from figurines.  A great effort was
made in landscaping to equal what had been done in
France or Spain, with a lake, for example, spilling
in waterfalls and coursing through well-fashioned
arbors and bush-flowers.  The water came from distant Monte Taburno as it flowed for nearly thirty miles
along a Roman aqueduct over the Tifatine hills, and
then along canals cut deep in the rocks or over great
bridges such as that across the Maddaloni valley.
After irrigating the land and embellishing the palace gardens, the water continued underground, till
it reached Naples and finally flowed out to sea.

It was somewhat ironic, perhaps, that Charles'
great masterpiece was not destined to be his permanent residence; this was to be reserved for his
successors.  He himself was to live out his days in
the great palaces of Spain by which he had been

inspired to create Caserta in the first place. But such irony was a small part of the picture. It would not be inaccurate to describe his reign as something of a golden age, embracing great painters from Liani to Panini and making Naples an important cultural center of Italy. And amid the climate of growing historical science, Charles became its chief curator of classified knowledge. It was indeed a pity that the serenity he aspired to was disrupted, as we have seen, by wars, plagues, famine and earthquakes, invoking innumerable acts on his part and that of his queen to relieve the people's sufferings. It was as if the thunder of guns sought deliberately to shatter the tranquility of his kingdom. Perhaps the greatest irony was the gaunt spectre of poverty in the grasp of a proud nobility, on whose support he had been forced to depend. But Charles was determined to probe deep for practical solutions, and we now follow his efforts.

The Palace of Caserta

# CHAPTER FOUR

## TENSIONS IN THE TWO SICILIES

There was a marked contrast between the royal
life at court, with all the glitter and flattery that
went with it, and the rural bleakness beyond; and no
one was more concerned at this than Charles himself.
His own close ties with the soil made him acutely
aware of the lot of the poor, from Lucania to Sicily,
and was resolved, with Tanucci at his side, to curb
the power of the nobles, reform the laws, and promote
industry and public works in general. He had been
brought up in the contemporary mode that preached of
enlightenment in princes, and his good intentions
are best summed up in his own words: "I rise in the
morning at five a.m., read and attend to reports till
eight, when I dress and go to the state council. I
hope to make this kingdom prosperous once more and
relieve it of taxes, especially since this year
1750. I have finished paying all the debts contracted
during the last war, and still have 300,000 ducats in
savings to put in my treasury. To prove this I have
refused the usual donative tax voted by the Sicilian
parliament, a larger sum than any voted previously,
telling them I do not need it; apart from which I
have cancelled another tax and wish to devote all my
attention to improving the welfare of my subjects,
since I want to save my soul and go to Heaven."[1]

Heaven aside, it need hardly be said that the
tasks he had set himself were formidable. The country,
as we have seen, was backward even by eighteenth-century
standards. Nobles, along with lawyers and merchants,
were all too resistant to any kind of reforms, a
legacy of civil wars in the past having left many
nobles stronger than ever. So entrenched were these
with feudal banality rights, tax-exemption privileges.
and arbitrary judicial power that the peasant was
little more than a serf. Their vast wealth, which
by some accounts comprised nearly one half of all
disposable lands, their constant fights over possession bringing legal confusion in its wake, the numerous
hunting and fishing rights vested in the hundreds of
petty princelings or their retainers -- all these
manifestations of a medieval way of life contrasted
with the land-enclosure type of society developing

66

elsewhere. Capital, like land itself, merely stag-
nated or passed passively from one hand to another.
Out of 2,765 townships assumed to exist in 1734, all
but fifty had come under feudal dominion from royal
or communal control, and by 1800 this figure was
barely four times higher.[2]

In Sicily, the picture was even bleaker. Here
such strong opposition existed to the government's
policy of trying to redeem noble-owned lands that
Charles was soon confronted with an important suit
between the powerful Gaetano family and the Sicilian
state. Anxious not to upset such nobles who had been
the mainstay behind his military conquest, Charles
bowed to a tribunal decision, and in 1740 issued a
decree favoring their claims including those to
allodial, or non-feudal, lands. The Gaetano case
was typical of strong landowners resisting redemption
by the state, though Charles got his revenge later
when he extracted from the Gaetano family a contribution of half a million ducats towards the construction of his great palace at Caserta.

Realizing that the nobles would violently oppose
even partial take-overs of their landed wealth, the
council of state chipped away at their prerogatives
instead. This was balanced by loading them with empty
honors such as the privilege of grandeeship or court
appointments; and as a sop to their self-importance,
many were invited to a commission for reforming the
law. In 1737, nobles could no longer extend their
patrimony by claiming succession through the female
line; and four years later, in an attack on osten-
tation, no noble or rich man could enter any public
place escorted by more than two serving retainers.
At the other extreme, absentee-landlordism came under
fire when many estates were placed under a commission --
the Farnese and Medici estates being cases in point.
One of the strongest weapons of seignorial jurisdiction was the *mero e misto* tribunal which gave the
nobles virtually unlimited powers over a defendant.
By mid-century, any new investitures of fiefdoms
were now deprived of this absolute jurisdiction, and
the right of appeal was granted. In further moves
against privilege, communes and municipalities were
supported by the state in their rights over redeemed

67

feudal lands, many of which were declared inalienable.

Charles also gave much leeway to Tanucci and Brancone in their attempts to curb the church's temporal power. Tanucci, whose views in the matter were far more radical, saw the church no less than the nobility as an obstacle to raising living standards. Nearly all the brilliant men of the age were critical in one way or another. A priest like Antonio Genovesi, following in the footsteps of historian Pietro Giannone, was proposing that the state take over some of the wealth of the religious orders, in an age when there were about 112,000 clerics in the kingdom of Naples -- 16,500 in the capital alone -- or over twenty priests per thousand of population.[3] The privileges and immunities of the church were considerable. These ranged from jurisdictional rights such as granting asylum to refugees from justice when hiding even in the buttery or kitchen garden, to tax-exemptions for bishops and their humblest retainers. Probably at least two-fifths of all disposable lands in the realm, exclusive of royal domains, were subject to church control in one form or another.

One big achievement was the concordat of 1741. It will be recalled that in 1737 Charles secured recognition from Pope Clement of his monarchy over Naples. Other objectives included some control over church appointments, reduction in the number of monasteries, and the release of revenues from lands held in perpetual mortmain. Although these demands were not met, the Pope did grant the much-coveted Bull of the Crusade whereby monies previously collected for Rome in respect of deferred obligations such as fighting in holy wars, fasting, and other religious duties were now accorded to the crown of Naples. This concession brought much needed revenue to the government. But a real breakthrough did not occur until the reign of the next Pope, Benedict XIV, with whom an important concordat was signed in June 1741. By its terms, a census was established to register church and secular lands, in which the church was required to pay taxes in the amount of one half of those collected under the secular category; the right to grant asylum to fugitives was drastically reduced, with the state

68

taking over greater powers to prosecute; while a mixed commission was to settle any disputes arising from the concordat.[4]

The census considerably curbed the church's temporal power. Though still unresolved were issues such as papal rights to investiture, tribute and benefices, the range of immunities enjoyed by church tribunals, and sheer numbers of clergy, yet the royal revenues increased by at least three million ducats. Less progress, however, was made in Sicily. When church properties were registered in 1747 and church produce under private franchise was assessed for tax, the laws were circumvented by adept Sicilian churchmen. Similar loopholes were devised with laws passed in 1738 and 1752 whereby vacant see appointments, which were now supposed to be filled by the state, passed only nominally under treasury control. Unlike in Naples, the governing panel established over the island proved rather ineffective in breaking down the church's fiscal autonomy.

Yet none of this deterred Charles and his ministers from their attacks on its power. The crown, for example, insisted on prior assent before papal briefs could be published; the number of priests was reduced (which by 1750 was aimed at a maximum of ten per thousand of population), along with church holidays; while by a law of 1756, the church was restricted in acquiring further property. But in the course of these measures a series of crises caught the government off-guard.

There was already in existence some degree of popular nationalism. This was prompted by the war of Austrian Succession and the natural diasters already referred to. And one of the policies which brought feelings to boiling-point was the admission of Jews into the kingdom. Seeking to attract foreign skills and capital, Charles published thirty-seven articles in 1741, permitting Jews to enter for fifty years, with virtual right of citizenship. They had been expelled by a decree of Emperor Charles V in 1540, and now two hundred years later the King was applying his new principle of toleration -- applicable to all provided his gospel of monarchy was left alone. The thirty-seven articles had the support of Tanucci, Montealegre, and some sections of the Roman curia, but they were unpopular from the start among the masses. The sufferings people were going through in the 1740's were taken as manifestations of divine anger, especially whenever the blood of San Gennaro preserved in the famous vial in Naples cathedral failed to liquefy. Triggered by pro-Austrian elements and religious extremists aiming to embarrass the government, popular resentment exploded into violence against the Jews who were held responsible for the disasters. Faced by riots which could only please the Austrian enemy, the government felt obliged to yield, and in 1747, reluctantly, Charles revoked the decree which had authorized the articles, giving the lame excuse that the Jews had contributed little to the economy.[5]

But others too felt the sting of popular anger. The riots were directed as much against segments in the church, when Pope Benedict XIV the previous year unavailingly tried to re-introduce the Inquisition, as urged by Cardinal Spinelli and the newly-established Order of bare-footed friars; and some protesters roundly condemned certain features of the nunciature which Tanucci and others had long been trying to get abolished.

In essence Charles was caught in the middle between religious extremism and anti-clericalism. Combined pressures, moreover, from Rome, France, and even by Tanucci himself led his government to come down on another group, this time the Freemasons. Their small upper-class society was suppressed in 1751, but there were few individual persecutions. Though scapegoats could easily be found when things went wrong, the government had learned that attacks against one group could provoke counter-attacks by another, for nationalism like Pandora's box had shown itself a potent and complex force, especially when dealing with all things foreign, whether from Rome, the Hapsburgs, or the Jews.

The radicalism of Tanucci, certainly more extreme than the views of the King, was yet out of touch with the masses when it came to popular fanaticism. But Tanucci at least made many aware of the church's huge mortmain wealth; and the basis was laid for the sweeping reforms he was to carry out after Charles' departure from Naples. With episcopal revenues to Rome drastically reduced, with priests no longer required to have a private income, and with marriage made additionally a civil contract, Tanucci in the 1760's was to secularize the state as far as any man could. As for Charles, loyal Roman Catholic that he was, he at least agreed with Tanucci in favoring some degree of jurisdictional independence from Rome; and his later opposition to Jesuit influence reflected the latent Jansenism which Tanucci had imbued in him. In a paradoxical way, then, fear of foreign influence was converging to shape the nationalism of the mob, the radicalism of Tanucci, and the regalism of the King.

One obstacle in the path of reform, was the entrenched professionalism of the lawyers. Along with magistrates, these cooperated only too willingly with landed interests. The very ambiguity of the law, moreover, provided a convenient smokescreen to confound reformers. There were a dozen legal codes in force, largely corresponding to the occupiers of southern Italy in the course of history -- Roman, Byzantine, Lombard, Norman, Swabian, Angevin, feudal, ecclesiastic, Aragonese, Spanish Hapsburg, and Austrian Hapsburg. Charles himself added a twelfth code in 1754 -- a well-meaning *codex Carolinus*, which yet put one more weapon of sophistry in the legal profession's hands. Indeed the fourteen provinces of the kingdom lacked an honest justice for the defendant, for whom immediate jail sentence with loss of property was usually the norm. Needless to add, Naples itself was crammed with lawyers and petty thieves alike, the latter comprising about thirty thousand, or one in ten of the population.

Despite its good intentions, the government through fear of revolt kept many of the tribunals which for so long had obstructed justice. Some were reformed or abolished, but retained were the treason or 'want-of-confidence' tribunal (*giunta d'inconfidenza*) designed to ferret out conspirators, usually pro-Austrian, along with that of poisons (*giunta de'veleni*) in which women were the main felons. Skilled officials were adept at securing proof of guilt. Since such costs were borne by the treasury, often involving extra judges at special trials, sentences were severe, and appeals mostly unavailing. Yet the government did allow appeals, especially at tribunals run by nobles, and it passed laws against harassment of debtors often flung prematurely

71

in jail.  Moreover it did its best to improve the jails
themselves -- damp surroundings, for example, being
banned for the convicted.[6]  Charles' regime was generally humane by contemporary standards, using force
to protect its reforming instinct.  Tyranny pure and
simple, with all the relish of dungeon and torture-
chamber, was more expertly indulged in by other rulers
of Naples.

Another shortcoming was the legacy of bad local
government, thwarting the enlightenment Charles envisaged.  A modicum of self-rule had existed since the
time of the Swabian Frederick II, which though noble-
dominated in the provinces included broader groups in
the cities.  Parliaments had arisen like the great one
at Palermo, whose rights had been conferred by the
crown in times past.  Convening at least once every
two years, their members could vote on such matters
as communal land rights, tax methods, and raising revenue for the crown.  There was also an office of Aragonese origin known as the syndic.  Voted on by the
taxpayers of each commune in a province, this served
to administer public funds through a pair of elected
officials, to examine the conduct of magistrates, and
supervise other matters in the public interest such
as the market places of Naples.

During the Spanish viceregal period, parliament
and local syndics could not meet all the financial
needs of the state.  In order to raise money and expand the army, the government had to sell offices and
titles and convert cities and communal lands into
fiefs.  But by dissipating and mortgaging its own
revenues, the viceregal government, like the crown
of Spain itself, got into debt from which it could
only escape by raising further mortgages.  A vicious
circle thus set in.  To anticipate future cash reserves it finally restored to the practice of selling
concessions known as *arrendamenti*, that is, sales to
individuals (or communes) of the right to collect
various types of tax for the public revenue.  This
practice of cutting off the state's direct taxing
powers and franchising them to tax-farmers may have
been a useful temporary expedient, but its effect on
the long-term economy of the nation was disastrous.
In depriving itself of future income, the government

was forced to rely on short-term annual revenues from arrendamenti. Human nature being what it is, powerful concessionaires were more interested in getting as large a rake-off as possible from the taxes collected, and it was not long before they used their enormous leverage to dominate the government. In the process they leased the lucrative business to sub-concessionaires, and the chain of tax-collection was passed on in turn, cutting back on revenues that belonged to the nation. With syndic power long since eroded, with parliaments suborned, officals corrupted and tribunals made arbitrary, impartial government under the Hapsburgs had become a sham.

The proper conduct of public officials being the first objective, Charles' government restored the syndic somewhat to its pristine beginnings by resuming the ancient custom of examining its officers forty days each year, during which time they had to answer any charges brought against them. But arrendamenti were another matter. Clearly the main task here was to reform the tax structure itself. In this regard, there were roughly three types of tax when Charles came to the throne -- enforced donatives (abolished in 1747), direct taxes, and indirect taxes -- a range of obligations that to say the least was highly inequitable.

Direct taxes were payable according to the hearths (*fuoci*) in a particular district -- such hearths reaching nearly 400,000 by 1760 -- and were collected from the head of each local family, but regardless of a district's aggregate wealth. Thus a richer, sparsely-inhabited, district might pay less tax relative to income or resources than a larger one which might be more populated and altogether poorer. Farmers additionally had to pay a land tax, plus a predial tax on the pasture of allodial domains. Nobles by contrast got off lightly. Owning nearly one half of all disposable lands, about the only tax they needed to pay was the annual *adoa* (in lieu of military service dating from Spanish times in the fifteenth century), together with a form of inheritance duty known as the *rilevio*. These totalled only about seven per cent of their revenues against at least three times this figure payable by most other citizens. And barely one tenth of direct tax money came from nobles in the first place. With similar exemptions enjoyed by royal, treasury, and church officials, as well as some professional groups, the load fell heaviest upon the smaller farmers and the poor.

Aware of inequities in the direct tax system, the government passed a series of measures to mitigate the worst abuses.[7] The first reforms were directed against collectors themselves. Zealous and rapacious by tradition, they were forbidden by an ancient law revived in 1737 to requisition more than sixteen horses in every covered mile. As to the hearth tax, with agricultural wages as low as thirty to forty ducats a year, this was curtailed when the maximum hearth tax per family was fixed at four ducats, 20 granos. By the 1750's, however, with population pressures growing, this went up by a further two ducats -- a trend that applied to most other taxes, though the government did try to hold it down for the poorest families, from Apulia to Sicily. At the other end of the scale, the government increased the land tax on wealthier estates in 1741, subsequently collecting from the nobles at least one half of any lapsed adoa dues as well as enforcing proper recording of the rilevio in the traditional register, or *cedolaris*. It also tried to impose a new tax on travelling salesmen and clerics. Displeased at both church and communes dragging their feet, and mindful of the census arising from the concordat of 1741, the government in the early 1750's appointed officals in every province to make sure taxes were kept up to the mark.

Indirect taxes comprised a wide range of dues and tithes stemming from feudal domains, but they were mainly included in the arrendamenti mentioned above. Collected by powerful concessionaires and market magistrates to whom the government, as we have seen, had sold such privileges in the past, these taxes were levied on the gross produce of items such as vegetable oil, olives, soap, silk, wines and brandy, tobacco, salt, fish, and even passageway tolls.[8] Needless to say, arrendamenti of this type provided a handsome living to those fortunate enough to possess them. By mid-century, arrendamento value

collected from salt and other products was approaching
15 million ducats, vastly exceeding the modest two to
three million ducats collected from direct taxes.  The
net proceeds from these arrendamenti yielded twice as
much to the concessionaire as to the treasury, all in
face of rising living costs which imposed great hardships on people in general.

The boldest of Charles' tax reforms was unques-
tionable the policy of redeeming the arrendamenti.
At first the government had little success, as when
in Sicily, laws passed in 1740 and in the 1750's tried
to reduce the number of tax-collecting franchises and
check corruption among officials.  Sicily was indeed
a hard nut to crack.  Much property on the island still
eluded the census -- the total value of untaxed property exceeded half a billion ducats -- while an absurd
export tax on silk injured what prosperity there was
in this field.  But elsewhere progress began to be
made.  The first positive move was in 1750 when the
government started buying back arrendamenti concessions on oil and soap.  Oil taxes alone were putting
up the price to the consumer thirty per cent or more,
and many an outraged merchant had petitioned Charles
to mitigate their harshness.[9]  The following year a
giunta was established for eliminating the concessions
altogether, starting with salt, followed by silk and
wine.  Though some arrendamenti were later returned
to private hands, the basis was laid for the eventual
redemption of the larger ones carried out by Tanucci
in later years, which for so long had alienated revenue from the government's jurisdiction.[10]

Despite the benefits of redemption, however, the
government was well aware that many hardships remained,
and this was especially so where producers were concerned.  There did exist mass cultivation of grains,
olives, mulberries, almonds, and vines, mainly in the
coastal areas of Apulia, Calabria, and Campania; but
the legacy of tax-franchise in the past, the conservatism of the peasant, confusions in land-ownership,
the poor roads, and restrictions in trade with other
provinces all hampered the chances for further plantation.  Too many farmers were unable to make ends
meet within the tight economic system.  Discouraged
by the bleak prospects of the countryside, many would

swell the ranks of absentee landlords, join the
floating population, or resort to open brigandage.

Even for those who persisted in arable farming,
a somewhat restricted market awaited them. There
was an institution termed the *annona*, that is, the
public storage authority for grain, whose function
was to ensure supplies to towns, communes, and stricken
areas before any of it could be sold elsewhere. To
offset ill effects from famine, decrees were issued
in 1743 and 1759 requiring the annona to submit before-
hand the exact stocks under its jurisdiction.[11] Hoarding was made illegal and a ready supply made available
for public baking ovens. The annona practice and the
laws that went with it were well-intentioned, but
since the prices were fixed by regulation and subject
to tax, the market was not very attractive to the
farmer, who as the immediate supplier had to trade
marginally and was often attached to some feudal fiefdom himself.

A traditional method for a farmer to secure a
market for his produce was by open contract, whereby
merchants in Naples would advance credit at prices
based on the seasonal average. This was usually fixed
at the end of the year. It applied to grain, olive
oil, silk, flax, tobacco, fruit, and fish -- severe
restrictions, incidentally, being imposed on their
export. The open contract practice was the only source
of liquid capital most producers could anticipate. The
Neapolitan merchants who funded it were themselves advanced credit from Amsterdam or London, often at high
rates of interest, so that the whole cycle of capital
was in large degree dependent on the big financiers
of Europe. Not surprisingly there was a tug-of-war
between the producers, anxious to maintain as high
prices as possible, and the merchants of Naples who
tried to bid them down. A related example was a dispute over storage charges of olive oil, which were
too great for the smaller producers to handle on their
own. The matter came to a head in the late 1730's,
and it ended with a victory for the merchant creditors
when a higher tribunal overturned a ruling in Otranto
by raising the interest from five to six per cent.
This dispute was symptomatic of the weak state of
capital-hungry producers. The work of Ferdinando

Galiani, *Della Moneta*, completed in 1750, upheld the
need for a more equitable credit system and paved
the way for the great economic reforms of Tanucci
in the following reign.

A brighter side of the picture was the growth in
olive oil production. Here Charles' government made
strenuous efforts to cultivate waste land and allodial
domains. Predial taxes were remitted for olive planters,
while penalties were enforced for olive trees cut down
without permission. Despite competition from Spanish
and Levantine oils, output increased nearly fivefold
between 1730 and 1760, by which year gross production
approached 55,000 *salme*, and exports extended to the
Adriatic and Baltic regions.[12] Increases in other
products included flax, tobacco, wines and brandy,
manna, saffron, salt, and fish (especially from coral
fishing near Vesuvius). There was a heavy export tax,
but internally many of these products became free of
arrendamenti. Rice, figs and other fruits, timber,
alum, marble and stones, pottery, leather, and textiles completed the modest list of exports.

Strenuous efforts, less successful in the end,
were also made to increase silk production. Traditionally one of the chief industries in the nation,
cultivation had been declining in face of burdensome
taxes at home and competition from abroad. When laws
were passed encouraging mulberry-tree planting and
forbidding its destruction, enterprising farmers
would adroitly intersperse the crop with fig trees
or the vine. The duty on every pound of silk was
already high enough, this being strictly based on
the volume of cocoons involved. It was later reduced, but with heavy transit and export taxes often
amounting to more than import charges, the point was
reached at which Neapolitan silk could no longer
compete with that of France, where at Lyons and other
places its quality became unrivaled in Europe. The
government tried to reverse the trend by curtailing
imports, at least for foreign residents, by improving
techniques in spinning and thread, and ending the
arrendamanto silk concession altogether. But it was
a losing fight. Contraband, corrupt inspectors, more
attractive profits to be gained from olives, figs,
and vines, and the indebtedness of silk producers to

77

the big merchants in Naples frustrated government efforts. Two million pounds produced in 1755 fell to one million by the 1780's as the value of silk exports shrunk to less than half the value of silk imported from abroad.[13]

French experts were called in to develop this lagging industry. And to stimulate trades in general, Charles' government invited other Europeans to come to Naples -- Italians, Germans, Dutchmen, and Englishmen. All these became actively engaged as craftsmen in such occupations as furniture-making, leatherwork, and jewel-mounting, all so dear to the King; and not the least important were foreign supervisors employed in mines and metal foundries for the expansion of a modest arms industry.

Domestic markets might have made more headway if communications had been better. Roads in fact were in a shocking condition. Little attempt was made to build fine highways radiating from Naples; and Charles himself, perhaps, can be criticized for thinking too much of the regal grandeur of the chase rather than commercial utility when he enlarged the strada di Puglia at the hunting seat of Bovino, along with similar roadways through Persano and Venafro -- the latter linked with the impressive strada di Caccia which spanned the Volturno river. Nonetheless some useful improvements were made. A new promenade was built along the Naples coastline, past Castel Nuovo, where before had been sea-infested shacks. Justinian's bridge was repaired to improve communications between Capua and Cagazzo, while south of Naples from Salerno, the via di Calabria was improved from Persano down to Reggio on the strait of Messina. A profitable rent was derived from the mails, run by a concession, which rapidly exceeded one million ducats as the service was extended over longer distances. Roads, bridges, and canals were constructed or repaired at many other places, though essentially the provinces remained desolate and untouched.

Desirous of unifying the market, the government by 1740 established a supreme tribunal of commerce consisting of a president and eight magistrates.

This was designed to promote trade through a policy of centralization, reform or abolish many cumbersome tribunals, and tighten up on customs and excise. But the very contradiction between trying to centralize trade and liberalize it at the same time was not lost upon the merchants. Many Sicilians complained that the sale of fruit and vegetables was now too tightly supervised to permit adequate profits; and as a result of petitions presented to the King by the viceroy and parliament of Sicily on behalf of the old ways, the supreme tribunal in 1746 was replaced by a consular authority. In the Naples portion of the kingdom however, the tribunal survived to regulate tariffs of national and foreign products, and to hear appeals. In 1751 it freed trade between Naples and Messina, where a commercial company was formed the following year. Customs and excise offices were enlarged at Naples, Salerno, Molfetta, Brindisi, and Taranto, to the chagrin of smugglers, for whom contraband especially in the silk trade was a permanent way of life; and to boost revenues, luxury goods were increasingly taxed at entry and exit through the ports. A final blow against feudal control over trade was struck in 1759. On October 4, the government passed an important law under penalty of a heavy fine which prohibited noble or merchant concessionaires from restricting the flow of sales in any territory under their jurisdiction.

Anxious to expand the marine, the government commissioned a number of ships -- the 1300-ton flagship *San Filippo Reale* and the 900-ton frigate *San Carlo* were cases in point -- and the port of Naples was correspondingly enlarged. A naval college was founded in 1741, with a code of commerce and navigation requiring, among other things, that the national flag be flown by all vessels. Ten years later a giunta of shipping was established. A new maritime code now required proper observance of shipping licences and of regulations for treating crews, while money was voted for the training of pilots and vessel-masters. Charles' idea was to have the modest Neapolitan navy a peacetime ally of the Spanish fleet, possibly partaking in its convoys and capable of reaching at least the ports of London and Amsterdam.

The tribunal of commerce mentioned above was as
concerned with foreign as domestic trade.  So many
foreigners were active in Neapolitan ports that it
was not long before new consular arrangements were
made with other powers.  Countries with which Naples
signed treaties of commerce and friendship in the
early 1740's included Spain, England and France, the
latter among other things providing a speedier mail
service to relieve the blockage through Rome.  Similar
provisions applied to an agreement with Turkey.
Following a visit to Constantinople in the spring of
1741 by envoy Conte F. Finochietti and his party a-
board the new ships, an arrangement with Sultan
Mahmud I allowed for communications between Naples
and the Ottoman Porte to be established through the
Albanian town of Durazzo; and a trade agreement afterwards was made with the Sultan's vassal the Bey of
Tripoli, who responded by sending lavish gifts of[14]
horses, camels, and lions to the court of Naples.
The Netherlands, Denmark and Sweden, along with other
countries, followed next in the last decade of the
reign, though it was not till 1787 that any commercial treaty was made with Russia.

To promote trade and coin circulation, the government reformed the currency in which, as with
weights and measures, a chaos of conflicting values
was the norm.  Gold and silver coins were debased.
To preserve more specie, severe laws were passed
against counterfeiting.  In the course of the reign a
number of new coins were issued, to the delight of
numismatists, including some six- and twelve- carlini
pieces (of 60 and 120 granos respectively), with the
head of Charles and Amalia engraved upon them.  Conflicting money-rates prevalent in the two portions of
the kingdom were to some extent standardized.[15]  These
measures also aimed at establishing a primitive common
market with Roman and Venetian products, to the detriment
of Austrian, Hungarian and even Spanish interests.

Improved revenues from taxes and trade contributed greatly to the number of welfare projects which
got under way in Charles' reign.  The metropolis received a liberal share of funds administered by such
bodies as the public works and sanitation commissions,

with equivalents established in Sicily by 1740. When plague broke out in Messina three years later, Charles promptly answered the appeals of the Palermo senate. His government also gave a high priority to reducing the vast number of beggars which infested the national scene; and laws against vagrancy and brigandage, trespassing on the royal chase, and unlicensed gambling lotteries were complemented by a wide range of protective poor laws. Near the famed Regii Studii in Naples, an impressive royal almshouse was begun in 1751, designed to accomodate some two thousand destitute of both sexes, including orphans, cripples, deaf-mutes and the blind.

Close to the Palazzo degli Studii by Constantine's gate, where a public library had been established, the new Bourbon-Farnese museum became richly adorned. Here among the treasures from Portici, lectures were given using first-hand sources of antiquity, foreshadowing the foundation of the Herculaneum and Pompeii Academy in 1753 and the Academy of Sciences and Letters in 1778. Though these institutions could never yet challenge the major universities of Europe, the many researches which Charles commissioned and the works of individual scholars such as Antonio Genovesi, who was the first to occupy a chair in political economy, made an enriching contribution to art, history, and the sciences.

Charles achieved a great deal in face of tremendous odds.[16] Most of the shortcomings -- social backwardness, maladministration, the lack of skills and capital -- were there when he arrived. During his reign, he was helped by a wise choice of ministers, not to mention his parents who sent him liberal sums for such purposes as expanding the army, or for the crown to redeem its debts. It was not forgotten how much had been lost from its many transfers of fiefdoms to nobles in times past. When Charles left, noble and church jurisdiction had shrunk, arrendamenti redeemed, the revenues increased. As a result of the one and a half million extra ducats of noble revenue, the census over the church bringing in three million ducats, and the vast savings derived from buying back the concessions, his regime by 1760 seemed to have more than doubled its net revenue to over ten million ducats, a no mean advance in face of so many adverse factors.[17]

While much of the gross was absorbed by continued redemption costs, yet Charles could show that he had his subjects' welfare at heart all along, as he had claimed. And if the peasant did not at once benefit from his reforms, if the capital city was not yet strong enough to finance productive industry, if commerce was still undercut by red tape and foreign competition -- in a word, if Naples was still a consumer economy -- it was a hard fact that people then, as now, had to wait some time before the momentum of growth and investment could bring results. Unfortunately, the new resources realized by Charles and furthered by Tanucci were squandered by foolish regimes in the future, for which Naples was to pay a high price in the nineteenth century.

Marchese Tanucci, engraving after an unknown artist

# CHAPTER FIVE

## STEPS TOWARD CASTILE

Philip V of Spain died on July 9, 1746, at the age of sixty-three. Charles was grief-stricken at his father's death (followed by that of a sister, María Teresa Rafaela, the Dauphin's wife, almost immediately after), and he soon learnt from this event that his chances of inheriting the Spanish throne were drawing steadily nearer. It was a prospect which increasingly troubled him at home.

The fact was, his half-brother, now Ferdinand VI of Spain, was proving disturbingly slow to beget children. It was no secret that his wife Barbara of Braganza was presumed sterile -- a charge that could equally be made then against Ferdinand, whose love of peace and solitude, exemplified by his fine playing of the violin, was marked by long spells of melancholia and sexual passivity. If he died childless, then Charles was next in line as the eldest son by Philip's surviving wife, Isabel Farnese. His great victory at Velletri had clearly saved his throne; and just when he had settled down to a reign with constructive reforms, he now faced the possibility of being uprooted from his kingdom. His main concern was thus the need to father a dynasty in Naples which would hopefully endure should he have to move to the senior Bourbon throne in Castile.

If he became king of Spain, what then would happen to his children in Naples? There were many predators in Europe anxious for the spoils of southern Italy. Maria Amalia, in addition to the two girls Josefa and Luisa, produced six boys by the mid-1750's. Felipe Pascual, born in 1747, unfortunately grew mentally retarded through alleged mishandling by his nurse. But there was Carlos who followed next year in November (the future Charles IV of Spain), while Fernando arrived three years later as the heir to Naples.[1] These last two, while physically robust, eventually turned out mediocre in the extreme -- mental inertia with the one, dissipation with the other -- and both showed a lack of political responsibility in later years. Whether their mediocrity was due to any peculiar strain in the Bourbons, though hardly in the House of Saxony, is difficult to say. Their parents, however, could take some comfort from the younger sons. There was Gabriel Antonio, born in 1752, and the apple of his father's eye; Antonio Pascual, who came three years later; and lastly Francisco Xavier, born in 1757, who was to die at the age of fourteen.[2] But at least Charles had a dynasty worth the name, and it was his job to protect it to the full.

In October 1748, the treaty of Aix-la-Chapelle (Aquisgrán in Spanish) had ended the war of Austrian Succession. Here, it is recalled, Parma, Piacenza and Guastalla had been given to Charles' brother Don Philip. This delighted Isabel, whose ambitions for her two sons to acquire a Bourbon inheritance had at last been fulfilled. But Charles saw scant cause for rejoicing. A serious snag had arisen from the treaty; for subsequent clauses, prompted by Louis XV, stipulated that in the event Charles were ever to relinquish Naples to become king of Spain, Naples should then pass to his next of kin -- a provision based on earlier agreement made in Vienna back in 1738 before he had any children. This 'next of kin' therefore could mean only Don Philip himself, who had married Louis XV's daughter, Louise Elizabeth. Parma, Piacenza, and Guastalla would then be divided between Austria and Savoy.

Charles bitterly contested the designs of other powers to expand at his family's expense; and now Savoy had joined in the pickings. Since Charles Emmanuel of Savoy had already acquired bits of Pavia as prizes from the late war, the King in Naples regarded it as an impertinence for his rival in the north, who was always changing sides, to expand his dynasty any further. Despite the betrothal between the latter's son Victor Amadeus, and Charles' own sister María Antonia, this tie did not overcome the distrust he felt, and he refused to sign these post-treaty provisions.

Charles was also annoyed with his half-brother Ferdinand. At Aranjuez in 1752, the Spanish king made a similar agreement with Austria and Savoy whereby in the event that Charles vacated his throne, Naples would go to Don Philip, Parma to Austria, and Piacenza to Savoy. A Bourbon-Hapsburg rapprochement was in the making. But this treaty still left Charles without any formal recognition of his family's rights. Though successful in the end, as will be shown later, Charles likewise refused to sign its provisions on the grounds that his children were being barred from succeeding to an inheritance; and he pointed this out in no uncertain terms to Ferdinand, who replied rather lamely that he was only thinking of what would be in his "dear brothers' best interests".[3]

The only point he was willing to yield, through the Pope's mediation, was his surrender of historic jurisdiction over the renowned Knights of Malta, a paltry loss indeed, seeing that the only annual tribute Naples ever managed to extract from the island's Grand Master was one thin falcon! Disgusted with his neighbors' conduct -- he even crossed swords with Austria over Tuscany to which realm he had once been the heir-apparent himself -- Charles contrived to seek the help of France through its ambassador the Duke of Duras in Madrid, who alone seemed willing to scheme against the Hapsburgs in Italy.[4] It is hardly surprising that there were raised eyebrows in Ferdinand's court.

Relations between Ferdinand and Charles were never close. Though the former on occasions could congratulate Charles on the progress he was making on the great palace at Caserta, and even settled an annual allowance of 40,000 pesos on the young heir Fernando now that Felipe's imbecility was common knowledge, memories of the past between the two relatives, each with their different backgrounds, still left their mark. If Charles' persistence to procreate annoyed both Ferdinand and Barbara, not to mention his interference in Spanish affairs of state, Ferdinand's treatment of the unwanted Isabel equally annoyed Charles. And the picture of his mother banished from Madrid and slowly losing her eyesight only increased the bitterness he felt. It was said in Spain that at Philip's death the reign of Isabel had ended and that of Barbara had begun. The treatment she had meted out to others -- Princesa de los Ursinos is a case in point -- now came full circle; and inasmuch as she represented a faction on behalf of her son had been banished by Ferdinand from the Buen Retiro palace, along with her children Don Luis and María

Antonia. There is little doubt that Queen Barbara had a hand in the affair. Seville, perhaps, would have been a happier place for the fallen matriarch, but it was La Granja, where the cold rooms of San Ildefonso palace looked out upon the bleak mountains of the Sierra Guadarrama. It was an undeserved punishment, recalling her powerlessness under Ferdinand, and one which she was not likely to forget.[5] Charles meanwhile, anxious to console his ailing mother and suspecting that he was moving closer to the throne of Spain, issued a decree from Portici on April 25, 1754. to the effect that in the event of his succession to the Spanish throne or in case of an interregnum, Isabel should be regent, pending a final decision by the government.[6]

Charles' involvement with Spanish politics was focused on rivalry of another sort which nearly caused a rupture between the two monarchs. This concerned a tug-of-war in Spain between two factions, one pro-English, the other pro-French. Ferdinand openly sided with English interests, but this scarcely improved relations with his half-brother in Naples, who as we have seen was tending to support the French faction led by Duras. That Ferdinand favored England was in no small measure due to the presence in Madrid of Sir Benjamin Keene -- the same British ambassador whom Charles would remember as a young man. Keene had many cards in his favor. Not only was he an excellent diplomat, but helping him to promote Anglo-Spanish friendship was an administrator and treasurer of outstanding merit, José Carvajal y Lancaster. The latter had awarded in 1750 the sum of 100,000 pounds to Britain in settlement of the South Sea company's claims upon Spain. This accord which Carvajal negotiated with Keene also gave British merchants the favored position of paying no higher taxes than Spanish subjects as well as lower tariff rates on certain imports which stemmed from earlier treaties in the previous century. All this was in exchange for winding up once and for all the Asiento contract, ceded at the treaty of Utrecht, which had entitled England to bring Negro slaves to South America and send the coveted permission-ship to Panama.[7]

Carvajal's policy was opposed by his rival,

Marqués de la Ensenada. As chief minister, the latter
wielded enormous power through holding the portfolios
of nearly every other department. Born Cenón de Somode-
villa in Old Castile, subsequently a successful banker,
Ensenada had served under Patiño as a quartermaster to
the navy and had been present at the victorious siege
of Oran. He helped Patiño organize the Spanish invasion of Naples and was architect of Spain's naval
expansion, rising thereafter to positions of still
greater responsibility. Though he had a natural flair
for intrigue, he yet ranks as an outstanding administrator. He did much to reform taxes, and achieved the
singular distinction of balancing the budget.[8] Generally
pro-French in his views, he regarded Carvajal's dealings
with England as tantamount to capitulating to foreign
interests, and cited as proof of his charges the fact
that British logwood cutters were being allowed to infiltrate Honduras in Central America. Carvajal's death
in 1754 briefly strengthened his hand against the pro-
English faction, especially when he alleged that British
influence was behind a treaty of 1750 between Spain and
Portugal which appeared to favor the latter's interests
at the expense of Spanish-held Paraguay. Ensenada secretly reported this to Charles, who promptly appealed
to Ferdinand to have the treaty annuled. Ferdinand resented the interference and relations between the two
monarchs were strained to breaking-point.

But Ensenada in the meantime had not reckoned with
Ferdinand, who took umbrage at his frequent anti-
British pronouncements. The king moreover had appointed in Carvajal's place a foreign affairs minister
who was just as Anglophile as his predecessor. This was
an Irishman named Ricardo Wall -- intelligent, ambitious,
and a one-time friend of Alberoni -- who having seen
service with the Spanish forces under Montemar, became
captain of Dragoons to Don Philip, official in the
Indies, and Spanish envoy in London before assuming
this top post in Madrid. Wall wasted no time in getting
rid of Ensenada. With the support of Keene and the Duke
of Huéscar y Alba, Wall charged Ensenada with defying
the king's policy, especially in regard to a secret
treaty proposal with the French including a plan against
the British in Honduras. On the night of July 20, 1754,
with the king's full authorization, Ensenada was arrested
in his bed and swiftly banished to Granada, his pro-
French accomplice Ordenaña sharing a similar fate.[9]

Whatever Charles thought about this affair, relations with Ferdinand improved upon the outbreak of a new international conflict, the Seven Years War. It began when Frederick the Great in 1756 invaded Saxony and once more started fighting with Maria Theresa, who was bent on recovering Silesia. This time the old antagonists were supported by different allies. With France gaining nothing from the previous war and with Austria equally disillusioned, the way was clear for Louis XV to become the ally of Maria Theresa, Bourbon at last burying the hatchet with a Hapsburg. Thus took place the famous Diplomatic Revolution ingenuously devised by the Austrian minister Prince Wenzel Kaunitz. While negotiations were proceeding, England became the ally of Frederick the Great in a novel London-Berlin entente, and this ultimately was to prove astonishingly successful on all fronts. Where Spain and Naples were concerned, the peace-loving Ferdinand was determined to stay neutral -- a fact not displeasing to Charles now that Don Philip of Parma, with the major powers once more distracted by war, stood a chance of holding on to his Italian duchies. By helping to consolidate Philip, Charles would strengthen his own position in Naples, where any transfer of his mandate would be more heavily weighted in favor of his own children.

Charles, then, in his letters to Ferdinand expressed pleasure that Maria Theresa, as well as Charles Emmanuel of Savoy, would leave Parma and Piacenza well alone, provided Spain kept to a course of strict neutrality. So long as she did, a breach between the two Bourbon monarchs was avoided. "May God give you guidance to do the right thing", Charles entoned prudently to Ferdinand in a letter couched in the usual terms of endearment, "With our brother Don Philip we are all in this together... The treaty of Aranjuez has now realized its purpose in Italy of reconciling Paris and Vienna ... and all we desire is tranquility".[10] Ironically, the tranquility Charles craved for was broken not by Ferdinand but ultimately by Charles himself when as king of Spain he later became embroiled in this war on the losing side. Great were the stakes indeed, with England and France fighting for supremacy in North America and India. Though none could forsee the outcome, the war was to raise England to the pinnacle of glory in the eighteenth century; at the same time Spain in her state of isolation was at this stage convenient to Charles, who despite his growing anti-English feeling was at least spared the nightmare of a possible British bombardment of Naples.

The two monarchs thus saw eye to eye; and though the pro-English faction had got the upper hand at the court of Madrid with the pro-French faction in visible disarray, this did not mean that Spain would join with England. It is true that at one point it was possible for Spain to have helped England recover the island of Minorca, temporarily taken by the French, in exchange for getting back Gibraltar -- an offer which British war minister William Pitt was known to have made. But Ferdinand clung to peace, and while independent of cousin Louis XV, he was not prepared to betray him. With the war going badly for England anyway at this stage, Benjamin Keene and others of his faction had a difficult time pressing home their advantage. Yet Keene's death in December 1757 came at the very time when the fortunes of war began to turn in England's favor.

This heartened her supporters, from Wall to the Duke of Alba; but what concerned them more was a new trend of events with which Charles became directly involved. Ferdinand and Barbara were both seriously ailing in health. The course of neutrality they were pursuing had its advantages in raising the revenue and few were proposing that the country change this policy -- Ferdinand was not at all a bad monarch who founded academies, botanical gardens, observatories, as well as scholarships for study abroad -- but new ideas were shaping among men in power who saw his hand behind Spain's weakening posture. With sovereign and consort slowly passing from the scene, it was Charles in whom they increasingly set their hopes for a successor. In this respect none was more hopeful than Isabel herself, who from her place of exile at La Granja was closely watching events.

Ferdinand was attended by that consummate physician from the university of Valencia, Andrés Piquer, whose incisive *Lógica moderna* (1747) and *Tratado de calenturas* (Treatment of fevers, 1751), made him an

outstanding man of his generation. The king proved
a long time dying; and it was Barbara who was the first
to go. Her face and breasts shrunken from the fever
she had contracted, the queen passed away at Aranjuez
on August 25, 1758. Bereaved, her husband retired to
the castle of Villaviciosa de Odón a few miles southwest of Madrid, there to lament in a state of chronic
melancholia, and unknown to the doctors of that day
and age, in a state also of chronic tuberculosis. For
this he was liberally treated with ass' milk, white de-
coction of Sydenham, quinine, and heartshorn jelly,
along with crushed vipers and cordials for strength.
As he grew worse with every passing week, Charles showed
fidelity to good form by suggesting that the sick monarch seek consolation in a new wife.[11]   Charitable as
this suggestion was to Ferdinand, it was hardly charitable to any future consort. For the king went steadily
mad, tearing up his bedclothes and refusing to be fed
or shaved as in his rage he hurled volleys of abuse inter
spersed with chamber-pots at the bewildered attendants
who tried to serve him. It was as if the castle of Villa
viciosa held a king possessed by a devil. On September 2
1758, Charles received word from Ricardo Wall, now Isabel
private secretary, that Ferdinand was losing his reason
and that the country was heading towards total confusion.
The intimation was clear, namely, that Charles should
make preparations without delay to take some part in
governing Spain.[12]

Urgent as Wall was sounding, he wisely refrained
from meddling in the delicate state of affairs in the
peninsula. To commit a rash act of intervention without a clear mandate from a provisional junta might prejudice not only his own position but that of his mother,
in whom largely resided the possibilities for his smooth
transition to the throne. When in December 1758 Spain's
council of Castile was being mentioned as the only executive organ which could govern, Charles carefully
instructed his envoy in Madrid, the Prince of Yaci, to
sidestep any involvement and convey to the council his
hopes for Ferdinand's speedy recovery.[13] Since everyone knew this was impossible, the ambassador's message
must have sounded somewhat bombastic, even to Spanish
ears. Carefully biding his time meanwhile, Charles
was kept fully informed of the situation through the

good offices of his mother, whose secret correspondence was relayed to him via a network of spies. As he shared these confidences with his family at Portici or Caserta, not excluding Tanucci to whom he had given the reins of full power since 1755, Charles knew that he could not postpone indefinitely some sort of reply to Wall's overtures. On February 13, 1759, he drew up a declaration from Caserta to the effect that in the event of Ferdinand's death leading to his succession to the throne, Isabel as queen mother should assume the reins of government in his absence and until he should arrive in Spain.[14]

Such a declaration was music to the ears of his parent. Stricken with rheumatism and approaching blindness after so many years of confinement at San Ildefonso, Isabel who had so often cursed Ferdinand's cruelty towards her now gloated over Ferdinand's cruelty to himself. She felt no pity, only longing for her son's return. With Ferdinand cutting himself with bits of glass and trying to eat them at the same time, it was only a question of waiting out the remaining weeks; though prolonging the tension was the fact that the patient in his madness would only talk with his lord chamberlain the Duke of Béjar, in whom pathetically the dying king could sometimes see a faint light of reason. As the council of Castile could get no sense out of Ferdinand, with neither abdication nor a will clearly naming a successor, with Spain in fact without a ruler, Wall wrote to Charles and invited him to take over the government.[15]

But despite promptings from his mother who now formed a little coterie with Wall, the Duke of Béjar, and others as they begged him to return in order to save the country from chaos, Charles held back that summer of 1759 postulating "certain difficulties", i.e., that it would be beneath a king's dignity to take over another country while its sovereign was still alive. By now all this was little more than pretense; Charles was being true to form for other reasons. While hesitance would keep the country waiting with mounting impatience until his triumphal entry, it was not easy to wrench himself away from his adopted Naples, and he well knew it would be even worse for his wife who was showing increasing signs of strain. But the end

for Ferdinand came at last.  Long stricken with the
final stages of tuberculosis, he was rapidly reduced
to a raving skeleton; and he died on August 10, 1759,
at the age of forty-six.  As one of the morticians put
it, "his skin literally came off with the sponge".
Charles was now recognized as king by practically the
whole country.

The following letter he wrote to Isabel in French
reflects his new authority: "... It is with the greatest
sorrow I received this morning your loving letter dated
the tenth of this month, giving me the very sad news
of the death of my dear brother the King on this same
date at past four in the morning.  I have indeed had a
long time in which to prepare myself for his final end,
and the love I have always felt only increases the great
sorrow I feel now, as Your Majesty may well imagine...
You were quite right to grant requests on my behalf and
to make the final funeral arrangements...  I can thus
rest assured that ...God will grant him eternal life,
as I trust He will also give me the strength to bear
as heavy a burden...  I humbly thank you for congrat-
ulating me on my coming accession to the throne and I
convey my thanks also in the name of the Queen...  Please
tell José Navarro to get us over in a good fleet and have
everything ready when we arrive at Barcelona.  I trust
God will give you strength to govern in my absence and
I am sure everyone will gladly obey you as if it were
me.  Forgive me for not writing more this evening and
for being spare of sentiment, but I embrace you with
deepest respect.  Your humble and obedient son...
P.S. Please have the corps of troops in Catalonia assemble
as soon as possible...but with minimum disturbance to
the people, so as to meet our scheduled arrival and
serve as escort...".[16]

Despite his absence from the country Charles was
duly proclaimed the new king of Spain on September 11,
1759, in the traditional ceremony at the Buen Retiro
palace in Madrid.[17]  The beating of drums, the waving of
flags and standards, was repeated elsewhere, variations
depending on local custom.  The alcalde would raise the
scepter of authority before the people, and making the
sign of the cross would ask them to declare their belief in God and to accept the absent Charles III as their
true sovereign.  To this the crowd would nod affirmatively

a procedure that was repeated two or three times. The
alcalde would then order free drinks from the town
casks of wine and brandy, and free corn from the public
granary, while the parish poor would receive the public
bounty in coin.

Among Charles' last acts before his departure from
Naples was a diplomatic one which reflected his astuteness. At the treaty of Aranjuez in 1752, it had been
stipulated between Spain, Austria, and Savoy that in
the event Charles became king of Spain, Naples would
pass to his next of kin in the person of his brother
Don Philip. Parma and the other Italian duchies would
then be divided between Austria and Savoy. As we have
seen, Charles had refused to sign, protecting the interests of his children. To make sure Don Philip would
retain his inheritance and not squeeze his own heirs
out of Naples, he first persuaded Charles Emmanuel of
Savoy to give up his claim on Piacenza by means of a
liberal compensation, depositing the funds in a Genoese
bank. He did likewise with Austria in regard to Parma,
at the same time persuading Don Philip to marry off his
daughter Isabella with the son of Maria Theresa -- the
future Emperor Joseph II. Such a neat arrangement protected Charles' heir in Naples, as well as satisfying
both Philip, Charles Emmanuel, and the Empress.[18]
A sequel to his diplomacy concerned Tuscany, another
sensitive point. After he went to Spain, a compromise
was worked out with Maria Theresa whereby his daughter,
María Luisa Antonia, became engaged to the younger
Hapsburg son, Leopold of Tuscany, in exchange for a
Hapsburg daughter becoming engaged to his heir in Naples.
While these arrangements confirmed the status quo in
northern Italy, at least Tanucci remained at the helm
to continue Spanish influence in the south and the two
sides at last drew closer together.

His dynasty assured, Charles and his family prepared to leave Naples as prayers were offered to
St. Anthony, the Virgin, and the city's patron saint.
As an added good omen in this last respect, the blood
of San Gennaro obligingly liquefied in its glass vial.
Farewells were exchanged as Charles' third son and
successor, the eight-year old Fernando, was placed in
Tanucci's capable hands. A regency in the form of a
giunta was established until he should come of age at
sixteen, which included Tanucci himself, the Prince of

San Nicandro (Fernando's tutor), and two secretaries of state. At the investiture ceremony on October 6, 1759, the boy-prince received Louis XIV's sword from Charles, just as Charles once received it from this father, and was formally proclaimed King Ferdinand IV.[19] The pitiable Felipe Pascual (Duke of Calabria) remained with his brother in Naples.

The next day the royal couple boarded the Spanish flagship *Fénix* accompanied by the two princesses, María Josefa Carmela and María Luisa Antonia (now in their early teens), and the younger boys, Carlos and Gabriel. The four-year old Antonio Pascual and the two-year old Francisco Xavier followed on the *Triunfante*. The Spanish fleet which took Charles to Spain conveyed an impressive array of notables, among them Castropignano, treasurer Squillace, the Duke of Losada (the lord chamberlain), Marquis d'Ossun (the French ambassador), and the King's confessors, the aging Father Bolaños and Father Eleta. Most of these figures in one way or another were to play an important part in Spanish politics and history. On October 17, the *Fénix* dropped anchor at Barcelona, the guns of Montjuich firing salvos of salute. The elite of the land were there to greet the royal pair, including Catalonia's captain-general (Marqués de la Mina), the Princess of Yaci, and two dukes besides -- Medinaceli and Medina Sidonia. With memories of the war of Spanish Succession long faded, the people of Catalonia who had once supported the Hapsburg cause gave their new Bourbon king a surprisingly enthusiastic reception, and this continued during the royal couple's journey to Madrid.[20]

There had been no music -- only Masses -- aboard the ships during the crossing, as if a feeling of trepidation pervaded the calm. Charles in fact had been out of touch with his native land for so long that he could not know at first hand what changes had been going on in Spain over the past three decades. One such change concerned the important class of grandees and senior nobles. These had been carefully removed from cabinet positions by his father, and instead there had emerged subordinate secretaries of state who were the forerunners of the ministers Charles was soon to employ in Madrid. But what he could not know was the slow recovery

94

of power by these nobles under Ferdinand, often pro-
Hapsburg in the past, who had gradually mixed in with
the new subservient nobility of some two hundred titles
which Philip V had created. By Ferdinand's time the old
and the new as a class were almost indistinguishable,
and both were naturally bent on retaining their privileges. They were often highly educated men. Feudal
yet juridical in outlook, absolutist yet believing in
the traditional rights of the regional councils of
which Castile and the Indies were the survivors, many
senior nobles, hand-in-glove with big merchant interests
and the military, sprang in spirit from the matrix of
Aragon and Valencia, lamenting the day when Philip had
taken away the conciliar privileges of these regions in
1707 as well as some judicial autonomy from Catalonia,
and hoping that Charles would reverse the process. Thus
for more than one reason he was cheered on his way to
Madrid.

But Charles had no intention of changing course:
to centralize the monarchy in order to reform the functions
of state was what his father, along with Feijóo and
Tanucci, had taught him; and though he was to give some
satisfaction to nobles in terms of local privileges, this
did not mean that they were to be restored to power totally
at the national level -- a policy that was to have severe
repercussions later.

Naples had certainly been a preparing ground for
what he intended to do in Spain, but the problems here
were to prove much tougher than he anticipated. Certain
features may have been similar, but the task of governing
was far more complex in Spain because of its greater size
and variety, its bewildering contrasts of development.
The essential fragility of his reign nurtured on Italian
soil was bound to put him to a severe test when he moved
to harsher and more divergent climates.

It was in many respects a painful return. Anticipation mingled with nostalgia. He and his wife remembered as they left the beautiful shoreline of Naples
how the people lamented their departure as much as they,
for the fact was that Charles had given the country its
best administration in two hundred years. A symbol of
the honesty of his mandate, like a tribute to the land
he would never see again, was his refusal to take even

95

a ring which he had found among the ruins of Pompeii --
a virtue rare in departing heads of state!  Pottery
and vases, perhaps, he could modestly take with him;
the atmosphere of Italy, never.  And though he also
loved Spain, for this was his country, he knew that
Amalia could not.  With ailing health she dreaded the
approaching solemnity, the somber austerity of Castile.
Charles' awareness of her state of mind was the heaviest
burden he had to bear.  Duty rather than ambition
guided his principles.  Coming from Spain he sensed,
though he could not accurately define, the difficult
tasks that lay ahead.  His wheel of fate had come full
circle.

Maria Amalia, by Francesco Liani

# CHAPTER SIX

## TROUBLED KING OF SPAIN

The arduous journey from Barcelona to Madrid in late 1759 already foreshadowed misfortune. Exuberant as Charles was in writing to his mother whom he had not seen for nearly thirty years, this could not mask the subdued tone of Maria Amalia, who revealed in her letters a state of exhaustion and mental depression. Aggravating this was the fever contracted by the children, Don Gabriel and María Josefa, so that the King's traveling secretary Leopoldo Squillace, expressed serious concern for the royal family's safe arrival.[1] But passing through Saragossa and Guadalajara, the party finally reached Madrid by December, where a formal entry with inaugural ceremonies took place the following summer.

The tumultuous greeting of the royal couple relieved anxiety, and Charles felt at home in the city of his birth; but the Queen's health steadily deteriorated. The gaunt blocks of granite, the long corridors of the palaces at Aranjuez or La Granja, seemed to Maria Amalia to cast the surrounding land in gloom, forming a sharp contrast to the sunshine of her adopted Naples. Though she played her role with Germanic fortitude, at heart she loathed Spain and implied as much in her letters to Tanucci, complaining of the rain, the wind, and the cold, or else of the suffocating heat.[2] Her antipathy grew worse as her health declined, and before anyone could realize what in fact was an advanced state of pleurisy, holy images were rushed to the Buen Retiro palace where she was confined. On the afternoon of September 27, 1760, Maria Amalia died at the age of thirty-six. A temperamental but intelligent woman, friend of conservatives but considerably more astute than most consorts of her day, she could have been of inestimable help to Charles in the troubled years ahead. Loyal and appreciative of his work, she once wrote to Tanucci that the department secretaries in Madrid now did more work in a single week than previously they had done in six months.[3] She also opposed Spain's involvement with either Bourbon France or Hapsburg Austria, favoring a strong isolationist position. Events were to justify her point of view in the immediate context, and Charles was deprived of much useful advice. He was deeply affected by her death, and it is a tribute to his high notion of love and fidelity that he chose to remain single for the rest of his years.

This tragic loss was but the beginning of his misfortunes. Over the next few years there was to occur an unsuccessful war with England, mounting inflation, and a serious mutiny known as the Squillace riots which nearly cost him his throne. Aware that this was not Italy, he yet underestimated the inbred conservatism of his native country. But a brighter side to these years was his reconstruction of Madrid, discussed in later contexts, including those moments when he stood by to watch the half-finished Royal Palace slowly taking shape. Begun long ago by his father to replace the original Alcázar which had been burnt down, the palace was now hastened to near-completion in memory of his wife, who had complained so bitterly of the drafty Buen Retiro -- the place where she had died. It was the best he could do to recall the lost days of happiness at Portici, where her porcelain figurines rivaling those of Sèvres or Saxony had once given meaning to their private lives. Inspired by Bernini's design for the Louvre, yet very Spanish with its huge blocks of granite and limestone (the work of Juvara and Sachetti), its rococo walls and ceilings decorated by Giovanni Tiepolo, it was Charles' grandest palace, the haunt of many distinguished artists of the neoclassic period, including Tiepolo's triumphant rival Anton Mengs.

Despite the grievous blow of his wife's death, the King continued to rule energetically, and not since the days of Ensenada was work expedited so speedily. Magnanimous reform was the mood of the hour. Various amnesties were granted, the public jails cleared of deserters, while in provinces such as Catalonia many autonomous privileges were restored which had been forfeit since the days of Philip V; and the nobles of that region, now displaying their once-forbidden family arms began to cheer anew their Bourbon king. The new monarch also met the claims of many creditors to whom the crown owed mounting sums of money accrued since Hapsburg times.[4]

    The secretary of the latter office was the Italian
named Leopoldo di Grigorio, Marchese di Squillace,
whom Charles brought over from Naples and who was
soon to become a scapegoat for the country's mounting
ills.  Unlike his fellow-countrymen, Charles was reluctant to blame foreigners when things went wrong,
and he viewed his subordinates for their competence
and loyalty regardless of nationality.  At the same
time he was reluctant to take on new people unless
he had known them for some time.  Thus he welcomed
the Duke of Losada as his lord chamberlain, an old
and trusted associate in Italy, who kept a sort of
balance between two rival factions developing at the
seat of government.  On the one hand there was the
coterie consisting of Ricardo Wall, Charles' chief
minister who had done so much to steer his course to
Spain, Julián de Arriaga, minister of the Indies,
besides Squillace himself; on the other hand there
was the ambitious Ensenada, exiled by Ferdinand but
now pardoned by Charles and given a job in the tax
office, but who was still hoping to restore himself
to power.  The King, meanwhile, was planning to introduce humbler politicians into the government with
a reformist cast of mind, when a crisis in foreign
policy interrupted this objective.

    The Seven Years war had been raging since 1756
in which the alliance between France and Austria, now
joined by Russia, had emerged into a huge continental
bloc against Prussia.  England came to Frederick's aid,
and this London-Berlin entente combining the strong
British navy with the strong Prussian army was proving
formidable on all fronts.  The war was particularly
disastrous for France, who had already suffered major
reverses at the hands of England in India and Canada.
All the great powers were involved except Spain, and
not surprisingly France was looking towards her for
help.  Charles was visibly shocked by news of the
British capture of Quebec and Montreal, but he had
wanted to remain neutral, if sympathetic to his Bourbon
partner.  As late as 1761 he was instructing Conde de
Fuentes, Spanish envoy in London, to negotiate a
settlement for the evacuation of British logwood
cutters who had intruded into Honduras and for recog-

nition of Spanish fishing claims in Newfoundland
waters; and it appeared at first that George III's
government was not averse to coming to some sort of
agreement on these issues. Circumstances, however,
were soon to persuade Charles to go to war disastr-
ously with England.

He certainly hesitated a long time. The fact
was that his cousin Louis XV, smarting over huge
losses in India and Canada, was hoping he would pull
the French chestnuts out of the fire when hardly any
chestnuts were left to pull out. But the obvious
reality that Spain's empire was next in line to feel
the threat of English arms, Charles' mounting frustration over the Honduras and Newfoundland issues while
trying to mediate the Anglo-French conflict during
tentative peace proposals, and what was probably the
last straw -- the rebuff by British minister William
Pitt of the attempt by French minister the Duke of
Choiseul to press Spain's claims on London -- were
some of the causes which led to the fateful decision.
In no way subservient to his French cousin, Charles
had a strong sense of honor and loyalty; and when
Choiseul, who was only too keen to drag Spain into
the war, implied through his envoys that Louis would
feel offended if his royal partner let him down after
having agreed to the Family Compact of August 1761
(subsequently joined by Naples and Parma), Charles
by December ordered that Lord Bristol, British ambassador in Madrid, be given his papers for departure.[5]
It was a risky step on Charles' part, for while France
had almost nothing left to lose, Spain had everything
to lose.

In the royal view this was the historic moment
that would decide once and for all who was to dominate
the New World. Wall was told to get on with the war,
despite his pro-English attitude to begin with, while
foreign minster Grimaldi was told to prepare plans by
the following month for an even closer Family Compact
with France. Charles had cast the die and would soon
know how well Spanish arms would fare. He was not to
wait long for the disappointing results. He had considerably underestimated British strength. Choiseul
had the somewhat ponderous Grimaldi to deal with, and

both were in any case eclipsed by Pitt, who unfortunately for the Bourbon powers proved to be one of the greatest war leaders in British history. Despite Pitt's resignation in October 1761 and the eventual predominance of the more moderate Lord Bute in the cabinet at London, the British war effort was in full swing by this time while Spain had barely begun to rearm -- a reversal of the positions England and Spain were in thirty years before.

But in economic power also, the British greatly exceeded Charles' estimates. Their commercial ascendancy in the New World had soon to be accepted, but they were strong around Spain herself, where smuggling was established practice. Charles now expelled enemy merchants and confiscated enemy ships, but he did not relish the idea of the French taking their place -- a distinct goal of Choiseul in his instructions to Marquis d'Ossun, French ambassador in Madrid. Neither was such a prospect appealing to many Spanish consumers, who were benefiting more from British imported textiles, hardware and leather goods in exchange for Spanish wines, than they were from the French, who needed little of peninsular produce. Charles was thus in somewhat of a dilemma. Nonetheless he cooperated with the French in trying to keep out British goods from Bourbon ports (excluding Naples); but it was a fruitless blockade because Franco-Spanish forces were simply not strong enough to enforce it. British commercial infiltration of Spain in fact continued during the war, and Charles afterwards did not see fit to abrogate the range of lower tariff privileges accorded to British merchants by the Carvajal-Keene treaty of 1750.[6] As for the French, Choiseul's bid for the same sort of privileges for their merchants under the Family Compact was doomed to greater unpopularity in Spain, where everyone knew the commercial advantages to be gained therefrom would be minimal. The fact was that the two Bourbon powers failed to reconcile their diverging economic objectives. Essentially Charles had the right idea in trying to curtail the influence of both England and France, but his strategy was at fault in resorting prematurely to arms against the British, where continued diplomacy might have made more headway. Answering the appeals of his French cousin thus got him into troubled waters, and he was not to redeem his position till twenty years later.

Ricardo Wall, meanwhile, directed the war as best as he could, soon feigning poor eyesight as a pretext fo retirement. But an early blow was struck at England's ally Portugal, under the command of Aranda who had been summoned from Warsaw to join the Portuguese campaign, and of whom we shall hear a great deal more later. The Spaniards took Almeida, but thereafter the war settled down to a stalemate. The only significant victory won by Spain was the capture of Colonia do Sacramento on La Plata river (near the present city of Buenos Aires), together with nearly thirty British merchant ships. Control of this Portuguese base, riddled as it was with smugglers, enabled the occupier to dominate a substantial part of the La Plata-Uruguay river system, and the two Iberian nations were to drive each other back and forth across this vital strategic point throughout much of the eighteenth century.[7]

Elsewhere the war went badly for Spain. Havana and Manila fell like ninepins. The former was taken by Sir George Pocock on August 25, 1762, the latter by Sir William Draper in the spring of 1763. Where Cuba was concerned, captain-general Juan de Prado was exiled after a Spanish court martial, which had to accept the fact of British occupation. Where the Philippines were concerned, bitter fighting ensued in which Draper's demand for a one million pound ransom to save the place from looting was countered by Simón de Anda's offer of a ten thousand escudo reward for Draper's head. The head was never taken, and the looting continued.

Faced squarely by these two defeats, Spain had no option but to join peace negotiations. Tentative proposals for a settlement were already under way in discussions between the Duke of Bedford, Choiseul, and Grimaldi at Fontainebleau in France, where it was known that George III of England was pressing for this end. The sentiment for a continental peace was shared also by Czar Peter III of Russia, and his consort and successor, Catherine, who did not feel antipathy towards Frederick the Great. Accordingly, with France and the three eastern combatants clearly exhausted. the treaty of Hubertsburg was signed in February 1763, by which Frederick secured Austria's recognition of his retention of Silesia.  At the same time a defeated France and Spain had to come to terms with England and Portugal.  The result was the treaty of Paris, signed on February 10 of this year.

The colonial powers settled the pieces across the world to the detriment of France, the repair of Spain's honor, and the triumph of England.  By its terms, France gave up her position in India and Canada to England who, as price for restoring Havana and Manila to Spain, received from this country all of Florida and virtually all Spanish holdings east of the Mississippi River.  Spain gave back Colonia to Portugal, recognized the right of English dye-wood cutters to be in parts of Honduras (provided they demilitarized their forts), and gave up fishing claims in Newfoundland.  Spanish ships captured by the British prior to 1761 were to have their prize value adjudicated in British Admiralty courts.  But Spain received from France the colony of Louisiana, the French king making good his promise made in October of 1762.  This vast undefined area west of the Mississippi, given in compensation for Spain's loss of Florida, was decidedly a burden to the bankrupt French treasury, and Choiseul, at least, must have been glad to get rid of it.

On balance the Spanish government redeemed by diplomacy much of what it had lost by defeat, and Louisiana in particular gave Charles a strengthened strategic position.  But the same could hardly be said of Spain herself; for here a severe revolt occured, once more cutting short the progress toward enlightenment, and serving as a sharp reminder that in this proud nation of eight million stubborn people, reforms could not be imposed easily.

One of Charles' policies was to give government posts to humbler professional men.  Their advancement to high office, to be based on merit, was part of the royal aim to modernize the country.  But many of the older nobility resented such a policy, for they saw this broadening of class as a step towards power by

103

centralizing officials and a threat to their own position. There were men in high places since Ferdinand's time, who having professed loyalty to Charles, now felt that their efforts had been in vain. A costly war only added to the resentment. Patriotic without being aggressively militant towards outside powers, these nobles had been lukewarm to the war with England in the first place, as indeed were many of the peasantry, not because of love for England but rather to deny France a more active role in penetrating the peninsula. In this they were supported by many merchants who were France's rivals. Yet in a curious way even Ensenada, the most Francophile of all past ministers, together with his following, must have felt slighted at being kept at arm's length by a king whose anti-English policies he had supported. There was thus a potential opposition made up of very different origins, whose common cause was enmity to a newer direction of policy.

There were deeper reasons for this opposition. Many nobles and churchmen of the old school had been educated at the expensive private colleges run largely by the Jesuits, graduation from which provided the indispensable entrée into government service.[8] In a word, collegians dominated the bureaucracy. Whether reform-minded or not, these collegians had patiently built up a considerable power-base among the councils, chanceries, and judicial courts since Philip V's time. Descendants in part of those who had been active in the councils opposing Philip's centralism, this elite had always cherished the conciliar traditions of government which in former times represented regions of Spain and the Spanish Empire such as Aragon and Flanders. They were particularly strong in the surviving and flourishing council of Castile. Now after a careful recovery of power, they faced a setback. Charles with his new policy did not exclude participation by nobles; but insofar as his aim was to circumvent their entrenched position and challenge collegian influence in the government, replacing it by an apparata of strengthened ministries, these nobles and their supporters were only waiting for a chance to embarrass the regime.

The humbler men whom Charles was promoting to power were dubbed *manteístas* on account of the long

cape they had worn as students at the universities.
Together with various hidalgos and lawyers, these
men had not gone to the expensive private colleges,
and had risen by merit rather than by patronage;
but they were educated men, often trained in history
and interested in economic theory as a means of bringing
about reforms in Spain.  Lacking family connections,
they cherished learning for its practical effect, not
as a passport to a sinecure; and on this account they
zealously supported regalism for furthering the secular advance of the nation.  Despising pretentious
sophistry, but not necessarily accepting every shred
of the new philosophy drifting over the Pyrenees, they
looked foremost to the King for moral guidance, and
the latter had much sympathy with their views.

It was bad enough seeing manteístas bypass the
traditionalists, in the view of many critics, but even
worse when these or their friends were upstart foreigners.  In this the opposition was not alone.  One
of the reasons for widespread unrest was clearly the
King's policy of employing foreigners at a time of
unsuccessful wars and rising food prices.  Seeking
to bring the machinery of government fully into his
own hands, Charles stood by his faithful subordinates
wherever they came from, and old veterans like Wall
retained their popularity.  But Italians such as
Geronimo, Marchese Grimaldi, who became secretary of
state upon Wall's retirement in 1763, drew a wider
range of critics.  Of Genoese origin, Grimaldi had
had experience as Spanish envoy in Sweden, The Hague,
and Versailles, and was at heart pro-French which was
enough to make him unpopular at this critical time.
Typifying the ponderous and legal-minded administrator
of his day, he was yet attentive to the sciences, and
had introduced the botanical works of Linnaeus and
Loeffling to Ferdinand's court.  His industry and
dependability made him so favored by Charles that he
survived the ill-fated Family Compact which he had
drafted with Choiseul, remaining chief minister till
1776.  British ambassador Sir James Harris once wrote
of Grimaldi that he was slow to act, having first done
everything possible to do precisely the opposite, no
matter how illogical such a move might be; he also
loved to play cards and scarcely concealed his anger
when he lost. [9] But what he was most patient in was

105

his unswerving support of Charles' ministerial
policies.

Another Italian was Marchese di Squillace.  Pur-
veyor to the Neapolitan army, chief treasurer and war
secretary when Charles was king of the Two Sicilies,
he had acquired a wide range of experience which should
have fitted him well for service in Spain.  He was likewise treasurer and war council chief in 1763, and next
to Grimaldi now enjoyed the highest offices in the
land.  The treasury, a lynchpin in any administration
and a delicate post for a foreigner to hold, was divided into a maze of halls, such as one for the
*alcabala* (sales) taxes, or that of the *millones* excise
taxes.  Both of these were disliked to begin with, and
here he cannot be blamed.  He was in fact an able administrator, but unfortunately did not understand the
Spanish people.  Foreigners can never be popular when
times are bad, but Squillace became indifferent to
public opinion, and worse, displayed an extravagance
to the point of indiscretion.  He would stroll about
Madrid alone -- itself something of an impropriety --
often assuming an insolent air when visitors called
upon his residence at the historic House of the Seven
Chimneys.10  His wizened face contrasted sharply with
that of his beautiful wife, Doña Pastora, who was in
the habit of giving sumptuous parties at their home.
Within a short time the Squillace family became associated with scandal, especially when unfounded rumors
arose that Doña Pastora was Charles' mistress.

There were other Italians brought over from
Naples, among them the able engineer, Francesco
Sabbatini, who had won renown for his work on the
palace at Caserta.  It had been said in jest, as a
reaction against the reign of Ferdinand VI, that what
Spain needed was reform in the six 'M's -- music,
medicine, ministers, mules, modes and *mujeres* (women).
To this might have been added a seventh -- Madrid --
and here Charles would have heartily concurred.
Sabbatini in fact was now commissioned to clean up
the city.  But this was only inviting more trouble
for the people loved their city as it was.  When even
Tanucci cautioned Charles to go easy on his subjects,
he wrote in reply, "My subjects are like children,

106

they cry when you wash them.!"[11] And he made it clear he was determined to go through with his policy of hygiene for Madrid, his favorite city and birthplace.

The capital of the Western world's largest empire, comprising some 150,000 inhabitants, certainly needed a good cleaning. Presenting a bleak spectacle against a background of grey snow-capped mountains, it was a sprawl of ill-paved streets and alleys infested with stray pigs, resembling in this respect the London of Stuart times. Slops and garbage tossed from the balconies would be accompanied by the eternal cry of warning -- '*Agua va* (water's coming down)'. The few streetlamps that did exist were at best an asset for the pickpocket. Nobody seemed to mind the filth -- a striking contrast with the Madrid of later times -- and doctors confidently told Sabbatini that the air in this condition was highly beneficial for the health. In these days of modern pollution, perhaps they had a point.

Obediently the council of Castile, highest executive body in the land, began implementing the King's wishes. Some quarter of a million reales being set aside for the purpose, royal decrees ordered streets to be paved and kept clean, providing for a proper system of refuse-carts and dumping grounds. Houses were to be kept tidy on all sides pending draining installation, while earlier laws were enforced requiring adequate streetlighting. Lanterns were to be placed on open stairways and balconies of the main streets which were to burn all night, at least through the winter and spring seasons; and an urban militia was organized to see that the new measures were properly carried out.

An even more urgent problem was the mounting price of food. The arrival from America of specie held up during the Seven Years war created such an influx that an inflationary spiral was set in motion, made worse by bad harvests in 1763 and 1765.[12] Squillace did his best to alleviate distress by importing grain from Sicily and stockpiling it in impoverished Castile and the south, but it was an uphill task. Already farmers and middlemen had forced him to relax price controls after the war, and a decree of July 11, 1765, established an internal free grain trade (a situation that more or less continued for the balance of the century). Squillace hoped that prices would stabilize; but the opposite happened, prices continued to rise after he had briefly reimposed a slightly higher limit.

Bread prices alone soon broke through their pre-1765 levels, bringing with them similar increases in cooking-oil, soap and candles -- all basic means of living for the Spanish peasant. It was not long before criticism of the treasury and its supply commission (or *junta de abastos* responsible for purchasing food and regulating prices in Madrid) rubbed off on to Squillace himself. In trying to please everyone, he had satisfied no one; and when it was remembered that his wife shared his extravagant style of living, and that his three sons were respectively a field-marshal, archdeacon, and senior customs official, he became not only a butt of lampoonery but the very object of popular vilification.

A composite example of all the satirical verse hurled at Leopoldo Squillace might go something like this:
"I Leopold the Great, Sr. Squillace of late,
rule Spain with a mere word, rule Charles the Third.
I do what I like with both, disregarding the truth,
whatever suits my whim, I can do to the two of them.
And when I 'reform', I make people conform,
and anyone's removal wins Charles' nod of approval".

Exacerbating the restless state of the people was the unpopularity of the foreign Walloon Guards, whose salaries were paid out of Spanish funds under Squillace's direction. Recruited in Belgium between the ages of seventeen and forty, Walloon guardsmen had to be at least fie feet three inches tall and to serve for about six years. Officeered by aristocrats of the old school, the regiment was a crack one, and its colonel-in-chief had to be a Spanish grandee.[13] In late 1765, nuptial ceremonies were held in honour of the marriage between María Luisa, daughter of the late Don Philip Duke of Parma (who had died after a fall from his horse) and Carlos, heir to the Spanish throne. Bullfights and musical comedies typified the occasion, and an immense crowd had gathered outside the Buen Retiro palace to watch the fireworks. Unfortunately some Walloon soldiers mistook these for firearms explosives, and in their zeal assaulted the crowd. In the stampede which followed several persons were killed. None of the soldiers were punished and public anger against the government reached dangerous proportions.

The situation was already tense when Charles and his hated Italians stirred up feelings further by deciding to simplify the national style of dress; and the measures they enforced now brought resentment to boiling-point. Their aim was reasonable enough -- to bring the country up-to-date by banning the broad-brimmed hat (not unlike the style of a French or Italian curate) which in half covering the face was becoming an anachronism. The cocked or three-cornered hat was encouraged instead, which was gaining ground among gentlemen of the period. As for the cloak, with its furtively long and copious folds so dear to Spanish males, this too was to be replaced by a shorter style of jacket more in keeping with current fashion in Europe. A further reason was to protect the public, for with so many knife-fights on the increase it was easy for a felon to hide his identity and purpose beneath his sloppy-brimmed hat and ruffled cloak.

The break with the past provoked violent reactions by Spaniards -- it was like waving a red rag at a bull. The men preferred to dress distinctively as also did their women incidentally, whose familiar mantilla and fan, embroidered costume, multi-folded skirt and sharp pointed shoes typified the fashion. The new style of hat, moreover, gave little protection against the sun or rain. A fiscal report warned the council of Castile that the changes would bring trouble and also annoy merchants, since the long gowns were made locally while the new jackets would largely have to come from abroad. It further cautioned against any decree being enforced by military means, contending that the best method to adopt would be via the civil power vested in crown officials and alcaldes.

At first Charles limited the use of the new style of dress only to royal employees. The decree of January 22, 1766, from the Pardo palace was in fact a repetition of earlier laws: 'It being repugnant to the King that subjects in his service are using long cloaks and wide-brimmed hats..., a style of costume which lends itself to easy concealment in Madrid and surrounding highways..., it is henceforth declared improper for the said subjects so to appear... Being determined to remedy these abuses so prejudicial to order and good government, We are sending directives..., especially to those in His Majesty's service in and around Madrid... that in future royal officials should wear proper dress, i.e., jacket or riding-coat with a wig or appropriate hair style, and with a cocked hat in place of the wide-brimmed hat, the coat to be worn in such a manner so as not to conceal anything. We hereby give warning that orders have been issued to arrest anyone in the King's service henceforth found wearing the forbidden style of dress... '.[14]

Ignoring the fiscals' advice against the changes, Charles and his advisers then proceeded to apply them even more widely in a proclamation of March 10, 1766, which was posted in all the public squares. No longer restricted to royal officials, the decree now declared that no man of whatever state could wear the forbidden dress, and came fully within the civil power's jurisdiction. Ironically this part of the fiscals' report was adopted. It meant that the king's government itself was now responsible, not just the army, and whose treasury officials were to supervise the new regulations. In the matter even of dress, there lurked in the public mind the shadowy figure of Squillace.

This decree was the final straw. Proclamations were ripped down as overworked alcaldes vainly tried to replace them. Slogans and lampoons directed at Squillace and his wife increased in vehemence; now he was satirized in mock burlesque as figurines with blue sashes and huge wigs were carried by youths chanting "Down with the prohibition rules", or "Give us Squillace's head." Round this angry mob rallied the guild of tailors who were incensed at being told that the cloaks they were working on would have to be a higher length from the ground, or else they would face fines and jail. Many customers were equally incensed when, after months of saving to buy a cloak, they were now told to have it cut short.

Still bolder men persisted in wearing the old style hat, while drawing the cloak prominently over the left shoulder and face. When T.S. Eliot wrote the famous lines "I grow old... I grow old... I shall wear the bottoms of my trousers rolled", he was expressing a free act of the will; but if the government had forced everyone by decree to roll the bottoms of their trousers, for whatever reason, there would have been a national outcry. Such was the mood of Spain in 1766, as angry defiance greeted the government on all sides.

Events took a more ominous turn when on Palm Sunday, March 23, some soldiers from the barracks in the Plaza de Antón Martín tried to force the wearers of the forbidden hat to turn the brims into the required three-cornered shape. After a scuffle, some thirty men raided the local barracks, disarmed the soldiers and proceeded to surge through the streets shouting, "Long live the King. Death to Squillace". Soon three thousand angry people milled about the Calle de Milaneses and the Plaza Mayor, smashing the newly installed streetlighting and hurling insults at Squillace and his wife, at the Walloon Guards, and members of the government. Confronting the Duke of Medinaceli, a grandee of much influence but now quite helpless, they told him bluntly to inform the King that he must get rid of Squillace or the latter must die. Extricating himself from the mob, Medinaceli, sweating profusely, rushed to the Royal Palace to convey to the astonished Charles what the people were demanding.

Squillace barely escaped with his life. There is little doubt that had he been caught by the mob he would have been torn to pieces. Luckily he was away when someone forewarned him of an attack on his house, and through a circuitous route he succeed in reaching the Royal Palace, where Charles offered him protection. Equally fortunate was Doña Pastora, who was taking a stroll with the Dutch minister and his wife just before the crowds approached her home. She boldly put on disguise, and having reached the House of the Seven Chimneys by a side door, gathered jewels and papers before anyone could catch up with her; and she finally took refuge in a nearby convent. The crowd now broke

into the Squillace home, threw furniture and portraits out of the window, and made a bonfire in the
street.

Grimaldi's house was the next target, in Cava de
San Miguel, where the people hurled insults outside
and smashed his windows. Thereafter they marched to
the palace itself where they knew Squillace had taken
refuge. Here the palace guard, mostly Walloons, fired
upon the mob. By the following day Charles was informed by Cardinal Lazaro Pallavicini, the papal
nuncio, of what had happened at the gates of the palace.
Walloon guardsmen had killed two women, their bodies
being afterwards solemnly paraded on stretchers, as
the crowds heaped insults on foreigners in the government, on the hated Walloons, and above all on Squillace,
whose immediate death they were demanding.

In the explosive situation, a hero of the hour
proved to be a Franciscan, Father Yecla. Entreating
the crowds as he marched along carrying a crucifix,
he finally extracted from them a clear consensus of
aims. Yecla agreed to approach the King, thus acting
as a go-between, and supported by other Franciscans
succeeded temporarily in restoring order.[15] The
people's petition contained seven definite demands:
1) dismissal and exile of Squillace and his family;
2) dismissal of all foreign ministers and their re-
placement by Spaniards; 3) dismissal of the Walloon
Guards; 4) freedom of dress; 5) abolition of the supply
commission; 6) immediate reduction of food prices;
and 7) acceptance of these demands by the King, who
was to go to the bakery building by the Plaza Mayor
and sign his agreement then and there or the city
would be razed to the ground. With tension escalating by the hour as disturbances in Madrid were
spreading to other parts of Spain, with barracks and
warehouses broken into, with Walloon guardsmen being
dragged through the streets and killed, the riots were
assuming the aspect of a revolution, more serious than
even the council fiscals had predicted. The king himself was getting perilously close to the target of
attack.

Though the Royal Palace was threatened with destruction, at least Charles knew such a threat could
never be carried out, so well was it built. It was

his kingly pride and joy, and now in the turmoil of
the moment the palace had become a sorry place, a grey
fortress besieged by angry faces. He was not going
to give in easily. Keeping his composure, he summoned
a council of war and asked its six members for a frank
appreciation of the situation. Three were for repressive measures, while three favored conciliation --
the latter including Conde de Revilla Gigedo, who as
a captain-general was also the war council's president.[16] Thus it was Charles himself who had to cast
the deciding vote. He at first considered the idea
of facing the crowds in person, but realizing the risk
of such an action he now voted for a more cautious
approach, agreeing to appear on the palace balcony
with his chamberlains the Duke of Losada and Conde
de Fernan Nunez, flanked by various officials.

The crowds below repeated in substance the same
demands as Father Yecla had conveyed, to which Charles
signified his assent. If bloodshed was to be avoided
there was little else he could do. Back inside the
palace, however, he was soon informed that they wanted
his assent in writing. When Charles appeared a second
time on the balcony, with Father Yecla securing the
royal signatures to the demands, the people calmed
down a little; and when they saw the Walloons retreating into the inner courtyard of the palace, they
consented to vacate the royal armory as many defiantly
waved the forbidden hats in the air.

The curtness of the demands as well as fear of
further demonstrations prompted Charles to leave Madrid
that same night for Aranjuez -- a bold decision recalling his days at Velletri and proving that he was
very much a man of action in a critical situation.
With Squillace keeping by him in the shadows, and with
the additional handicap of having his half-blind
mother with him, now in her seventy-fourth year, Charles
managed to follow the planned route with the help of
loyal chamberlains and friends. The trio presented
a dramatic picture at 2 a.m. on March 25, 1766, as they
groped their way along the underground passages and
secret vaults by the Campo del Moro, heading for Puerta
de San Vicente where coaches were waiting to take them
to Aranjuez. The litter carrying the stately Isabel
had to be handled with great care, its wooden poles

113

sawn off to permit freer movement round the curves of the winding passageways. But they successfully reached the coaches which took them safely to their destination. Charles was an old hand at the game of escape -- a striking contrast to Louis XVI's disastrous flight with his family to Varennes in 1791.

When the news leaked out that the King had gone, the people thought that they had been tricked and that an assault by troops was imminent. Accordingly they set up roadblocks and barred any royal officials from leaving the capital. At the same time they called on bishop Diego de Rojas, president of the council of Castile, to bring back Charles by force. Fearing treachery, the ringleaders then changed their minds and instead forced Rojas to write a message to the King. With trembling hand the powerless president at pistol-point fixed the blame for everything upon Squillace -- the war with England, the scarcity of grain, the new dress rules, and those for sanitation and streetlighting in Madrid. The King was to accept unconditionally in writing the seven points contained in the petition and grant clemency. A freed convict called Diego Avendaño then took this communique in the name of the council to Aranjuez, where Charles informed him he would accept the petition and give him a pardon.

The city of Madrid waited in a state of extreme tension for a reply. It was without a government, its troops powerless to take action. At last on the morning of March 26 Avendaño returned, to the city's great relief, and Diego de Rojas from the bakery on the Plaza Mayor read out Charles' message. This was to the effect that in exchange for granting clemency and his people's requests, the King expected public order to be maintained and riots to cease immediately. And any violations would only cause him to revoke this concession.[17]

Quieted by this address, with conditions for a general pardon repeated more than once, the crown returned their stolen arms and began to disperse. The government had obviously yielded to popular pressure, but without losing too much face. Bloodshed had been narrowly averted thanks to Charles' swift action in leaving Madrid and negotiating from a distance. He had conveyed his acceptance of -- i.e., surrender to --

the petition through an intermediary, thus preserving an air of legality, and had diplomatically combined a peace offering with the continuing fact of his authority, which pleased both sides. Nobody had wanted him to abdicate exactly, but at the same time through all the verbiage of conciliation everyone knew where the relationship stood: the King could continue to govern as an absolute sovereign but only when absolutism's terms had been dictated through force by the mob.

In more precise terms this meant that Charles had to get rid of Squillace. It was a hard decision for him to make, but with grain riots in cities like Cuenca and Guadalajara spreading to the rest of Castile, and indeed to practically all of Spain's thirteen provinces, and with satirical slogans warning that if Squillace stayed and the Walloons returned the Bourbons would no longer rule in Spain, abdication might have been the only other alternative. It was a situation that had rarely happened in Spain. Despite his outward composure Charles had been badly shaken by events. By plucking out the thorn of Squillace from the flesh of Spain, much as it hurt his principles, he could at least persuade the people that they were parting with a major ill. A reorganization could then proceed if he was to push reforms without a revolution.

Squillace with his family went post haste to Cartagena, where a ship took them to Naples; and he subsequently became ambassador to Venice. Charles well knew that he had been a victim of politics and never doubted his ability. His extravagance at a time of chronic rising prices had been his undoing; yet as treasurer he had stockpiled corn supplies, apprehended vagrants, forbidden the carrying of weapons without a permit in the interest of public safety, helped veterans, widows, and orphans through lotteries and other forms of charity, promoted reform of the universities, and endorsed the royal plans for the cleaning-up of Madrid. In plaintive tone Charles could write to Tanucci that Squillace was being dismissed as a necessary sacrifice under very trying circumstances, having served both himself and his heir the Prince of Asturias in an exemplary fashion.[18]

There was little choice now but to shift policy direction. The new treasurer was Miguel Múzquiz from Navarre, a compliant administrator having some links with Aragonese noble circles, and who at least was a Spaniard; as was also Gregorio Muniain from Extremadura, who as a former minister to Don Philip in Parma was now promoted to chief of the war council. Grimaldi in fact became the only Italian of importance left in the government. But riots still persisted in the starved central parts of Spain; and though a cooperative church ordered the sacramental monstrance to be carried through the streets to quiet the crowds, it was obvious that strong measures were needed. On April 11, 1766, the King appointed Pedro Pablo Abarca y Bolea, Conde de Aranda, as president of the council of Castile.

Born in Aragon of noble lineage, Aranda was destined to leave an indelible mark on Spanish politics. As a reformer with a liberal cast of mind and thus pleasing to Charles, he was yet a law unto himself, for he fell between the conservative nobility from which he had sprung and the humbler men of government who were equally anxious to capture the reform spirit of the times. Aranda opposed these humbler 'manteistas' whom he regarded as centralist upstarts, favoring instead the more traditional form of the regional councils. A man of wide experience in the army and diplomacy, he had served under generals Montemar and Gages in Italy, rising to full colonel by 1742. As director of artillery under Ferdinand VI, he was largely responsible for introducing the Prussian system of drill and tactics into the Spanish army. He had served as envoy to Frederick's court; and subsequently to the courts of Lisbon and Warsaw. His views on enlightened progress in the arts and sciences stemmed from his contacts with Frederick the Great and from French philosophers whom he had met in Paris, and he was familiar with the works of Voltaire, Diderot, and d'Alambert. Enlightened militarism would partly describe Aranda's philosophy; but an uncompromising quick temper got him into trouble with so many notables of the day that even Charles kept him at arm's length until now. Yet aware of his abilities through the Duke of Alba, among others, the King ordered Aranda as captain-general of Valencia to assume command of the army of Castile in Madrid -- an order which Aranda insisted should be accompanied by political responsibility. Somewhat to the chagrin of the Duke of Alba who coveted the post himself, Aranda became president of the council of Castile and shortly after took the ceremonial oath.[19]

In considering the complex sprawl of government which had built up over the centuries, a clearer picture can be given of the difficult task facing Aranda and the King. The council of Çastile, situated in the Uceda palace, was the highest executive and judicial body in the land. It had long absorbed the other regional councils of Aragon and Flanders (between 1707 and 1715), and expedited the royal decrees, besides making rules of its own for royal promulgation. About thirty senior magistrates comprised its membership, drawn from the intendants, judges, lawyers, crown agents and the like, and whose salaries could reach 60,000 reales per year. Its functions, shared with an inner chamber, were to authorize such matters as appointments and inspections, prosecutions and pardons, royal and landed privileges, and the summoning of the Cortes or parliament; and often when the council was not in full session, its chamber would attend to specific details, meeting every day for about three hours. It also contained a number of halls or *salas*. Of these, the *sala de Alcaldes de casa y corte* regulated the court of Madrid and its buildings, while the *sala de Gobierno* was the council's chief executive agency. Here its many administrative and police powers could be freely delegated to the provinces. It also had supreme appelate jurisdiction (its famous hall of the Fifteen Hundred being so-called because each litigant had to deposit this sum in pesos before he could lodge an appeal), with a fiscal and attorney-general office; while a number of smaller halls dealt with rights such as those of widows and orphans. The council was indeed formidable, responsible for virtually all law-making, decisions in lawsuits, public administration, and appointments before such matters reached the king's hand for final ratification.[20]

There were also the five other councils to contend with -- State, treasury, war, justice, and the

Indies together with the marine -- each under a minister whose title as such was beginning to replace the traditional term of secretary. By the end of Charles' reign these ministries forming a cabinet were to eclipse the great council of Castile, just as they had already eclipsed Spain's historic parliament, the Cortes. The latter had represented the three traditional orders of clergy, nobility and burghers; but in sad contrast to its great days of the fifteenth century, it had ceased to exist as a legislative body and was now purely formal, its last notable act being to validate Charles' entry into Madrid.

The Uceda palace housed other councils besides that of Castile -- the treasury and Indies among them. Yet another, important for its social implications, was the royal council of the military Orders of Knighthood comprising six in all, of which those of Santiago, Alcántara, Calatrava, and Montesa, were the oldest. The fifth order dating from the sixteenth century was the famous Order of the Golden Fleece (*toisón*), while the sixth, that of San Carlos, was created by Charles himself in 1760 as a follow-on from the Neapolitan Order of San Gennaro. Like the toisón, this was a senior one and composed mostly of grandees, the hereditary blue-blood principle being here preserved. But the orders as a whole were designed to promote brotherhood, awarded as they were for some special service to the nation, and replacing their purely military character which in former times was expressed through surrendering to the king, as grand master, the traditional tribute of lances and ducats to help him carry on his crusading wars. Grouped round or near the palace were other agencies, among them the important council of commerce and money, a board of public works, a board of tobacco and one for forests, though the discredited supply commission was abolished in response to the rioters' demands. Last but not least was the awesome Inquisition and other church agencies associated with it.

We may pardon the King and Aranda for excessive haste in getting things done; in normal times procedures were slow even for urgent matters. Sometimes a decree or regulation, whether by royal order or in council, would lack proper examination of its merits; and it was not unknown for state papers to be submitted to the king in a haphazard manner without anyone properly aware of who had compiled them in the first place. Despite Bourbon attempts at verticalization, with scores of fiscals, judicial officers, and secretaries of despatch to reinforce it, a strong chain of command was somehow lacking. Rather the government sprawled horizontally, in which the councils with their ministers had overlapping powers. The council of Castile, for example, supervised the church and in many matters clashed with the Inquisition; that of the Indies, truly giantesque in its responsibilities, frequently clashed with both; while other councils such as war or treasury were often in conflict with the council of Castile. Matters were usually patched up in committee but much time was wasted in the process.

Once a ruling filtered through the top of the bureaucracy it eventually reached the provincial intendants, there to be passed on by crown agents who supervised the districts into which the thirteen provinces were divided. Though disputes of interpretation could be tardily dealt with by the judicial courts or *audiencias*, everyone was caught up in the government's network of inspectors and spies. This was indeed so large that grandees and powerful merchants would distribute favors on a liberal scale in order to channel legislation in the desired direction. Mid-century Spain and the England of Sir Robert Walpole or the Pelhams were alike in one respect -- both countries ground slowly towards their administrative end, smoothed by graft and corruption on the way. Not surprisingly, it was Charles' intention to cleanse the system through new ministerial reforms.

A few times a week the King would receive visitors at the Royal Palace. Pomposity of ceremony underlay these occasions. Royal officials from chamberlain to majordomo would enforce the strictest rules of dress and etiquette -- black cloak and collared jacket, knee-breeches and silver-buckled shoes, the hat carried in hand to prevent disturbing the wig -- formalities which were disliked by the King and Aranda alike. The latter would often break council-presidency rules by neglecting to carry his gold-pommeled baton, or would wend his way to the theatre and bullfight with the curtains of his

coach drawn apart, whence he would chat with passers-
by. Aranda in fact was liked by the masses, and
Charles made no objection to these violations of the
traditional rules nor denied him the right to the coveted 'footstool' session at which he would have the
close attention of his sovereign.

Without delay Aranda proceeded to restore order
and find out who was responsible for the riots. Summoning three regiments into Madrid to enforce the rules
against long cloaks and broad-brimmed hats, he singled
out one or two of the most violent ringleaders and
without Charles' knowledge had them executed. To
reinforce the point he made the public executioner
wear the forbidden style of dress, and with this grim
reminder few dared to protest. The people put away
their long cloaks and wide hats, and any man brave
enough to defy the ruling was hounded out of his city
by the alcaldes. Under penalty of stiff jail sentence,
moreover, similar laws were passed against gambling
and other forms of amusement prejudicial to public
order, as well as against clerical gossip and unlicensed print.

Yet spurred by the King, Aranda made serious
efforts to get to the root of the nation's problems.
In the important question of grain prices for farmers,
the government by a decree of May 5, 1766, annuled any
previous price reductions, thus effectively removing
controls at a time when supplies were at last improving,
and Spain fortunately was to be spared the nightmare
of further riots which were to bedevil France in the
years ahead. But consumers also had to be protected.
To ensure that food supplies reached the public, edicts
were issued calling for deputies of the people, or
syndic procurators, to join with local town councils
in seeing that justice be done at all levels, any disputes being settled by the higher audiencia courts.
Each parish was to select about a dozen men who would
then vote for these deputies. There were to be two
for townships with less than one thousand residents,
four deputies or more in excess of this figure, and
an impetus was given to local self-government which
Charles had learned from his experience in Naples. A
further measure of Aranda's was to divide Madrid into

eight clearly-defined precincts.  Each was under an
elected alcalde armed with police powers to enforce
public order, including the new sanitation and streetlighting regulations.[21]

With farmers and consumers at least partially
appeased, the nation was slowly getting back to normal.
Slogans faded on the walls of Madrid, and the capital
began to affirm loyalty to the King, appreciating his
general pardon.  His absence only seemed to strengthen
this feeling.  He stayed away that summer to mourn his
mother's death on July 11, 1766 at Aranjuez -- a sad
and fitting time to reflect after so many shared experiences with her, and after so much turmoil, serving
to quell passions further.  Following a petition by
the grandees and merchants of Madrid that he return,
Charles complied later in the year, and as if perceiving his desire to forgive, the crowds acclaimed
him.  A sense of mutual trust, as well as self-pre-
servation, affected sovereign and subject alike.  The
government had reneged on its freedom-of-dress clause
contained in the rioters' petition, but Spaniards had
largely replaced the Italians, Walloon guardsmen were
kept discreetly in the background, and with bread
prices stabilized (though at somewhat higher levels),
the people considered it a fair exchange.

The new national mood had papered over the cracks
of a deeply-divided society.  Now it was time to ask
whether there had been a conspiracy.  It was Aranda's
job to unearth one.  Hence an intensified search for a
villain when the truth was that nearly everyone had
felt a grudge of one sort or another against the government.  Nobles of the old school resented manteista
influence in the councils as they watched the riots
from the sidelines, hoping that the King would be
forced to change his policies.  Along with collegian
churchmen, many nobles also resented Aranda, for in
tending to oppose the emerging centralism of the state
in favor of the older, more regional, conciliar government preferred among Valencians, Catalans, and
Aragonese, they felt let down by the man who had been
moulded by this same tradition.[22]  Aranda's policies
also challenged their influence over municipal government -- reforms which incidentally also annoyed

the powerful trade guilds of Madrid which now stood
to lose predominance over food prices and other items
because of the increased local autonomy.[23]  The guilds
also resented the French who had a large stake in the
Spanish domestic market, while many Spanish merchants,
incensed at the near-monopoly wielded by the guilds
and French alike, felt a certain sympathy for the cause
of the rioters.

As for the masses in Spain, all they wanted was
to be left alone. Generally honest and unspoilt by
money, they had little patience with reforms they did
not understand. To some extent they resented the French
for their power in the economy, and they certainly resented the Italians for their power in the government.
It was no secret, moreover, that shouts had been heard
among the masses during the riots demanding the recall
of Ensenada. But all these disparate elements had
never acted as a concerted group and were certainly
now unwilling to reopen a healing wound. When faced
with the search for a conspiracy which Aranda was conducting, therefore, they all tended to close ranks and
point the accusing finger at others as a way of avoiding
any incrimination themselves.

Much of the tension with all the class cleavage,
was closely observed in Madrid by British ambassador
the Earl of Rochford and his staff, and it is ironic,
perhaps, that residents in another country can often
see things more clearly than its own nationals, especially when complex issues concern foreigners themselves.[24]

Charles' reliance on foreigners had been one of
the main causes of the explosion. His alienation of
much of the noble elite had been the other. Moreover,
while he understood the rivalries in government --
conservative noble versus manteista lawyer -- he had
completely overlooked the masses as a factor in politics
with their nationalistic fervor. There was thus a trio
of forces to contend with, not a duality of forces
as he had incorrectly judged, and herein, perhaps,
lay another great mistake. Though Charles could not
know it, history was to show other empires falling
through popular fears, especially of foreign rule.
For the time being, however, he had sorted out Spain's

problems which involved issues only in a relatively narrow sense -- let the people be fed and kept clean and tidy, let them wear the same as the rest of the world. The question was not how to create a new society, but how to cope with an existing one. For this purpose Charles was still supreme, the machinery of government firmly in his hands. If its centralism was disliked by many, it was now Spaniards, not foreigners, who were to be accountable; and any future problems the King might be confronted with was for him alone to settle, now that he had kept his promise of a general amnesty. But it had been an amnesty extracted by force; and though the people had been obliged to yield in the matter of dress, everyone knew by instinct the limits that had been drawn. Supported in spirit by many nobles, the riots had been a spontaneous conservative outburst by the masses who for the first time in many years had directly influenced politics. Reflecting the national mood, they had given back to the King his mandate to rule, asking only in exchange the right to retain their way of life.

Yet Charles had made his moves cleverly and with luck. He now emerged in a considerably stronger position than before, having shown astuteness in choosing Aranda, who as a noble combining swift military justice with swift reforms had the common touch as well; and the way had been cleared for other men with also a reformist cast of mind to enter the government. But in the last analysis it was the people themselves who had been the main activists in the Squillace riots. Since Charles made it clear to Aranda that the people were not be be blamed -- to do otherwise would only invite more trouble -- the search for a villain became more urgent than ever. The penalty was to be reserved for others -- a ready expedient based on vague assumptions and pleasing to most because it offended the least number of social groups. Vindictive as this policy was, it worked because of its conciliation towards everyone else. Thus by an unlucky fate it was members of the Society of Jesus for whom was reserved a needlessly stiff decree of punishment.

123

CHAPTER SEVEN

THE FALL OF THE JESUITS

An atmosphere of purge hung about the corridors of government in April 1766: Aranda had just summoned an extraordinary session of the council of Castile to determine the true nature of the Squillace riots and to track down the conspirators. The immediate scapegoats were the council's own former president, Diego de Rojas, as well as Ensenada, whose Jesuit friendships now contaminated him with treason to the state. They were both exiled, the latter spending many lonely years at Medina del Campo before his death in 1781. But the banishing of these men was only the beginning; and why it was the Jesuits who suffered a similiar fate and why so magnanimous a monarch as Charles could turn so harshly against them is best explained by examining Spanish Catholicism itself.[1]

With all its faults of over-zealousness, this religious force was no less nationalistic than that of other nations; and while supremely loyal to the Holy See it was just as keen to retain its tradition of separateness. Few portraits of the Pope adorned Spanish chapels down the ages; and the same was true in the eighteenth century. Crusading patriotism, personified in monarchs like Isabel I or Philip II, was always strong in a nation which ruled half the world, and as such there was a double bond binding the subject to his prince as Christian overlord and to his prince as chief executor of the church's temporal domains. The church did indeed retain enormous privileges in Spain, but in the final analysis it was the Spanish national courts, receiving historic grants of power given the kings by the Pope, rather than the Holy See itself, which remained the arbiter in many issues.

The Jesuits who arose in the sixteenth century served Spain well for several reasons: they extended the missionary, hence temporal, power of the nation, especially in the Americas, and they fought against Spain's Protestant enemies in a bitter struggle which lasted well into the following century. Though the nation was declining, temporarily at least in Europe, as its kings kept doggedly to the ideal of making

124

the world safe for Catholicism, there were great Jesuits like Francisco Suárez or Luis Molina who were stressing the contract theory of society and the doctrine of free will with as much vehemence as the Spanish character was asserting its creative independence. But with the coming of the Bourbons, Jesuit relationships with the crown slowly began to change.

In the eighteenth century the forces of the Counter-Reformation had long been spent, and the new monarchy influenced by the centralizing ideas of Louis XIV needed less priestly internationalism to strengthen the state. Absolutism was still the order of the day -- the old precepts were simply cast in a new mould -- and it still needed Jesuit power; but the presence of a friendlier France and the growth of secular concepts of sovereignty were paving the way for more critical modes of thought as expressed by great writers like Feijóo. Scientific curiosity was stirring anew in Spain, if only because continued stagnation would have been the only alternative.

Though enlightenment had not yet fully arrived, the ideal of enlightened monarchy had already done so. Strengthening the new views were the philosophers of France who were later to reveal to Spaniards that God did not exist as a detached entity but was understandable from the mechanical laws which moved the universe and hence adaptable to human reason. And it was Voltaire, no longer the harmless playwright and historian, who set people thinking about social justice, as Montesquieu was earning an equally wide reputation with his *De l'esprit des lois,* published in 1748. Even Charles himself when a king in Italy, without subscribing to all the new views, did not oppose the precepts of the philosophers whenever they extolled the monarch as the natural head of an orderly state. If few Catholics in Spain condemned the latest thought it was because they had never heard of it; but those who were reading their Feijóo at least approved freedom from superstition, the trend toward scientific enquiry, and the current interest in economic problems. French philosophers had only a limited influence on Spain at this stage, but once the new mood got under way, moral and social questions about the relation of church and state gathered momentum, and passions were often heated.

Indigenous to the growth of the new outlook was Spanish regalism. Loosely influenced by what in earlier French circles was termed Gallicanism and Jansenism (so named after the Flemish scholar Cornelius Jansen, who stressed the predestination tenets of St. Augustine), regalism subscribed to conventional Catholic doctrine; but in extoling monarchy and its role in educating the nation, it played down the international character of the church whenever the two were in conflict. At many points such views were opposed by the Jesuits, who also advanced regalism to preserve their influence. Jesuit and non-Jesuit were thus rivaling for control of the regalist position; but at the opposite extreme, the supremacy of the Pope became the watchword of the Jesuits, while regalism pure and simple became the watchword of their enemies. Just as regalism tended to become the yardstick of orthodoxy in Spain, so the Jesuits tended to label as Jansenist anything which departed from the *ecclesia supra omnia* principle.

The Inquisition also played an important part in upholding church supremacy; but it would be incorrect to regard this awesome institution as wholly in Jesuit hands. Rather it was Dominican-influenced after it was first founded in 1251, since which date it had steadily grown to include Spain and her dominions as an important branch of the Holy Office. Though waning in the eighteenth century, its powers were still formidable, not merely for its formal autos-da-fe but secret censorship. In this function it was assisted by the Spanish Index, or national branch of the index department in the Holy Office. The Inquisition in Spain contained a tribunal under an inquisitor-general with five councillors, including at least one Dominican sitting on the panel. In addition were four secretaries (two for the council proper and two for an inner chamber), together with a procurator, high constable, receiver, two recorders, two examiners, and a host of consultants, agents and spies. Its headquarters were in Madrid, but it had branches in all the big cities of Spain.

The question of releasing works from the Index at Rome had always been a busy issue, and the Jesuits were invariably at odds with the other Orders over works deemed Jansenistic. Perceiving that the Popes had given support to rival missionaries, the Jesuits flirted with regalism additionally to secure from the Spanish crown missionary rights of their own in the Americas. The heirs of Ignatius Loyola who claimed to be the standard-bearers of the Pope had to tread very carefully in their relations with the Spanish kings, whose majesty and power still held sway over much of the world, and they were quick to rebut any charges that they were anti-monarchist. Since they were influential with both the Spanish Bourbons and the Index in Spain, and since the Popes on various occasions were favoring the rights of the other Orders, a veiled conflict was in the making between the heads of the two opposing forces -- the Spanish monarch and the Pope.

A case in point was the controversy over the work by Enrico Noris, an Augustinian. His *Historia pelagiana* published in 1673 was an attack on the Spanish Jesuit, Luis Molina. When in 1747 the Pope yielded to Augustinian pressure and ordered the Spanish inquisitor to remove the work from the Index, the latter refused to obey, and for ten years the papal order was defied by king and Jesuits alike. A further victory for regalism, with Jesuit support, was the famous concordat of 1753, which permitted the crown in place of the Pope to receive taxes from the *Cruzada* (the historic tribunal set up to collect indulgence money in lieu of going on the crusades) as well as more monies from various mortmain lands and missions; in addition, the crown received the right to appoint certain church offices.[2] With King Ferdinand insisting on royal assent before a papal instruction be made legal and on tighter control over the nunciature, regalism was making significant advances. But where the Jesuits were concerned, they were playing dangerously with fire in smoothing over differences between the international papacy and the Spanish national crown. It was their misfortune eventually to fall right in the middle of the conflict and end up its victims.

Surprisingly, their first big defeat occured not in Spain but in Paraguay. Here their missionaries

for well-meaning motives encouraged the Guaraní Indians
to resist a joint Spanish-Portuguese invasion designed
to force them into the Portuguese sphere east of the
Uruguay river as a result of a treaty made in 1750 between the two Iberian powers.  Known as the war of
Seven Reductions, the terrible struggle was made meaningless when the treaty was annuled eleven years later,
and Paraguay with the missions was restored to Spanish
sovereignty.  The net result of all this, meanwhile,
was that the Jesuits in antagonizing both powers at the
same time not only earned their dismissal from Portugal
at the hands of the reforming minister Marquês de Pombal,
who in the wake of a plot expelled them from that country's entire dominions in 1759, but growing hostility
from Spain as well.

The Jesuit missions of Paraguay brought into focus
their alleged design to set up a theocratic state independent of the civil powers.  A detailed examination of
all the charges would be irrelevant in this context,
but suffice to say their enemies believed what they
wanted to believe, and it was not long before complaints against them were echoed in Spain.  Briefly,
the charges included:  treasonable words against the
Spanish king; unlawful tenure of benefice; immunity
from certain taxes while undercutting merchants in
Mexico and Peru (already chafing at taxes and price
controls); illegal deals with British merchants; opu-
lence and monopoly in too much trade; employment of
foreign missionaires (chiefly Italian, Swiss and
German); attacks on serfdom, polygamy, and witchcraft
among the Indian tribes, but without proper clearance
from governors, thus upsetting the latters' relations
with native chieftains; undue influence in Rome, bypassing official channels in Madrid; and secrecy of
organization in what smacked to many as an international state ruled by an autocratic Father-General
through provincial congregations.[3]

To do the critics justice, the Jesuits had undoubtedly built themselves into a powerful elite, and
had aroused widespread opposition in the process.
Forgotten was their humane role in protecting the
Indian, or that manpower shortages in Spain simply

obliged the Order to recruit outside help. Neither was it true that the Jesuits were excessively wealthy. But what annoyed many a non-Jesuit was the seeming hypocrisy by which the Order could adopt a holier-than-thou attitude in condemning abuses to the Indian at the hands of white men in America, while at the same time appearing to uphold the class structure in Europe.

This double standard was particularly resented in Spain, where it was frequently charged that the Jesuits were behind the advancement to high office of upper-class churchmen and nobles educated at the best colleges (*colegios mayores*). Charles himself, as we have seen, wanted to change this practice to the extent of promoting humbler men to positions of responsibility in the government. Coming from Naples he had already been imbued with some degree of anti-Jesuit feeling through his long contact with Tanucci. The latter still had a Jesuit confessor, but he was quick to point out that members of the Society of Jesus were inimical to royal interests and that it would be a bad policy for a king to have as his confessor one of their Order.[4] Such a contradiction between private confessional practice and public attitude well illustrates the dichotomy existing at this time. Statesmen needed Jesuits to buttress their influence at Rome and to have them as a source for personal advice; but with their vast power as an institution, the Jesuits also had the power to undermine. In this situation, they were feared by reformers who saw in their international brotherhood a means for asserting church-dominated interests above the regalism of the state.

When Charles came to Spain, the pro-Jesuit attitude of his mother and the older nobility deterred him from an openly hostile stand. Yet before long events again brought into focus the inherent conflict between church institutionalism and regalism, and this time the Jesuits stood ominously in the way. One question at issue was the catechism by a French abbot, François Philippe Mésenguy. Since the Holy Office at Rome had this work on the Index because of Jansenist denigration of both the papal claims and the Jesuits, the Pope in 1762 sent word of the ban to the nuncio in Spain, where the inquisitor-general, Manuel Quintano y Bonifaz, proceeded to publish the Pope's brief to this effect. This made the King angry as he had expressly forbidden the brief to be published. As a result, he had Bonifaz temporarily banished and insisted on the royal assent before papal instructions could be validated. Though Charles then softened his stand, he finally insisted on this ruling, just as Ferdinand had done before him.[5] It was no secret, moreover, that the King felt the Jesuits in Rome were somehow behind the ban on Mésenguy's catechism and that they were clearly an embarrassment in his relations with the Papacy. What in effect had happened was that the Spanish crown and the Papacy, now visibly at odds, were each reversing their position on Jansenism since the Noris affair of 1747, and the Jesuits, this time the friends of Rome, were losing their hold over regalism in Spain.

A more personal controversy was bringing Charles still nearer to an openly anti-Jesuit stand. In 1753 Friar Joaquín de Eleta, a Franciscan from Burgo de Osma in Castile, left for Naples to become eventually Charles' chief confessor. Now serving his sovereign in Madrid, Father Eleta reminded him that an earlier bishop from Osma, Juan Palafox y Mendoza, had had many quarrels with the Jesuits when he was bishop of Puebla in Mexico during the previous century. Palafox soon became a subject for beatification in Rome -- a cause intensely desired by the King, whose reformist objectives in no way diminished his zeal as a Catholic. Enemies of the Jesuits no doubt encouraged the cause in full knowledge that they would oppose it, and so bring down Charles' wrath upon them. Delay by Rome in fact resulted, and the King blamed the Jesuits for the obstruction.

Diverse forces in Spain, meanwhile, were swelling the anti-Jesuit tide. Not the least of these were many young manteístas whose careers in government Charles was favoring, among them two procurators in the council of Castile -- Pedro de Campomanes and José Moñino (later Conde de Floridablanca). Campomanes came from Asturias of modest origin, had graduated in history and law, and was subsequently appointed assessor of the mails and a treasurer before his promotion to fiscal, for which promising career he owed a great deal to Ricardo Wall. A keen patriot and regalist, highly critical of the church's hold over mortgaged property, Campomanes sought to purge the nation of its prevalent poor, and to this end he used history and the historic parallel as a basis for polemics. His judicial training convinced him that only by training humanity and structuring institutions to facilitate this education could Spain's ills be remedied, and that it was no use blaming other people when the fault lay within the nation itself.[6] Campomanes was essentially a practical intellectual, impatient with the present, and in combing the past to justify his faith in regal centralist aims was much in tune with Charles' policies.

Moñino who came from Murcia was also of modest origin; and having studied law at the university of Salamanca practiced his father's profession of notary before entering government service. Like Campomanes, Moñino had a legal cast of mind and shared many of his views; but his whole frame of reference was more related to current political issues, in whom the influence of Voltaire, the Jansenists, Augustinians, and Freemasons was not without effect.[7] Essentially a diplomat rather than a writer, he was astute enough to conceal his leanings from the King, and at the same time win his confidence in a number of issues, playing down hostility to the church except when it coincided with Charles' own criticism. Events were to be with Moñino in the future, and as diplomat, lawyer, and politician, he rose to be one of the greatest statesman of the eighteenth century on behalf of his country's interests.

There were many others in the vanguard of reform, but two more of the same ilk deserve special mention. Senior to the above was another lawyer, Manuel de Roda. Born in Aragon, Roda received his doctor's degree in law at the university of Saragossa before becoming secretary of justice in 1765 -- an important post in that this council of 'grace and justice' was also empowered to process royal grants and favors. Roda had two distinctive features, seemingly contradictory. On the one hand he was deeply distrustful of Roman Catholicism's formalism and power, which won some degree of admiration from Campomanes and his friends; on the other hand he was extremely mercurial in the political spectrum, having close ties with Aranda and his Aragonese circle, so that one never quite knew his degree of manteista sympathies. But one thing beyond dispute was his personal honesty and integrity.[8] A fourth member of this group was another Aragonese, José de Azara, Spanish procurator at the Pontifical court in Rome, of gifted intelligence and whom Charles exhorted to get on with the beatification cause of Palafox. Azara kept in close touch with his compatriot Roda, informing him of his intense dislike of certain ceremonial at Rome. All these men were fired by a burning hatred of Jesuits in particular, whom they regarded as obstacles in the path of progress. Their chance was coming now that Roda and Campomanes were among the thirty magistrates sitting in judgment on Aranda's special session of the council of Castile. Indeed their hatred exceeded that of Aranda himself, whose attitude to the Jesuits, like that of Grimaldi, was one of rational moderate criticism largely stemming from patriotic loyalty to his king.

Many nobles who supported Aranda resented the intrusion of these lesser mortals into the government. A notable example was Marqués de Campo Villar, secretary of justice, who failed to block Roda succeeding to this post before his own death in 1765. But sensing the changing times, they were by no means averse to the developing regalism of the period and were only too anxious to support their king lest their manteista rivals capture the spirit of the conservative-reformist trend. Though educated at the better private colleges in Spain where the ultra views of the teaching clergy were well-known, many of them had traveled abroad and learned about the suppression of the Jesuit Order in France. Here Choiseul, under considerable pressure from the Jansenists, had extracted a royal decree to this effect in November 1764 -- an action which was subsequently condemned by the Pope -- and by the time Aranda became president of the council of Castile, writers like Denis Diderot and Jean d'Alambert were being read by a widening circle in the government, the Duke of Alba and many diplomats included.

Extremists lauded the works of such philosophers as a challenge to international clericalism, while Charles, smarting over the beatification setbacks, saw the Jesuits behind every action of the Pope.

Under these circumstances it was becoming fashionable to cast aspersions on the Order at the slightest provocation. Now that the Squillace riots were over and there was a hushed silence over the land as if people were waiting to see what would happen next, a sort of competition got under way among the council politicians in which each tried to outbid the other in their protests of loyalty to the King. Isabel's death that summer of 1766 removed the last restraining hand of pro-Jesuit influence at court, and the Society was now looming larger than ever as the common enemy. Politicans saw the chance they were seeking: the louder the complaints made against it the more the King would listen to the advocates of this or that political group. Patricians like the Duke of Alba were betraying the Jesuit affiliations of their class to form common ground with plebeians like Roda, whose friends in Rome were sending back the latest accounts of the stalled beatification cause of Palafox.

As the council under Aranda, meanwhile, intensified its efforts to investigate the causes of the Squillace riots, several Jesuits were singled out for banishment on the flimsy grounds that they had been seen on familiar terms with the crowds. Priests were to return immediately to their parishes, while bishops were to forbid any criticism of the royal family or government. By September 18, 1766, Aranda instructed the fiscals Campomanes and Miguel de Nava to draw up a decree against anyone in the service of God disturbing the public peace.[9] What the council had in mind were still more Jesuits deemed sympathetic with the rioters, when certain clerics from other parts of Spain had been seen mingling with the crowds, including exotically-dressed citizens taken to be secret agents in disguise. In the tense atmosphere a consensus was emerging that the Jesuits, if not absolutely guilty for the riots, were absolutely guilty for the ills of Spain. To the many groups of accusers must certainly be added individual members of the other Orders -- Franciscans, Dominicans, Capuchins, and Augustinians among them -- who all had grievances of one sort or another against their enemy. All that remained was to find a bit of tangible evidence to indict them as a whole, as a follow-up to the banishment of the few that had already taken place. By picking on the Jesuits, reasoned their enemies, both church and state as well as the people would each be exonerated in the eyes of the other; and as the time was ripe to reassert the crown's historic role over the church's temporal power, Charles himself increasingly became a party to this feeling.

Searches were accordingly carried out for subversive and satirical literature. At Vitoria, what appeared to be an illegal printing-press was found by agents of Aranda's council. Here also, the rector of the local Jesuit college had sent the non-approved work *Cartas del doctor de la sapiencia* to Father Mauro de la Fuente, a fellow-Jesuit living in Saragossa, who then by means of a relative and a senior secretary in the Inquisition proceeded to get the work approved. The blame in this case was fixed upon the rector at Vitoria for having bypassed the local authorities in the first place. A rector in Saragossa, Father Payons, was also indicted, incidentally, for having distributed copies of a satirical work attacking the anti-Jesuit Choiseul, as well as Louis XV himself. Another case concerned Francisco Ramón Solano, curate of San Juan near Pamplona and a relative of the local Jesuit rector, who had apparently entered a work in a library titled *Anales de los Jesuítas* without the proper formalities on the ground that he was doing this as a special service for the Inquisition.[10] The council of Castile used such cases to argue that the Jesuits were especially favored by the Inquisition, and by implication was willing to launch a double blow at both Jesuitry and what was considered its fellow international conspirator, the Holy Office itself.

Unwilling as Charles was to go this far, he nonetheless gave the council further powers in October 1766, increasing tribunal membership in both its hall of justice portion as well as in the so-called chamber of conscience. With rumors escalating each passing week, the government would now stop at nothing to convict as many individuals it could lay its hands on, Jesuit

imposters included. Some charged that the Squillace
mutineers had been in the pay of the Jesuits, that
the latter were everywhere printing satirical pam-
phlets to be smuggled out of their colleges, while
others went so far as to charge that they were planning to kill the King. Francisco Suárez' *Defensio fidei*
and Juan de Mariana's *De rege* were resuscitated and construed to mean that all Jesuits were advocating not
merely the contract theory of society with the sovereign, but the right of society to rise up and murder
him whenever it suited its purpose.[11] Under these
circumstances it is not surprising that the King approved Aranda's extraordinary session of January 29,
1767, at which the council began preparing a proposal
or *consulta* for banning the Jesuits altogether and
getting Rome to sanction their universal suppression.

The final draft for the decree of expulsion was
ready the following month, and all that remained was
the King's signature. He hesitated a few days before
signing, announcing that the full reason for his decision would remain 'locked in his breast'. This delay
may have been due to his secret fear lest the Society's
father-general, Lorenzo Ricci, threaten to reveal his
alleged illegitimacy through his mother's liason with
Cardinal Alberoni, and fear also that the Jesuits were
planning to assassinate him and members of his family.[12]
Amid such a flurry of rumors, ill-founded as they were
for the lack of corroborative evidence on the part of
either Ricci or his enemies, another possible reason
for the delay was, if not an inner struggle on Charles'
part over so drastic a step, then at least a play for
time in order to prepare a reply to Pope Clement XIII's
plea for mercy.

We shall never know who precisely planted the false
idea that the Jesuits had incriminating evidence against
the King or that they were planning to kill him --
some say it was Roda's idea, others that it was
Choiseul's, and certainly the Duke of Alba was not above
suspicion in slurring the Society's name. But one clear
point emerged from the situation in which Charles
found himself. If it were publicly revealed that he
was illegitimate, then in accordance with Philip V's
will that his heir be born in Spain, the next in line
would be Charles' younger brother Luis, who had earlier

taken holy orders as the Cardinal Archbishop of Toledo
but who by this time had been released from his vows.
What Luis thought of all this is difficult to say,
but this much is certain: though relations between
the two brothers were friendly -- Luis made an excellent hunting companion -- the idea of having to
surrender the Bourbon throne to a kinsman who had once
taken the cloth, with an uncertain future even if he
married later, must have weighed heavily on Charles'
mind. It would have been wiser, perhaps, to let the
smoke of rumor die down; but in the midst of his per-
plexity, the King had already determined where the
fire was coming from and was resolved to put it out.

Accordingly on February 27, 1767, he signed in
secret the fateful decree banishing the Jesuits from
Spain and all her dominions. Parts of the decree were
entrusted to children who could not read them, the
printers put under close guard.[13] Though much of the
wording of the original consulta has been lost --
practically all that remains is the second part dealing with methods for carrying out the Jesuits' banishment -- enough evidence has survived to reconstruct
the charges levelled against them. These included responsibility for the Squillace riots; diffusing maxims
contrary to royal and canon law; sedition and political
intrigues; treasonable relations with the English in
the Philippines; monopoly of trade; illegal with-
holding of taxes and other abuses; pride and vanity
in support of certain doctrines against the King;
advocacy of the right of tyrannicide; and aspirations
for universal monarchy.[14]

Unaware of their fate, the Jesuits were suddenly
told to get ready by March 31; and with their properties registered and exit routes planned by Aranda
and his aides, they were conducted the next day in
batches of tens and conveyed in cartloads to their
embarkation, escorted by soldiers acting under orders
of strictest secrecy. Similar procedures were applied
to the Jesuits in the Indies later in the year, where
in Mexico severe riots occured at their expulsion.
The King showed a spark of human kindness -- and it
was only a spark -- providing an annual pension of one
hundred piasters for the exiles and their families, a
matter to be arranged in Rome through the Spanish envoy
there and not through officials of the papal nuncio.[15]

No such consideration, however, was to be given to Jesuitry as a world-wide institution. In this respect the matter had been clinched in Charles' mind, there could be no turning back. He had called a crusade against his collective enemies, and he became the most militant of sovereigns in insisting that the entire Jesuit Order be expunged from the earth. At the end of March he replied to Pope Clement's plea for leniency, asserting that his decision to expel the Jesuits from his kingdom was an act which he regarded as a civil necessity, and he begged the Pope to understand his reasons -- a request in which Clement revealed himself to be as stubborn as the King. The Pope responded by defending the Jesuits with his pontifical letter *Tu quoque fili mi* in which he asked for an impartial hearing, but it fell on deaf ears. The King hit back with a reply in June that he would not restrict the decree to just a few individuals but that proofs abounded to indict the Order as a whole.[16]

It was an argument which amply reflected the wording of another consulta drawn up by special session on April 30. It maintained that all the trouble came from the government of the Society, and upon this corrupt mass its individual members depended for their actions like so many puppets in the hands of their superiors. The consulta stressed the fact that were the Jesuits individually being tried for the Squillace riots alone, this would not be sufficient evidence for condemning the whole Order. It was the pride, fanaticism, and false doctrine of their teaching for which the Jesuits were being condemned, and any king who tolerated these evils would fall victim to their whole organization, no matter what the Roman curia might say; and in a later context the consulta stressed that in the struggle between the preachers of ignorance on the one hand, and enlightened men of wisdom on the other, the state would either succumb to the political malaise by which it was infected, or else must expel the Jesuits altogether.

As if seeking defense for his actions elsewhere the King wrote to Tanucci in July, "... facts speak for themselves... I can assure you that the Jesuits by their maxims and system are the enemies of every

sovereign".[17]   But before Charles could muster support
among the sovereigns of the world and appeal to their
consciences, he first had to clear his own; and this
involved disposing of Jesuits in as harmless a way as
possible.  The original idea was to banish them to the
Papal States.  This is clear from the same letter to
Tanucci in which Charles expressed approval that his
old friend was preparing a like fate for the Jesuits
in Naples.  At the same time he cautioned Tanucci
that no news from Rome meant bad news inasmuch as
Cardinal Torrigiani of the nunciature had probably
received orders to oppose the landing of the Jesuits
by force -- an assessment of the situation which proved
correct.  Clement XIII in fact, much as he sympathized
with the Jesuits' plight, had not forgotten that Pombal
had dumped the Portuguese Jesuits on his territories
eight years before and had never settled the bill.  He
was most reluctant to repeat the same mistake.  With
relations between the King and the Pope steadily wor-
sening, Charles denied all audiences with Hippolito
Vinzenti the papal nuncio, who could only deal with
Grimaldi, and attempted to coordinate a common strategy with Louis XV and Tanucci for the disposal of the
exiles. Corsica was the place temporarily agreed upon.

Rejected as they were from the port of Rome, the
Jesuits went via Orbetelo to Corsica, where the Spanish
captains landed them rather carelessly amid confusion
on the island.  Here Pasquale Paoli had been fighting
an abortive war of independence from France, which
finally asserted its rule by a treaty with Genoa in
1768; but France did not want the Jesuits to remain
in Corsica.  With other exiles joining them from the
Americas, the Pope eventually consented to allow them
to settle in Bologna and Ferrara.  Leaving the island
and passing through Genoa, Pisa and Florence, thousands of hapless Jesuits, many of whom died from sheer
exhaustion after so many arduous journeys, found a
haven in these areas, much to the uncharitable annoyance of the local clergy.

Adding insult to injury, the Spanish government
now organized carnivals to greet their departure, at
the same time applying harsh measures against anyone
voicing sympathy.  Campomanes prepared the legislative

drafts. Capital punishment by hanging for crimes of lese majesty, was extended in October 1767 to any Jesuit refugee daring to seek asylum in Spain; nuns educated by Jesuits were banned from the country; mock trials were staged and a further census taken of ex-Jesuit printshops and other properties.[18]

It is estimated that five thousand fathers, brothers, and novices were expelled from Spain and outposts in north Africa; with four thousand more from the Indies and nearly one thousand from Asia and the Pacific, the total number of Jesuits uprooted from the Spanish Empire must have been at least ten thousand. In addition were those expelled from Naples in November 1767, and from Parma and Malta the following year.

Some idea of their suffering is best revealed by the Jesuit, José Francisco de Isla. Author a decade previously of *La Historia del famoso predicador Fray Gerundio,* he now shifted his attention from satire on preachers to an appeal for justice, which took the form of a Memorial personally directed to the King. Having written this at Calvi in Corsica in February 1768, Isla was well familiar with the Jesuits' plight. With incisive reasoning he pleaded for an investigation by impartial judges, allowing the defendants enough time to prepare a defense so that the charges against them could be given a chance for rebuttal, with all the proceedings published. But Isla was only wasting his time. Too much had been done, too many consciences made firm by a sovereign committed far beyond the point of compromise. A heavier blow awaited the Jesuits now that Charles was planning to get the Pope to dissolve their entire Order.

Seeking the church's corroboration on this point, the King's government next sounded out the views of individual clerics in Spain. It was not forgotten that a group of these, admittedly non-Jesuit, had defied royal polcy when in April 1767, Isidro Carvajal y Lancaster bishop of Cuenca, along with others, had written to Father Eleta, the King's confessor, protesting the gradual undermining of the church in recent years. Their complaints included the excessive

levy known as the *excusado* amounting to two million
reales a year which had to be paid to the crown, and
the loss of control over certain church preferments
and titles to mortmain land.[19] All that the worthy prelates received for their efforts was banishment from
court, and few clergy dared thereafter to protest.
Armed with this victory, the council of Castile collected signatures from a number of influential churchmen endorsing its moves against the Jesuits, and followed this up in 1769 by polling the entire hierarchy
on the question of the Jesuit Order's extinction. With
forty-two of the fifty-six votes, including Father
Eleta's,cast affirmatively for the royal policy, Charles
received a mandate from the Spanish church to proceed
with his overtures at Rome.[20]

Clement XIII was not going to give way without
a fight. True, he had made a serious mistake in trying
to assert authority over Parma, which upset Charles'
ruling nephew Ferdinand, and whose minister F.G. de
Tillot, hand-in-glove with Roda and the French encyclopedists, was forthwith instructed to expel the
Jesuits from this duchy. All of this brought Bourbon
courts closer together, including Portugal and even
Austria, in the question of the crown's right to have
a veto over papal briefs; and it led to the occupation
of papal Avignon by France, and of papal Benavento by
Naples. But when Clement breathed his last in 1769,
Charles was still without the sanction for Jesuit dissolution.

The cause of Palafox, meanwhile, was equally at
a standstill, and this had prompted procurator José
de Azara with his cynical wit to comment to his friend
Roda that about all he could get out of Clement XIII
was a papal bull to digest.[21] Azara was reinforced by
Tomás Azpuru as Spanish envoy, supported by Cardinal
Bernis of France and Cardinal Orsini of Naples; and
now the three Bourbon courts made a joint attempt to
influence conclave politics in favor of a compliant
Pope. Their candidate was Lorenzo Ganganelli, a
former consultor of the Holy Office, who had given
vague promises to secularize the Jesuit Order if elected; but when he ascended the pontifical throne as
Clement XIV, he proved just as stubborn as his predecessor.

The trio of envoys duly prepared a request for the suppression of the Order. But the new Pope gave an evasive answer, fortified by a brief *Coelestium* granting the Jesuits further privileges overseas. This angered Charles, who had already upbraided the Bourbon delegates for their slowness. "What Orsini has written to me concerning the delay in presenting to the Pope the petition for the Jesuit Order's suppression has displeased me greatly... especially in view of the inconstancy with which Orsini and Bernis have conspired to collaborate", Charles complained to Tanucci in August 1769, his feelings now bordering on an obsession.[22] Absurdity was reached in circles around him when the Jesuits were blamed for the false rumor that he was going to ban hairnets, as well as silk kerchiefs worn round the necks of his subjects.

The months, the years, dragged by without progress being made. With the cautious François Bernis now working in slow collaboration with the Marquis d'Ossun and Conde de Fuentes (the French and Spanish ambassadors accredited to each other's courts), Pope Clement still resisted, and tried to drive a wedge between the two Bourbon monarchs, Louis XV and Charles III, by appealing to their consciences. Though Louis remained loyal to the general plan, still no progress was being made until in 1772, almost in desperation, Charles turned to his able fiscal lawyer, José Moñino. "Now that Moñino is going to Rome, we shall surely see the steps he will take", he wrote confidently to Tanucci, and this time his confidence was justified.[23]

Now ailing, and confronted by the persistent Moñino who had solid grounds for stressing the indebtedness he should feel towards the Spanish king for his present office, the Pope finally gave way. On August 17, 1773, he released the famous bull *Dominus ac Redemptor Noster*, which dissolved the Jesuit Order -- a decree that was to last for almost forty years. An unhappy man, the Pope died a few months later, knowing that it was Moñino who had extracted from his conscience the betrayal of the Order, and that it was Moñino who had prepared much of the papal wording.[24]

Having received a copy of the bull, Charles wrote jubilantly to Tanucci that "it was very good news and necessary for our holy religion and family... as well as for the security and tranquility of our realms".[25] As for Moñino, he was created Conde de Floridablanca for his services -- a name that applied to a parcel of his estate -- and he shortly became Spain's chief minister in a role that was to last through the end of the reign. Azara too was rewarded for his successful work on Palafox by being appointed a councillor in the Spanish treasury. By contrast, the Jesuit father-general, Lorenzo Ricci, lingered in an Italian jail and died soon afterwards, though hospitality to many Jesuits was given by sovereigns like Frederick the Great and Catherine II of Russia who did not share the dilemma confronting reforming monarchs in Roman Catholic countries.

The question might finally be asked to what extent the Jesuits were guilty of the charges made against them. Two parts to this question arise -- the degree of their complicity in the Squillace riots, and the degree of conspiracy and corruption of which they were accused in a general sense. Taking the Squillace riots, we know from the correspondence between the nuncios Cardinal Pallavicini in Spain and Cardinal Torrigiani in Rome that certain unidentified priests from outside of Madrid were seen mingling with the crowds, presumably inciting them to riot. Other reports make mention of exotically-dressed civilians urging on the rioters, paying for drinks all round. Pallavicini commented that many of the dying and wounded brought into the hospitals during the riots told officials that they saw no sin in what they were doing because they were not being condemned for their actions from the parish pulpits or the confessional. It would appear then from Pallavicini at least, that while the Squillace riots were basically spontaneous in origin, certain groups opposed to Charles' reforms had infiltrated the masses to stir up trouble and hopefully bring down the government, with many local clergymen watching from the sidelines as sympathetic spectators.[26]

It is highly doubtful that any significant number of the Society were involved, beyond those who were friendly with the crowds and had a personal understanding of their problems. True, it was well established that in a few cases Jesuits were distributing literature that could be construed as subversive by the standards of the time, as in the instance of the printing-presses discovered at Vitoria and Saragossa; and some were probably acting treasonably in the Basque lands. But none of this could make the entire Order guilty of planning a conspiracy, and the magistrates sitting on the council probably knew this quite well. The fact was that no master mind planned the Squillace riots at all. Originating with the masses, the riots nonetheless were spurred on by diverse individuals, by men who shared the resentment of nobles like the Duke of Alba or his circle who were being excluded from the highest posts, and on that account only too anxious to embarrass centralist rivals once the crisis had broken. Once the crisis had healed, it was easy to make scapegoats of the Jesuits in the subsequent wake of the riots.

When Pope Clement XIII asked for a fair hearing against any of the separate accused, Charles replied, as we have seen, that the expulsion was not being limited to a few individuals but that grounds existed from expelling the entire Order from Spain's dominions forever. Complicity in the Squillace riots, then, was not the Jesuits' main crime apparently, for the charges against them covered a wider range, thus considerably diluting their immediate specific guilt.

Referring to the second part of the question -- their culpability in the world order of things -- their chief fault lay in a high-handed attitude, which because of their undoubted power aggravated the other Orders, as well as merchants, and stood in the way of regalist reformers. Least guilty of all, perhaps, were the men in the field doing excellent work in bringing the better side of Western civilization to the American Indians. From Spanish Jesuits like José Cardiel who had been in Paraguay, to foreign ones like Johann Baegert or Ignaz Pfefferkorn who had been in northern Mexico, their incisive reports written in exile defending their actions and explaining their enormous hardships would have moved anyone other than those sitting in judgment on the council of Castile. It was only the structure of the Order, not its achievements, which interested officialdom. Rising food prices, the riots, and now the tension after the riots, demanded that justice be meted out with minimum disturbance so

that the wrongs be expiated. To have castigated the
people would have invited revolution; hence the resort
to secret methods of enquiry in which the charges
could be made impersonally, without the defendants
as a whole being physically present. In the prisoner's
dock before the magistrates stood the invisible force
of Jesuitry with all the moral implications resting
with its accusers; and this whole force was whisked
out of Spain as silently as the charges made against
it. If the Order was thus guilty at all, it was because through faults in diplomacy -- with a little
vanity thrown in -- it had fallen victim to the fight
between international church power and the power of
the state, which quickly blamed the Order for the national ills of Spain.

Tempting indeed would it be to exonerate Charles
from blame. The best of Spanish monarchs, he was
seeking to bring his country more in line with the
advanced nations of Europe, and in his defense one
can appreciate that the Jesuits were viewed by others
beside himself as a dangerous and reactionary faction
within the state. The words of the great historian
Manuel Danvila y Collado are here relevant: "The
collision had to come and did come through the inevitable contact of two powerful forces. The expulsion
was thus brought about by the ideas, policies, and
attitude of the Society of Jesus; and the Spanish
monarch was guarded over his reasons. But we can
affirm that an essential change of policy for genuine
reasons of state prompted the expulsion, which often
concealed great injustices."[27] In other words, the
church's most powerful international force was being
sacrificed to further Charles' program of reforms.

Acting ruthlessly in suppressing the Jesuits,
the King was yet scrupulous in disbursing their proceeds, and much of their confiscated wealth was used
to enlarge the very colleges and charities they had
founded. In attacking the elite of Christianity, he
reasoned with circuitous logic that his own monarchy
would emerge more Christian. In the immediate perspective, then, some gains were made. Primary education became compulsory after October 1767; while

the way was clear for cutting down on the privileges of the private colleges, when by decrees in 1766 and 1771, teaching chairs were thrown open to fairer competition. This trend prompted Azara to write joyfully to Roda, "Long live the condemnation of that learning which is destroying us ... and long may our Sovereign live to raise us up from the ignorance and barbarism which has enslaved us";[28] and Tanucci said as much when in lauding Charles' action against the Jesuits, he looked forward to a sweeping-away of backward 'Gothic' learning which encumbered the nation. In other respects, the expulsion did give the King a pretext for shunning conservative nobility raised on Jesuit traditions; and men like the Duke of Villahermosa openly lamented being excluded from power because of his past connections with the Order. In curbing both the bureaucracy and the church of excessive elitism (including whittling down the church's own jurisdiction), Charles, as it were, was killing two birds with one stone.

Commendable as his objectives were, it is doubtful whether these gains insofar as they incurred Jesuit expulsion outweighed the losses in the long run. The university chairs, for example, now filled by non-Jesuits, did not necessarily improve academic standards, and the crown lost one of its mainstays of support. In banishing many worthy prelates, Charles deprived Spain of gifted men who by a careful policy could have been brought into harmony with the needs of the state. The example of Russia or Prussia showed how it was possible to employ a Jesuit elite capable of useful service without prejudice to the national goals. What was needed in Spain most of all was a scientific impulse. This came in due course, but not because of the Jesuits' downfall; on the contrary, the Order had never been opposed to the sciences.

The King, then, could have furthered his aims not simply by crushing this force to extinction. Admittedly he felt a keen dislike combined with a genuine fear; yet the Inquisition also qualified in these respects and Charles made no real effort to curb its retarding presence beyond a few side-attacks, even when the council of Castile implied its willingness to do so.

He could have made a whipping-boy out of freemasonry which existed in a small way in Spain, as in Naples, and which he was closely watching.[29]  He could have attacked foreign merchants which still enjoyed many privileges within the empire.  But he did none of these things.  He was too magnanimous to want a victim as such, though victims the Jesuits became.  His decision to vent full wrath upon them may have been welcomed by some segments of Spanish society, but at best it can be seen as an ill-chosen option which not only came near to causing a schism in the Roman Catholic world, but which ultimately was to backlash upon the fortunes of the Spanish Empire.  Though Charles could not know it, of little avail would it be in the future to call upon the Society to help preserve the imperial grandeur of Spain which collapsed so suddenly at the turn of the next century.  The unnecessary sacrifice was the King's own doing.  In his inner secrecy, greater than the secrecy of his victims, lay a blemish, or serious misjudgment of policy, which obscured his otherwise fine statesmanship.  At the bar of history, the portentous events surrounding the decrees against the Jesuits in 1767 and 1773 must rank in the long run as a defeat for an enlightened king.

A small clue to at least a part of his secret can be gleaned from the following incident.  After his return to Madrid from Aranjuez when the Squillace riots were long past, Charles heard noises in the street one night from his palace and got out of bed to ask his Italian attendant, Almerico Pini, what the trouble was. Pini replied that it was St. Peter's day when people amused themselves by dancing and celebrating in public. Satisfied, the King retired but it was observed afterwards that he never returned to Madrid from Aranjuez until well after St. Peter's day, it being his custom hitherto to return between St. John's day and St. Peter's.[30]

The Squillace mutiny, them, was to haunt him long after the event.  And deeply embedded in these fears, almost certainly, were sinuous figures belonging to the Jesuit Order.  The two were inextricably linked in his mind.

146

# CHAPTER EIGHT

## LAND AND THE ENLIGHTENMENT

As if to get away from his problems, Charles continued to spend much of his time hunting. As in Italy, he loved the open country where he could go on fishing expeditions or live in the mountains; but soon came the inevitable shoot when he would spend his pent-up energy with full force upon the innumerable wild animals which stalked the land. It was as if he saw his abomination, the Jesuit Order, behind every target. Certainly the wildlife 'pests and vermin' marked down for extermination, convinced him he was doing the world a service, though it would be interesting to speculate on his views were he living in the later twentieth century. No other monarch seemed so dedicated to the task. "Here we are all well, thanks to God", he would write to his mother from Cuerva near Toledo during her last years, "and we've returned from our hunting trip highly successful... having slain a male wolf, a she-wolf, seven cats, two wild boars male and female, besides six young boars, two deer, and two vixens".[1] The list of trophies would be repeated a hundred times. Weatherbeaten from the dry air and sun, his face a reddish-brown about the bulbous nose, the lively blue eyes, Charles played on, triumphantly holding back the infirmities of age. "If only people knew how little I sometimes enjoyed hunting", he wryly mumbled "they would pity more than envy me for this innocent pasttime".[2] This as much as anything explains his obsession -- love of blood-sports inherited from his forbears purged the mind of gloom and introspection, making it one with nature, enabling the body in perfect health and strength to perform the high tasks at hand, a quality he would like to see in others.

Yet in attaching as much importance to the hunt as to a field campaign, he was not merely keeping himself in trim; he was also escaping the relentless ceremonial at court which he hated. "Thank God it's all over", he was wont to mutter, his regal robes scarcely hiding the hunting-jacket underneath, the gold-braided silk waistcoat, the black buckskin hose. It was an embarrassment his courtiers had learnt to put up with. As one witness described him: "... His dress seldom varies from a large hat, gray segovia frock, buff waistcoat, small dagger, black breeches, and worsted stockings; his pockets are always stuffed with knives, gloves, and shooting tackle. On gala days a fine suit is hung upon his shoulders; but as he has an eye to his afternoon sport and is a great economist of his time, the black breeches are worn to all coats. I believe there are but three days in the whole year that he spends without going out a-shooting, and those are noted with the blackest marks in the calendar... No storm, heat or cold, can keep him at home... Several times a year all the idle fellows in and about Madrid are hired to beat the country and drive the wild boars, deer, and hares into a ring where they pass before the royal family".[3]

Happy was the day when Charles drank a lot of water at breakfast, for this could only mean a day of rest from the hunt, his attendants at least spared the royal relievings of nature on the way. But these occasions were rare. The greatest sufferers at court were the majordomos who would literally be swept off their feet as the slavering hounds at supper-time rushed forward to get at their bowls of food. And Charles would feed the hounds himself with tidbits from the table, having trusted the servants to do exactly what they were told in the matter of preparing meals for man and dog alike. Indeed he was quick to detect any lies or deceptions. Inwardly smarting whenever a valuable piece of china was smashed and painfully reminded, perhaps, of Maria Amalia's bad temper whenever her underlings transgressed in this way, he would never lose dignity beyond delivering a mild reprimand, and the humblest menial felt at ease in his presence.

Prudence and self-discipline were his characteristics. Roused at six o'clock by his Italian bedroom attendant, he would dress, say prayers, then greet his lord chamberlain the Duke of Losada. By seven he would be saluted by gentlemen of the guard, and then have breakfast, which regularly included hot chocolate, Viennese-style. At other mealtimes, incidentally, his diet changed but little -- soup, veal, eggs, a

good salad, with toast which he invariably dipped
in Canary wine before draining the glass, though on
occasions sugar-coated cakes would be washed down with
diluted Burgundy; and as was the custom of the time,
he always dined in the presence of palace officials.
Meals, like prayers and daily audiences, were things
he attended to on time, as if omission of them would
earn him punishment. The breakfast over, there would
follow the tedious chat with his doctors, after which
he would hear Mass, greet his children, and be ready
for work by eight o'clock. This continued till eleven
when Father Eleta would be around to hear confession.
He would next give audience to his ministers, chiefly
Grimaldi and Aranda, along with church officials and
foreign ambassadors; while others if they were lucky
might squeeze in an appointment after lunch if he was
in a good receiving mood. The siesta over, the proverbial hunt would then commence. Here he would
often be joined by his brother Luis and his son the
Prince of Asturias, and not till the end of the day
would work resume in earnest when he could attend to
all his private correspondence. Later he would greet
his family again and sometimes play cards, never for-
getting to say his prayers at night before going to
bed. He was a devoutly religious man who could keep
sacred relics under his pillow -- so devout in fact
that on one occasion he allowed a priest who was
carrying the Host to ride in his coach while he walked
behind.

As J.F. Bourgoing, a visiting contemporary, once
put it; "Charles led a highly regulated life; use of
each moment was calculated, and nothing ever varied.
Hunting, fishing, his religious devotions, his work
with his ministers, always followed the same pattern".4
Devoid of sexual interest for the pleasures of this
world, he never ceased to mourn his wife; and rumor-
mongers, searching eagerly for the slightest sign
that he was contemplating marriage again or thinking
of taking a mistress from among the prominent dancers
and actresses of Madrid, drew an absolute blank.

But Charles had one supreme passion. As a true
*Madrileno,* he loved his city more than any other Spaniard.
Indeed Madrid had already come a long way, now clean-
sed of much of its dirt and some of its sins, and
Charles had the satisfaction of seeing it shaped to

become a capital worthy of a great empire. He certainly planned with great care. With his favorite trees and shrubs he even ordered roads to be laid around them, as if defiant nature was to be commemorated by the works of man. In 1768 the Prado was under way -- the work of José Hermosilla and Ventura Rodríguez -- which leads from Atocha to the city-gate of Puerta de Alcalá, itself a Carolinian accomplishment. A new post office was built, along with a treasury and hospital, close by the Puerta del Sol with its tree-lined avenues and fountains. Aranda wanted to use such buildings as fortresses against rioters; and it is interesting to recall that they became centers of popular resistance against the forces of Joseph Bonaparte in the years to come, as much as centers of acclaim when the Duke of Wellington passed by in triumph later.

As patron of fine buildings, Charles encouraged the latest neo-classic architecture, where arts and sciences could be taught in impressive surroundings. An expanded royal academy of San Fernando with a new Fine Arts center in the Calle de Alcalá, innumerable trade schools, colleges of medicine and pharmacology with the San Carlos college of surgery founded by 1780 -- these were some of his many projects and interests. Slowly there began to appear in the capital such novelties as optical equipment and even a steam-engine factory. There was also an astronomical observatory near Atocha, designed by Juan de Villanueva. Assisted by a team of engravers, Villanueva also designed the Prado botanical gardens with the famous museum of red brickwork and white stone, which in those days housed a magnificent natural science collection. Here were sent all the flora, fauna, and mineral treasures the government could lay its hands on, and the museum's director, the Peruvian Indian Pedro de Avila, passed on the King's wishes through the council of the Indies that overseas viceroys should do likewise. Alone among the sciences, perhaps, it was in botany and geology where Spain shone brightest and where the great name of Antonio Cavanilles comes to mind. Many other buildings of Madrid were designed in the grand manner, and mark a rich chapter in Spain's institutional history as much as Charles left his own unique stamp upon the city.

To achieve such goals, he gave a high priority to education; in doing so Spain could catch up with the outside world and play her rightful part as a great power. Elimination of Jesuit influence, of collegian monopoly in government, was to be accompanied by making educational posts available to wider sectors of society. The curriculum was to be modernized, a work-force expanded, and even the church was to give ground if it stood in the way. Some progress at the primary level had been made already, as when in 1767 school attendance became compulsory; and teacher certificates, as soon as approved by church and local authority, had additionally to be endorsed by the council of Castile. At technical schools, mathematics and science instruction was on the increase, with a teacher college under way by 1780, but elsewhere sciences were being neglected in general, especially at the provincial universities.

There were twenty-three universities existing at this time, of which Salamanca, founded in the thirteenth century, was the most famous. Like similar universities abroad, their rectors and professors were faced with an out-dated curriculum designed to train primarily clergymen and lawyers, but happily or resignedly they accepted the status quo, tending to ignore the new scientific trends. Theology, civil and cannon law, logic, metaphysics, and physics -- the last three included in 'arts' -- still dominated their classrooms. Scripture, decretals, and rhetoric completed the picture. Chairs in mathematics, medicine, and cosmography existed, but the faculties of theology and law which gave entry to jobs in church and state had much more pay and prestige. Systematic theology, reams of dry Roman law, and Aristotelian logic and metaphysics formed the not very palatable fare for the average student; and it was not long since that there were disputed such problems as to whether the milk-white substance which sprang from the heads of martyred saints like Paul was ordinary milk, or something of a higher celestial order. As for degrees, these were very demanding in time and diligence and costly to obtain. A licentiate in theology or law, for example, might take three or four years, while a doctorate required largely money, often involving an outlay of 20,000 reales. Degrees were indeed passports to advancement, but in the academic world at least, it took a long time to amortize the investment.[5]

Frustration reached deeper levels with the great colleges (*colegios mayores*). Formerly semi-monastic and intended for poor students, these had long become bastions of privilege, as noted already. Financially independent, they had close links with the nobility and religious Orders, in which the Jesuits had been prominent, and this gave them access to a network of formidable influence and power. Costly ceremonies, formal debates which were sometimes rigged, and unnecessary fees such as paying for bullfights when taking the doctorate, were some of the aggravations earnest students had to put up with. Promotion came by slow seniority. Chairs in the faculties of theology and arts were rotated by college, and secured for the 'right' candidate through nepotism and personal influence. Well over half all chairs in the more prestigious subjects of theology and law, for example, went to collegians. Frequently their salaries including stipends and benefices were much in excess of the four thousand reales accorded to less exalted faculty members from the ordinary universities. Senior chairs, moreover, such as those in law were tenured and proprietary, and collegians in these influential positions often purposely blocked the careers of humbler students whose only weapon was merit alone.

It was Queen Maria Amalia who once said that collegians as a whole were even more tightly-knit than the Freemasons, retarding the advance of the sciences.[6] Protected by nobles and higher clergy who largely dominated access to careers, collegians had great advantages in the formal debates termed 'oppositions' which were the first steps to chairs and benefices. Such men were not generally lacking in ability, nor was the practice of oppositions without some merit, but collegians too often used chairs only as stepping-stones to careers in church or government, not to teaching or scholarship. Non-collegians on the other hand were obliged to climb laboriously up the long ladder of academic rank, or battle without friends for political or church appointment. In vain would reformers speak of 'democracy' as a harmonious functioning of the three social orders; and no wonder such modest regalists as Roda or Azara would curse the privileged from behind their desks, lumping many a collegian, along with the Jesuits, as 'apostles of darkness'.

Influenced by Squillace and Father Eleta, Charles had already directed the council of Castile on October 16, 1766, to revive some old laws of his father whereby chairs were to be appointed "according to rigorous justice" and to be no longer rotated by seniority. Competition for chair was eventually made wider, regardless of college connection or theological school, whether of Aquinas or Scotus or Suárez. But while the later 1760's saw the universities remedying such abuses as fraudulent transcripts, poorly supervised exams, rigged oppositions, and illegal holidays, the root of the problem -- privilege versus non-privilege -- remained. In this respect, certainly the expulsion of the Jesuits had not solved it.

Two prominent educators from Salamanca, meanwhile, entered the picture. One was Francisco Pérez Bayer, former professor of Hebrew at this university and now keeper of the royal library at the Escorial as well as tutor to Charles' children.7 Pérez Bayer's memorial, "In defense of the liberty of Spanish learning" (1769) did more than anything to tip the scales in favor of sweeping reforms at colleges and universities. Charles being won over, Pérez Bayer met Father Eleta personally on the stairs of the Royal Palace who told him that the King required him to prepare a draft immediately for cleaning up the colleges; and assisted by Roda the secretary of justice, Bayer hurriedly got to work lest the King change his mind. The result was the important decree of February 23, 1771. Aimed at restoring the colleges to their original purpose, this called for regular inspections, fairer competition for chairs, and the dismissal of some of the older recalcitrant fellows who could still use court influence to defy the reformers.

The other educator was Felipe Bertrán, bishop of Salamanca, now appointed chief college inspector to enforce the decree. Despite vehement counterattacks led by such prelates as the dean of Saragossa (Tomás Lorenzana), which managed to win over the vacillating Father Eleta, the reformers won their victory. Not only was there incriminating evidence at hand to prove collusion with certain members on the council of Castile, but Bertrán was armed with Pope Pius VI's brief *Motu proprio* (1777) in support of educational

change.  The colleges as a group were a long time
dying, but their doom was surely laid.  By the turn
of the century they were driven to extinction by the
crown, their assets taken over to help pay off the
national debt.  In the meantime, the more equitable
methods of chair apportionment weakened collegian
strongholds in the government.

While these reforms were in progress, the universities themselves were being brought into line with
current trends.  Already in 1770 the council of Castile
ordered all universities to introduce more courses in
jurisprudence -- natural law, Spanish law, and public
law -- as well as in mathematics, moral philosophy,
and experimental physics.  The next year on August 31,
a great plan of studies was drawn up by Campomanes,
aimed chiefly at Salamanca which the government considered was dragging its feet.  In essence a compromise with the resistant faculty, the plan made a place
for science in the fundamental arts curriculum, called
for basic Thomism and positive theology in place of
speculative scholasticism, and insisted that legal
studies be more functional and regalist.  It modernized medical and anatomical studies, and imposed more
administrative diligence in supervising credit and
degree-granting.[8]

The plan was then broadened for Salamanca to include more chairs in mathematics and the sciences,
and this reinforced the excellent work being done in
the faculty of medicine.  The university of Valencia
also took a lead in teaching the new subjects, having
an enrollment of 2,500 students as against Salamanca's
2,000, and by the end of Charles' reign, it had a
wide number of chairs ranging from mathematics and
moral philosophy, to physics and the law of nature
and of nations.

In response to the decrees of 1771, the San
Isidro college of royal studies was reopened in
Madrid, replacing its Jesuit predecessor.  Essentially
preparatory in scope, it offered instruction in logic,
physics, and law, with Charles insisting that lawyers
attend courses here for one year before they could
practice in Madrid.  It drew many illustrious figures,

among them the Duke of Almodóvar -- diplomat, historian, and translator of Raynal. Such an atmosphere typified the new spirit, in which scholastic and speculative theology was slowly giving ground to the new studies, though not without heated debate between conservatives and reformers.

As for the professors, their lot was considerably improving, for though salaries remained modest, at least there was stepped-up competition for their services -- an enviable state of affairs. They had of course to tread very carefully in face of the many titles on the Inquisition's banned list, which usually applied not to pure scientific writers such as Newton or Linnaeus, but to those writers who drew dogmatic conclusions from the science of others. But though they might be on the Index, the works of Locke, Swift, Grotius, Montesquieu, Voltaire, Rousseau, Pufendorf, Helvetius, Vattel, d'Alambert, and all the rest, could with permission be consulted in the universities' growing libraries; and there were lawyers in high places such as Francisco Peñaranda who openly praised them.

Charles personally did not like the Inquisition, but he viewed it as a useful tool to serve the national interest. Hatred of heresy in any case was shared by a majority of Spaniards. The institution could perform the function of censoring books coming in from abroad, leaving the government to decide what books to license inside the country. No bishop could now stamp a book with the imprimatur unless first approved by the state, authors having the right of appeal thereto, and the Inquisition after 1770 was confined more and more to purely religious cases coming within its jurisdiction. Crown officials became largely immune from its powers, while no one caught up in its net was to be jailed for long periods until clearly proven guilty.

Yet to destroy the Inquisition entirely was never the government's intention; and a stern reminder of its still awesome presence was the heresy trial in 1778 of a Peruvian named Pablo de Olavide, charged with moral depravity. Friend of Voltaire, d'Holbach and the French encyclopedists, Olavide was an intendant in Seville before supervising some settlements in the

Sierra Morena (of which more later), and whose problems
he handled with great skill.  He was a popular figure
and had enjoyed the patronage of both Wall and Aranda.
But his clashes with the local clergy, including
Capuchin inspectors of these settlements, and his
sumptuous style of living at Seville made him many
enemies, who soon accused him of being tainted with
the wrong sort of philosophy from France.  Their
charges were confirmed when paintings of very nude
women (of whom he was inordinately fond) were discovered in his possession.  With other incriminating
evidence at hand, Olavide was subjected to an *autillo*,
and his trial was the most sensational of Charles'
reign.  Nearly a hundred witnesses were called, including the Duke of Almodóvar; but because everyone
knew that the works of French philosophers were being
furtively read in Spain even by the prominent witnesses present, Olavide in the end was merely banished
to a monastery with loss of property, whence he subsequently fled to France.[9]

Men like Olavide, of course, did not die at the
stake, whose fires in any case were fast passing into
legend by the later eighteenth century.  Only four
persons were burned during Charles' reign -- the last
victim on record being an old woman from Seville
accused of witchcraft in 1780 through having had inter-
course with the Devil.  In England, incidentally, justice was quite happily burning women as late as 1786
under the normal processes of criminal law, usually
for murdering their husbands.  But devils and husbands
aside, the blot on freedom of expression in Spain came
from the Inquisition, which continued to apprehend
persons accused of moral offenses.  Outright confiscation of property was rare, but victims in the meantime suffered through not knowing exactly what the
term 'moral offense' meant.  Was this merely unusual
unorthodox behavior, people were asking, or was forni-
cation included as well, in the grand Olavide manner?
Many were quick to point out that university statutes,
for example, often separated the two.  And what if
sexual laxity involved no heresy?

Yet with regalism all triumphant, reflecting as
it did Charles' own impeccable conduct, the church
itself was gradually becoming more subordinate to the

state.  There were strong arguments for reducing its
privileges.  In some parts of Castile and the Basque
provinces nearly one quarter of all arable revenues
was under its control.  Elsewhere in the interior
including León, it owned about a seventh of all the
land, perhaps one twelfth in Spain as a whole, much
of it in mortmain.[10]  The clergy comprised about
200,000 persons, or nearly two and a half per cent
of the population; and though this number was declining by the end of the century, the church's income remained substantial -- estimated at well over
a billion reales.  Of the vast rent money it controlled,
critics charged, barely one fortieth part ever reached
the treasury; and in devising loopholes for avoiding
its just share of taxation, it often pronounced against
others investing at interest, which was one important
way the government, by borrowing, could redeem the
loss which the church was causing in the first place.
To many, it was a double standard when the church held
huge investments of its own in mortgages, tithes, and
other liquid assets.  Yet for all its wealth, the church
did adhere to a high moral tone, funding a vast amount
of its income for charitable purposes; and there were
many gifted churchmen -- Ramón Pignatelli, for instance,
canon of Saragossa cathedral -- who became reconciled
to Charles' regalism.

It was precisely the question of charity hand-outs
that disturbed reformers, for without productivity,
here was a further drain on national resources.  In
this the church played a defensive role, trading off
loss of jurisdiction as the price for retaining its
wealth.[11]  As a landowning force, it was simply too
powerful to be felled in one blow.  But the church was
shifting with the times.  In the field of welfare it
devoted so much of its wealth to, it was prepared to
share, if not to shed, many of the obligations the
state was willing to assume, especially in curbing
vagrancy and social delinquency.

Helping Charles in this direction were manteístas
like Campomanes.  Friendly with Wall and Aranda, and
whom we have already seen at work on the council of
Castile, Campomanes was a passionate critic of church-
owned lands held in mortmain.  In 1765 he published
his *Tratado de la regalía de la amortización,* tempering his

anti-clericalism and hatred of the Inquisition by an ardent regalism, but not without being cautioned by his superior, Floridablanca, in the process. Champion of education for the masses, he called for a vocational training plan to develop a skilled labor force. Like other reformers, he struck out against permitting thousands of vagrants to plague the countryside, pleading to uproot from the wasted soil its human illiteracy and ignorance. To the main pillars of economic theory such as land and capital, he added another -- use of human resources through fomenting a national industry. The result was his famous *Discurso sobre el fomento de la industria popular*, published in 1774, followed by similar *Discursos*. [12] In these works he lamented Spain's depopulation, and also castigated restrictive organizations such as the shepherds' guild, in which he later held the highest office. Eventually becoming governor of the council of Castile, raised to the rank of count in 1780, he had such a deep grasp of his country's problems that he can be regarded as an economic centralist of major rank.

Bernardo Ward with his *Proyecto económico* paralleled Campomanes in attacking vagrancy and unemployment, in which he praised the English system of parish workhouses. Ward also proposed a national lottery as a charity-funding institution, though this was as much the brainchild of Squillace, who borrowed the idea from Naples. The first drawing, incidentally, took place on December 10, 1763 before Charles extended it to Mexico seven years later; and this became very much part of the national scene in Spanish-speaking countries.

Burning with impatience, Campomanes along with Ward had long been condemning the policy of punishing vagrants when there was not work for them to do at home; and they urged productive jobs at a wage of four reales a day paid from state funds, in lieu of church charity. There is little doubt that Charles via Floridablanca listened to their ideas. In 1778, for example, he created a royal junta of charity to clean up his beloved Madrid, in which wanderers were to be sent home within two weeks and the poor and disabled properly cared for out of parish funds; but the important feature here was that the administering of this junta was to be shared by state and church alike.[13]

Clearly, the latter was retreating from its monopoly over charity. Already critical of certain abuses going on at its own welfare banquets and fiestas, it even considered the question of cutting down on the number of feast-days -- another theme dear to Campomanes who was quick to calculate how many work-hours were lost through having ninety-three idle days in the Spanish church calendar. The way was clear for harnessing more human resources to industry. As Ward put it, it was the 'soup of the convents' which was the biggest obstacle to the establishment of factories.[14]

In this respect, Charles clearly aimed to help wider numbers of people. He travelled a great deal around Madrid, whence he could visit such places as Toledo or Cuerva and see at first hand the difficult tasks that lay ahead. In January he would stay at the Pardo, replete with its rich seventeeth-century tapestries and frescoed ceilings and looking out on the Sierra de Guadarrama. By Palm Sunday he was back again in Madrid, and after Easter would depart for Aranjuez where he usually stayed till June. Returning to the capital, he would then leave for San Ildefonso for the rest of the summer, putting up at the Escorial en route and again in October on his way home. With winter approaching he would be back in Madrid once more, having spent three-quarters of the year in the countryside on his regular round of visits.

It was occasions like these that gave him full scope to survey the land of Castile. Here he would come in close contact with peasants and mountain folk, with men and women from simple walks of life as they scratched a living from the soil. Sympathy for their plight and an underlying feeling of equality in a spiritual sense prompted him to talk with them on familiar terms, and this was reciprocated, much to the annoyance of his hidebound entourage. He genuinely wanted to broaden the basis of society. Giving people a fairer share of the land's wealth would open new avenues and perhaps herald the ultimate luxury of more liberty in enterprise and social expression. On one occasion he rebuked a governor of Castile for procrastination, commenting that without prejudice to any class he would like to see maximum attention given to the poor.[15] It was the first time in many years of Spanish history that a king had said such things and actually meant them.

But it was easier said than done. Enlightenment would not stay just because the Jesuits had departed. There were forces among nobility and people alike who could use Catholicism -- sacrosanct to all including Charles himself -- as a strong weapon of counter-attack. Members of his government, while honest in a personal sense, were devious in practically every-thing except in their zeal to let things stay as they were. Rooted in a fixed rural society, too many of them resisted attempts to introduce new techniques in agriculture and industry, remaining unsophisticated except in sophistry itself. There were learned men in Spain, and there was wealth, but little had been done to transform the soil into that of a modern state. Muddled tax practices was the norm at home, while a-broad the limitless specie from the American colonies was too often syphoned out of the empire to make way for foreign products.

The area of Spain, some 195,000 square miles, was then divided into thirteen provinces, of which Old and New Castile were the largest. Among the ob-stacles to progress are the interlocking mountains averaging two thousand feet, forming an arid plateau with little moisture draining off except around the edges of the peninsula. Here quite fertile valley regions are to be found. The coastline itself was always fairly well developed, its many capes pro-tecting the ports and hinterland. But it was in the starved central part of Spain -- Castile, León, and the huge area southwest of Madrid -- where backward-ness was most evident. Here sheep-raising, wheat, leather goods, pottery, and an occasional royal fac-tory were about the only signs of activity to illumine the otherwise bleak picture.

Spain's assets elsewhere included cattle, grains, fruit, wines and minerals, largely in the south. Textile production was widespread in Valencia and Catalonia, the Barcelona region turning out a wide range of manufactured goods. Across the north of Spain, the many cannon foundries and shipyards de-pended on the local resources of iron ore and timber,

while hemp and flax, also in abundance, supplied the
cordage, linen, and sail-cloth which could be seen
as far west as the port of La Coruna.  Salt-fisheries
dotted the coastline, largely Catalan-owned but worked
by Galician hands.

The population according to Aranda's census of
1769 was over eight million, of whom about two million
peasants with their families lived directly off the
land.16   The interior and the south were largely semi-
feudal, and here the church, nobility, and military
orders were still highly influential.  Though somewhat weakened by the intendants set up by Philip V,
these traditional orders of society had lost little
of their economic power.  Even where great cities had
shrunk into smaller towns, many were still governed
by hereditary nobles.  With all their privileges or
*fueros*, these wielded enormous power among elected town
councillors (*regidores*), though in Aragon at least, city
officials could be appointed by the crown.  Seignorial
jurisdiction aside, one of the biggest problems was
the prevalence of huge estates with tax-exemptions
accumulated over the years.  Huge estates of course
were typical of the eighteenth century everywhere;
but in Spain's case the gap between the rich and the
poor was made worse by an unproductive management of
the land even when good resources lay upon it.  The
crown could do little to reverse the situation because the kings in the past had sold large parts of
their royal estates to powerful nobles in order to
raise money for carrying on the government.

There were many good señores devoted to agrarian
reform -- the Dukes of Medinaceli, Infantado, and
Alba were three cases in point, the latter owning
vast tracts of Andalusia -- but elsewhere a desire
not to be bothered with the running of estates was
too often a chief fault of the Spanish aristocracy.
Absentee landlordism was rife.  More numerous than
the clergy, the nobility comprised about eight per
cent of the population in the 1780's, though its
numbers were declining.  Of the six hundred senior
nobility about a hundred were grandees, and these
were strong in Castile and the south where the
biggest estates were to be found.  The north of
Spain by contrast had more of the minor nobility

and hidalgos; but the pride of caste prevented too
many from engaging in simple manual trades, so that
thousands were lost to industry. People preferred
cosier jobs in church and government -- or simply preferred not to work at all.[17] This state of mind was
even stronger in the interior, where at the bottom
of the scale some 140,000 vagabonds and beggars led
unproductive lives. With more emphasis given to social
prestige than hard work, it would have been a caustic
joke to comment that there were two nobles for every
one beggar in Spain!

Along with social attitudes was a general resistance to change, especially to English techniques.
There was a popular saying -- 'you can't work with
English-style implements'. As in Naples, the absence
of a fixed labor force made harvest-gathering irre-
gular, and this, combined with the uneven landscape,
impeded distribution and encouraged hoarding. One
contemporary observer, Edward Clarke, described the
haphazard state of affairs. After glowing words of
praise for the cattle and abundant wild game, for the
swine fed on chestnuts "giving it a most exquisite
flavour", for the sturdy oak trees, for fruits of all
kinds, for the excellent wine and cork, and for a
climate "good for the dry cholic", the author in the
same breath could comment that despite the flour being
as fine as any in England, it was sad to see so much
good land going to waste from the little labor bestowed
on it. The cut corn would lie about for six weeks at
a time, when Spaniards would amuse themselves at night
by the huts and threshing floors, some playing the
guitar, others dancing to *fandangos*, while the corn was
trodden out by the most primitive methods.[18]

But it was not all a tale of wilful abandon.
Many were being driven off the land by force of cir-
cumstance, even those willing to work for pitifully
low wages; for the population was steadily rising
(approaching ten million by the year 1800), so that
a growing land hunger was pushing up the price. It
was becoming more difficult to earn a livelihood, and
many tenants could not afford to employ even seasonal
labor. Adding to the peasant's woes was an unproductive method of land tenure which consisted of no less

than six different types of possession, many of them overlapping.

There were crown lands (termed the *patrimonio real*), much of it in wasted areas and whose better parts the kings since Arab times had sold to private interests; church lands (*señoríos eclesiásticos*), which included benefices, chaplaincies, and cathedral chapters, in large degree held in mortmain; private lands (*señoríos legos*), owned mostly by nobility, and strong in southern Spain; municipal lands (*comunidades*), also strong in the south, but probably the most widespread of all; and entailed lands (*mayorazgos*), strong in the interior and the north, also very widespread and possessed by private families as well as by the church. Finally there were the lands of individual tenant-proprietors, of whom there were about 300,000, representing one seventh of the two million tillers of the soil. These lucky few with guaranteed land tenure were prevalent in more prosperous Catalonia, Valencia, Aragon, Navarre, the Basque lands, as well as Granada, where they could comprise nearly one half of all farmers in these areas.[19]

A great hardship was the growth in land enclosure. Larger private owners at a time of increased competition for land, tools, and luxuries to sustain their way of life, were driving out many tenants not merely to acquire more pasture, but more profitable arable farming. Enclosure abuses were very prevalent among municipal lands. Peasants would graze their cattle in the common pastures and some had received leases, but powerful local magnates strong in these municipalities were tending to push them out. To protect the public interest, Aranda's administration in 1766 (as Charles had done in Naples) authorized syndic procurators to check city financial accounts, while provincal intendants were to ensure impartiality in the courts on behalf of the peasants' right to land. But this had limited success. Peasants had slim chances in a court where money talked, and many would end up as hired hands to the very landlords who had displaced them. Charles then instructed his fiscal lawyer Floridablanca to prepare a plan by 1770 for distributing arable town lots for farmers with enough livestock and equipment to succeed on their own.

163

Good as this law was, inflation continued its
upward trend, and even where farmers could get double
the price for their crops -- animal products alone
trebled in price during the later eighteenth century
-- rents were often rising faster than income.[20] The
tenant was indeed in a vulnerable position. Landlords
pressured by the price squeeze would resort to the
practice of selling a part of their estate along with
the lease itself, without regard to the rights of the
holder, simply by filing the transaction with the
registry of land titles. '*Venta deshace renta* (the sale
voids the lease)'. went the saying, as tenants' rights
were virtually auctioned to the highest bidder.
Lapses of rent payment, moreover, which were tolerated
in the past as a time-honored practice, would now
most likely find the offender in court, and fore-
closure cases abounded. Even when rents were frozen,
as in Galicia and Asturias or when Charles decreed
in 1768 that no leaseholder could be deprived of
his land without just cause, tenants to make ends
meet often resorted to sub-leasing, so that the rent-
burdened peasant at the bottom of the scale might end
up as a water-carrier in some nearby city, or simply
lapse into vagrancy.

The poorest of all were probably the casual day-
laborers of the south, where seasonal employment was
sometimes available on the larger estates. Here
wages ranged between a mere three to four reales a
day, though skilled workers such as carpenters could
command three times as much. But elsewhere, wages
for regular farm workers were barely increasing one
fifth, at a time when prices were rising at a considerably faster rate.

Confused land tenure with all the other abuses
contributed to the depopulation that was going on,
especially in such areas as La Mancha or Andalusia.
There could be seen all over Spain hundreds of square
miles of abandoned land -- a sad reminder that worthy
people for one reason or another had long since emi-
grated. "Why in our town and villages are there men
without land, and in our countryside lands without
men?" critics were asking.[21] Evicted peasants, forlorn drifters making do on piece-work, beggars and
brigands would have provided the answer. Tenant

was at the mercy of landlord, with thrift and the
initiative to make improvements self-defeating.
The gap between the rich and the poor was widening.
For those peasants who remained, there was only the
fatalist acceptance of poverty or famine, the simple
faith in miracles, consoled as they were by well-
meaning priests whose status was higher but whose
education was barely above the level of their own.22
It was a world of inequality, lightened by the hope
that in the next one all would some day meet on
common ground.

Pockets of prosperity did of course exist, especially near rivers or the sea -- the plains between
Córdoba and Seville for instance, rich in wheat, vines,
and olives -- and there were well-kept farmlands and
orchards to be seen around Madrid and in the south,
dappled with neat whitewashed cottages roofed with
thatch. Luckiest of all were tenant-proprietors in
the more prosperous parts of Spain who had a hereditary lease or some protective clause against disposs-
ession. But often elsewhere, from Castile to Extremadura, the evil effects of Spain's land-tenure systems were only too apparent.

Charles of course, along with Ward and Campomanes,
was not alone in recognizing all this injustice. There
was Ignacio de Luzán, long enthused about Voltaire from
his contacts in Paris, as well as Antonio Muñoz (probably a pen-name for the soldier Enrique Ramos), who was
equally enthused about Montesquieu.23 Indeed the
French philosophers were being read by an ever widening
circle, from Aranda and Roda to the critical Duke of
Alba, now director of the royal Spanish Academy. All
these men were calling for fairer laws, improved education, and more applied systems in agriculture which
would strengthen the nation against idleness and attri-
tion from the land. Similar appeals in varying degrees
were made by Miguel de la Gándara and Nicolás de Arriquibar, as they blamed the Hapsburgs' disastrous tax
policies for Spain's ills, proposing a liberal policy
within the empire as the best means of combating foreign goods which flooded the market.24 Last but not
least was the fiscal Vizcayno Pérez. In the 1760's
he attacked Spain's stagnant land system in which the
peasant was enmeshed in a parasitic web of mortgages

and quitrents (*censos*), proposing instead that these tied-up rent monies be released for productive enterprises such as banks and a better grain disribution, and hitting out at guilds and monopolies in the process.[25]

Soon the names of reformers became legion. The influence of France continued to be felt, but it was the field of native economic theory rather than social philosophy that yielded the richest harvest. Familiar complaints -- wasted resources, uneven development, the draining away of specie -- no longer sounded like hollow clichés. Less abstract, hence less incriminating, economic scholarship generally escaped the Inquisition, and there were secret 'radicals' of the day apart from Campomanes or Roda who enjoyed immunity from prosecution. Activity of all sorts was encouraged so long as it conformed to social orthodoxy, there being a bond of a sort between regalism and the Inquisition in order to preserve the status quo of society in this pre-revolutionary era.

Private enterprise in particular responded to Campomanes' patriotic appeals. Conditions here were ripe for development. Basques, Catalans, the French themselves, were particularly active. An important landmark was the Basque Society of the Friends of the Nation (*Sociedad Bascongada de los Amigos del País*), founded in 1765. Various notables who had been to France formed meetings to promote scientific progress, and they prepared a constitution at Azcoyta and Vergara for submission to the King. A royal charter was processed by Grimaldi, thanks to the efforts of founding members led by Conde de Peñaflorida; and with the support of others such as Marqués de Peñafiel, the Society spread rapidly. All social classes were involved, along with upper-class women, and nobles were expected to engage in farming or trade.[26] The young also were invited to join as junior associates, candidates being examined in Latin, French, chronology, geography and physics. Prizes up to a thousand reales were awarded for the best monographs; and here interests ranged from flax cultivation, cattle-breeding, sheep-raising, soil sampling, tree culture, and control of farm prices, down to such novel ideas as meat refrigeration and improved bellow techniques in iron foundries.

The Society's impact was contagious. Branches sprang up all over northeastern Spain, with new seminaries offering chairs in the sciences, economy, and law, in rivalry even with some of the universities; and it was not long before Charles himself was caught up in the general enthusiasm. Anxious to keep ahead of French influence, he authorized in 1775 the establishment of the royal Economic Society of Madrid. Campomanes had a hand in its creation, and the Society soon served as a model for others. It enjoyed Charles' personal endowment of three thousand reales annually for prize money and medals, besides funding for such worthwhile projects as spinning schools for girls. Numbering hundreds of members, including Charles' own sons, Gabriel and Antonio, the Society did much good work in furthering industry and vocational training, reflecting as it did direct royal commitment to the reform spirit.[27] In the course of the reign, nearly sixty economic societies were founded, the ones at Segovia, Seville, and Majorca being particularly active. The King meanwhile started other pet projects of his own, from irrigation works to forestry plantations, while at Aranjuez he set up a model farm to experiment with the latest techniques in cultivation.

One commendable feat was the founding in 1767 of settlements in the Sierra Morena region of southern Spain. Supported by Campomanes and Muñoz, the plan envisaged the immigration of foreign workers on a large scale, much like Frederick the Great's plan to colonize parts of Prussia. Already there was a Bavarian living in Spain, Colonel Johann von Thürriegel, who had proposed to Charles a colony of Germans in Puerto Rico, though this idea was turned down. The chosen region of Sierra Morena was a wasteland lying west of La Mancha not far from Bailén, and whose barren heights spanned the waters draining down through Cordoba into the Guadalquivir river. The region was infested with brigands, the mountain passes so dangerous that coaches arriving there had to discharge their passengers who then were obliged to proceed perilously on horseback.

It was Campomanes who drafted a constitution for the new settlements. Divided into communities,

the immigrants were to be given enough land and
cattle for their needs, with scores of acres for
larger families, from which roving herdsmen were to
be excluded. Electing their own officials, the immigrants would pay only minimum taxes, would be required to send their children to primary schools,
and as Roman Catholics were given full facilities
of their religion. Money for the project came from
excise taxes, with the treasury granting a subsidy
of one and a half million reales to include travel
expenses for the immigrants coming in from Germany,
France, Switzerland and Greece.

The task was enormous as the immigrants struggled
in unfamiliar terrain. Toiling with hoe and axe and
spade, unable to use oxen because of the stubborn
soil, and craving not for Spanish wines but for the
good continental beer they had left behind, many immigrants died from sheer exhaustion. Despite these
hardships the settlements slowly took shape, and
over two thousand colonists survived to build up
about twenty communities of which La Carolina, perhaps, was the most famous on account of Charles'
formal founding of this site commemorated in the
painting by Victorino López. The colonies slowly
became self-supporting, and after ten years comprised
nearly sixty villages which dotted the region over
an area some one thousand square miles. In the process the settlers had planted a quarter of a million
olive trees, half a million vines, besides innumerable mulberry bushes; while their local industry
turned out such items as clothes, hats, lace apparel,
lamps, soap, and pottery, down to nails and needles.
Despite friction with local church inspectors and
although many of the colonies died out later (with
Spaniards eventually outnumbering the foreign immigrants), the experiment was one of the most remarkable in Charles' reign.[28]

Among the many posts which Campomanes held in
his later years was the presidency of the shepherds'
guild, or *Mesta*. Unrestricted pasture grazing --
which would have included the Sierra Morena region
had not his constitution prevented it -- was the
chief activity the Mesta supported, and in view of

the government's priority given to arable farming, this guild became a big obstacle to reform. Owning no livestock as such, it existed to protect the rights of the migratory herdsmen. Their sheep -- some five million of them -- would be moved southwards for the winter whence they would return the following spring to be shorn at such Castilian centers as Segovia. The fine Merino wool would then be exported to northern Europe through Bilbao. Favored since the time of Ferdinand and Isabel, the Mesta had grown enormously rich when grazing had been profitable; but now that the raising of crops was taking its place the powerful landlords and municipalities viewed the herdsmen as a threat, especially when the latter intruded upon common lands which many townships had taken over.

Sharpening the conflict was the role of the itinerant magistrate (*entregador*), whose judgments were often slanted in the Mesta's favor. Traditionally supported by the crown, the entregador was not unknown to accept bribes from the townships to keep away from his circuit; but as he was handsomely rewarded by the other side as well, this role of dishonest broker led to heated lawsuits brought against the Mesta -- often unsuccessfully -- by the town. The Mesta upheld its traditional privilege to graze at will, protesting the many wool taxes and tolls it had to pay, while the townships protested the immunity from prosecution given to Mesta trespassers under a collective law by which, in the event of damage to property, the individual was virtually absolved from guilt. Herdsmen would behave like rustlers, it was charged, who would steal livestock and trample crops under cover of night. The cry went up that Mesta graziers were outright thieves who were putting up the price of food for everyone. In an age of rising land values these complaints had much support, and it was not long before matters came to a head when in 1771 certain towns in Extremadura finally won redress of grievances in the provincial court.[29]

Like the Jesuits before them, the graziers -- perhaps with more justification this time -- became the general target of attack; and with Campomanes as president of the Mesta pressing for its dissolution, Charles himself, along with Floridablanca, became

inevitably drawn into the conflict. He had to choose
between two evils -- allowing trespassing by the Mesta
or enclosure by the townships -- and in the end he favored the latter option. First the townships, then landlords in general (respectively in 1783 and 1788) won
their right to continue enclosing common lands, while
in 1786 the Mesta lost its right to 'squat and possess '
altogether. The office of entregador moreover was finally abolished. The Mesta's demise did not take place
till 1836, but Charles with his reformers was moving
in the right direction, and it was to his credit that
he was willing to forego much revenue from the Mesta
in order to thwart its oligarchy of outdated privilege.

Yet in the process other forces were inevitably
strengthened -- the big landed estates and municipalities. Furthering crop cultivation certainly improved
Spain's resources, but with prices ever rising the
smaller farmer felt the pinch, entwined as he was in
a mesh of mortgages and landlord rights too deeply embedded to be unravelled in one generation. Despite
a five per cent tax on landholdings, some ten thousand towns and villages remained under seignorial jurisdiction by 1790, along with so many estates still
entailed, all of which was precisely the opposite of
what the government intended.[30]

But it is doubtful if any other regime could have
done any better when faced with the sparseness of the
soil, the conservatism of society, the stoicism of
the inhabitants. That erudite Dominican, Father Andrés
de Valdecebro, expressed it aptly for the eighteenth
century when he wrote: "As the beauty of the hand is
in the disparity of its fingers, so the greatest harmony of a commonweal lies in its unequal parts dis-
tinguishable by kings and vassals; just as among the
creatures, from elephants to storks and cranes, it is
the older and the wisest that guard the rest. And
witness the miracle of the bees... If it were not for
inequality the world would be worse off, for spiritual
ruin sets in when flesh is made equal to the spirit.
And just as the inequality of chords makes harmonious
music, so the surrender of differing passions makes
harmony in the soul. There is nothing less equal for
existence than equality, nothing more really equal
than the inequalities in existence".[31]

Truisms, perhaps, as only a Spaniard could express them. And herein lay Charles' own dilemma; he who had once nearly been toppled from his throne knew only too well that if he stirred the morass of rural backwardness too deeply, then another revolt, this time by country patricians instead of city plebs, could not be altogether discounted. Thus too many peasants whom he vowed to help stayed poor amid the bleak pasturelands of Spain.

Already much had been achieved in face of deep-seated opposition. He had broadened education and reduced the power of the private colleges, thus reducing the power of collegians in government itself. Manteista careers were correspondingly advanced. He had protected peasants' rights by limiting evictions, founded new settlements as a check on depopulation, and restricted the activities of the shepherds' guild -- all to conserve labor resources and promote agriculture. With much the same end in view, he had released labor resources from church charity organizations, which as a sincere and faithful Catholic he saw no contradiction in doing.

In this last respect it is worth noting that, sensing the changing times, Pope Pius VI in a special bull of 1780 conceded the crown's right to collect up to one third of the income from royal-nominated benefices, and to invest it jointly with the church in public credit agencies known as *montes de piedad*. Millions of reales from royal sources, sale of church properties, and sale of pardons during Lent (the *indulto cuadragesimal*) enabled these agencies to build schools, hospitals, and poor-houses. Three years later these montes de piedad were ordered to supervise church charity confraternities, long under attack by Campomanes and Ward for being too labor-wasting and costly to the taxpayer. Included also were the more secular social-aid brotherhoods, which among other things extended loans and insurance to their members. All of this of course was a blow to free social enterprise as confraternities and brotherhoods began to wither on the vine, but Charles' regalism had triumphed without opening new wounds with the Pope, and a firm basis laid for harnessing human resources to national industry.

Clearly new currents were stirring.  Reformers
of every hue, from Castile to Catalonia, were demanding cheaper bread, better land use, more scientific training for the nation as a whole.  If they
could not master, at least they could try to control
the forces of economic change.  The remarkable burst
of industry and trade (reserved for a later chapter)
was the result of the convergence of regalism and
the reform spirit, in which a constructive national
policy enhanced Spain's capacity to influence external events.

Conde de Campomanes, artist unknown

# CHAPTER NINE

## STATECRAFT AND REARMAMENT

Charles was determined to strengthen his country much more among the powers of Europe. It was no easy task, for although other countries had problems, Spain as we have seen, had a liberal share of its own. His two chief ministers, Aranda and Grimaldi, heads of the councils of Castile and State respectively, were at opposite ends of the political spectrum. Aranda and his circle led the so-called 'Aragonese' faction, largely noble and conciliar-minded, while Grimaldi led the 'manteistas' (or *golillas* as they came to be called), who were fully behind the King's centralist policies. The terms Aragonese and golilla were rarely used in official parlance to describe the factionalism, but the lines became drawn once a crisis developed. Sharpening their rivalry was Charles' own son the Prince of Asturias. He scarcely hid his preference for the Aragonese faction which soon became an embarrassment to royal policy.

Yet despite his centrist position, Charles was surprisingly even-handed in his choice of ministers. Members of either group could be considered for a job so long as the demands of loyalty were fully understood; and there is no evidence that he deliberately played off one against the other. The authority of his kingship was unquestioned. He was in fact an astute executive; and guided almost by instinct among the mass of memoranda before him, with Father Eleta hovering in the background, he usually had the insight to get to the root of a problem. The familiar features -- prominent nose, bushy eyebrows, bent and narrow shoulders -- were becoming more marked as he grew older, but his vivid blue eyes and benevolent manner were so compelling that everyone obeyed him with willingness. He had long become a peculiarly engaging character. A contemporary, Joseph Townsend, once commented that the only time Charles lost his temper was when he was detained from the chase by the two days in Passion Week.[1]

Allowing much rein to his trusted ministers Múzquiz, Roda, Muniain, and Arriaga, heads respect-

ively of the treasury, justice, war, and the Indies
-- Charles would listen patiently to their advice,
though perhaps less so when listening to Aranda, who
was fast becoming overbearing. Generally forgiving
by nature, he could be beautifully caustic on occasions. Unpunctuality in all things, bullfights ex-
cepted, has always been the proverbial custom in
Spain; but it went against the grain for a meticulous
king like Charles to tolerate tardiness in his ministers, some of whom were apt to take advantage of his
generosity. When Muniain was absent from council
duty at the palace, the King once quipped: "Don Gregorio must greatly rely upon my aversion to change,
otherwise he would never have dared to provoke me by
these proofs of disrespect!"[2]

The fact was that once out of royal earshot, government matters were often haphazardly conducted. The
ministers of the main councils were either at cross-
purposes with one another, or else if harmony prevailed,
they might conspire together and withhold embarrassing
facts. Too many office-seekers buying supporters with
sinecures, young army men wasted in staff jobs, inadequate rotation in committee membership, all tended
to impede Charles' reforms. What was needed most of
all, perhaps, was a man of confidence who could unify
the councils' many procedures and bring the issues
to royal attention; and though Grimaldi with Eleta
partially did this, it was not till much later that
this was fully done by Floridablanca. Charles of
course was no fool and was well aware of all the back-
stairs intrigue, no doubt relayed to him by old servants like Wall, who long after his retirement was
still on hand to give advice before his death in 1777.

When the afternoon hunt was over, the King would
devote much of his time to private correspondence in
which he would unfurl his grievances with painstaking
care. Among the young members of his family was his
son and heir, Carlos Prince of Asturias (the future
Charles IV), who in December 1765 had married María
Luisa of Parma, precocious daughter of Don Philip.
Relations between father and son were never very close;
the father's austere way of life was too restrictive
for the easy-going Carlos. Reared in Italy with his

sisters and brothers, and none too bright to begin
with, Carlos must have had mixed feelings at his impending uprooting from Naples. The family's move to
Spain, the tragedy of his mother's early death, and
turmoil of the Seven Years war were all occasions
when closer attention might have been given to the
prince, for whom teen age had its usual problems.
In the crises of these years the father was somehow
absent from the boy's formative and lonely youth.
Carlos for his part did not lack total aptitude --
he scored highest when assisting at the hunt -- but
his somnolent existence in the shadow of the throne,
his disinclination to study and natural jealousy of
the younger, more studious Gabriel whom his father
obviously preferred, bred in him a kind of lazy, fur-
tive, indifference to his father's many problems and
turned his feeling of neglect to one of slow hostility. Thus when marriage came, it came as a relief,
breaking down his sense of isolation. Here at least
was a real woman and a lively one, who in some measure
could replace the lost Maria Amalia and shine through
the haziness of the dreamy, tinselled, semi-world in
which he lived. Though the father cannot be blamed
exactly -- it was perhaps as much the chance of cir-
cumstance that had done the damage to the prince's
adolescence -- the damage for whatever reason had been
done; and these two first cousins of nearly the same
age were to prove disastrous to their country in the
end.

The King was sorely troubled by the tactless conduct of his daughter-in-law. It was bad enough when
her emancipated ways clashed with the stuffy traditions of the court, but even worse when she drew together conservative factions opposed to his own reforms. She and her husband were fast becoming courted
by nobles of the old school who remembered the care-
free happy days of Ferdinand VI, and who hated the
manteista class of politicians (dubbed *golillas* on
account of the white ruffled collar they wore) now
riding high in the royal favor. Such parvenu types
were clearly distinct from the upper-class Aragonese
led by Aranda, who largely came from the private
colleges. Aranda certainly communicated with Carlos
to impress him with the ideals of toughness and efficiency, but it would be fair to say that Aranda as

a reformer himself was only loosely associated with this noble Aragonese faction, and then only in virtue of his high lineage. Many conservatives in fact were hiding behind his back in order to hide their opposition from the King. But there is little doubt that Charles saw through their designs, that they were using his family as a tool to serve their interests. Since Carlos was not in the least disposed to check his wife's conduct, it was not long before friction arose between father and son. Repeatedly he counselled Carlos to be on guard against this rivalry of factions (i.e., Aragonese versus golilla), but the son was blind to his admonitions.

The gnawing anxiety Charles felt at home was somewhat relieved by his correspondence with relatives abroad. These included his fond sister María Ana, wife to Joseph of Portugal, who had resided in this country since 1729 as a faithful ally of Spain; and his other sister María Antonia, wife to Victor Amadeus of Savoy, who did her best to assuage any anti-Spanish sentiment in a husband whose dynasty for many years had sought to play arbiter to the rival Hapsburgs and Bourbons in Italy. He also had a daughter in Tuscany, son in Naples, nephew in Parma, not to mention his cousin Louis XV of France, and without this rapport he might have felt considerably thwarted by the complexities of governing.

There were important foreign policy matters to consider. Grimaldi had been instructed to seek commercial treaties with the courts of Europe aimed at a general peace, but an equally important task in those days of dynastic interest was to sound out the chances for marriage alliances. The trouble here was that eligible Catholic royalty was not so easy to come by. If Charles was to marry off his children outside his own line, then the distinguished Hapsburgs of Austria as the senior House in Europe seemed a risk worth taking.

Long association with Empress Maria Theresa who had been the Bourbons' ally in the Seven Years war had diminished Charles' ancient enmity; and with Parma, Piacenza, and Guastalla being additional gains for Spain by secundogeniture since 1748, apart from

Naples itself, the time seemed ripe to cement the status quo: Austria could be predominant in the north of Italy, with Spanish influence predominant in the south. To this the Empress responded favorably, an important reason being her fear of both Romanovs of Russia and the Hohenzollerns of Prussia. Already in the 1760's the two monarchs were negotiating to pair off their children on a mutual basis. Maria Theresa's progeny by Francis of Lorraine, greatest dilettante and wine connoisseur in Europe, proved so sturdy that Charles hoped this quality would be reproduced in his own line. His twenty-year old daughter in fact, Maria Luisa Antonia, had been married in 1764 to the younger Hapsburg son Leopold, Archduke of Tuscany and a future Emperor. By this union his first grandson Francis was born four years later at the Pitti palace in Florence, evoking happy memories when he once resided there himself; and the Spanish ambassador, Marqués de Viviani, proudly represented him as godfather to the regal infant (destined to become the first Emperor of Austria proper in 1804).

This marriage was consolation indeed. But trouble soon came when Charles' son was married to a Hapsburg female. Austrian daughters of the redoubtable Empress contrasted strongly with carefully brought-up Spanish infantas, and three of the swept imperiously into the Bourbon fold. Maria Carolina, following the death of a sister, married Charles' son Ferdinand of Naples in 1767, and with her fifteen years of age proved adept at intrigue to a dangerous degree. Despising her irresponsible husband who was ever fond of droll pasttimes, she made not the slightest pretense of behaving as a dutiful daughter-in-law to Charles (somewhat like Maria Luisa of Parma), and made no secret of her anti-Spanish feelings. On more than one occasion Charles had to admonish his son (as with the Prince of Asturias) for letting things get to such a sorry pass: "I would never have believed that disorder and indecency could reach such proportions, so dangerously affecting your health and your reputation which is the most important thing to preserve, especially in sovereigns ... I am ever grateful to the Empress for her advice, which shows her love for you and our family through putting most of the blame on her daughter, and whom

it is your responsibility as her husband to restrain
... Enjoy innocent pastimes in company with people
of good character ... I have implored you many times
as you well know...to listen to the advice of a servant so loyal and devoted as Tanucci...".[3]

But it was all rather in vain.  Carolina had
never forgiven her father-in-law for interfering
in her private life, and this resentment was also
shared by her husband.  In defiance of her elders'
concept of how a queen ought to behave, she developed
such strong political preferences that the path was
laid for the retirement of Tanucci himself after 1776,
though Spanish influence was a long time dying.  Nonetheless, as with the Asturias couple so with the Neapolitan, and both unions were to prove highly disad-
vantageous for Spain in the long run.

Another Hapsburg daughter following imperial footsteps to Italy was Maria Amalia, who married Charles'
nephew Ferdinand, the Duke of Parma.  Like her strong-
willed sister in Naples, she too was determined to
have her way, and once again with chagrin in his heart
Charles had to counsel a husband to rule his capricious
wife by force of authority -- "a principle grounded in
reason", as he entoned rather simplistically," from
which you will soon see order and discipline coming
into your household".[4]  But it was easier said than
done.  From Naples to Parma, the Bourbon males seemed
a poor reproduction of the originals, a far cry from
the resplendent Louis XIV.

A third daughter of Maria Theresa, the ill-fated
Marie Antoinette, became engaged in 1770 to the
Dauphin, the future Louis XVI.  In constant touch
with his French cousins, Charles celebrated the event
by three days of festivity at Aranjuez.  Louis XV
and Charles III were both great grandsons of Louis
XIV, but in their looks and behavior they were poles
apart.  Rule through a coterie of mistresses was not
in keeping with Spanish tradition and it is possible
to say that, despite Louis XV's natural intelligence,
the French king had let in too much corruption to
reverse the course of decline.  Nevertheless Charles
was indebted to him for many bright ideas in the past.
It was Louis who had helped Philip V and Isabel recover

influence in Italy and who had given Louisiana to Spain; and if both parties to the Family Compact veered off course at times for purely self-interested reasons -- Charles was in no way subordinate to Louis -- both Bourbon partners generally stood together, from joint actions against the Jesuits to joint strategy in the event of war with England.

Maria Theresa's eldest son, Joseph II, co-sovereign since 1765, had been married to a Bourbon relative, but Charles regarded him as cynical and pretentious. In his correspondence with Tanucci he referred to "the unspeakable conduct of the court of Vienna", calling Joseph "unworthy of imitation, either as a Christian or as a man of beneficence".[5] Charles blamed Joseph for secret visits to Rome and Naples, above all for not being hard on the Jesuits, failing to take into account that his reluctance to act against them was partly to prevent the secular clergy from seizing the spoils. In any case Joseph's tolerance and concern for their plight was shared equally by Frederick the Great and Catherine of Russia. To his fellow-monarchs, Charles' exhortation for the Jesuits' total supression must have appeared as pious doubletalk when in the same breath he was so often admonishing the world to respect religion and the laws of Christian morality. He appeared unappreciative of the motives behind Joseph's quarrels with his more conservative mother, or that his aims were really the same as his own -- to modernize the state. Resistance to change on the part of their subjects was a problem affecting them both, and in time Charles' attitude softened.

Frederick the Great's aggressive conduct was equally displeasing to Charles; but he viewed the warrior-king more dispassionately. If the latter had violated Charles' concept of monarchial relationships, it was the fortunes of politics rather than personal dislike that had placed them apart. Memories of earlier days in Naples when Charles as a warrior-king himself was Frederick's ally, mollified the estrangement. Certain similarities between the two great men subsisted. As each strove to develop their thinly-populated countries, both had comparable ideas of what constituted an enlightened king -- a servant devoted to the state in a spirit of industry, armed efficiency, and personal virtue. If it was not government by the people, then at least it was government for the people, and the directory at Berlin had its equivalent at Madrid where the council of Castile was to function in the best interests of the nation. As for Frederick's views on Spain, while these were often critical, he could praise her abundant resources of warm fruits and plants as natural assets for an enlightened monarch; and affectionately refering to Charles, once quipped to Spanish envoy Simón de las Casas that Naples with its warm climate could be a fitting abode for the most senior king in Europe.[6]

Religious differences would not deter Charles from praising a Protestant, Gustavus III of Sweden, who by a military coup had imposed a strong regime, partly against Russian designs. Lauding such successes, Charles was outraged by the ill fortunes that had attended Catholic Poland, whose former king Augustus III had been his own father-in-law, and whose partition in 1772 by the surrounding powers of Russia, Austria, and Prussia, seemed contrary to reason, justice, and morality. "In relations between nations", Charles wrote to Tanucci in a collective slap at the three eastern monarchs, "religious precepts, good faith and respect for treaties should prevail, and not just power or ambition".[7]

If countries such as Prussia and Sweden could be turned into potential friends of Spain, Russia like a huge shadow was a potential enemy who needed careful watching. Charles expressed constant fears lest this empire form an alliance with some other power such as England. Thus as early as 1761 he charged Almodóvar, Spanish ambassador to St. Petersburg, to report in detail on Russia's attitude to the outside world, for "the mutual silence of London and St. Petersburg seems highly suspicious".[8] Almodóvar was quick to report on the new empress Catherine, commenting that "she had illusions of grandeur...her head full of chivalrous novels and romances". But Charles had no illusions about the grandeur of Russia, whose empire straddled three continents and was far less dispersed than his own. After the Seven Years war it was no secret that the Duke of Grafton, supported by William Pitt, was flirting with its govern-

ment in pushing for a commercial treaty; and Prince
Masserano, Spanish envoy to the court of St. James,
related tentative proposals made in 1765 whereby naval
equipment and timber was to be accorded by Russia to
England but denied passage to its enemies in time of
war.[9]

Catherine soon showed herself in her true colors.
Displeased about the way she had deposed her husband
in the first place, Charles frequently complained to
Tanucci of her unbecoming conduct, her haughtiness,
and uncontrolled ambition. Catherine's aggrandise-
ment on many fronts, her wars with Sweden and Turkey,
the turmoil of the Pugachev revolt, and the breakdown
of international standards of morality over Poland
seemed to confirm his suspicions. "There is a marked
absence of even Orthodox Christian scruples in Russia
in face of the new malevolent way of thinking and
doing things which have arisen in that country", Charles
commented somewhat helplessly to Tanucci;[10] and exaggerated warnings by Spanish envoys in St. Petersburg
that a Russian thrust on China or Alaska might have repercussions on the Philippines or Mexico only increased
his fears.

If Charles could not check Russia in the east, at
best he could try to do so in the Mediterranean, and in
these circumstances it was natural that in conjunction
with his French partner he preferred suggestions of
friendship with Turkey. In the course of the decade
Spanish agents at the Ottoman Porte were instructed to
secure a commercial treaty with that empire, achieved
between 1779 and 1782, as part of a common Bourbon policy of deterring any Russian thrusts through Constantinople.[11]

As for Great Britain, that country was apparently
unperturbed about Russian expansion; but adding to
Charles' difficulties was British expansion itself,
which in the eighteenth century loomed as a very visible reality. To contain the Albion tide Charles abortively offered disarmament proposals, though actually
George III of England, despite occasional war speeches
in London, had personally very little to quarrel with
him about. Both were concerned with dissidents in
their own empires; and one wonders whether George,

keen intellect that he had, might not have approved
of Spain's absolutist government, preferring it to
his own.  To the Hanoverian king, parliament was
often a nuisance.  Yet paradoxically there were more
deliberative bodies applying absolute rule in Spain
than there were similar bodies applying constitutional
rule in England; and by the same token Charles might
have envied his counterpart in London, playing politics with a determination that matched his own.

He had to put up with a lot of trouble in Spain,
as we have seen.  Backchat even from some of his ministers was not uncommon.  When he once called Aranda
an Aragonese mule, the testy president replied that
he knew of someone more stubborn still and that was
His Majesty himself!  George III might have taken less
kindly to such audacity, while Charles laughed about
it afterwards, having learnt the hard way to take as
good as he gave.  And if both monarchs were fond of
farming and the soil, were moral and frugal in their
private lives, Charles as the older man was altogether
the better diplomat who was to achieve much in face
of tremendous odds.  George III created his own obstacles even when things might have gone his way.  He
was destined to lose an empire while remaining popular
at home; Charles III who was once nearly overthrown
at home managed to expand an empire overseas.  If
George loved music and went mad, Charles loathed
music and kept entirely sane.

But despite their good formal relations as fellow-
kings, the fact remained that England was growing at
an alarming pace, forcing Charles to join with France,
and if necessary with Austria, for adequate response
to British power.  In his view the three Catholic
nations of Europe should cooperate to preserve stability on the continent.[12]  And many besides Charles
had the mistaken notion that in America there was going
to be a showdown, a final colonial struggle for supremacy, this time between England and Spain herself,
the only major powers left in the field.

It was to forestall such a contingency that the
Spanish government gave a high priority to armaments.
The legacy of Ferdinand VI for all his good inten-
tions had been to leave the country in disarray when

Charles assumed the throne. Ineptitude and over-confidence had borne their bitter fruit in the Seven Years war, and Charles was resolved not to be caught out again. The regular army at this time consisted of over seventy thousand men, though hardly more than fifty thousand were in a state of effective readiness.[13] Of the forty-seven regiments of infantry, about one quarter were foreign, comprising Italian, Irish, Swiss, and Flemish-Walloon, the latter including the famous regiment of Walloon Guards which had earned such opprobrium at the time of the Squillace riots. The native regiments (named after the regions of Spain) usually consisted of twelve hundred men apiece, divided into two battalions and whose pairs of colors varied from among red, white, or blue, and occasionally green; but they were often rather ill-equipped or lacking in combat training. Infantry strength approached sixty thousand men. Of the cavalry, there were thirty-two regiments of Horse and Dragoons, mostly of about two hundred and fifty men apiece usually divided into two squadrons, and totalling nearly nine thousand men. A further complement of five thousand or so came from the royal halberdier guards, artillery, and engineers, as well as independent companies from outposts in North Africa. In addition to the regular army were thirty-three regiments of militia, mostly named after the cities of Spain and totalling some 23,000 not very fighting-fit men. In other respects, regular soldiers were good in action, the plug-bayonet rifle performing well in their hands since it was introduced in 1703 in place of the musket and pike, about which time incidentally the regiment itself as a system came into being. But building up an army based upon recruiting one man per hundred of the population was bound to prove a long and costly process. The payroll reached one hundred million reales a year, with total government expenditures approaching three times this figure;[14] and as time went on, military defense-spending took a heavier toll of the budget, to the joy of Muniain but to the chagrin of treasurer Múzquiz.

Charles well understood that the nobles and members of the military knighthoods, weakened as these semi-feudal orders may have been, still played an important part in maintaining Spain's defenses. Thus nobles like Aranda and his fellow-Aragonese and cousin, Conde de Ricla (war minister in 1772 following Muniain's death), were encouraged to reorganize, with the assistance of army inspectors. There was certainly a great deal to reform. Despite impressive achievements of Spanish arms in the past -- the capture of Oran, the brilliant invasion of Naples, the battle of Velletri -- one of the most serious drawbacks was lack of manpower; and in this respect, the necessity to rotate regular units to and fro across the Atlantic to garrison the vast Indies, which powers like Austria did not have to do, considerably weakened Spain's immediate effectiveness. At home, despite the bravery of her men, the overall picture was one of disorder and neglect of talent. The army was top-heavy with too many officers, while ill-paid soldiers being allowed to engage in private business to make up for arrears, were all too prone to desert from their units. To ease this problem, Charles directed the council of war to replace the volunteer practice by a draft known as the *quinta*, by which one man in every five was subject to service for a term up to eight years.[15] Good as this reform was in answering manpower needs, it also had the effect of promoting bribery to avoid the draft. Those actually recruited tended to be vagabonds or criminals, many of them impressed through forced levies as a form of punishment. Desertion countinued to mount, and the army's ranks were thinned still further when men were granted leave for as long as a season to help with the gathering of the harvests.

Veniality in all ranks came under heavy fire from Aranda. As a former captain-general he had seen at first hand the corruption that went on. With characteristic brusqueness he corrected men in high places, not excluding his cousin Ricla, for tolerating nepotism, office-seeking, and an over-abundance of staff officers more interested in a career at court than on the battlefield. The war council's eight chief staff members, Aranda charged, should be accountable to the King for their performance, instead of playing generalissimos with paper soldiers. By proper procedural methods of voting and attendance they should ensure that men and supplies duly reached the field; to do otherwise was to nullify reforms such as the Prussian system of tactics, with more rifles and guns ordered

for garrison locations.[16]   Aranda in reminiscing here
with the Prince of Asturias certainly made his points --
unmanned defenses left the coasts of Spain dangerously
exposed to attack -- but he so overplayed his critic-
isms at the time, and so openly tried to pack the council of Castile with his Aragonese supporters, that he
gave his enemies the chance to plot his downfall.  Not
a few of the *golilla* faction saw in him the very buttress
of noble and upper-class military power they as civil-
minded rationalists were opposed to.

The struggle in fact between these Aragonese elements led by the Prince of Asturias and Aranda on the
one hand, and the golillas led by Grimaldi and Floridablanca on the other, was growing more acute, and
Charles had to keep a balance to prevent either side
getting too much its own way.  Granted that Roda and
Father Eleta were somewhat mercurial in the middle,
he naturally inclined more to the golillas because he
needed support for his reforms such as the dissolution
of the Jesuit Order which he had long been forcing upon the Pope.  Favoring the Aragonese elements, however, was the latent anti-French mood in much of the
country at a time when Charles desperately needed
Louis XV's support in a number of other issues.

One such issue was a dispute with England over
claims to the Falkland Islands.  This was bound to
put added weaponry in the hands of the Aragonese, more
anti-French than anti-English, who tended to see in
France the villain behind the King's ministerial policies.  England's predominant strength did not at
first deter Charles from taking a firm stand, in
which he abortively counted on aid from his French
cousin.  Though wiser counsel prevailed, the issue
in the process brought to a head the confrontation
between Grimaldi and Aranda, in which the latter's
over-zealous behavior led to his downfall.

On the Atlantic side of South America facing
Patagonia, lie the Falkland Islands (termed Las
Malvinas by the Spaniards), where the British had
intruded in the wake of cod and whale fishing by the
French.  The latter had withdrawn in response to protests from Madrid, leaving Spanish and English settlers
each ignorant of the others' whereabouts in the storm-

swept islands. The crisis came in 1770 when Grimaldi ordered the governor of Buenos Aires to expel the English from their base at Port Egmont. This provoked the British admiralty into sending a fleet, leaving Prince Masserano, Spanish ambassador in London, faced with a difficult task.

War now seemed inevitable. Charles' appeal to Louis XV had only been answered by evasion, and for various other reasons, by the dismissal of Choiseul. The last thing Charles wanted was to take on England alone; and he was immeasurably relieved when James Harris, Earl of Malmesbury, arrived from London under instructions from George III to negotiate a settlement. The fact was that the British themselves were divided on the issue. The incoming prime minister Lord North favored moderation, with support from George III, while secretary of state Lord Weymouth backed by the opposition leader William Pitt favored stronger measures. Amid the bellicose atmosphere -- Weymouth and Pitt had their opposite number in Aranda who as leader of the war party in Madrid cited the anonymous "Letters of Junius" as evidence of anti-Spanish sentiment in London -- Lord North secretly assured Charles that if only Spain could give satisfaction for her affront in expelling the Port Egmont settlers, then the British would evacuate the islands as soon as public wrath died down. The settlers came back in 1772, but true to his word, North removed them two years later. Both England and Spain continued to claim titular sovereignty, but as the latter maintained a few effective settlements till 1811, and England did not, the arrangement went a long way to mollify Spanish objections.[17] The islands were thus prevented from being used as a base for an attack on the mainland, at least during Charles' reign.

It might be supposed from these events, meanwhile, that Aranda as leader of the war party would shine as the champion of Spanish patriotism against the wickedness of London; but with his usual singularity he only succeeded in isolating himself from many of his own (moderately pro-British) Aragonese compatriots, while his attacks on Grimaldi for backing down on the issue of going to war only annoyed Charles. When Aranda's attacks included criticism of the King himself on the

186

same issue, Grimaldi and his golilla friends needed
no punch behind their counter-attacks, for the King
fully resolved that Aranda had to go.  He had exceeded his powers as an essentially internal minister.
Telling him to mind his own business in the matter of
conducting foreign policy, Charles dismissed him from
the council of Castile presidency in June 1773, and
packed him off to France as ambassador to that country.
His place was taken by Manuel Ventura de Figueroa, a
controversial churchman sympathetic with the golillas,
and whose appointment Grimaldi subtly advanced.[18]

Aranda received his just punishment, but in many
ways he had the last word.  Two years later, as if
fulfilling his observations about military careless-
ness, the Spanish army met with a severe reverse in
an attack on Algiers, and in the aftermath the way
was laid for the downfall of Grimaldi himself.  What
the Falkland Islands affair had been to the one man,
the Algiers affair was to prove to the other.

Relations between Spain and North Africa were
always important, for neighboring Morocco shared the
entrance to the Mediterranean, while the Barbary
states along the coast engaged in piracy and slavery
which called for delicate and often fruitless negotiations.  Spain was in possession of Ceuta, Melilla,
and Peñón de los Vélez in Morocco; but here its Sultan,
Mulay Sidi Mohammed who reigned from 1757 to 1790, was
an intelligent monarch whose ambitions for dominating
neighboring Algiers and for trading with the Indies
were greater than his resentment of these Spanish garrison strongholds in his country.  Aranda along with
treasurer Múzquiz favored giving up these strongholds
in order to release the six thousand troops for duty
elsewhere, while Floridablanca, along with Arriaga and
Ricla, favored their retention to preserve immediate
positions of strength.  An important treaty had already been signed with Morocco on May 28, 1767, establishing the basis for a freer mutual trade between the
two countries, and this was largely the work of a
Spanish naval officer and scientist, Jorge Juan y
Santacilia.  He had once been on an inspection tour
in South America and well understood the Sultan's
wider commercial objectives.[19]

In view of this treaty, it seems surprising that the Sultan should have subjected Melilla to a strong siege between December 1774 and February 1775; but the continued presence of such garrisons on his soil, the activities of Riff tribesmen and others who were calling for a holy war against Christians, and the activities of pirates under the Spanish flag who in Morocco's eyes were every bit as bad as Barbary ones, were all motives behind the attack. In essence, the Sultan was simply probing Spain's defenses. Melilla held triumphantly (as did Ceuta) largely because the Spanish navy controlled this part of the straits. But in the meantime the Sultan made a patched-up alliance with his fellow-Moslem rival, the Dey of Algiers, and upon this pirate city Grimaldi was persuaded to deliver a knock-out blow.

An expedition of twenty thousand men was accordingly launched under the command of Alejandro O'Reilly, a former governor of Louisiana and army inspector of high repute, and with a great fanfare it set off to its secret destination. But tragedy was awaiting the Spaniards, for the Algerians had been tipped off in advance by merchants in Marseilles. The attack was repulsed with crippling losses in that sweltering heat of July 1775, which prompted one Spanish sergeant to comment wryly that "they landed us as if we had been invited to drink coffee with the Moors".[20] The disaster all but finished the career of O'Reilly, whom Charles quickly posted to a remote district to get him away from the fury of the mob. What arms had failed to accomplish, however, was later achieved by patient diplomacy. The Sultan always looked upon Spain as a potential ally against Algiers, and this was a factor behind a further treaty of friendship agreed between Spain and Morocco in 1780; while five years later, a treaty was signed between Spain and Algiers itself, thanks largely to the Sultan's good offices. Eventually, piracy and slavery were both drastically curtailed on all sides, thus freeing the Spanish coast for peaceful development.

As for Grimaldi, meanwhile, this was one setback he could not long survive. Aragonese supporters joined the mounting spate of criticism hurled at the discredited minister, at O'Reilly, at golillas in

general, in which increasingly it was the Prince and
Princess of Asturias who openly took the lead. Prominent men and women surrounding the royal couple or
holding positions in their household came from illustrious families such as Medina Sidonia, Sotomayor,
Arcos, and Aguilar, and their names were frequently
heard at court blaming the King for his policies.
Last but not least was Ramón Pignatelli, canon of
Saragossa cathedral, whose relatives had a close rapport with María Luisa and the Duchess of Alba, and
whose pique at his brother's rejection as the council
of Castile's president when Aranda fell from grace
only added more fuel to the anti-Grimaldi fire.[21]
His brother was the diplomat Conde de Fuentes, who had
much experience in England and France; and it was left
to Floridablanca later to ease the bitterness felt in
the family by working tactfully with Pignatelli on his
pet project of the Aragonese canal.

There were other reasons for Grimaldi's downfall.
Aranda himself from Paris was not above doing mischief
by conveying to the chief minister via the Asturias
household what lines of policy he ought to follow,
such as an invasion of Portugal (with whom Spanish relations were then at a low ebb), and which Charles,
already annoyed by Aranda's intrusion into foreign
affairs, had no intention of sanctioning. But the
unpopularity of Grimaldi was becoming ever more apparent. With singular clumsiness, he incensed the Duke
of Villahermosa by passing him over in favor of another person of lesser rank to be secretary of the
fine arts academy of San Fernando.[22]   This was the
last straw where Aragonese patience was concerned,
and the slur prompted many of the upper nobility to
close ranks still further against the common enemy.
Grimaldi moreover was getting isolated in his own
cabinet. Múzquiz, Ricla, even Roda all had close
ties with the Aragonese, while Arriaga, who had similar ties but who alone might have helped him, had
died soon after the Algiers fiasco. As for O'Reilly,
military men in general had old scores to pay off
against him and who above all was of foreign origin
like Grimaldi himself.

The last thing Charles wanted was another Squillace mutiny on his hands; and though he had already

decided that Grimaldi would have to go, this did not
mean giving way to the Aragonese. Holding his son
responsible for the crisis between the factions --
Aragonese versus golilla -- the King in injured tones
censured his indiscretions, which he saw as violating
his own august view of monarchy: "... Between a father
and son, a King and his heir, there is no place for
diversity of interests... A ship cannot progress if
its sails are set against the wind; the same applies
to a State where disunity prevails ... where envy,
hatred, and personal malice play havoc at court, and
in the end it is the sovereign and nation that suffer.
Think of how ... self-seeking people have tried to
win you over by their cunning,... making out it is I
who am hiding the facts... Those who criticize my
government when mistakes are made ... only promote
lack of confidence among their fellows ... for then
criticism will spread to all its other operations...

Even if no one has actually gossiped to you or
your wife ... in the way I suspect, the point is that
the public has inferred it ... and the fact that you
and your wife have coldly received those whom I favor
... and vice versa only makes our differences all the
more regrettable ... I would gladly go over with you
all the qualities of those I support ... and if you
can show me wrong I'd gladly change my judgment, only
tell me in confidence ... rather than confiding in
others ... which can be more damaging than you realize.

Everything ... counts in princes; on external
appearances the public bases its image. By treating
well those who so deserve, then sovereigns and princes
can win over their subjects' hearts; bad treatment
only alienates them and it is better to be served by
love than by self-interest. Rightly or wrongly ... it
is believed that there are two factions at court ...
which does great harm especially to you since one day
you will inherit. If people believe now that factionalism exists between father and son, then there will
be men in the future who ... will try to do exactly
the same in turning your family against you...

Remember two points, my son: first, almost all
matters of state can be judged pro or con ... and thus
those near you can easily put a bad complexion on a

worthwhile issue... getting out of you ... some word
or gesture indicating your concurrence; second, those
who approach you with lampoons ... or gossip ... are
not fit to serve God or King, for real or apparent,
our disunity would only ... bring discredit to the
monarchy and benefit the enemies of Spain ... Thus I
do trust ... you will set a good example in respecting
decisions of government ... so that when your time
comes to rule you will be equally respected and obeyed. One thing more: women are by nature weak, fickle,
ill-informed, and superficial, too easily impressed
by designing and ambitious flatterers ... If you pause
to examine things dispassionately and hear all sides...
then you will become more circumspect as I have become
after many years of arduous experience.

I assure you, my son, that I feel better in un-
burdening myself to you in this intimate way; I hope
you will respond to my affection, expressing the message of this letter each day in your words and actions,
with the strict proviso that you show it to absolutely
no one in the whole world, except to your own son and
heir ... as the need arises ... Your affectionate
father, Charles".[23]

The King's distrust of party government and of
women in power must be taken in its context, for his
view of enlightenment, autocratic as it was, could
surely be considered far better for Spain than the
petty factionalism indulged in at court. It was still
an age when government stood apart from, instead of
being part of, everyday problems; and any attack on
its policy was made not by a courtly group resorting
to force, though this could never be discounted, but
by setting a royal prince against his father. It was
close to the fashion in England whereby the Prince of
Wales personified opposition to the sovereign. But
the very lack of a legislative parliament in Spain
pushed important issues into the background, promoting
gossip and slander behind the shuttered windows of
the Asturias household. In such a situation it was
difficult for a minister to defend himself against
invisible attacks.

Yet Charles had inherited the system and was determined to make it work, though it certainly hurt him to let old servants go. When Grimaldi, prompted by the King, noted that his sixty-seven years were making him feel too old for the job, his resignation was accepted.[24] But his place was taken not by an Aragonese but by José Moñino, Conde de Floridablanca, a man twenty years younger who fitted perfectly Charles' idea of a manteista-golilla reformer. Assuming office in February 1777, he had been recommended by Grimaldi himself, with behind-the-scenes support from one of the ministerial secretaries, Bernardo del Campo; and as Grimaldi departed for Rome to serve as Spanish representative to the papal court, it was with a feeling of mellow satisfaction that he had turned his last trick on behalf of his king and the manteista cause that went with it -- as an Italian a not very popular figure in Spain, but as a diplomat a man of devoted loyalty and service to the country of his adoption.

Floridablanca's brilliance as a lawyer in Madrid, his reports for Aranda on the disorders at Cuenca during the Squillace riots, above all his work in getting Pope Clement XIV to dissolve the Jesuit Order for which he received his title in 1773, were all factors in his advancement to high office. As a manteista, Floridablanca represented for Charles an alternate choice to the officials still coming from the noble-dominated private colleges. The choice was indeed a good one. He was a man of outstanding ability who correctly gauged the relation of a minister to his monarch. Less aggressive than Aranda, especially in foreign policy, but more attuned to his master's 'enlightened despotism' in which he showed the constitutional skill to understand and interpret, he yet continued the policy of rearmament, appropriating more powers from the war council, and expanded the training of officers in the new schools of infantry, artillery, and engineers. Aranda had always been quick to point out what was needed; now it was Floridablanca who fulfilled the needs. As a result, the army steadily grew in numbers and quality of weapons. His cool 'cabinet' manner -- his enemies could call it a disguised form of ministerial despotism -- was more congenial to Charles than the fiery Aranda had been, and the two statesmen crossed swords on a number of occasions. But the clinically correct minister

of State usually triumphed over the irascible exile
in Paris. In appointing him to this high office,
which included also the portfolio of foreign affairs,
Charles was choosing an adviser strong in ministerial
reforms and centralization, and his duration of power
which lasted into the early 1790's was to leave a deep
impression on Spain's government structure.

Another manteista lawyer who rose to power at
the same time was the able José de Gálvez. By 1776,
the storm had burst with a vengeance in North America
as England grappled with the mounting rebellion there,
and Charles needed strong-minded advisers in the event
of war with that country, an assumption which proved
correct. This same year, Gálvez was appointed minister
of the Indies, succeeding Julián de Arriaga. Born near
Málaga of humble stock, Gálvez took his degree in law
at Salamanca, rising thereafter in this profession by
a combination of sheer merit and intrigue. His many
French connections, including a French wife, soon made
him one of Grimaldi's circle, and he became an *Alcalde
de casa y corte* by 1764, subsequently joining the council
of the Indies. His appointment as inspector to Mexico
the following year, where he carried out a number of
important reforms, earned him the full gratitude of
the King and hence his eventual appointment as minister
of the Indies. Not the least of his achievements in
Charles' eyes was his ferreting out information in
Mexico relating to the beatification of Palafox.

Gálvez was not above turning against his old patron
Grimaldi to the extent of standing by while his colleagues roundly denounced O'Reilly, thus undermining Grimaldi's position.[25] He carefully befriended members of
the Aragonese faction like treasurer Múzquiz, no doubt
with the aim of taking Grimaldi's place -- a strategem
which Floridablanca later observed in his own case and
which he deftly countered by suitably rewarding Gálvez'
family and friends with offices or titles. Where
Charles was concerned, the minister's sheer competence transcended factional loyalty -- his manteista
background was simply a good alternative to the aristocratic one of Aranda or any of his circle -- and his
record was to prove brilliant. Together with Pedro
de Castejón (in charge of the marine department which
was to become separate from the Indies ministry),

Gálvez at once prepared for the coming contingency of war.

Where the navy was concerned, ships of the line were increased from the forty or so then existing, thanks also to the earlier efforts of Ensenada and Arriaga; while ports were improved from Barcelona to Vigo, with better beacon lights installed. But one big defect was the shortage of manpower. A weak merchant marine only added to the problem, which normally would have provided manpower reserves, like the impressment policy practiced by the British. Spanish seamanship moreover, marksmanship in particular, left a lot to be desired. Apart from Galicia and the northern provinces, Spaniards generally made better soldiers than sailors, for being an essentially inland people they tended to look landwards rather than across the oceans, which for them had largely been already explored. To some extent, the same applied to Spanish Americans; and it is significant that, unlike English practice, the army and not the navy was considered the senior service in the empire. Even Spain's best seafarers -- Galicians, Asturians, and Basques -- preferred fishing to fighting for their king. Under these circumstances, recruitment problems plagued the government; and with naval personnel furloughed for long periods when ships were in port, which gave them release from the rampant scurvy and other discomforts, it was not surprising that the rate of desertion was high.

Total crew strength, much of it on paper, amounted to about 55,000 in 1762, with annual expenses steadily rising from a level of 65 million reales.[26] Needful of better crews and commanders which its huge commitments demanded, the government made strenuous efforts to bring standards up to the mark. Fishermen were drafted, cannoneers given longer training, potential officers screened. Among the many cadet schools enlarged, none was more famous than the academy of marine guards at Cádiz. The best naval advisers were sought after, and officers were sent to study abroad. All ranks were treated well by the standards of the time, discipline being far more relaxed than with the British navy; but in exchange for paying everyone on time, giving benefits to families, and extending shoreleave, better performace was expected at sea.

Evidence that the government was paying close attention to foreign techniques can be seen in the *Examen marítimo teórico y práctico* by Jorge Juan -- the same naval officer and scientist who had been to South America and who had helped frame the Spanish-Moroccan treaty of 1767.[27] Reflecting the ideas of many British naval writers and the Swiss scientist Leonard Euler, he impressed Charles and Grimaldi with his appeal for lighter ships than were being built at the time, as well as for imperial reforms in general. He also helped found the San Fernando naval observatory, and was a member of the Royal Society of London and the Academy of Berlin before his untimely death in 1773.

Scientists like Juan, together with an equally distinguished colleague, Antonio de Ulloa, had an international touch about them. They never forgot old friends like Ensenada, but in stirring their compatriots they above all represented hopes for Spain's future. Much as the King had accomplished -- modernization at home with manteistas in power, dynastic ties with Austria in Italy, and good relations with the other powers of Europe cemented by trusted nobles in his diplomatic service -- still more social and technical development was needed if Spain was to keep abreast of current trends. This was especially so in the Americas. In the Falkland Islands dispute with England, Charles had shown wise statesmanship in avoiding what might have become a more serious threat to the security of the continent; but without the transmission of skills and benefits he was trying to implant at home, then all the good work in arms and diplomacy could be self-defeating. Jorge Juan had sounded the warning. The pluses and minuses of Charles' rule in the Americas are therefore next examined, for here a real test of strength would shortly come. It was to be as much a tussle between big merchant interests on the one side, and centralist elements on the other, as between Spanish subjects in America and the imperial authorities themselves.

# CHAPTER TEN

## CHARLES III AND THE INDIES

Charles' great fear in the New World with all its riches, was encroachment by foreigners -- British, Russians, and Portuguese among them -- and this lay behind his motives to drastically reorganize the Indies. This decision in many ways was an extension of what he was doing at home, and it was commendable, but it was given such a high priority that deeper social problems were neglected. Here he was faced with greater complexities than he realized. It was like his earlier troubles in Spain only on a very much larger scale. That he acquitted himself well was due to his flexibility, which called for the kind of swift decisions he was always good at making once the tensions erupted into open crises.

A cardinal feature of his policy was one of strong defenses, for a strong America would mean a prosperous Spain. To help raise revenue for this purpose, mercantile principles were to be relaxed in favor of a freer trade, Spanish settlements expanded, administration made more centralized. Despite the ambivalence of some of these aims, Charles sought out the best advisers he could, and the record in the context of his own reign was to prove a successful one. But not before a series of upheavals from Mexico to Peru was to shake the empire to its foundations. In face of revolts by Indians and whites alike, the conflicts were resolved, the cracks cemented over, and fortunately, he did not live to see the edifice tumble down at a later epoch in history.

It lies outside the scope of this book to trace the causes of the empire's demise in the Americas, which stem more immediately from conditions prevailing in the earlier nineteenth century. A more relevant purpose is to depict the features of discontent in Charles' own day, when everything seemed so bright on the surface. Certainly Spain had implanted her language and institutions deeply enough. Among her soundest achievements was the great code of laws published in 1680, which showed a meticulous concern for the welfare of the Indian. Paternalistic as it may have been, it was far in advance of any other code drawn up by a comparable country. It also laid bare what was perhaps Spain's greatest dilemma -- how to reconcile this concern with fear of Indian revolt provoked by white intruders, whether officials, missionaries, or settlers.

What Charles personally thought of the Indians is hard to say, though he never minded employing them in high positions in Spain, and it might be added on his behalf that the threat to the Americas posed by foreign powers took up much of his time. Where pacification was concerned, as in the Sonora war of 1770 against hostile Indians in northern Mexico, he urged gentleness, ordering that captured Indian women be used to bear gifts to their menfolk as a way of inducing them to lay down their arms. Though this met with little success, he favored the more moderate policy of building a line of garrisons to defend settled areas, instead of sending out punitive expeditions.[1] But it must have been clear to him, as it was to Arriaga, minister of the Indies, that any attempt to apply the good laws too literally on behalf of Indian rights might only provoke hostilities by the white settlers themselves.

To resolve this problem, it had long been the policy of the government to separate the races where possible, in the hope that the Indian would catch up with his more fortunate white brother. Deemed virtually a free minor by the Spanish crown, he was not to be abused nor subjected to the Inquisition. Unfortunately things did not turn out in the idealistic way intended. Wherever separation was achieved Indian complaints were ignored, while conversely, where the two races met, there was considerable exploitation by the conquerors over the conquered.

Charles' inheritance included a landholding structure modelled on Spain's own. In typical feudal fashion since the sixteenth century, the Spaniard had been given a grant of Indians termed the *encomienda*; but to balance this practice local Indian chiefs were given similar powers over their own people. As time went on, crown officials instead of these chiefs began

197

to collect the coveted tribute money, and thus deprived of economic power especially in Mexico, the latter drifted into the Hispanic community. Here they were soon joined by other Indians. To escape their incongenial burdens, including a forced labor draft, many fled to the rising townships, their womenfolk giving rise to a mixed-blood or *mestizo* element in the population. Those who remained were not all tied to the land -- small creole estates were often in debt themselves -- but these very changes point to the unrealizable goal of separate equal coexistence, for the Indians were too badly needed as a cheap labor force for the stronger conquering class.

The labor draft mentioned above was known as the *mita*.[2] It applied to factories, public works and mines, from Zacatecas in Mexico to Potosí in Peru. Regulations carefully prescribed the number of Indians to be sent away from their villages, the length of service (about a third of the year with alternate working weeks), the maximum distance to be travelled, and wage rates, usually at subsistence levels though sometimes with remission of the tribute tax. Legally the Indians were supposed to return home after doing their time, but the laws were often bypassed. While conditions were particularly harsh in Peru and Paraguay -- the only way of dodging the draft was to pay a mita tax instead -- those in Mexico receded in severity as time went on. Here voluntary and increasingly well-paid labor slowly took root in the mines, so that by the eighteenth century, following the Mexican pattern, voluntary labor was in evidence even among the Andean Indians. The mita still existed at Potosí, alongside free labor, but it is significant that Mexican production exceeded that of Peru, not merely because of its greater population and reserves of mercury, but more efficient work force.

In many cases, then, the races were living side by side; but too often Indians were serfs, either on plantations or as mita draftees, with American-born Spaniards (*creoles*) and home-born Spaniards (*peninsulares*) staunchly upholding their privileges. It was a vicious circle, for Spain and the settlers both needed each other in the event of foreign attack, so that the social order could scarcely be changed. In this situation

the most savage Indian saw no reason to come out of
his natural habitat in order to be a mere third-class
citizen. The mestizo whom he saw emerging seemed a
despised outcast, employed as a menial on plantations
or in the great burgeoning cities.

A distinctive feature of this American empire
was the diversity of its peoples, for apart from
Indians, whites, and mestizos, there were large numbers of blacks; mixtures between whites and blacks
(*mulatos, morenos* or *pardos*); and for good measure, mixtures between Indians and blacks. By the end of
Charles' reign there were over seventeen million Spanish subjects in America, of whom nearly eight million
were Indians, and about three million were whites.
With scarcely more than fifty thousand immigrants
coming over from Spain at times during the eighteenth
century, it was inevitable that Indians and mestizos
predominated.

Of the blacks, there were at least a million in
Spanish America at mid-century. All at first were
slaves, and the only ray of light in the somber picture was the rare missionary work done by such saints
as Pedro Claver, S.J., who labored as apostle to the
blacks at the slave-center of Cartagena (Colombia)
in the seventeenth century. Here Britain received
the right to import Negroes for thirty years, by
the treaty of Utrecht in 1713, but the English were
well established in other parts of Spanish America,
ostensibly to regulate the traffic, in reality to
snatch up other commodities. By the time of Charles'
reign, the Spanish government was anxious to replace
the monopoly surrendered by Britain. There were various plans to supply Peru with black slaves, for example, to replenish the dwindling numbers there; and
Floridablanca himself later proposed using Spanish
islands off the west coast of Africa as a springboard
for this purpose.[3] Some success was achieved, but the
price of slaves was too high for the average Peruvian
landowner to afford them. Scarcity of blacks in fact
explains why their lot slowly began to improve. Many
of them could be seen engaged in useful arts including
medicine, from Vera Cruz to Quito, though because of
racial discrimination they were debarred from higher
education. But free blacks were on the increase, and

could now join the militia, whose many privileges gave them a new-found sense of dignity and purpose.

The multi-racial texture of this vast emporium, far more composite than the thirteen English colonies to the north, called for the highest degree of skill on the part of the Spanish government to hold it all together; and it is perhaps in some degree due to the experience gained that, despite all the abuses, the empire lasted as long as it did.

At the top of the hierarchy was the council of the Indies, dating from 1524. It had three chambers -- one for Mexico, one for Peru, and one for judicial affairs and appointments, linked directly to the king through its governor and minister. Conscientious if slow-moving, and staffed by experienced officials, the council was absolute, and not even the church could dispense benefices without its consent. Yet absolutism was slowly defeating its own ends, for it was a near-impossible task to make the excellent laws work effectively. Overlapping jurisdictions and opposition from local vested interests often frustrated government efforts. The council's range of duties, moreover, was enormous -- settling land and inheritance claims, running the navy, regulating tariffs, and authorizing such matters as suppression of revolts, wars and peace treaties, tours of inspection, voyages of exploration, money grants for institutions, down to collections of rock and flora in the vast regions under its control. To ease the complexity, a ministerial junta was formed in 1763 which met once a week to ensure efficient management of the Indies.

Responsible to this council were the big four viceroyalties, the original ones of New Spain (Mexico) and Peru being supplemented by that of New Granada (Colombia) in 1739 and Río de la Plata (Argentina) in 1776, the latter created by Charles himself. In addition were about eight captaincies-general at various times, including the Philippines, each with a wide range of defensive responsibilities.

Severe checks were imposed against any abuses of power by the resplendent viceroys. During their term of office they could be called to account by a

judicial review known as the *residencia*, though this
procedure was often waived in their case. Assisting
the viceroys to rule were the *audiencias*. These
were essentially courts of law each under a president
(and under a regent after 1776), which could transfer
appeal cases to the council of the Indies as well as
legislate in the event of a viceroy's absence or
death. Their judges had a right to review viceregal
accounts, and if alienated could always use the threat
of unfavorable testimony in any residencia. But in
practice they seldom censured the viceroy direct, preferring to communicate on a more or less power-sharing
basis. The residencia (or its equivalent) was applicable to any royal official, including judges themselves, which combined with inspections from Madrid
known as *visitas*, had the effect of keeping everyone
on their mettle. Under these circumstances, while
graft did of course exist, it was difficult for a
high official to get too rich too quickly.

Not a few viceroys were men of outstanding ability
in Charles' time. Among them may be mentioned Antonio
de Bucareli of Mexico (commemorated to this day by a
street-name in Mexico City), or the American-born
Ambrosio O'Higgins, who rose from a president in Chile
to viceroy of Peru. Creoles could sometimes reach the
highest ranks of office, and it was an age when their
faith in the Spanish Empire had not yet been shaken.

Creoles in fact participated in colonial government on a significant scale. This was marked at audiencia level, where peninsulares -- strong elsewhere
in commerce and mining -- were not always in the majority. They were proud of their posts, for administration was a coveted prize, and rather than be sent to
another country with all the uncertainties before they
could rise in rank, many of them preferred to stay in
their own localities.

They were also strongly represented in town councils or *cabildos*. Self-elected for terms up to six
years, often to family seats in rotation, creoles had
a strong sense of municipal pride. Ironically, having
inherited this from Spain, they often resisted the
dictates of Spain's own policies. '*Obedezco y no cumplo*'
went the saying, as they tried by every means to thwart

royal commands in such matters as taxes, respect for Indian land rights, or recruitment of local militia.[4] One reason for their attitude was shortage of funds from the provincial treasury. With their purchased municipal offices hardly worth the expense so little was the pay that went with them, cabildo members or *regidores* had to beg for the meager grants of money handed out to them via the district magistrate (*alcalde mayor*), and the result was cabildos' political weakness in an otherwise promising pattern of elected local government.

The church and the law were other avenues of opportunity for creoles, and here they were well provided for in entering schools of higher learning. A test was required to determine purity of heritage, clear of any blood-taint, though this prerequisite was increasingly relaxed and it never applied to qualified Indians. By the eighteenth century about ten major universities had been established in the colonies. These included the prestigious senior one of Mexico (founded in 1551), Santo Domingo, San Marcos in Lima, Bogotá, Guatemala, Caracas, Havana and Santiago de Chile (the latter founded in 1747). Chuquisaca and Córdoba were of Jesuit origin, while many others were founded by Dominicans, including Santo Tomás in Manila. Some fifteen smaller universities and colleges, in addition, were run by Franciscans. Seminaries for the sons of Indian nobles existed in Guatemala, Cuzco, and Lima, while various institutions in Mexico and elsewhere accepted Indians in general.

The universities mainly followed the statutes of Salamanca in Spain (with one or two following those of Alcalá), and offered chairs in the seven basic disciplines -- theology, scripture, canons, laws, decretals, rhetoric, and arts (i.e., logic, metaphysics, and physics); but as time went on, grammar, philosophy, and Indian languages were added. In Charles' reign a great impetus was given to the neglected field of medicine, as when in Mexico for example, the famous school of surgery was created in 1768 offering chairs in anatomy, physiology, and operations. This was followed later by an academy of botany and pharmacology. Methods of degree granting were similar to those in Spain, oppositions being held every four years in competition for the available chairs. It is estimated that by 1775 about 150,000 students had taken degrees at colonial universities, with 30,000 receiving their Bachelors from Mexico alone.[5]

Intellectual activity reflected trends in Spain, now more concerned with observation of nature, with its effect on sensation and change, than with Aristotelian metaphysics. But this is not to say that the doctrines of Aquinas or Descartes were being discarded. Academicians were still largely conservative, more interested in political justice than social ethics, let alone revolution; yet it is from this Western Christian tradition that the democratic spirit was eventually to be born.

Spanish thought itself had its great Feijóo, Sarmiento, and Piquer, but there had been much criticism penned by other Spaniards, angry at stagnation and racial injustice. Melchor de Macanaz, a minister exiled in the reign of Philip V, published his *Testamento de España* in 1740, biting with satire at Spain's imperial structure which weighed heavily upon the Indian. Though forced to live abroad, Macanaz loved his country well, and in the final analysis considered that the Spanish record in America was in no way worse, in some ways better, than the record of France, England or the Netherlands.[6] More fortunate officials like Jerónimo de Uztáriz or José del Campillo favored capitalist enterprise to reduce the empire's dependence on foreign trade, and by developing the soil, to elevate the Indian from a mere serf to a more prosperous consumer. In this respect, there were visitors in the field like Jorge Juan and Antonio de Ulloa who gave an appalling picture of conditions among mistreated Indians in South America (discussed in the next chapter), and whose prophetic warnings for the future the Spanish government might well have heeded. Bernardo Ward and Antonio Muñoz echoed the above pleas, stressing specie as a productive medium for imperial trade in raw materials and finished products, which without harming Spanish industry could undercut competition from Europe.

Reformers' criticism seemed to strike root initially with the creoles. At mid-century there was a revolt in Venezuela under Juan de León against the Basque-founded Guipúzcoana company of Caracas. Here in typical mercantile fashion, raw materials like cocoa, tobacco, indigo, leather, vanilla and silver were being sent to Spain in exchange for imported Spanish manufactured goods, but the complainants charged that the company was robbing Venezuela by paying too little for these native products and charging too much for the goods it imported from Spain. After the uprising some prices were relaxed, and to discuss such problems many company meetings were held in Madrid with Arriaga presiding, who was captain-general of Caracas before he became minister of the Indies.

An interesting defense of the company's position can be seen in its report of 1771, when it affirmed that big monopoly firms did a better job in supplying consumers' needs than private traders did.[7] But the fact that it had to defend itself against Venezuelans and Spaniards alike showed that its days as a monopoly were numbered. Though the ports serving Caracas were not yet open to free trade, the way was clear for the break-up of the Basque monopoly in this region by the 1780's.

The Caracas revolt was an early example of the dilemma facing the Spanish government as to how much freedom to give monopoly merchants trading in the colonies. But the problem grew more complex with Charles on the throne, when the need for a stronger Spanish posture in the Americas caused by British expansion required more revenue. Clearly the aim was to develop more trade, but doing so posed the central question: whether to further monopoly control at the expense of smaller traders and keep Spanish America strong against foreign attack, or whether to further smaller traders' enterprise at the expense of monopoly, and run the risk of an even stronger America asserting some degree of economic independence. It was no secret that many loyal subjects of differing backgrounds were prepared to take this risk, among them the Chilean audiencia president, Ambrosio O'Higgins, or the Italian explorer, Alessandro Malaspina.

Monopolies indeed were becoming a heated issue as more and more merchants were clamoring for company privileges themselves. But while Charles with his advisers subjected big companies to closer scrutiny, especially if they yielded insufficient revenue, he had no intention of allowing smaller private enterprise to take their place if this meant dismantling the Spanish Empire. In view of the commercial rivalries in so vast a market, with all the cross-currents of conflict between the larger merchants and the smaller ones, between national and foreign interests, and between peninsulares and creoles, the government chose to steer a middle course. This was to promote government monopolies (e.g., tobacco) and royal joint-stock companies at the expense of unsatisfactory private monopolies, and at the same time to encourage smaller merchants, provided no harm was done to the prime task of protecting national industry.

Already traditional monopolist views were losing ground. The old idea had been to strictly channel trans-Atlantic trade through certain colonial ports, where the goods were subject to a rigorous duty process. The same applied to the chief home port of Cadiz, to where the clearing and accounts departments comprising the Board or House of Trade had been moved from Seville in 1717, and where big monopoly interests in the colonies still had a big stake. But the effects of this stringent control were all too apparent by the eighteenth century: monopoly interests were stifling smaller private enterprise, in which official bottlenecks and outright smuggling abounded, all to the benefit of French, British, and Dutch investors who were taking a major share on the returns of the trade. 'Spain kept the cow while the rest of Europe drank the milk' was an apt description of affairs prevailing at this time.[8]

Even before Charles' reign there had been strains in the rigid pattern of convoyed fleets (*flotas*) by which these tightly-knit policies were enforced. Until 1740 these lumbering convoys would cross the oceans at certain times of the year, bringing back bullion and other goods to the mother country. The

normal pattern would provide for one fleet to sail
from Cádiz to Vera Cruz (Mexico) in the spring, detaching vessels on the way to make contact with Honduras. Another fleet would sail for Porto Bello (Panama) in the fall, detaching vessels bound for Cartagena and other ports of the Caribbean protected en
route by what was termed the *Armada de Barlovento*. After
wintering in America the two main fleets would then
reassemble in Havana and return to Spain early the
following spring. In the intervening period, galleons
would ply between Acapulco (Mexico) and Manila, and
between Panama and Lima, whence goods could reach as
far as Buenos Aires. Mindful of the inadequacies
of these fleets which weighed against the smaller
trader, and whose under-manned crews exposed them
to enemy attack, the government suspended fleet operations between 1740 and 1754, relying on smaller
independent ships; but under pressure from the big
merchants, the system was revived three years later
to include the Vera Cruz (but not the Porto Bello)
fleet. After 1778, its use declined rapidly till
its final demise in 1789.[9]

By licensing more independent ships in the meantime, including regular packets to Havana once a month
and Buenos Aires every two months, Charles with his
advisers was slowly promoting the growth of the smaller
private sector. The capture of Havana by the British
in 1762, who promptly threw the island open to free
trade, had shown what private enterprise could do.
Three years later on February 14, a blow was struck
at the big monopoly interest at Cádiz when a technical junta informed the King that the whole fleet system was outdated and hindering Spanish commerce in a
number of ways, that the high duties levied on such
exports as wine were harming Andalusian vineyards,
and that the high import duties on bullion and other
American products were contributing to the vast increase in smuggling. Accordingly duties were scaled
down to an *ad valorem* instead of bulk rate; and on
October 16 this same year Charles ordered ports in
Cuba, Santo Domingo, Puerto Rico, and Trinidad to be
thrown open for trade with the Spanish ports of
Barcelona, Alicante, Málaga, and La Coruña.[10] All
of this portended a number of merchant ships sailing
at their own risk.

But the battle for a freer trade was by no means over. A limiting factor here was the smallness of the Spanish fleet, whose strength of about five hundred ships ascended to barely a thousand by the end of the century. This only made things worse in enabling the Dutch and British carrying trade to continue capturing more markets. But perhaps the biggest rival facing the smaller merchant was the Spaniard himself -- the powerful mercantile traditionalist who had a strong lobby in the council of the Indies.

The Caribbean was indeed a region where monopoly interests flourished. Both the royal trading company of Havana and that of Barcelona had huge investments, the latter having received a license to trade with the Spanish West Indies and Honduras in 1765, promoted by Catalan sugar interests. Among monopolies in Spain, none was more resented than the trading company set up two years previously by the big five guilds (or *gremios*) of Madrid, whose immense resources extended to southeast Asia. In this region too, monopoly interests eventually won. Here in Manila, traders had been buying Chinese goods with silver, draining away specie intended for Spain -- a practice condemned by the junta of 1765 mentioned above. A short-lived scheme thereafter did allow private merchants on their own account to trade their sea otter skins for Chinese mercury, which was badly needed in Mexico for the production of silver. But the conflict was resolved in favor of state-backed monopoly, when in the 1780's Charles authorized the royal Philippines company as a joint-stock enterprise with a capital of 160 million reales, to which much Basque money was diverted from Caracas. Designed to improve trade with the Far East through exchanging such items as Mexican silver for Oriental muslins and supplementing the Manila galleon with one by way of Cape Horn, this company too became a target of attack by rival merchants, especially in Peru, though it proved a tough organization to crack and lasted well into the early nineteenth century.

Meanwhile demands were becoming more vociferous for freedom to trade. In 1767 an explosion came from an entirely unexpected quarter, this time not from Spanish creoles, as in Caracas, but from French ones.

As early as 1720 Spaniards had moved into Texas, establishing garrisons and missions among the Indians, with the additional aim of checking the spread of French and English influence in this region. With the vast area of Louisiana also acquired in 1763, which extended indefinitely along the Mississippi and Missouri rivers toward Canada, Charles now secured virtually all of North America west of the Mississippi as a counterweight to British expansion. But what took him by surprise was the resistance of the French to Spanish rule, especially in the capital port of New Orleans. Excluding Indians, soldiers, and black slaves, the population could not have exceeded eight thousand, their products ranging from sugar, tobacco, rice and buffalo skins which were exchanged for guns, knives, and such typically Gallic demands as mirrors and cosmetics. With the French treasury bankrupt after the Seven Years war that now had few funds to honor depreciated bills of exchange presented to it in good faith by the creole merchants of New Orleans, Choiseul was glad to divest himself of such a liability as Louisiana. But the creole merchants thought otherwise, and were incensed at what they regarded as a betrayal of their interests by the mother country.

Into this situation stepped Antonio de Ulloa, former *visitor* to Peru, who assuming the Spanish command in 1766 proceeded to strengthen defenses along the Mississippi. But great intellect that Ulloa had, he was not the sort of governor to understand the intricacies of French colonial problems To make matters worse, merchants were restricted in trade between New Orleans and the French West Indian islands of Haiti and Martinique at a time when Spain was beginning to relax her own trade. Now boiling with resentment the colony erupted, and Ulloa had to flee by fastest sail to Havana, leaving the nominal French governor, Philippe Aubry, looking on helplessly while the rebels began running the colony as an incipient republic. Faced by this act of defiance, Charles had little option but to take firm measures. In 1769 he sent Alejandro O'Reilly, visitor-general in the Antilles (an illustrious soldier whose reputation was to tumble in the Algerian disaster previously described), to restore

order with two thousand troops. In the wake of
heavy tropical storms which struck the coast where
he landed, O'Reilly coolly exaggerated the number
of his men so as to frighten the rebels, and having
induced Aubry to read out his letters of authority
from the balcony of the governor's mansion, succeeded
in pacifying the colonists; but not before he had
tricked the rebels into submission by offering a
reception and then having the ringleaders arrested.
In all five persons were shot, the remainder receiving prison sentences or amnesty altogether.
O'Reilly nonetheless won support among the French.
He upheld the trading privileges granted by Charles
to Louisiana merchants the previous year, appointed
creoles to high office, and encouraged the immigration of more settlers.[11]  Following Ulloa's footsteps,
he liberated Indian slaves forthwith and organized
regiments of mulatos. With the creation of a firm
and stable government, its defenses strengthened
against foreign attack, the region was drawn securely
into the Spanish orbit.

It might be supposed that France and Spain hereafter would work harmoniously against their common
rival England, but this was not necessarily the case.
French proposals for closer economic ties whereby
France could purchase the raw material of the Indies
in exchange for selling her industrial goods at low
prices could only harm Spanish national industry.
Wool and silk in any case was about all France wanted
from the peninsula itself, and on balance her merchants would gain at Spain's expense.[12]  Choiseul
nonetheless had friends in Madrid, among them Abbé
Beliardi; and not the least of Francophiles was José
de Gálvez, who was to become a central figure in
Charles' reorganization of the Indies.

Friendship with Grimaldi, an influential French
wife, and determined ambition were all factors in
Gálvez' astonishing rise to power; and from his position on the council of the Indies it was but a step
to his appointment as visitor to Mexico, with a salary of 12,000 pesos a year, a post he occupied from
1765 to 1771.  Charles' instructions to Gálvez of
March 1765 were spelled out via Arriaga in detail.
He was to check procedures at law of the audiencia

judges, reform the collection of revenue, improve public order, and work with viceroy Marqués de Cruíllas and the military inspector, Juan de Villalba, in organizing the defenses of the colony. Gálvez' devious technique of hiding his ranges of authority from the viceroy (who quarreled with both the visitor and Villalba), his drastic uprooting of venial corruption at the customs of Vera Cruz, his development of a crown monopoly in tobacco which brought him into conflict with the viceregal fiscal, perhaps belong in detail more to Mexican history than to Carolinian. But what is relevant is his decisive imprint upon the whole imperial structure.

In essence the visitor typified the newly-trained bureaucrats whom Charles was sending out to the colonies. What the King had been doing for Spain in favoring a new generation of manteísta politicians was now being applied to the empire at large. The aim was fiscal and administrative centralization. Yet when we consider the explosive effect which a similar British policy via Parliament was causing in the thirteen North American colonies at the same time, it is not surprising that there were clashes with the Mexicans in a number of ways. Moreover, Gálvez had already belittled creoles by his ill-concealed opinion that these were too bound by local family ties to be entrusted with high authority. Now he scored a further triumph by forcing Charles' hand in the matter of getting rid of both Villalba and Cruíllas, in which, incidentally, the latter's residencia cleared him of any serious charges of nepotism.

The way was now clear for Gálvez to work in harmony with a new viceroy. This was Carlos Francisco, Marqués de Croix, who ruled New Spain from 1766 to 1771 and as a Frenchman more in line with the current administrative trend. Much progress was made in redeeming the revenue which was being soaked up by corrupt officials. Various duties, taxes and municipal finances were placed under direct control of the crown instead of being handled through tax-farming leases, and this practice was gradually phased out as the leases expired. Proper bills of lading were enforced as a check on smuggling, along with the correct stamping of the royal arms on

210

shipments, while improved bookkeeping methods were enforced in counting-houses where previously chaos had reigned. But trouble was soon to come. The *alcabala* tax was now to be paid at the point of entry into Mexican ports instead of at the point of sale in the interior, and this was reduced from six to four per cent. But since the larger merchants had taken their cut from this sales tax instead of passing its due share to the crown, they not surprisingly were incensed at such reforms; and complaints from their guild (or *consulado*) in Mexico, with its following of Basques and Montañeses who had always benefited from this tax at the capital, soon reached the ears of the council of the Indies, where monopoly interests were strong.[13] The tug-of-war between centralists and traditionalists was now emerging into the open.

While judicial conflict was pending in Madrid, storm-clouds were gathering among the Indians of Mexico. Here Gálvez, busily planning the expansion of crown revenues from new tobacco, playing-card, gunpowder, salt and pulque monopolies, made matters worse by imposing tighter methods of tribute collection and higher excise duties. The country was already tense when on May 30, 1767, the visitor received word from Croix that he was to carry out a systematic expulsion of the Jesuit Order which had been so staunchly protective of Indian rights. The ban on carrying arms only inflamed feeling further, and severe riots erupted, mainly in such mining regions as San Luis Potosí, Guanajuato and others, in which hard-worked alcaldes and militia could only with difficulty drive back the mobs. In all, about eighty Indians were hanged on the personal orders of Gálvez -- a dark stain on his record, and whose defense afterwards was that a full-scale Mexican revolution was imminent.

Outwardly, this would appear so. Indians aside, creole merchants were incensed at the downgrading of colonial industry, and at the lack of freer trade incentives in which Gálvez so far had only opened the ports of Campeche, Yucatán, and a few others to European goods from Vera Cruz. The clergy were incensed at attacks on their immunities which the visitor charged were being used as a cloak for profiteering and smuggling; militiamen resented being recruited; while miners were angry at production going down because of the riots. The Spanish government in fact was playing with fire in disturbing the warp and woof of colonial society, generally respectful toward the Jesuits, and for which the King must take some responsibility. But although the cabildo of Mexico City in 1771 went so far as to declare that Castilian law was no impediment in the promotion of Mexicans to high office, and that Spaniards ought to be excluded, a national revolution against the monarchy itself was a long way off; and Charles in the end did many good things for the country. Mexican creoles, unlike Anglo-American settlers to the north, had an Indian majority in their midst, and this of necessity bred a sense of reliance upon the mother country at a time when potential British expansion and Indian raids seemed to threaten the security of the viceroyalty.

This same year, royal plans for colonial reorginization assumed a decisive phase. On April 20, 1771, Floridablanca and Campomanes, fiscals on the council of Castile, declared roundly in favor of Gálvez and his revenue policies against charges by the council of the Indies that the visitor had wielded undue influence on viceroy Croix, had confounded the laws, and injured the rights of the consulado and cabildo.[14] Essentially, the charges were a petition to annul the grants of power accorded to Gálvez by instructions of February 1767; but in this the judicial plaintiffs failed dismally. The verdict in fact was a foregone conclusion. By a subtle maneuver on the part of Grimaldi, with Charles' blessing, the case had been passed directly into the council of Castile's hands, where manteista centralists were strong, and away from the council of the Indies and minister Arriaga, with his traditionalist friends among the merchants.

The judicial verdict closed the chapter of the Gálvez visita, when Croix was replaced by Antonio de Bucareli, an excellent viceroy and diplomat, formerly governor of Havana, who proved adept at preserving some of the old ways without directly contravening orders from Madrid. It was a time of critical debate, for the triumphant Gálvez had struck deep with his reforms, and with the support of treasurer Múzquiz

was to become minister of the Indies in 1776.  The
sweeping changes he made, especially in raising the
revenues, reflected Charles' basic overhaul of the
entire empire in America.

Gálvez can be credited with the flow of more
merchant capital into Mexico and all the colonies.
The artificial scarcity of foods caused by slow convoyed shipments to Vera Cruz, which also encouraged
smuggling, was broken down by curtailing the fleet
system, and as a result the port took on a new resilience.  This easing of controls enabled commerce
to bypass traditional centers such as the trade fair
at Jalapa, where big monopoly merchants had an important stake.  Smaller men, including mining entrepreneurs, were thus given a better chance to contri-
bute to Mexican development.  Reflecting these trends
in America as a whole was perhaps the greatest single
achievement of the new minister -- his liberalized
trade regulation of October 12, 1778.  This opened
most Spanish American ports to free commerce with
Spain (extended by 1789 to those of Mexico and Venezuela, thus ending Cádiz and Basque monopoly interests
in these regions respectively).  Though goods still
had to be carried in Spanish ships, the regulation
relaxed many import-export duties, and allowed most
ports to trade with one another.  The enormous resultant increase in commerce bound the empire closer
together, which was a main aim of Charles' policy,
and checked the leakage of some 12 million pesos
annually lost to the crown revenues because of smuggling in the New World.[15]

Another achievement of Gálvez was his promotion
of the mining industry, especially in Mexico.  He had
been charged to expand this when he was visitor there,
and his reforms included various tax exemptions, price
reductions in gunpowder and mercury (the latter brought
over from Spain and Austria), properly paid officials
to supervise production, and tighter discipline in
the ranks of labor enforced by a recruited militia.
In 1776 delegates were summoned from the chief mining
camps of Mexico to establish a mining court and guild,
with headquarters at the capital.  The court had independent jurisdiction and soon became wealthier than
any merchant consulado.  Seven years later, the King

authorized the publication of a new mining code. Designed to increase silver production, assert crown control over subsoil deposits, set patent rights of discoveries, and regulate such matters as labor relations, financing, and liability of operators, this exerted a considerable influence on other mining codes as they developed later in North America. The basis was also laid for a technical mining college, which got fully under way by 1792. As a result of these reforms there was a substantial increase in Mexican gold and silver production, which in terms of mintage value ascended from about 12 million pesos in 1770 to nearly 20 million pesos two decades later. Royal revenues were derived from the *quinto real* (virtually a one-tenth tithe on bullion and precious stones), besides various mintage charges, seigniorage duties, and sales from mercury and gunpowder; and these reached an annual average of nearly five million pesos by the end of the same period.[16] The most resplendent figure in all this, perhaps, was Charles himself, whose patronage of the arts and sciences led to many foundations of which the royal academy of Noble Arts, under way by 1775, and the academy of San Carlos, under way by 1783, are but two examples.

Military and strategic reforms also showed an encouraging picture. The regular army was becoming a force to be reckoned with, as well-trained units were sent across the Atlantic in rotation to reinforce colonial garrisons. Here creoles could receive commissions up to the rank of colonel; and alongside peninsulares they now enjoyed a wide range of privileges (*fueros*), such as those codified for Mexico in 1768, which included some immunity from ordinary court jurisdiction and certain tax exemptions. The militia was enlarged by royal ordinances for both provincial and urban units, in which mestizos and pardos, whose morale had never been high at the best of times, were also given fueros. The introduction of more units of the regular army, and the additional recruitment of militia begun by Villalba increased the total number of men under arms in Mexico from 14,000 in 1766 to 40,000 twenty years later.[17]

These figures exclude the new northern command, brainchild of Gálvez, who in face of Indian attacks proposed detaching the northern provinces of Mexico from direct viceregal control; and over Bucareli's initial objections, these were organized by 1776 into a commandancy-general for the purpose of fighting the warlike Apaches, Utes, and Comanches, as well as Caddos between New Mexico and Texas, who were ravaging the region. Arizpe was the capital, occupying an ideal central position. Consisting of California, Sonora, Nueva Vizcaya, and New Mexico (to which were later added Coahuila and Texas), the region was linked by a chain of garrison presidios -- a policy decided on by Charles through royal orders issued on April 25, 1770, and September 10, 1772. Thereafter its commandants achieved significant success in pacifying the enemy.[18]

Charles' plans also included the occupation of the Mississippi valley and the California coast. Experience with the Sierra Morena settlements in Spain already formed a basis for colonizations in lower California, where Gálvez as visitor had distributed communal lands to Indian and Spaniard alike. Aiming to compromise between imperial restrictions and a freer activity for his subjects, Charles with Gálvez opted for the policy of extending colonization by slow stages. Outposts were to be linked by troops and missionaires, thus holding back Indian attacks, while at the same time subtly outflanking European rivals. It was a painstaking process, but in this way the North American hinterland could be gradually tapped in close concert with a visible defense force, in which everyone would be protected beneath the shield of the advancing Spanish flag.[19] From Santa Fe to San Antonio, also in the Caribbean and South America, presidios and ports were being strengthened in anticipation of foreign attack.

Charles had England very much in mind with these policies. British claims to territorial sovereignty were based on effective settlements, and this clashed at every point with the Spanish view of territorial sovereignty based on historic grants and precedence. Now Charles would apply the tactics of the enemy. Indeed he saw conflict as inevitable, providing him with an eventual pretext to annul past treaties with this country. Not for nothing had British logwood cutters moved insistently into Honduras, which was vaguely permitted by the treaty of Paris, arousing Charles' acute fears lest they expand their holdings in this region. Already at home he had ordered British merchantmen to be searched when entering certain Spanish ports; while in the south Atlantic, as we have seen in the previous chapter, trouble was brewing over claims to the Falkland Islands.

Relations with England were further strained over terms for settling the one million pound ransom originally demanded by Admiral Draper as his price for averting the sack of Manila during the Seven Years war, and which sum the British were still trying to collect as a post-condition for the city's return. Following consultations at the time with his ministers Grimaldi and Squillace, Charles had refused to pay it on the grounds than any yielding on the issue had never stopped the looting; but it remained a sore point with the British government, and delighted the opposition in Parliament led by William Pitt, who could always use the failure to collect the Manila ransom as a means to embarrass the cabinet.

Security in the Pacific had always been a prime objective of Spain, who still regarded this vast ocean as her own preserve; and a classic case of the Gálvez policy of 'search and occupy' can be seen in the advance up the California coast in order to locate a securer haven for the Manila galleon which had to navigate past the treacherous rocks of lower California on its way to Acapulco. But an additional reason was Charles' fear of penetration by England, whose vague claims to 'New Albion' dating back to Sir Francis Drake's historic visit to this region had not been forgotten. Charles also had a great fear of Russia, which Spanish diplomats at St. Petersburg did nothing to assuage. With everyone aware of how sensitive he was on this subject, it needed only the slightest hint to convince him that the Russians were coming. In painting visions of British Redcoats rushing to embrace leering Muscovites, greedy for empire in California with its sea otter and pearls, Gálvez and his friends were possibly working up a little mischief of their own, for in Spain, as always, one needed to exaggerate to get things done.

216

It certainly seemed to Charles that unless he
could somehow ward off his British and Russian rivals,
whom he feared in about equal proportions, by offering
superficial friendship with both, then Spanish America
would be threatened on two fronts -- with the British
thrusting westwards from the Mississippi, the Russians
thrusting eastward across the north Pacific. The biggest nightmare of all would be a concerted alliance
between them. Though his fears were misplaced, enough
was known of Russian activities for Charles to give
credence to the rumors Gálvez' friends were circulating
and to put Indies minister Arriaga fully on the alert.

In the wake of Bering's historic voyages to the
north Pacific earlier in the century, a number of
Russians -- Gvozdev, Glotov, Krenitsyn and Levashev
among them -- had been making expeditions to Unalaska,
Fox Islands, and Kodiak, in the course of which on
March 2, 1766, Empress Catherine made a formal claim
to Alaska itself. Frequent winterings by Russian sea
otter traders (using Aleutian forced labor), attempts
to rediscover lost Russian colonies, and sheer imperial expansion were the motives for these expeditions, which would form the basis for a tighter administrative control. Because of official secrecy surrounding them, Spanish ambassadors in St. Petersburg
such as Vizconde de la Herrería were understandably
vague, if alarming, in their coded despatches to
Grimaldi about the exact limits of their penetration;
and it was not until later in the decade that Herrería's
successor, Conde de Lacy, could piece together with the
help of paid spies a finer, though still inaccurate,
description.[20] This very lack of certainty about the
shape of the Alaskan coastline as a springboard for
Russian activities southward was enough to increase
Charles' fears and spur him to do something quickly
to confront the Russian threat.

Accordingly a plan was evolved in 1768 for his
forces to occupy the California coast, and then proceed northwards to find out how near foreigners really
were; and Arriaga passed on these orders to viceroy
Croix, charging him to caution the governor of California to be circumspect in all things and to report
every suspicious detail.[21] Gálvez himself when still
visitor ordered the occupation of San Diego this same

year, which was duly carried out by governor Gaspar de
Portolá and the Franciscan missionary, Junípero Serra.
The latter spread both Christianity and the yellow
mustard-seed with equal tenacity, heralding the many
crop plantations which were to be the fruitful products
of the twenty-one Franciscan missions eventually dotting
the region.

It was while Portolá and his men were searching
for a land route to Monterey further up the coast, that
in November 1769 they stumbled upon the magnificent bay
of San Francisco, Shrouded by mist, which explains why
the Spaniards never discovered it before, it provided
perfect facilities for a colony and port. This impression was confirmed when it was later explored, among
others, by Juan Bautista de Anza who had made an eight-
hundred mile trek from northern Mexico to Monterey,
and under orders from viceroy Bucareli to lead a company of settlers was now searching the bay region for
a suitable site. Near a steep white rock at the tip
of the peninsula, a presidio and mission were built;
and on the historic date of July 4, 1776, San Francisco
was officially founded.[22] Spain's hold upon the coast
enabled the hinterland to be opened up, providing a
nexus of land routes for settlers in the years to come.
In this regard two worthy Franciscan friars, Silvestre
de Escalante and Francisco Domínguez, set out from
Santa Fe (New Mexico) this same year in an attempt to
find a land route to the new missions at Monterey; and
although they failed in this object, they yet explored
much of Colorado and the Utah valley.

Meanwhile the way was clear for a further phase
of the King's plan, that of sending sea expeditions
up the coast which could be supplied from the bases
being built on land. Headquarters for these operations
was at San Blas, about 140 miles west of Guadalajara
on the Mexican Pacific coast. Here a remarkable group
of navigators, including the Peruvian Juan Bodega y
Quadra who was in full command by 1790, won signal
honors for their country. There was Juan Pérez, who
with eighty men touched Vancouver Island in 1774 and
reached the fifty-fifth parallel, the first Westerner
to do so. The next year Bruno de Heceta, besides
visiting many islands towards the Canadian coast discovered the Columbia river, also the first Westerner
to do so and anticipating the American, Robert Gray,
by ten years. Among these men none was more intrepid
than Francisco Mourelle from Galicia, in whom was bred

something of the traditional sea-dog. Spaniards as a whole, perhaps, have never been quite at ease on the oceans compared with Britons, Portuguese, or Dutchmen, but Mourelle and his companions were exceptions. Determined to carry out orders to the letter during Heceta's expedition, he forged ahead on his own after parting company with the equally intrepid Juan Bodega, almost reaching the required sixtieth parallel, and subsisting with his men on rice, beans, and lard for ten long months as they all crouched below-deck for survival in a tiny storm-tossed vessel. Mourelle also served as pilot on José Arteaga's voyage of 1779 to the sixty-first parallel, which touched Prince William Sound in the gulf of Alaska; and the following year saw him in the south Pacific on a visit to the Spanish Tonga Islands and Fiji.[23] He covered so many leagues that he can worthily be compared with the celebrated Captain James Cook. The latter, incidentally, touched Nootka Sound on Vancouver Island in 1778, under strict orders not to disturb Spanish waters to the south. The American Revolution was on and Britain wanted to avoid trouble with Spain.

Cook's visit to this island where he received two silver spoons from the Indians given them by members of Pérez' crew in 1774 provided the Spaniards with a tangible claim that they had got there first. Thus was set in motion a famous controversy with England which led to a mutual (if temporary) abandonment of the island twenty years later. As for the Russians, it was not till 1784 that a firm foothold was secured close by the Alaskan mainland when the merchant Shelikov established his trading post in Three Saints Bay on Kodiak Island. Not surprisingly, there was fevered activity in Madrid to continue exploring. But no hostilities with the Russians occured, and the friendliest of greeting were exchanged with them by Estéban José Martínez and Gonzalo López de Haro during an expedition to the Alaskan peninsula in 1788, whereon the Russians had established a firm but peaceful presence.[24]

Spain's brave navigators, still operating well into the 1790's, not only brought back a treasure-load of scientific information; they also traced

219

the limits of discovery made by other powers, including France, and whose proximity to the Spanish dominions was not nearly so close as had been imagined. Yet thwarting any rival attempts to penetrate further, these men had turned the Pacific flank of California into an effective barrier designed to block any hostile power which might be tempted to overrun it.

In the final analysis, the real challenge came not from rival European powers, but from within Charles' own empire; for in 1780 occured a devasting revolt by the mistreated Indians of Peru, whose tutelage and welfare the Spanish government had pledged to uphold. Far worse than anything experienced before, it was in essence a protest against abuse, and echoed the warnings of earlier reformers that all was not well within the system. A solution in part was an extension of the intendance practice, which was a final facet in Charles' reorganization of the Indies. It is this type of reform, along with other topics treating South America, which require some comments before a balance-sheet on Charles' rule in the Indies can be made.

CHAPTER ELEVEN

CRISES AND CONSOLIDATION

The turmoil throughout Spanish South America
stemmed directly from internal problems, and Charles
must take some blame for not dealing with them in time.
But complicating the scene was the American Revolution
and Charles' war with England (discussed in the next
chapter), so that his attention was focused on many
fronts simultaneously. His manner of dealing with the
turmoil is what concerns us here, and this completes
the essential picture of his legacy to the Indies as
a whole.

By way of prologue to troubles ahead, Spain was
first at odds with Portugal, who was England's ally
and apt to take advantage of this in the New World.
The two Iberian powers had long been engaged in conflict below Brazil. The Portuguese were pressing along
the Paraná-La Plata river system, which had led to
various posts being overrun first by one power, then
the other. Where the Paraná was concerned, the Spaniards had founded missions in northern Paraguay at an
early date, but the Portuguese had intruded, capturing
both Indians and cattle with impunity. Where La Plata
was concerned, the Spaniards had long founded Buenos
Aires, but on the river's east bank toward the con-
fluence with the Uruguay, the Portuguese were busy
settling Colonia do Sacramento, with the help at various times of England and France, who were cashing in
on its lucrative smuggling.

Ferdinand VI of Spain had unsuccessfully tried
to end the rivalry in a treaty of 1750, by which seven
Jesuit missions east of the Uruguay up-river were
given to Portugal in exchange for Colonia being given
to Spain; but the fierce opposition by the Guaraní
Indians and their Jesuit guardians in this part of
Paraguay, who feared the Portuguese slave-raiders,
inflamed the region with rebellion. The result was
a joint Spanish-Portuguese military effort in 1754
to enforce the treaty; but hardly had this succeeded
with terrible devastation, when in 1761 the treaty
was annulled. After the two powers fought each other

221

in the Seven Years war, this annulment was confirmed by the treaty of Paris in 1763, when Paraguay with the seven missions was retained by Spain and Colonia was returned to Portugal.

With the expulsion of the Jesuits completed in the 1760's, the way seemed clear for cooperation between the two powers, but this did not materialize. One reason for this was the ambition of the Portuguese reforming minister, Marquês de Pombal, whose rise to power took place during the reign of Joseph I. Despite the policy of Jesuit expulsion he shared with Charles, Pombal had been scheming for some time to build up a strong position south of Brazil at Spain's expense, in which he hoped to count on British support. Another reason for the continuing rivalry was the extensive smuggling carried on at the Portuguese outpost of Colonia, which upset the Spanish settlers of Buenos Aires to the south who alleged that Portuguese and British traders were robbing them of legitimate business. In response to their complaints and needing a fortified region against Portuguese expansion, Charles in 1776 created the viceroyalty of Río de la Plata and placed strong forces there under the command of Pedro de Cevallos, who had recommended this policy.

Charles and Pombal, each as shrewd as the other, were heading for a showdown; but the latter was dangerously isolated with Britain's hands tied by events in North America, and this gave Charles a unique opportunity to press home his advantage. Cevallos in fact with nine thousand men and a strong naval force was able to take Colonia on June 4, 1777, after a two months' siege. Having thus broken Portugal's bastion for a second time -- the first was during the Seven Years war -- Cevallos proceeded to reinforce Montevideo on the estuary of La Plata, and on his own initiative to improve trade relations with upper Peru.[1]

Strengthening Charles' hand, meanwhile, was a combination of factors which led to Pombal's downfall. Despite the gratitude which the Portuguese monarchs owed Pombal in the past, conflict with Spain was not popular at court; and Joseph's death early the same year was followed by the regency of the queen mother,

222

María Ana, and by the accession to the throne of their
daughter María, neither of which ladies were favorably
disposed to Pombal when it became known that he was
now scheming to undo the female succession.  Nor was
Charles the sort of monarch to forgive such treacheries.
Queen mother María Ana was his favorite sister, and he
fully used his influence to put an end to the high-
handed actions of the Portuguese minister.  With conservative nobles also eager to pay off old scores
against him, Pombal's doom was sealed.  This same
year, 1777, he was promptly dismissed and later exiled
by the new young queen, who with her mother's blessing
thus got rid of a man with great talent, but whose
ambition and duplicity in politics had made him too
many enemies.

     With Pombal removed, friendly relations were soon
established between the two powers.  By the treaty of
San Ildefonso concluded on October 1, 1777, Portugal
ceded to Spain all navigation rights on the Paraguay
and Paraná rivers up to where the Pepiri Guacu flows
into the Uruguay, all navigation rights on the La
Plata river, and gave up Colonia.  Spain on her part
ceded Amazon territory around the Yapura river to the
north, and in southern Brazil, portions round Laguna
Grande and also the island of Santa Catalina.  The
boundary delimiting Brazil's frontier with Paraguay
was fixed from the Paraná southward along the Pepiri
Guacu, crossing the Uruguay and Negro rivers, thence
along the Grande to Brazil's southernmost tip.[2]

     After so many years of bitter hostility, the way
was now clear for a personal celebration.  Thus took
place the historic meeting between Charles and his
sister near Badajoz in Spain the following month.  The
rendezous was in the vicinity of Galapagar on the
Guadiana river; and the story goes that Charles in
his impatience to greet her grabbed the correspondence
from the mail-courier to ascertain any last-minute
details, but on seeing that the envelopes were addressed to Floridablanca, he quickly restrained himself with the remark, "Take them man, they're not
for me but for my minister"![3]  Composure and correct-
ness soon gained the upper hand in one who was every
inch a king.  María Ana was festively entertained by
her brother in Madrid, the city where they grew up

together, and they discussed old times as well as
the possibility of future marriage alliances among
their children.  In bidding her farewell Charles had
cemented new ties with Portugal, and on March 24, 1778,
a further treaty was signed as a follow-up to the one
of October the previous year.

Ratified in the Pardo by Floridablanca and the
Portuguese envoy, F.I. de Souza Coutinho, this treaty
bound each party not to form an alliance prejudicial
to the other, to promise neutrality in the event of
either going to war with a third party, and to accord
the other the most favored-nation status in commerce.
Portugal additionally ceded to Spain the islands of
Annobón and Fernando Po off the west coast of Africa.
Both treaties were important, for they marked the end
of hostility between the two powers, assuring that in
the event of Spain going to war with England, as in
fact happened in 1779, the latter would be deprived
of Portugal as an ally.  The price for this was a
slightly enlarged Brazil, but the treaties safeguarded
Spanish control of the La Plata region for another
generation, as well as foreshadowing the frontiers of
Spanish-speaking Argentina, Paraguay, and Uruguay
as we know them today.

The viceroyalty of Río de la Plata was a fruitful product of the foregoing events.  Freed of control
from far-away Lima, it gave Spain greater scope for
defensive action, while the liberalization of trade
decreed in 1778 was of inestimable benefit to Buenos
Aires.  Its hinterland, now a channel of commerce
with upper Peru, could be seen crammed with all sorts
of goods from hides to vicuña wool bound for ship-
ment to Spain, while less commendably, black slaves
streamed in the other direction.  Mercury also began
to be imported from Spain via Buenos Aires.  The
city's strong defenses, moreover, could withstand
any attempt by Britain to dominate La Plata in time
of war, or to infiltrate it in time of peace.

The able Cevallos was succeeded as viceroy by
the Mexican-born soldier, Juan José de Vértiz, whose
administration in Buenos Aires was a brilliant re-
plica of what Charles and his advisers had done for
Madrid.  Vértiz gave the city better sanitation and

streetlighting, a theatre and printing-presses, besides founding hospitals, institutions for orphans and the poor, a medical school, and the college of San Carlos for higher education. The sturdy settlers had much to be grateful for; but impatient for wider opportunities they continued to fan out into Indian country, pursuing herds of wild cattle in the gaucho manner as they slew bulls by the hundred, and then and there would barbecue them to their taste. Quarrelsome and independent, these settlers yet did much to foster the growth of the viceroyalty, bringing it nearer to the modern form of Argentina. Its burgeoning industries of cattle-hides, leather-goods, and horse-breeding portended a rich future for a vast and promising land.[4]

Peru by contrast presented a depressing picture at this time. The senior viceroyalty of Spanish South America had been dealt a severe blow, for the region of Charcas which included Potosí, La Paz, and other districts of upper Peru, with all the mineral wealth contained therein, had been detached along with Tucumán, and included in the new La Plata viceroyalty. The loss of upper Peru in fact (the equivalent of modern Bolivia) seriously dislocated Peruvian trade, as was evidenced by the significant fall in the outflow of silver and sugar to Lima, which went to Buenos Aires instead. In a word, Buenos Aires was eclipsing Lima as a commercial center. With a population of just over a million -- one fifth that of Mexico -- Peru was now unable to exert the same degree of political pull over the rest of the continent which had been her privilege in former times.

In Lima, a closely-knit creole society of land-owners, merchants, and office-holders was riddled with corruption and resistant to all but the most determined reformers. Defiance of Spanish law was common, as expressed by the *obedezco y no cumplo* principle; and Madrid was wont to protest such lapses of obedience as when, for example, a cargo ship from Spain might be held up for months in port while the audiencia, hand-in-glove with commercial interests, would verify its voyage-permit with painstaking slowness in order to allow time for merchants to dispose of previous stocks. If sale of office was standard practice, plenty of

225

other abuses abounded among creoles and Spaniards alike, and cases to settle grievances were frequently quashed through bribes being passed to the attorney's office.  The network of corruption embraced all ranks of society.  So much profiteering went on in mining circles at the mercury base of Huancavelica that Antonio de Ulloa who was once governor there likened the situation to "an old woman slowly losing her teeth". Manuel de Amat y Junient, capable viceroy of Peru from 1761 to 1776 and who incidentally was the first to build up a militia in his kingdom, agreed that things were bad; but while his famous *Memoria de gobierno* put the blame squarely on the commercial greed of audiencia officials in the provinces, he showed no desire, any more than Bucareli did, to hand over power to a meddlesome visitor or intendant.[5]

It was this stagnant conservatism which prompted Gálvez as minister of the Indies to send out Antonio de Areche, who had been with him in Mexico, as visitor to Peru; and he duly arrived in 1777, charged with the task of reforming the judicial system, improving the revenue, checking on Indian abuse, and stimulating mining and agriculture.  But all this was to prove an uphill task.  Areche soon found out, as Gálvez did in Mexico, that revenue reforms do not come easily when special interests see their tax loopholes in jeopardy. He was strongly opposed by the new viceroy, Manuel Guirior, who like his predecessor preferred older-tried methods, in which he was pleased to show a revenue surplus of over a million and a half pesos by 1779.

But such niceties in the meantime did not impress Areche; and matters came to a head when the visitor increased the alcabala sales tax from four to six per cent, transfering its collection from inefficient local officers to a central customs house.  This was bitterly opposed in Lima not only by the viceroy, but by the audiencia, cabildo, and a whole range of merchant interests, who like their counterparts in the Mexican consulado had long been taking their cut.  Areche's collection methods, his application of the new six per cent levy to grains and foodstuffs, higher taxes on rum and brandy, and the erroneous belief among mestizos that they were going to have to pay Indian

tribute led to riots in Arequipa, Cuzco, and elsewhere early in 1780. The main impetus here, be it
noted, came not from the Indians but from the wealthier
creoles angered by the loss of control over taxes; and
it is plausible to suggest that if creoles had been
excluded from such control in the first place, government might have been less corrupt.

Areche so far succeeded in restoring order. He
also managed to have Guirior removed, with whom a
personal struggle for power had developed, and who
like viceroy Cruíllas of Mexico was eventually subjected to an exonerating *residencia*. But his success
was short-lived. Hardly had the crisis passed when
there occured the most critical explosion of all, the
famous Indian uprising of Túpac Amaru, whose causes
were directly related to a long list of unredressed
grievances. There seems little doubt that had Areche
not been so involved in disputes with the viceroy,
audiencia, and the merchants, he might have done more
to lighten the burdens of which the Indians were for
so long complaining. Now it was too late. The new
viceroy, Agustín de Jáuregui, looked on helplessly
while Peru was in turmoil, faced as he was with having
to deal with a difficult visitor, and tied to the
coastal region expecting an English attack as a result
of the war which Spain had declared.[6]

The chief cause of the trouble was the greed of
the district magistrates or *corregidores*. These would
purchase such items as cloth, mules and iron implements from merchants at Lima, then sell them by intimi-
dation to the Indians at excessive prices. This
forced sale of goods was known as the *repartimiento de
comercio*. The more Indians involved, the bigger the
profits. Adding insult to injury was the inclusion
of totally unnecessary wares, from economic diction-
aries to volumes of Feijóo, which for all the erudi-
tion contained therein was unlikely to bear much fruit
on alien soil scratched by descendants of the Inca.
The corregidor's role was supposed to be judicial
but in fact it was absolute, and the Indians had a
slim chance of successful appeal to the audiencia of
Lima when its judges (*oidores*) were themselves bound
up with merchant interests who financed the goods
to the corregidores in the first place. Over five

and a half million pesos' worth of merchandise was
tied up in Peru in this way; and although corregidores paid the alcabala tax on purchases at the ware-
house, they were still free to charge the Indian what
they liked.

In fairness to the accused, there were instances
where repartimientos did provide the Indians with a
modicum of subsistence, without which they would have
starved or resorted to brigandage; and there were
viceroys like Bucareli who defended the practice.
Corregidores' salaries, moreover, were pitiably low
-- barely more than a thousand pesos a year against
a viceroy's salary of 80,000 -- thus inviting rapacious
profits to make ends meet. But despite pleas by reformers such as Ulloa and Amat to abolish repartimientos
altogether, nothing was done in time to stop the revolt.
Viceroy Jáuregui in fact abolished repartimientos one
month after the revolt erupted in November.

The *mita* system, outlined in the previous chapter,
was another grievance. Owners of mine, estate, and
factory, taking advantage of weak local government,
would exploit this levy of cheap labor, in which unscrupulous corregidores would then advance food and
clothing to the Indians who had no hope of paying all
this back. Default would result in their indefinite
confinement to cloth factories, where yet more irrever-
sible credit awaited them. Reduced to debt-peonage
by this vicious circle, Indians would suffer the
additional burden of having their families uprooted
through an unwarranted interference with their communal
land rights. Yet another abuse was corregidor collusion with the local *cacique* chieftain, who minimizing
the number of able-bodied Indians on the official list
for tribute (amounting to a few pesos per head as
part of revenue collection), would keep the real
number of Indians on another special list, where much
of the tribute would end up in private pockets. There
was little doubt whose pockets these were. Indian
and the treasury alike were being fleeced at the expense of human rights and needs.

The unkindest cut of all was the failure of the
Spanish government to enforce its own laws on the
Indians' behalf. It had indeed been warned, for in

the 1730's the two distinguished naval officers mentioned in previous contexts, Jorge Juan and Antonio
de Ulloa, gave a startling account of Indian exploitation by corregidores and churchmen in Ecuador; and by
mid-century Ulloa wrote a similar report on the appalling conditions of forced labor in the mines and on
estates of Peru.[7]  But little was done to put things
right.  Together these two great officers showed such
a deep understanding of the causes of tension between
Indians, creoles, and peninsulares that they were able
to correctly forecast future revolts.

Perhaps the biggest villain was the imperial system itself, in which the council of the Indies, staffed
by experienced men among the viceroys, captains-general,
governors, oidores, corregidores and scribes sincerely
tried to cope with all the problems inherent with repartimiento practice, but without effect.  The budgetary
appropriations had to come from someone; and the Indian
paid more than his fair share -- a share that might
have been more equitable if rapacious middlemen had
been taking less and lower officials paid a decent wage.
All these defects were being closely studied by Areche
during his *visita,* and who was urging the introduction
of tighter methods of control when this worst revolt
of all suddenly occured.

On November 4, 1780, near Tungasuca in Tinta province, Peru, José Gabriel Condorcanqui (descendant of
the Inca king Túpac Amaru, meaning Resplendent Serpent,
whose name he adopted), ambushed and seized a cruel
corregidor named Antonio Arriaga.  The attack was a
surprise for the two men had just attended a dinner
in honor of Charles III's name-day.  Using Arriaga as
a device for raising funds, Túpac Amaru then hanged
his captive in the public square.  He professed loyalty
to king and church, declaring his intent was only to
redress Indian wrongs, but he failed to win over the
creoles who considered his demands too excessive.
These included the removal of corregidores, an end
to the repartimiento and mita systems as well as Areche's
visita, and the creation of a new audiencia at Cuzco
so that justice might be done to the oppressed.  His
freeing of blacks, moreover, was hardly conducive to
winning support from plantation slave-owners.  Of huge
stature clad in scarlet riding-jacket and mounted on

his white charger, a medallion of the sun dangling
from his neck, Túpac Amaru seemed the very image of
an Inca emperor come to life. With sixty thousand
Indians flocking to his standard, it was not long
before news of his revolt spread like wildfire throughout Peru. Alarmed by the growing challenge to its
power after a rebel victory near Cuzco, the Spanish
government organized an army of all ethnic strains,
including units from the viceregal command in La
Plata; and this was entrusted to General José del
Valle, reinforcing Gabriel de Avilés who early in
1781 was already on the scene in Cuzco with detach-
ments of militia. Soon the Andes mountains became
dotted with the campfires of the warring sides.

Túpac Amaru's decline thereafter was as much due
to his dilatory tactics as to sporadic massacres of
creoles committed by his followers, in which he wasted
time trying to negotiate with Areche and the bishop of
Cuzco instead of advancing on the city. Lacking good
advisers and trained officers, he suffered a big defeat
near Checaupe in 1781, and was finally captured with
his family in the mountains near Tananico. In May of
this year, Areche and an oidor from Lima ordered his
execution in Cuzco's main square. After some members
of his family were put to death before his very eyes,
his limbs were then tied to four horses each moving in
different directions; but he possessed such enormous
physical strength that he resisted for a while this
ghastly form of execution, as rearing like a giant
spider in the air he bravely met his end. But it was
Túpac who had the last word. Although the revolt
sputtered on for two more years, when his brother
Diego and family were either hanged or imprisoned even
after viceroy Jáuregui had given them a pardon, a
number of immediate reforms mitigated the worst abuses.[8]

The attitude of Gálvez towards the revolt, like
that of Areche (who had been recalled in 1781), combined brutal harshness to its leaders with a sympathetic understanding of its causes. But restoring order
had to come first; and an important response was the
introduction of seven intendancies based on an ordinance issued for La Plata in 1782, and applied to
Peru two years later. The idea was not new, as intendants had already been posted to Havana, Sonora,

and Louisiana in keeping with the institution in Spain, in which the idea was now to parallel the two systems. Many viceroys saw in this a challenge to their power, just as they had done with the visitas, and largely because of Bucareli's forceful arguments, an ordinance for twelve intendants was not issued for Mexico till 1786.[9] It was only in the same year that Chile received an ordinance, while one planned for New Granada was never put into effect at all during Charles' reign. Yet the policy prevailed. Charged to safeguard the laws, promote the revenues of crown and colony, and maintain firm control over public order and local administration, these intendants were really super-governors over the entire judicial, financial, and military machinery of the provinces assigned to them. In keeping a close watch on things and reporting back to the crown, they became a strong force in the viceroyalties, and brought to fulfillment the centralizing policy of the Bourbons begun by Philip V.

Meanwhile in Peru, the powers of the hated corregidores were gradually merged with those of the intendants' subordinate officials, termed subdelegates, who were each responsible for a part of the intendancy. Corregidores were then phased out altogether. As for repartimientos, these had already been abolished by royal order of May 25, 1781, and confirmed in the ordinance of each respective viceroyalty; but as the new subdelegates still received an inadequate salary, the problem of their having to supplement their income through trading with the Indians remained. Subdelegates were certainly better than the corregidors whom they had replaced, but as they were still impelled by economic necessity, repartimientos continued to exist illegally, albeit in a diluted form.

The mita system, another Indian complaint, was not fully phased out till 1812, but in the meantime conditions of enforced personal service were very much improved. No Indian could now be transported more than thirty miles from his home or be moved to a higher altitude than what his health was used to; while only one-seventh of the able-bodied population in a district could be used for labor at any one time. Moreover, better judicial appeal was given the Indian by

231

the creation of the audiencia of Cuzco in 1787, over
objections from Lima.[10]  This was yet another of Túpac
Amaru's demands, and showed that the Spanish government
was following the footsteps of the great patriot whom
it had so ruthlessly struck down.  As if seeking a way
out of its own dilemma of conscience, it ordered a surviving son of his to be brought to Spain and educated
in style.

A less pleasant voyage to Europe awaited two Frenchmen, Antoine Berney and Antoine Gramusset, who conspired
with others in 1781 to set up a liberal republic in
Chile.  Together with José Antonio de Rojas, a Spaniard
just arrived from the peninsula, they proposed establishing a senate, introducing popular suffrage (to include
Araucanian Indians), and reducing taxes.  To complete
their plans, a letter was to be sent to Charles III
politely informing him that Chile was independent.
The governor of Santiago was not impressed, and the
incipient rebels soon found themselves sent to Peru
for trial.  Berney died in a shipwreck, but Gramusset
survived to spend his days in a Cádiz jail.

This event shows the earliest influences of the
American Revolution, which at this stage affected only
a tiny minority of activists.  In coming to grips with
subversion in his own colonies, Charles was taking no
chances, and through the council of the Indies he secured the appointment of viceroys more in keeping with
the new centralizing trend.  Such a one was Teodoro
de Croix, a protégé of Gálvez and nephew of Francisco,
the former viceroy of Mexico.  As commandant-general
of the northern provinces of Mexico, Teodoro de Croix
had been busy pacifying the hordes of Apaches and Comanches who besides fighting one another, wreaked havoc
on the Spanish settlements.  Under these circumstances,
the new viceroy was hardly sympathetic with the abstract
idea of liberty when he arrived in Peru in 1784, especially when faced with taxes to raise caused by wars
and revolts; and reinforced by a decree the next year
proceeded with the Inquisition's help to seize all
subversive books he could lay his hands on, including
works by Machiavelli, Raynal, and d'Holbach.  Despite
this, Croix imparted a new cultural and scientific
spirit to the kingdom.  Creole society flourished,its
young men encouraged to come to Spain, while Charles

himself in 1786 created forty scholarships for the
education of upper-class Spanish Americans, many of
them Peruvians, at the royal Seminary of Nobles in
Madrid.[11]  Peru in fact recovered a little of its lost
glory.  There was Lima's academy of youth, its comedy
theatre, its achievements in botany and medicine in
which the great name of Hipólito Unanue comes to mind.
Despite loopholes in the law, things were improving
sufficiently for people in general to continue their
loyalty to the Spanish crown; and it is significant,
if not ironic, that Peru was one of the last South
American nations to relinquish it.

The viceroyalty of New Granada to the north, meanwhile, was also in a troubled state at the time.  Created
permanently by 1740 to protect the Spanish Main, the
realm enjoyed a 'Pax Hispanica' under such able viceroys as Sebastián de Eslava; and Manuel de Guirior had
served here in the 1770's before his move to Peru and
his fatal clash with Areche.  The viceroy was now
Manuel Antonio Flores.  Like his predecessors he spent
much money on the defenses of Cartagena, which the
English had not dared to attack since their fiasco of
1740; but it was in the interior of the viceroyalty
whence trouble came, giving Flores a severe problem
to deal with at a time when his resources were already
strained to the limit defending the coast, and doing
what he could to assist the audiencia of Guatemala
during Spain's current war with England.  Indeed troops
had to be sent to Flores from the Caribbean command to
help snuff out what became known as the *comunero* revolt.

As usual, it all started with a visita -- this
time one made by Juan Francisco de Piñeres, who with
the same sort of zeal as Gálvez had displayed in Mexico,
proceeded to set up royal tobacco and salt monopolies
in order to raise the revenues, but which hurt the
smaller entrepreneurs in these fields as much as it
hurt everyone else who had to pay the new taxes.  In
March 1781, the townsmen (*comuneros*) of Socorro and
other places, joined by Indians excited at the news
of Túpac Amaru's revolt, rose up under the leadership
of Juan Francisco Berbeo, who with 20,000 rebels of all
ethnic strains eventually drove out the hated visitor.
In what resembled a truly national movement, Berbeo
and his men approached the audiencia of Bogotá and

demanded essentially three things. These were: 1) the removal of the audiencia's unpopular regent; 2) abolition of the new tobacco rates and the scaling down of various other taxes; and 3) full participation by creoles in the public functions of government. To all this the audiencia hastily agreed on June 7, through the mediation of Archbishop Caballero y Góngora, and which became known as the pact of Zipaquirá. The rebels thereafter dispersed, but the government later reneged on the terms, claiming that the pact had been extracted by force. Thus the flames of rebellion were fanned anew, and a more extreme leader emerged, José Antonio Galán, who had refused to accept the pact in the first place. He directed his efforts mainly north of Bogotá; but excesses committed by his Indian following as well as the arrival of fresh troops from the viceroy turned the scales against him by the fall of 1781, and he was captured and shot in February the following year. After a reign of terror by the avenging audiencia -- with many a rebel head stuck on pikes just as a reminder -- the weary Flores was recalled, and it was left to the next viceroy, Archbishop Caballero y Góngora mentioned above, to bring about peace and stability to the region.

Under the archbishop's wise rule, the last years of Charles' reign ended here on a happier note. A keen supporter of the sciences, the viceroy founded mathematics chairs, expanded colleges, and organized the botanical expedition of José Celestino Mútis. The trail blazed by the latter and his companions was followed by the visit of the famed mineralogist, José d'Elhuyar. With relatives such as Fausto he had been commissioned in 1780 to conduct mining missions designed to give Spanish America the benefit of technical improvements in refining silver and gold by amalgamation with mercury.[12] The Elhuyar family did much to foster metal studies in New Granada as well as in Mexico, where Fausto, incidentally, became director-general of the mining court in the 1780's.

In considering the total perspective of Charles' reign in the complex Indies, it should first be noted that Spain was fighting England on many fronts, which considerably taxed her resources as well as drawing attention away from Indian problems. On this account the government in Madrid cannot be blamed exactly for all the excesses committed on both sides. Granted Spain's successes in this war, it was with military strategy, trade and colonization where Charles scored highest marks, rather than with social change. Yet even here the record was good in terms of what he tried to do in peacetime, which was to make the Indies prosperous and purged of as many abuses as possible. In the long view his record was less successful, but this was due more to Spain's subsequent decline and the faults of administrators than to anything inherently wrong with the policy he imposed.

In regard to matters affecting creoles, Charles sought to further imperial unity by promoting Spaniards to high office, regardless in theory of class or continental origins. For this purpose, it was previous experience in the empire, not purchased local offices, which would serve as the prerequisite for promotion. Peninsulares and creoles, hopefully working in harmony, could thus advance their careers in an ascending rotation of appointments and compete for the highest offices based on merit. There were variations from this ideal, as with intendants for example, who were nearly all Spaniards from Spain, but many of the subdelegates were creoles; while the appointment of Juan de Vértiz as a Mexican, who became viceroy of Río de la Plata, or of Ambrosio O'Higgins, an Irish-Chilean who became viceroy of Peru, shows that there was no bar to a non-peninsular representing the King's highest mandate in the New World.

Yet in fact there was a certain bias in favor of home-born Spaniards. It was an attitude born of the circumstances of the time, in which Europe was the center of the Western world, and Spain still an important part of this center. Charles and his ministers held the implied view that since the ratio of educated males between Spain and the Indies was nearly three to one (given a population in Spain of just over eight million and a creole population in the Indies of just under three million), it was natural that the majority of senior appointments anywhere in the empire would fall to peninsulares. Creoles, moreover, if visitors' reports meant anything, were not inclined to govern

235

impartially. Yet Floridablanca and Campomanes favored
attracting creoles to the peninsula for their training,
giving them church or chancery posts in Spain while
sending skilled penínsulares to the Indies for the
senior offices.13  Charles agreed with this in principle, but was also influenced by the arguments of
Gálvez and Father Eleta in favoring the three-to-one
ratio rather strictly -- i.e., limiting the creole
share of bishopric, chancery and other posts in the
empire to one third, sometimes to less than a third
among audiencia posts, while reserving for surplus
creoles the new viceroyalty and audiencia appointments
in La Plata and Cuzco respectively.

Such a policy was bound to ruffle creole feelings.
With many estates mortgaged up to the hilt, with big
business largely in the hands of peninsulares, and
with army commissions rarely offered above the rank
of colonel, creoles had only the meager jobs in law or
the church to look forward to as careers, unless they
competed for government posts.  Even here the plums
of high social office were only too often elusive.
Under these circumstances, many a young aspiring creole
-- and this might include peninsular Spaniards as well
-- would seek to marry into a local landed family, as
in Chile for example, thus adding to the elite of
colonial society.14  Such a lucky entrée would eliminate
the need for prior service elsewhere; and to the extent
that the government's insistence on this point was
taken by creoles to be discriminatory, or at least
a burden, resentment was felt in colonies as far apart
as Mexico and New Granada.

Yet Charles' policy becomes more understandable
when the precise nature of creole objection is more
closely considered.  What colonials wanted most of
all was not necessarily the highest jobs in church
and state, but rather a chance to be promoted in their
own native region.  A creole would thus be indifferent
as to whether it was a peninsular or a Spanish-American
from another part of the Indies who enjoyed the higher
post above him, the resentment would be equal in
either case.  Imperial strategists countered this
view by holding that local appointments to the higher
offices in the same region could lead to a native

resident developing a vested interest in his post --
through intermarriage with the local elite, through
bribery and nepotism, and no less applying to a peninsular if he stayed too long in one place -- thus
thwarting the very purpose for which imperial administration was designed. Only through the widest
spread of appointive responsibility could subjects
of the empire, it was felt, develop a true sense of
belonging.

In examining this point of view, it is worth
taking a brief look at the ratio of appointments
between creole and peninsular in audiencia positions
under Charles' rule. The picture least favorable to
creoles, perhaps, can be seen in the Mexico audiencia,
where between 1779 and 1789 membership in its sixteen-
man team consisting of regent, dean, nine oidores,
and five criminal judges included only four creoles.
There was thus a disparity of four to one, though it
is worth mentioning that the senior post of regent
was finally won by a creole, and that out of eight
titles of mining nobility created by Charles in this
country, five were awarded to creoles as against three
to peninsulares.[15] In Peru, by contrast, the picture
in Charles' reign was brighter. In 1779 (following
the dismissal of four creole judges in the Lima audiencia deemed incompetent in a report sent by Areche
to Gálvez), the ratio among the sixteen members stood
at seven creoles against nine peninsulares; but by
1787, when the audiencia membership had been reduced
from sixteen to twelve, there were seven creoles
against five peninsulares.[16] What Peruvians in any
case were demanding was not a monopoly of all offices
by nationals, but a one third to one half allocation
of senior posts among the judgeships, cabildos, and
the military. In this respect they were less insistent than the Mexicans, who in the name of loyalty to
the Spanish crown would have liked to push the Europeans
out altogether. Yet if demands were rising for national control over local affairs -- and this was a legitimate grievance -- the charge that the King himself
discriminated against creoles just because they were
creoles seems to carry little weight. Peninsulares
themselves were also under fire because of their
entrenched monopolies, for Charles with his new policies

sought to strike at the roots of medieval privilege, regardless of the ethnic background of those who exercised it.

The chief spokesman for the imperial strategy was of course Gálvez, "with his knowledge, experience, and devotion to the present ministry of the Indies", as Charles was prompted to note, "in whom I have the highest satisfaction".[17] Yet creoles must have hated him as they saw in his peninsular appointments a threat to their own participation in government. The very nepotism he accused them of he himself indulged in, for his brother Miguel became envoy to Russia, another brother Matías was a president in Guatemala, while his nephew Bernardo (Matías' son) became governor of New Orleans, who as we shall see, played a brilliant role in the war of American Independence. Yet here again there are exonerating circumstances where Charles' position was concerned. The King needed a tough and able leader who could build up a strong defensive position and increase the royal revenues for this purpose. Only then could Charles tread on safe ground in any war situation with England which he regarded as inevitable. Gálvez supplied this need, and his reforms were to pay off handsomely when this war began. Perhaps it would be fairer to say that Gálvez was not so much anti-creole as anti-anybody who didn't come from Andalusia. He had many enemies in Spain also, not least of them being the circle around Martín de Mayorga, viceroy of Mexico from 1779 to 1784, whom he treated with undeserved contempt and whose appointment by a chance of fate he failed to prevent before Matías and Bernardo de Gálvez became successively the later viceroys of this kingdom.

Criticism of Galvez, justified as much of it is, should not obscure his otherwise great achievements. His increase of revenue to the crown in Mexico, his creation of the northern commandancy there, his part in the creation of Río de la Plata, his great free trade regulation of 1778, and his role in the intendancies were all important features of the new administration. Under his ministry the royal coffers were not wanting in funds.[18]

238

Yet Gálvez did not succeed in everything. In later life he failed, for example, to reduce permanently the power of the viceroys. One of the key measures set forth in the ordinances to the colonies was the appointment of a royal treasury superintendent, senior to the intendants and empowered to take treasury responsibility away from the viceroys. The latter strongly resented such a policy, for although they were burdened by many tasks already, they had long seen in Gálvez, with his fondness for ordinances, a challenge to their power. The new official was to be assisted in each viceroyalty by the audiencia regent and a fiscal, replacing a broader junta which had included members from the mint, audit, customs and tribute authorities as an alternative to an earlier secretariat existing before 1780. Either way, it was the viceroys who had dominated them. Gálvez now briefly changed all this, the last new official sent abroad being one posted to Mexico in 1786. The viceroys, shorn of money powers, were thus reduced to a shadow of their former selves. Yet Gálvez' death on June 17, 1787, give the conservative-traditionalists the chance they were waiting for; and the royal treasury officials were recalled one by one, the last of them being withdrawn from Buenos Aires in May 1788.

The surviving juntas became staffed by older men more in keeping with the conservative spirit. Feeling they were dragging their feet, viceroys like Croix of Peru and the Cuban-born Revilla Gigedo of Mexico, while opposing many features of the intendancies, became well attuned to the new mood of efficiency. Indeed Revilla Gigedo, friend of Floridablanca and perhaps the greatest economic thinker sent out by the Bourbons, looked upon his junta as the source of all evil in New Spain after he took office in 1789.

Many viceroys thus became the very reformers whose power Gálvez had tried to check; conversely, many bureaucrats whom he had appointed slipped back into the old ways. Unwittingly he had allowed his policy to strain the existing mechanism of government. A further example of this can be seen in the dilution of the audiencias' judicial powers, whose control over such agencies as excise, the mails, courts of audit, and the mining guild became weakened by exemption privileges (*fueros*) from ordinary courts of law enjoyed by many of the new bureaucrats. The military in particular, whether peninsular or creole, had so many fueros that despite its patriotism almost seemed to lose respect for the law itself. Audiencias in fact became less able to protect society in matters of contentious litigation, and this was a morally weakening factor. The result of all these changes was a recovery of viceregal power, but at the same time there was an increase of jurisdictional confusion between intendants, juntas, and audiencias, and this obscured the more positive aspects of Charles' reorganization program.

There are indications that in these later years the coteries in council circles were as sharply divided as ever. Floridablanca as the minister in power clearly supported most of the reforms and appointments, but the hand of Aranda can also be seen, with his close ties to conservatives. While each differed in many aspects of foreign policy, they together appreciated Gálvez' constructive work, but here their common ground with him as a reformer ended. Both men in varying degrees felt that his arrogation of power could only accelerate the currents of discontent since the King began his reforms in the 1760's. Aranda was perhaps the most pro-American of all Charles' ministers. Outspoken as he was, he clearly saw the dangers, and he later suggested dividing Spanish America into three great sub-monarchies each ruled by a Bourbon relative, an impractical idea which Charles rejected. In his letters to the Prince of Asturias written during the American war, Aranda argued that the King could get to know the Indies better once its affairs were relayed directly to the five corresponding ministries (State, treasury, war, navy and justice), and pleaded for more consultation on behalf of his American subjects. Mistakes could be avoided if the Indies council's laws were brought up to date, and the best reformers sought after. For every good administrator there were a hundred bad ones, weakening the overseas foundations on which Spain's power rested. Creoles coming to Spain for careers, Aranda continued, were treated like natives, despite their right to as

much protection by the crown as European Spaniards
enjoy, with the result that they return home sufficiently disgruntled to foment future revolution.[19]

Prophetic words indeed. As if in response to
criticism from Aranda and his circle, the very bastion
which had made all these changes possible -- the ministry of the Indies -- came under political fire in
July 1787, one month after Gálvez' death. With old
scores to pay off against the memory of the man who
had held it for a decade, conservatives pulled the
centralists with them and broke up this office by
dividing it into two halves -- one for grace and justice headed by Antonio Porlier, the other for war and
finance headed by Antonio Valdés.[20] Three years later,
the colonial secretariats which had already eclipsed
the old House of Trade at Seville were dismantled
altogether and distributed among the five regular
ministries. The council of the Indies, or what was
left of it, was the only remaining body concerned exclusively with the Americas, but it now had merely
consultative, judicial, and fiscal duties.

Indian affairs as well as church appointments
came under Porlier's department, and these were handled more efficiently. But though the Indian himself
had been the cause of so much change, it is doubtful
if these late developments could change him much
further. The feeling seemed to be growing that he
would one day count among rational adults and that
at least he should pay his alcabala tax when engaged
in trade; but he was still otherwise exempt from a
wide range of obligations. As for his tribute, this
was now collected by ordinary town officials instead
of defunct corregidores, whose evil deeds were fast
passing into legend. In other respects, as we have
seen, there was considerable curtailment of the mita
and repartimiento practices, and the latter was still
the subject of heated debate, Revilla Gigedo holding
that the best way out of the difficulty was to abolish
the practice altogether and pay subdelegates a living
wage. Yet it was symptomatic of the times that the
Indian's welfare became increasingly the focus of
attention by conservatives and centralists alike, who
saw in his progress the guidelines for the progress
of all. His feudal chains had at last been loosened,

from Louisiana to Peru; and the best that can be said is that, while Charles personally was always mindful of his role as protector of the Indian -- the case of Pedro de Avila as director of the Prado comes to mind -- the age had not yet dawned when he could be fully incorporated into contemporary society. Spain was a long way from the Indies, and the government's instinctive concern for his betterment, as Great Britain's in regard to the North American Indian, was continually thwarted by encroaching settlers.

As for Charles' subjects in general, the Spanish presence must have given them some sense of security against further disturbance. But with many still cherishing the earlier days, when the church, perhaps, was less powerful as a landowner and mortgagee, and when sale of appointments, a longer tenure of office, and the right of officials to freely engage in trade were unchallenged practices, Charles' success in winning over the general public seems all the more remarkable.

The answer largely lies in the increasing prosperity at hand. There was an enormous growth of commerce which the great free trade regulation of 1778 did much to foster. This filtered down to local levels so that more creoles, along with mestizos and Indians, had a greater chance to share in the economy. Even cabildos now had more funds available, as from Mexico to Buenos Aires they felt a new sense of direction, many of them becoming strong bastions against foreign attack. In overall terms, there was an increase in population and skills on both sides of the Atlantic. Horizons were expanded and the Americas became more important as a protected market for Spanish industry. To the tobacco, sugar, cocoa, and tropical fruits of the Caribbean, to the wheat of California and the livestock of La Plata, to native industries like leather goods and furniture, can be added all the cotton transformed into finished textiles exported back from Spain; while a host of other Spanish exports included wine, oil, iron goods, and mercury from Almadén.[21]

Another promising feature was the remarkable growth in Mexican silver production. This outflow

242

might have brought disadvantages to Spain as in former times, impairing local resources; but she was now a developing country as trade continued to advance as far as China via Acapulco and Manila, and the precious supportive metal flooded the world's markets. Thus the silver piaster, the gold piece of eight, remained the world's international currency. Though Spain was simply too small to supply all the needs of an expanding American market, where colonial consulados not unnaturally began to feel less dependent on the mother country, yet the overall volume of goods and services soared within the empire, approximating to a four-fold growth where Spanish exports were concerned. These increased to the Americas from a mere one-eighth of the total in 1700 to about one half of the total in 1788, by which date their export value reached 300 million reales -- a figure which had jumped thereto from a mere 75 million reales ten years earlier. This impressive growth was capped when measuring the total value the other way round -- from Spanish America to Spain -- which reached nearly 800 million reales by the end of Charles' reign.[22] Only the mother country's need for increased funds with which to meet the empire's rising costs kept the colonies from reaching their maximum potential in terms of net gain in trade.

Yet economic progress and political strategy were helping to bind the empire closer together; and though the seeds of revolution were being laid everywhere in the eighteenth century, we must judge a monarch's work in relation to his own age. Seen in this relationship, Charles' reforms had a revoluntionary life-cycle all their own. Monopoly privilege had been curbed to make room for smaller merchants, creole and Indian reconciled to his regime, and a higher standard of justice, honesty and efficiency enforced by his intendants. Economic dispersal and political centralism had both been squared. Seen beyond this relationship, perhaps the root cause of the empire's final collapse was due to the collapse of the monarchy itself, which lost its force as a unifying principle during the Napoleonic wars.

But all this lay ahead.  At the time of the
American war, the monarchy was strong; and Charles'
triumphs here were to outshine the unknown future
and leave a final mark on world events.  In the
overall context, then, of his legacy to the Indies,
it was in defense, commerce, and imperial expansion
where his efforts shone brightest.  Deeper social
issues were to await another day.  As for his subjects, if they were holding the frontiers of the
Spanish seas for the last time -- and the gulf of
Mexico was to be indisputably a Spanish lake once
more -- they were opening new frontiers on land for
the first.  Everywhere there were signs of coming
vitality and prosperity.  The age had not yet dawned
when intendants from the peninsula were to provoke
successful movements against the mother country that
sent them.  From California to Patagonia the empire
reached its maximum extent in the New World and
glowed with a veritable Indian summer of glory.

Conde de Aranda, artist unknown

# CHAPTER TWELVE

THE SHOWDOWN WITH ENGLAND

Anyone surveying the vast course of the Mississippi river back in the 1760's might have reasoned that sooner or later England and Spain would be locked in mortal combat for mastery in North America. Charles had been forced to concede that the continent east of this river now belonged to England; he was determined not to yield sovereignty west of it.  The peace of Paris in 1763 had settled nothing permanently, the wrangling continued, and just as Choiseul and Grimaldi thirsted for revenge against England, so now it was to be the French minister Vergennes and his Spanish partners who were to work together for the same end.  Yet the crisis when it came caught everyone by surprise.  That it was the English colonists themselves who were in revolt against their own mother country shook Europe to its roots, but it nonetheless gave the Bourbon powers the vital chance they were seeking.

Where Spain was concerned, the first inkling that something was afoot came not from England's thirteen colonies on the Atlantic seaboard, but rather from those in Canada, and then only in a loose sense of resentment felt there against big monopolies.[1] The last thing Charles wanted was trouble above the Mississippi region which might bring on British reinforcements, hence British expansion, to the north of his dominions.  Resentment against privileged companies, moreover, was a painful reminder that all was not well in this regard throughout his own empire, and indeed this was an underlying cause, among others, for the American Revolution itself.

Whatever the foremost cause of this great explosion, he sensed that discontent was rife, if unable to pinpoint exactly where the problem lay.  And when the Boston Tea Party aboard the East India company's ship led to open conflict, Charles was not so much delighted at the harassment of his old enemy as disturbed by his own dilemma: how could he help the great rebellion against this enemy without in the long run fanning the flames of similar rebellions

245

against himself? The rumble of discontent in his own
empire, as we have seen, was an ominous sign of things
to come. Yet if he gave no aid at all and the Americans won, almost certainly with the help of France,
then these powers would profit at Spain's expense.
On the other hand, if the British won, then the position of England (and also of Russia if she joined her)
would be immeasurably strengthened throughout the
whole continent.

Charles' initial reaction, then, was to try to
isolate the disturbance and ward off its effects
elsewhere. But his efforts were short-lived; for as
the storm gathered momentum, culminating in the Declaration of Independence and the British defeat at
Saratoga the following year, the French were becoming
ever more enthusiastic to come in on the American
side. Charles was not in the least disposed to have
his French ally back again on the Mississippi; and
his fears sharpened lest the war involve other powers,
including his own. Prepared as Spain was, he was
not nearly so keen for another full-scale conflict,
as unlike France he had much more to lose.

Two rival policies at this stage were evident
in the Bourbon camp. The 'hawks' were led by Vergennes who slowly won over Louis XVI, the new French
king since 1774. Vergennes had ample backing from
Aranda, the Spanish envoy at Versailles, and from
José de Gálvez, minister of the Indies in Madrid.
In varying degrees they were impressed by the appeals
of such representatives of the Congress at Philadelphia
as Benjamin Franklin, Silas Deane, and Arthur Lee,
during their visits to Europe to get support. The
'doves' were led by comptroller-general Turgot in
France and Floridablanca in Spain, and who like Charles
himself advocated a policy of 'wait-and-see'in the
hope that the British Empire would tear itself to
pieces. Even before the battle of Saratoga, the
hawks had taken the initiative when Aranda passed
on to Madrid urgent French requests for armed cooperation in the Caribbean and for financial aid to
the American insurgents. Gálvez accordingly was
instructed to send eight thousand reinforcements to
the garrisons at Havana, Vera Cruz, and Campeche,
and to put the fleet on the alert; but the question

of financial aid was somewhat tricky if trouble with the British was to be avoided.[2]

France had already sent supply credits worth a million livres (about 43,000 pounds sterling) to the Continental Congress. This was done by merchant Caron de Beaumarchais who was working hand-in-glove with Vergennes. Spain then devised a subterfuge in August 1776 whereby Aranda deposited an equal sum in the French treasury, passing on the receipt to Vergennes who promptly issued a letter of credit made payable to the order of Beaumarchais.[3] Spanish involvement was thus completely hidden in what appeared on the surface as a purely French internal transaction. This not only helped enormously to finance much of the French fleet; it also contributed a great deal to American victories themselves -- an indirect debt which perhaps has never been sufficiently acknowledged.

American overtures to Madrid, meanwhile, were also meeting with some success. What Benjamin Franklin and Silas Deane were to accomplish in France, Arthur Lee was to do in Spain when he visited this country in 1777. A distinguished Virginian who had been to Eton and the university of Edinburgh -- though somewhat less distinguished in letting down his old school -- Lee asked for all-out aid against his British enemy, and he duly met Grimaldi at Burgos in March of this year. Everything was asked for, from equipment to money itself, and credits were duly granted through the services of a merchant from Bilbao, Diego de Gardoqui.[4] Lee nonetheless had a rough time in Spain. The Old Etonian from the New World, with more than a touch of Anglo-Saxon condescension, openly complained of harassment by the many fleas and bugs with which Spanish inns were infested; and he was aggravated further by being told to keep away from Madrid and get out of Spain as soon as possible lest the British get wind of what the Spanish were doing. His place as representative of the Continental Congress was subsequently taken by Silas Deane, and then John Jay, but his work had not been in vain, and he was soon to play an important role in finally bringing Spain into the war.

247

Grimaldi, now retired, was succeeded by Floridablanca, and it was during this time that there shaped
in Charles' mind the idea of offering himself as me-
diator in the American conflict. A grateful George III
would then be able to retain some tenuous link with
his rebellious colonies; Spain would be in a position
to influence the newly emergent States diplomatically
and economically; and a grateful world at large would
undertake to return to rightful Spanish ownership
such places as Gibraltar, Minorca, and Florida --
a highly optimistic but not unreasonable course of
action as it seemed at the time. The moderate Floridablanca took the view, unlike Vergennes and Aranda who
were calling for an outright alliance with the Americans, that in the event of any British attack, the
combined Franco-Spanish fleets could deal with it,
but that a concerted strategy need not draw Spain
right into the war; rather the policy should be defensive in character. Reflecting his sovereign's
line of thought, the chief minister in a subsequent
memorandum held that Spain could certainly benefit
by mediating the conflict; but cautioned that although the Americans might be persuaded to support
her re-occupation of Florida in exchange for all
the aid given them and who could be helped in fram-
ing their new government, yet the combined strength
of their States might one day eclipse, even threaten
Spanish America, and that the best course to pursue
was to encourage a separatist feeling among them in
respect of one another.[5]

Events were moving swiftly however, for on
February 6, 1778, with a Patriot victory looming
distinctly nearer as a possibility, France without
waiting for Spain signed a treaty of commerce and
alliance with the Americans by which London would
be required to recognize the complete independence
of the United States. Deeply disturbed by the French
actions -- Louis XVI, after all, was junior to himself as head of the Bourbon family -- Charles sounded
out the views of Floridablanca and Gálvez, in which
the chief minister still clung to moderation, warning that to involve Spain was premature so long as
the full terms of the Franco-American alliance were
not made known to his government. Gálvez by contrast, continued to be the most forthright in

proposing aggressive action. In the spring of 1778, meanwhile, Lord Stormont, the British ambassador to France, received his passport, and in the summer France formally declared war on England.

These unilateral actions by the French undoubtedly reflected their impatience with Spanish procrastination. The new French ambassador to Spain, Comte de Montmorin who had replaced the aging Prince Ossun, told Floridablanca in no uncertain terms that His Catholic Majesty should follow the action of His Christian Majesty King Louis in supporting the historic Family Compact -- an attitude which the Spanish government deeply resented in the light of past disasters suffered in its name. To Montmorin's insistence on united action, Floridablanca evasively replied that the Indies treasure fleet, including one convoy from Buenos Aires, had not yet arrived and that it would be folly to expose such cargo needlessly to enemy attack. The truth behind Spanish evasion was simply, that much as Charles was fond of his devoted 'nephew' at Versailles, and much as his country was in fact prepared, the French action had considerably set back his hopes to mediate the American war.

Foiled in his objective by France, Charles next turned his attention to England. He was similarly doomed to disappointment. The question of the return of Gibraltar was raised, which had been in British hands since 1704, but on point of honor Charles could not agree to enter the war on England's side as the price for its recovery, any more than the British at this stage were willing to return it as the price for Spain's neutrality. Despite chords of response from London here and there, the war of American Independence by 1778 was monopolizing all attention as it now escalated into a full-scale land operation, far larger than the British government had expected; and however friendly George III may have felt towards the Spanish king, London's olive branch to the Americans in the form of Lord North's Conciliatory Propositions failed to achieve its purpose. The war thus went on. King George's friends in fact were fighting with their backs to the wall not merely vis-à-vis the Patriots in America, but many opponents at home, from William Pitt, Edmund

Burke, and Charles James Fox, to aristocratic peers like Richmond and Rockingham. But with the Whigs in Parliament also in disarray, it was not surprising that the new Spanish ambassador in London, the Duke of Almodóvar, could get nowhere in proposing on behalf of his sovereign that the British make a temporary truce with the Americans and the French.

Floridablanca, obedient to his instructions meanwhile, continued to convey to France and England various proposals for mediation which each court could modify to the satisfaction of all parties concerned.[6] But he was soon informed by the British ambassador in Madrid, Lord Grantham, that this was impossible so long as France kept sending troops to North America; and Grantham then informed Lord Weymouth (temporary secretary of state in London ) that Charles and Floridablanca believed the stumbling-block to French withdrawal was the escalating war, and that once a truce was made between Britain and her colonies, then a truce could easily follow between Britain and France.[7]

With no progress being made at all on the mediation issue -- the war raged on in America as both the seceding colonies and France determined to bring it to a successful conclusion -- the attitude of Charles began to harden towards England. Nonetheless he instructed Floridablanca to make one last try at seeking some acceptable formula. Accordingly in the spring of 1779, the Spanish government informed Lord Grantham of a final offer of mediation. There should be an indefinite suspension of hostilities (originally proposed as extending up to twenty-five years), not to be broken without a year's notice on any side, and followed by a multilateral disarmament; within thirty days, peace negotiations were to begin covering such disputes as the exact status of the separated colonies, restitutions, compensations for prizes etc., for which purpose the King of Spain was willing to offer Madrid as the place of meeting. The Spanish government would guarantee whatever was settled with only the precondition that a 'yes' or 'no' be immediately given to these proposals by the British government.

Commendable as Charles' efforts were, they came at the wrong time. Neither England, much less France or the United States, with the war's outcome still hanging in the balance, were in the least disposed to come to Madrid for an international conference to discuss terms for a compromise truce. As the King saw Gibraltar and Minorca slipping through his fingers, he began to listen to the hawks of France; and by the early summer the British government received wordy complaints delivered by Almodóvar to Weymouth of various incidents suffered by the Spaniards at the hands of the English in Honduras and along the Mississippi. With Britain in her plight giving evasive replies, Almodóvar was instructed to formally withdraw his sovereign's mediation offer, "His Most Catholic Majesty having done everything he could to conform to his earnest desire of serving mankind".[8] To which Lord Weymouth added curtly "I have nothing to add to the subject".

The impasse was such that Charles by now had become thoroughly frustrated, and in May, with Gálvez triumphantly present, he affirmed his adhesion to an agreement with Louis XVI worked out by Montmorin and Floridablanca the previous month. By its terms, the following objectives were to be pursued jointly by France and Spain: affirmation of the Family Compact; capture of Newfoundland by France; defense of the French-held islands of Haiti and Dominica; abrogation of all trade concessions given to Britain at the treaty of Utrecht; recovery of Gibraltar and Minorca; recovery of Florida; revocation of the 1763 logwood-cutting agreement with Britain in Honduras; expulsion of the British from Mosquitía in Guatemala; Spanish support for the Franco-American treaty of commerce and alliance signed on February 6, 1778; and independence of the United States.[9]

Charles' growing decision to go to war with England was finally clinched by none other than Arthur Lee, who in a forceful memorandum of June 7, 1779, addressed to the Spanish government, called for Spain to end neutrality, commence hostilities with England, and openly espouse the cause of American independence. Spain could protect her lifelines of commerce with well-armed convoys, for which purpose

the French navy could close the Channel and the
Spanish navy could close the straits of Gibraltar,
thus bottling in the enemy. A few days after
studying Lee's memorandum, Charles instructed his
government to declare war on England, and this was
done on June 16, 1779. The American theatre of
operations will be considered first.

Impressed as he was with Lee's arguments, the
King had no intention of making a formal alliance
with the United States; this would have made a
mockery of his own imperial position. Instead he
opted to give them all-out aid short of actual
troops -- a policy that had the effect of preserving the dignity of monarchy while at the same time
delivering heavy blows against the common enemy.
His aim was to clear the lower Mississippi valley,
and recapture Florida and Honduras together with
any adjoining territory where the British had intruded, along with Gibraltar and Minorca in Europe.
He might have achieved all these objectives if his
empire did not have one big weakness -- Spain's
coasts were dangerously exposed to British attack,
while supply-lines across the Atlantic could all
too easily be cut by an aggressive British fleet.
But this maritime weakness showed up less where
America was concerned. By agreement with Louis XVI,
joint Bourbon commands were to be put under a Frenchman in Europe, under a Spaniard in the Caribbean,
and in the latter respect Charles had confidence
in men like Bernardo de Gálvez, governor of New
Orleans and José's nephew, who foremost among
Spanish commanders was to win distinguished honors
for his country.

Granted that the Bourbon powers did not always
see eye to eye and that there was insufficient liason
with the Americans, the British for their part had
weaknessess too: thanks to poor diplomacy they were
fighting without a single ally. In the Caribbean,
moreover, Spanish and French bases lying leeward
to the Antilles considerably outnumbered the enemy's.
The only good British naval repair base was at
New York, and this so remained till the end of the
war. Getting to the West Indies at all was a formidable task in the days of sail. British ships

took a westbound route from Europe at a lower latitude than along which they returned, and this put
them in the trade wind envelope and exposed them
to enemy attack. The British main port of call was
Barbados, just as Havana was to the Spanish. Here
the convoy would split up, one part going to the
Windward Islands (protected en route by the British
equivalent of the *Armada de Barlovento*), the other to
Jamaica. The difficulty here was the near-impossi-
bility of the Jamaica fleet sailing eastwards to
join the Windward convoy because of the strong north-
easterly wind. British ships from the Windward convoy could sail from St. Kitts back to Europe along
the west wind route, but ships from Jamaica had to
run the gauntlet of the Spanish patrols in the Gulf
stream and the strait of Yucatán before they could
veer round and pick up the west wind route for
home. Under these circumstances, with their widely
dispersed toeholds in the West Indies, the British
were at a disadvantage aginst the vigilant Spanish
and French vessels, whose superior windward position
could harass their men-of-war desperately needing
repair so as to miss the hurricane season between
July and October.[10]

In view also of Spain's good strategic position
in the gulf of Texas region, it was not surprising
that things went well from the start. As early as
1777, governor Bernardo de Gálvez impounded British
cargoes in the Iberville part of the Mississippi,
imprisoned the crew, and then expelled British
traders from New Orleans altogether.[11] All of this
drew sharp protests from their consul, Thomas Lloyd,
especially when the governor gave sanctuary to American privateers. More tangibly, Gálvez gave the
Americans considerable aid short of actually sending
troops -- a policy begun by his predecessor Luis de
Unzaga, who secretly supplied the Patriot forces
which had enabled them successfully to hold off
Loyalist assaults at Forts Pitt and Wheeling. Gálvez
now authorized an American agent by the name of
Oliver Pollock to receive the equivalent of $70,000
for materiel to be despatched to the Virginia command,
and to the army of General George Rogers Clark who
was fighting further west. Here over a thousand-
miles stretch from the Ohio and Illinois countries

and along the Mississippi, Clark stormed many a Loyalist outpost in a way he could never have done without Spanish aid and relying on support from Virginia alone. The Spanish outpost of St. Louis on the Missouri river, moreover, which Unzaga had fortified against British fur traders coming down from the Great Lakes, now acted as a base for Americans supplied from New Orleans, whither arms and provisions of all kinds -- guns, powder and shot, uniforms, corn and vegetables -- began to flow in from such ports as Havana and Vera Cruz.[12]

The entry of Spain into the war in June 1779 gave Bernardo de Gálvez a much freer hand. Gathering his forces, he audaciously proceeded with the plan drawn up by his uncle José and the King to expel the British entirely from the Mississippi valley and the Florida peninsula. The Mississippi part of the plan was achieved with relatively little resistance. By August, with Baton Rouge and Natchez fully fortified, some two thousand men were sweeping the lower part of the valley clear of enemy troops. While this offensive was under way, another Spanish expedition struck at a higher latitude, destroying British stores as far north as Fort St. Joseph on Lake Michigan which forced Britain's Indian allies there to remain neutral. By the end of the year 1,200 miles of territory extending from the Great Lakes to the gulf of Texas had been cleared of the enemy, while many a Patriot refugee from Georgia was given welcome asylum.

Successes, meanwhile, attended Spanish arms elsewhere. There was fighting in Central America where the British had been trying to enlarge their toeholds upon the audiencia of Guatemala (which included Honduras and all this part of the Hemisphere except Panama), and whose president was Matías de Gálvez, Bernardo's aging father. Since the seventeenth century, Britons had been encroaching below Campeche and Yucatán and into Honduras along the Hondo and Mosquito rivers mainly for log cutting and dye extraction purposes. Their sphere of penetration was vaguely defined at the treaty of Paris in 1763, but they were not to militarize their forts or strike deeper into Guatemala; in fact they were threatening to do both. They had also occupied the

islands in the bay of Honduras -- a task made easier
by the abandonment of Trujillo on the part of Spaniards who had given up trying to evangelize the
fierce Mosquito Indians of the interior. But Spaniards had since built a nearby fort called San Fernando de Omoa; and after war was declared had driven
out the British settlers from the bay of Honduras in
September 1779. Though the English under Major Dalrymple and Captain Luttrell captured Omoa the following month, the Spaniards retook it soon after, and
throughout 1780 good tidings from Central America
reached Charles' court.

This was especially so in Nicaragua. Here an
ambitious British plan got under way to strike at
Fort Immaculada on the upper reaches of the San Juan
river. The fort was not far from Lake Nicaragua,
which guarded the approaches to the rich city of
Granada. Capture of this city, together with León,
would have the effect of cutting Spanish communications across the Guatemalan province. In charge of
the operation was a young naval officer by the name
of Horatio Nelson, of future immortal fame, who had
already been to the Arctic and had served with distinction under Sir Peter Parker. Setting out from
San Juan del Norte in the fall of 1780 and striking
up-river towards Lake Nicaragua, Nelson and his brave
six hundred men, armed with pistol and cutlass, pushed
stubbornly forward. But they were greeted with tor-
rential rains and mud, decaying leaves and vegetation,
not to mention the snakes which hung ominously from
the trees, and equally annoying Mosquito Indians who
were no more eager to join with the British than they
were with the Spanish. Though Nelson and his men captured the fort, yellow fever then decimated their
ranks, and the whole venture had to be abandoned.[13]

"Praise God I have received the best news from
the Indies as one could expect, my commanders having
recaptured Omoa and expelled the English completely
from the coasts of Campeche, destroying all their
settlements... "[14] Thus did the King relate the
happy events in Honduras to his old friend Bernardo
Tanucci. Now eighty-two years of age and living in
dignified limbo since his downfall at the court of
Naples in 1776, the grand statesman was still on hand

255

to extract good tidings from Charles' voluminous
letters and pass them on to Ferdinand and his Span-
ish-hating consort. Tanucci's days may have been
numbered, but there was still a bond between himself
and his former master, the loyalty of the one matched
by kingly understanding of the other that fellow
mortals besides exchanging memories of bygone days
could also, while there was life, serve a common plan
-- the plan of serving Spanish Bourbon interests.
On top of this came exciting news of the English
debacle in Nicaragua. This too Charles relayed to
Tanucci, unable to forsee the irony whereby the same
court of Naples was one day to be linked, via Lady
Hamilton, with the name of Nelson himself: "My
troops have captured the forts which the English
held among the Mosquitía Indians ... thus implementing the previous peace treaty (1763) accounting for
the many prisoners ... taken at Fort San Juan del
Norte and despatched in safety to Vera Cruz ..."[15]
Nelson, ill with fever, was invalided home.

Minor as these successes were in Central America,
greater victories were forthcoming in Florida, and
the capture of Pensacola in May 1781 particularly
swelled the royal pride. Following the clearing of
the Mississippi, Bernardo de Gálvez next swung eastwards with nearly a thousand men to strike at the
British outposts in the Floridas. This was the
second part of the plan, a much tougher one to accomplish but which he executed brilliantly. In West
Florida (approximating to the coastal region of present-day Alabama) Mobile had fallen by March 1780,
despite a relieving expedition under Campbell who
arrived on the scene just too late. With Pensacola
as his main objective, Gálvez pushed along the Mobile
river and approached the provincial capital by the
autumn, but heavy rains there postponed the main
attack until the following year. By March 1781 the
governor landed in Pensacola bay. Here he assembled
some five thousand Spaniards and Frenchmen, who successfully eluded the pursuit of Admirals George Rodney
and Sir Peter Parker. After an initial thrust by
Campbell against the lines of the crack Mallorca and
Hibernia regiments (the latter commanded by that
redoubtable Irishman Arturo O'Neil), Gálvez launched

a powerful counter-attack.  A Spanish shell hit and
exploded the British powder magazine and the enemy
key positions were stormed.  Pensacola as a result
fell on May 8, 1781; and within two days Campbell,
Chester the governor, and some eight hundred Britons
were taken prisoner.[16]

"I am very pleased to tell you, that I have received word of the capture of Pensacola on May 8,
with all the garrison taken prisoner, as you will
read in the gazette...", the King wrote to Tanucci
at this important Spanish victory; and the following
month he went on, "I appreciate all you say about
the capture of Pensacola by Don Bernardo de Gálvez
and by Solano as well as the thanks you have given
to God who always rewards those who ask of Him ..."[17]
Thus Charles continued in jubilant vein, Solano receiving the title of Marqués del Real Socorro for
having brought up vital supplies from Havana, just
as Bernardo's uncle, José, was to be made Marqués de
Sonora later.  We may allow Charles his grounds for
rejoicing.  With West Florida now secured, it was
only a matter of time before the flank was turned
in East Florida (approximating to present-day Florida);
and exactly a year after Pensacola's seizure, a Spanish trust under Manuel de Cajigal, commandant of Havana, assisted by that aspiring liberator, Francisco
de Miranda, temporarily captured New Providence in
the Bahama Islands.  The prestige of Spain shone
brilliantly in the Antilles, and the name of Bernardo
de Gálvez, incidentally, is perpetuated in the Texas
city of Galveston.

In conveying to all that divine providence was
on his side, Charles felt pleased that God was also
favoring the Americans, whose juncture with the French
under Marquis de Lafayette had forced the British into
a corner.  In Chesapeake bay, Virginia, the combined
allies now predominated on land and sea.  At Yorktown on October 19, 1781, the British commander Lord
Cornwallis surrendered to General Washington with
seven thousand men.  The war was virtually over.
By November Charles in familiar style was writing
to Tanucci that he had received the very good news
that the entire body of troops commanded by Lord
'Cornualis' had surrendered and been made prisoners-
of-war.[18]  It was a well-deserved elation, for the

Spanish fleet had played a significant part in
Europe intercepting British convoys trying to help
the crumbling Virginia front.

Where Europe was concerned, Charles was bent
on recovering Gibraltar and Minorca, both of which
places had been given to England (temporarily in
Spanish eyes) by the treaty of Utrecht. Spain's
performance here was perhaps less brilliant than
in America. This was partly due to the shortage
of first-rate commanders; and though successes
were achieved, these were obscured by Charles' own
abortive attempts to win back Gilbraltar, his prime
objective, where he staked all in a supreme effort
after every trick of diplomacy (short of betraying
his French ally) had failed.

Philip V, incidentally, had tried very hard
to do the same thing -- the siege of 1727 was his
biggest effort -- and at other times might have secured it by diplomacy had not his wife Isabel been
only too willing to sacrifice it in order to gain
British support for her designs in Italy, ironically
enough on behalf of Charles himself. Now the mood
was different. One of the first things the King did
upon entering the war against England in June 1779
was to instruct Floridablanca to proceed immediately
with the siege of Gibraltar. Here Conde de Revilla
Gigedo, an able royal adviser and later viceroy of
Mexico, was to lend assistance. About one hundred
and thirty battalions were available, though many
would be needed to defend the coasts which were
highly vulnerable to enemy attack. Great preparations were indeed made. About twenty thousand men
comprising one fourth of all disposable forces were
stationed two miles from the Rock at camps between
San Roque and La Linea, where Martín de Sotomayor
was put in charge. Antonio de Barceló conducted
the naval blockade using fireships and gunboats
armed with rockets, and he also had at his disposal
a number of frigates and smaller craft stationed between Algeciras and Cádiz. Surrounding nations were
successfully made neutral. Charles had already
cemented friendly relations with his niece, Queen
Maria of Portugal, while Sultan Sidi Mohammed of
Morocco granted Spain special commercial privileges

at Tangiers and Tetuan late in 1780, thereby closing important markets to the besieged Gibraltarians.[19]

On the British side the defending governor was Sir George Elliot, a man of incomparable skill and daring, to whom the successful resistance of Gibraltar was primarily due. Supported by a force of nearly six thousand men, Elliot and the inhabitants began to make feverish defense preparations, digging trenches, installing gun batteries, and rationing supplies in anticipation of a long siege.

The Spaniards meanwhile kept on tightening the noose, constructing shell factories nearby, and Barceló at first was able to report considerable progress with his blockade. The British were on tight rations and scurvy became commonplace. So confident was Sotomayor of starving the garrison into surrender in his letters to Floridablanca that Charles promised all-out aid to the besiegers; but he was soon to find out that the historic fortress was a hardier bastion to crack than all the British forts in the Floridas.

Reinforcing his objectives was the general plan worked out with France to sweep the seas clear of British convoys bound for the American front. For these purposes France could count on about sixty ships of the line and thirty-five frigates, while Spain had almost the same armament -- fifty-five ships of the line and thirty frigates -- which together about equalled the enemy's. Of Britain's one hundred and twenty ships of the line, eighty were patroling the high seas, the balance stationed in home waters, which was enough to put Bourbon naval men in a somber and sober mood.[20] It was an axiom of French and Spanish policy that only by working together could the two nations hope to defeat England in time of war.

Spain's navy, nonetheless, was a force to be reckoned with, and its growth deserves some comment. From a figure of almost zero in 1700, its ships of the line had risen to forty half a century later, thanks to the efforts of men like Patiño and Ensenada. But Spanish victories in the Caribbean when England slept under Walpole were more than offset by English victories in the Seven Years war when Spain slept under Ferdinand; and it was Charles who then instructed his ministers to hasten a further build-up of the fleet in order to try to close the gap with Britain. Thus with a figure of nearly sixty ships of the line by 1780, all but ten of them then ready for action, this was a solid achievement and indeed they made an impressive sight. Termed *navíos*, and averaging 170 feet in length by 50 across with gross tonnage up to two thousand, the double-decked giants could command seventy bronze cannon or more, mounted on recoil launches and fired by the traditional powder-and-shot method through the ports. If poor maintenance and not enough skilled training was the curse of the Spanish navy, at least techniques were advancing fast -- bow and poop, for example, were now being built lower to gain more maneuverability at sea, with less array of figureheads in gilded relief which especially adorned the stern. In peacetime navíos were used as escorts protecting the declining convoys across the Atlantic which conveyed emigrants and supplies one way, and bullion the other. Now it was war, and first-hand witnesses testified that, despite defects, they were in no way inferior to British ships as products of craftsmanship.

Spain's single-deck 30-gun frigates averaging one thousand tons were fast and effective as escort fighters, being also based on the latest designs. Similar attention was given to other kinds of craft -- packet-boats, sloops, brigs, cutters, tri-masted xebecs, and rocket launches. Neither were facilities neglected. Shipyards were busy with sail and rigging, foundries with cannon and anchors. Where timber was concerned, both France and Spain had imported much of it from Russia via Baltic ports and were among that country's best customers. The two Bourbon powers now planned a common strategy for an incursion upon England itself; and though Charles' ships played a somewhat passive role in this, their performance by the end of the war was at least more promising than during the previous one.

This incursion -- brainchild of the French though hardly of the Spanish -- turned out feckless in its execution, though not without provoking alarm in southern England, portending the great invasion scare of 1804, and more ominously in the distant future, that of 1940. The idea was to effect a juncture of the French and Spanish fleets and assemble at Le Havre a task force of some fifty thousand men for the expedition.[21] By early August, 1779, all was in readiness. The great armada of sixty-six ships of the line was entrusted to the French admiral Comte d'Orvilliers, assisted by Comte de Guichen, with the Spanish admiral Juan de Córdoba posted in reserve. Of these big ships, some twenty-six were French, twenty-four were attached to d'Orvilliers' command from Córdoba's home fleet at Cádiz, with Córdoba himself in charge of sixteen reserves from Juan de Arce's squadron at Ferrol. France and Spain were thus committing half of their combined Home and Atlantic fleets to the formidable task, when a more sensible policy would have been to attack over a wider area enemy convoys crossing the ocean. It was no secret that Charles himself was lukewarm to the whole idea. Concepts of honor bound him to the French plan, and no doubt he felt relief that a French commander was to bear the responsibility for the whole affair, as agreed upon with Louis XVI for operations in Europe, and not his favorite, the monkish and over-cautious Córdoba.

As for d'Orvilliers, he gave a very poor showing as he sailed along the Channel, allowing convoys under Admiral Keppel's command to slip right through his fingers; neither did he attack Admiral Hardy's ships stationed near Spithead when it was obvious that the latter were heavily outnumbered. A spectacular blow delivered commando-style upon Plymouth or the Isle of Wight, perhaps in Ireland, would have raised the morale of the Bourbon forces, as in the great days of the Dutch when in 1667 they boldly sailed up the Thames and burnt the naval dockyards at Chatham. But nothing of this kind was even attempted. Their only achievement was to prove temporary predominance at sea as they swept the Channel clear of enemy ships carrying supplies to America, which also permitted the safe arrival of a Spanish fleet from the Indies. Without a direct thrust upon the British Isles the armada failed in its purpose, and as a result d'Orvilliers was demoted for incompetence. [22]

But worse was to follow. In the early days of 1780 there emerged the illustrious figure of Admiral Rodney, the same who was to pursue Solano in vain through the West Indies, but who now was to successfully elude the Gibraltar blockade right under Córdoba's nose and bring in urgently needed supplies for the beleaguered garrison. Rodney's brilliance shone in inverse proportion to Spanish and French naval mediocrity in Europe (distinct from personal bravery or the quality of ships) which seemed so disappointing at critical times. Putting to sea with twenty-two ships of the line, Rodney had already captured a Spanish convoy when approaching Cape St. Vincent on January 18 he suddenly came upon a Spanish force of only ten ships of the line commanded by Juan de Lángara and cut it to pieces. After gallantly defending the main ship *Fénix* (the same that had once brought over Charles from Naples), Lángara struck his colors and was taken captive to Gibraltar, where he remained a distinguished guest till the end of the war. If Córdoba had not been so keen to follow orders from Floridablanca, he might have risked coming out of Cádiz despite poor weather in order to assist Lángara, caught as the latter was in a fog, without proper intelligence of the enemy, and heavily outnumbered by him. "Have patience," Córdoba was reported to have said, "today the English are rejoicing; tomorrow will be our turn".[23] But the turns seldom came, and when they did were made with the slow precision of a chess tournament, with only occasional flashes of brilliance, like a game played in a monastery at sea. Meanwhile Rodney had come and gone with scarcely a Spaniard to touch him.

There is little doubt that the relief of Gibraltar disposed the British government to protract Lord North's tentative offer of the Rock's return, first considered in the fall of 1779 in exchange for Spain's neutrality -- an offer which Charles could not possibly now accept. For the purpose of continuing this question, an Irish priest by the name of Father Thomas Hussey (Almodóvar's chaplain in London and a confidant to secretary of state Lord Hillsborough) visited

Madrid in 1780, and here he was later joined by Richard Cumberland (an aide to Lord Germaine, secretary of state for the American colonies). Their job was to work out a settlement with plenty of strings attached -- Gibraltar in exchange for Ceuta, Puerto Rico, and Omoa, but if Spain offered cooperation, then Florida plus Newfoundland fishing rights into the bargain -- conditions that Charles absolutely could not meet without compromising his honor both to himself and France; and with Floridablanca being instructed to insist on Gibraltar's return *sine qua non*, with minimum concessions elsewhere, it was hardly surprising that the talks which dragged on until early in 1781 came eventually to nothing.

Another reason for Spain's hard line over Gibraltar was a stunning victory at sea. Córdoba's words had not been wholly in vain. The anti-Catholic Gordon riots were raging in London in June 1780, and these were seen in Madrid as heralding bad times for the British government as it also faced a deteriorating situation in America. Now it was Spain's turn to strike at the enemy; and the naval victory off the Azores on August 9, 1780, considerably raised national morale.

Two large British convoys, one bound for India, the other for Jamaica, and whose weak escort was correctly gauged by Floridablanca, were ordered to be attacked, and this was carried out by Córdoba in a rare display of brilliance. Sweeping in upon the enemy as private merchantmen were scattered in his wake, he captured the 70-gun ship of the line *Ramillies*, overpowered its escort of two 36-gun frigates, and despatched to Cádiz the entire contingent of sixty sail with two thousand soldiers and civilians on board, eighty thousand rifles mostly bound for America, and merchandise to the value of nearly two million pounds sterling.[24] British prisoners of war, incidentally, were sent to camps in Seville and Ecija for the duration, where those not converted to Catholicism were classed as 'heretical subjects with special skills' if they showed a desire to work. Many of them did so, more from a desire to get away from the camps than from any higher motive, and were offered good positions in the royal factory at Seville.

The victory off the Azores did much to bolster Spain's prestige, particularly in the eyes of France, who was quick to blame her partner for any failures. Some idea of the undercurrents of distrust between the two was conveyed by Richard Cumberland to Lord Hillsborough. Spanish soldiers at San Roque by Gibraltar, he reported, were brave in action against Elliot but were hampered by Barceló's unpopular fire-ships and feuds with the French. Cumberland took an extremely dim view of d'Estaing, who cut a poor fig-ure in Cádiz with his meddling, quarreled with Cór-doba, and sailed away over his protests. The French and Spanish were like two terriers sporting for a fight. In Cumberland's view, the Spanish would be about as glad to see d'Estaing and Guichen defeated as they would be to see Gibraltar retaken. They would give anything to get this back, even if it meant spiting the French. Only their recent cap-ture of the English Jamaica fleet off the Azores had kept their morale going ...25

Another victory of a sort, a diplomatic one this time, further raised spirits, at least in gov-ernment circles. This concerned Russia and her Em-press, Catherine the Great. Following Barceló's seizure of some Russian ships in the straits of Gibraltar blockade which the Spanish had imposed since July 1, 1779, the Russian minister in Madrid, Stepan Zinoviev, successfully demanded reparations for this violation of neutral rights at sea. What started as a Spanish blunder, however, was soon turn-ed to good effect. Despite Catherine's toasting of Rodney's victory over Lángara at a festive ball in St. Petersburg, the Empress condemned the British for similar practices, and she soon became the champ-ion of aggrieved neutral nations who had suffered injury at sea from both the warring sides. With the British and Spanish envoys in St. Petersburg (Sir James Harris and Pedro de Normande) each bidding for her support, it was but a step to her declaration of February 28, 1780, which led to the famous League of Armed Neutrality. This upheld the right of neutral ships to pass virtually unhindered to bel-ligerent ports through any paper blockade -- 'the flag protects the merchandise' as the saying went -- in defiance of Britain's interpretation of its

right to search. It was Spain's action in seizing
the Russian ships in the first place which had prompted the declaration, and this Sir James Harris
found out from a secret informant whom he paid to
ascertain Catherine's motives.[26]

Spain along with France could now exploit the
situation in their favor. In proclaiming sympathy
with the League's principles (jointly with the Netherlands which declared war on Britain in December),
they were considerably more in tune with neutral
feeling than Britain, who had much more to lose from
this threat to her command of the sea. The island
nation in fact was now alone against all Europe. And
though Spain failed to win Catherine's support in
the planned attacks on Gibraltar and Minorca --
Aranda went so far as to suggest tempting Russia
with bases in Morocco and the Caribbean -- Catherine
did respond to Charles' offer of direct trade access
to Spanish ports in the Mediterranean. This is evidenced by Charles' letter of January 1781 to Marqués
de la Torre, the new ambassador to Russia who had
been with Sotomayor before Gibraltar. In it,
Charles exhorted Torre to curry favor with Catherine
over the liberty of the seas issue (hoping to provoke a crisis with England), to watch Harris very
closely, and even the French, and to work with Normande while perusing Conde de Lacy's files. Spanish-
Russian trade should be opened via the shorter Black
Sea route from the Mediterranean as Spanish wines,
for example could begin to be exported, while trade
through the Baltic could be resumed during the final
peace negotiations.[27]

Conditions were favorable for improved trade
with Russia, for Spain needed naval items such as
timber for masts, as well as pitch, iron, and rigging,
while Catherine was ambitious to expand her maritime
register. In 1779 for example, over one half of the
nearly forty Russian ships leaving St. Petersburg
for trade abroad were destined for French or Spanish
ports. Charles and Floridablanca were thus willing
to accord Russian ships full honors due to their flag,
and this shift in policy, without actually driving a
wedge between Russia and England, yet had the effect
of preventing a close concert between them vis-à-vis
the Bourbon powers.

Meanwhile the siege of Gibraltar was mounting
in intensity during the spring and summer of 1781,
when something like a thousand shells a day were exchanged between the English lines and Barceló's artillery gunboats. But Gibraltar still held, especially
since Admiral George Darby's relieving squadrons safely reached the Rock on April 21, thus repeating what
Rodney had done the previous year. As a result Spanish fury began to die down, the firing rate now being
reduced to three rounds a day, which were hailed as
greetings from the Holy Trinity by the surviving but
triumphant British soldiers. A victory was becoming
more urgent than ever, and Floridablanca felt the
time was ripe for submitting a plan to his sovereign
for the conquest of the other great objective, the
island of Minorca.

A large armada was accordingly prepared in secret
at Cádiz, the French being informed by Aranda of its
true destination only at the last minute. All was
ready by July 1781 as over fifty transports with fifteen thousand men on board sailed out of the harbor,
with Ventura Moreno in charge of fleet operations
under the overall command of the Frenchman, the Duke
of Crillon.[28]  The latter was a wise choice on the
part of Floridablanca for he was a man of imagination
and daring -- qualities rather rare with the Franco-
Spanish command in Europe -- who had distinguished
himself in Italy and Flanders and had served in Portugal on the Spanish side during the Seven Years war.
The British defending general was James Murray, who
unfortunately had less luck than Elliot at Gibraltar.
Commanding barely three thousand men, he was heavily
outnumbered from the start with no relief on the way,
and his ranks were soon depleted to less than a thousand as a result of scurvy and the casualties of
battle.  The invasion in fact had achieved surprise,
and it was not long before Fort Mahon was taken, together with Fornell and Ciudadela.

The fort of San Felipe was the next target, and
here siege operations began in November, one month
after the battle of Yorktown in America.  This time
the Spanish forces were aided by four thousand Frenchmen under Baron de Falkenhayn sent by Louis XVI, who

had got over his pique at not being informed in advance of the invasion plan.  Supported by Ventura Moreno's blockade squadrons, Crillon launched a powerful attack on San Felipe, destroying the munitions dumps and reducing the garrison to rubble.  On February 5, 1782, Murray surrendered.  Passing down the lines of Crillon's triumphant army, the surviving infantrymen, artillerymen, and sailors earned the respect of the conqueror as much as the latter displayed humanity to the defeated.  The islanders everywhere welcomed the invaders, and one of Crillon's first acts was to restore their privileges in the name of Charles III.  He was later created Duke of Mahon by a grateful king, who now put him in charge of the siege of Gibraltar over Sotomayor, with the able Ventura Moreno as one of his aides.  The Spanish nation needless to say was jubilant at the victory, tarnished only by the death of colonel José Cadalso, inspiring poet who was killed in one of the sorties at Gibraltar.

In England meanwhile, with the loss of the thirteen colonies dwarfing Minorca to insignificance, Lord North's ministry fell the following month, eventually succeeded by the Earl of Shelburne's in which Lord Grantham became the new secretary of state for foreign affairs.  Negotiations for peace were going to prove stubbornly tortuous because George III's obsession was resisting the notion of American independence as much as Charles' obsession was now the recovery of Gibraltar.  As Floridablanca quipped to Marqués de la Torre early in 1782; "King George III will only recognize American independence when the French have occupied the Tower of London; and he supposes that the only Gibraltar we shall ever get back is Gibraltar Square in Madrid itself!"[29]  Such a comment barely concealed the fact that it was also Charles' determination over Gibraltar that was proving a stumbling-block to peace, for in the royal view the Rock had to be taken at all costs.

The King's firm confidence in victory was no doubt strengthened by news from Córdoba that a further British convoy of twenty-seven ships bound for America had been attacked on June 25, 1782, and all but eight of them captured.  Minorca had already fallen; God

267

would not let him down over Gibraltar. When even
his old friend Tanucci expressed doubts, Charles
assured him that a great display of arms would soon
accomplish what so far a blockading siege could not.
And in a subsequent letter, he told of the chief preparations being completed by mid-August, involving
minimum casualties, with the further good news that
the Bahamas had been taken on the other side of the
ocean.30   Charles, incidentally, had a genuine concern for the lives of his subjects, and this was
why there had been a lull in the attacks, but now he
was to stake all on a final spectacular effort.

Preparations were indeed impressive when the
grand assault began on September 13, 1782.  Command
had been given to Crillon, despite earnest appeals
from Aranda via the Prince of Asturias that the command should be given to himself.  Judging by the
negative response, it would appear that the Prince's
team was fully overshadowed by Floridablanca, who
fulfilled Charles' wish that Aranda be kept in Paris
where he would do least harm and handle the triumphant
negotiations that must inevitably follow.31   Meanwhile
Crillon had at his disposal ten ships of the line, besides frigates, gunboats, landing-craft, xebecs, numerous artillery, and thirty thousand men, all vastly
exceeding the 7000-man defending garrison under the
redoubtable Elliot.  Nor was this all; for notables
from all over Europe attended, including the Prince
of Nassau, the Duke of Bourbon, and two future kings
of France -- Louis XVIII and Charles X -- respectively
then known as the Comte de Provence and the Comte d'
Artois.  Engineers by the score had submitted plans
for the Rock's recapture, including one by Sabbatini,
though most of them were more noteworthy for their
imagination then practicality.  There were such crank-
ish ideas as the construction of false reefs to trap
enemy ships or of the laying of underground mines to
blast the Rock to pieces, though none so bizarre as
the calculations made in one plan for erecting a
mountain of earth higher than the Rock itself.

What had attracted most attention and fatally
put into practice were the floating battery-ships --
brainchild of the Frenchman Michaud d'Arcon, and

foisted by the court of Versailles on Floridablanca, who then pressed the idea on the King. Ten of these boats were built between May and August for the assault landing. Capable of holding seven hundred and fifty men apiece, they were equipped with an all-embracing top cover made of hide, with wooden-plated sides one meter thick containing twenty guns, and defended at each end by walls of cork to protect the gunners from shrapnel. A novel contrivance was a tubular water-cooling system designed to annul the effects of the red-hot shot fired by Elliot's men, and which d'Arçon claimed made the batteries fireproof. Crillon was sceptical from the first and said as much to Floridablanca, and his words proved justified.

Everything in fact went wrong from the start. Elliot's red-hot shot set fire to one battery-ship after another with mortal accuracy, wreaking havoc upon the attackers, d'Arçon giving the genuine excuse but which sounded rather lame at the time, that the water-cooling system as well as the caulking of the vessels' joints still required a great deal of experimentation. With only a few battery-ships left after three days, and with over three hundred men taken prisoner besides many killed, it was obvious that the great assault had failed. "Has Gibraltar fallen yet?" Charles would ask anxiously of Floridablanca, but the minister averted his eyes. Adding insult to injury was a third British relieving expedition, this time under Admiral Lord Richard Howe, which safely reached the Rock by October 1782. In eluding Córdoba despite the forty ships of the line at his command, Howe put paid to any further chances of success.32

Charles was still adamant over getting back Gibraltar; but now that the fiasco of the battery-ships became fully known in Europe, his task grew progressively more difficult. British reluctance not unnaturally was hardening; and whatever conciliatory gestures George III might be tempted to make, he had to reckon with Parliament, the lords of the Admiralty led by Keppel, and other influential hardliners like the Duke of Richmond. At this juncture an emissary named Gerard de Raineval came to the fore, a general

given civilian rank, and sent to London by France to
sound out chances for a peace settlement. Here he
was later joined by Ignacio de Heredia as his Spanish partner. Through Raineval, Charles proposed exchanging Gibraltar for Oran in North America, an
offer that now lost its attraction with the Rock
firmly in British hands. Instead, prime minister
Lord Shelburne proposed exchanging Gibraltar for
Puerto Rico, a much richer prize, with Britain also
retaining Minorca and the Bahamas; Spain could keep
West Florida, but if she wanted to keep Puerto Rico,
then she should have to give Trinidad to England
and Santo Domingo to France.[33]  But either option
was too high a price for Charles to pay, since this
would involve losing lynchpins in Caribbean defense
-- Puerto Rico to one country, Santo Domingo to the
other -- which islands Charles held to be almost as
important as Gibraltar itself.

With the King still adamant, with Vergennes at
odds with Aranda over the same issue, and with the
Americans suspicious of French intentions in the
Ohio and Mississippi regions, it was not surprising
that a wide range of propositions crossed the diplomats' table, and that from the ensuing stresses and
strains in high places talks about a separate peace
were in the air.  Each country in fact was pulling
in different directions.  The first to break their
commitments were the Americans, who despite their
understanding with France not to make a separate
peace but suspecting her designs, came to provisional
terms with England on November 30, 1782, by which
their independence was recognized.  Such a move had
the obvious effect of straining Vergennes' commitments
to Spain, for it would logically be in France's interest to favor a swift conclusion of the war at
England's expense.  It also strained Aranda's loyalty
to his sovereign now that he was torn between pursuing the receding possibility of Gibraltar's return
and achieving through diplomacy with France some
credit for a victorious end.  Only two days previously
Aranda was huddled in conference at Versailles with
Vergennes and Raineval, who had just returned from
London, over what to do about Gibraltar.  The conference lasted seven hours and nerves were getting frayed.

There is no doubt that Aranda would have liked to wash his hands of Gibraltar altogether; and he must have been immensely relieved when on December 9, 1782, he received a letter from Floridablanca couched in terms which definitely revealed Charles' softening stand at last, asking what advantages Spain could get from a peace treaty, should the King for any reason forego the commitment of trying to get back Gibraltar.34 The King had obviously been seeking a way out of his impasse, prodded by Shelburne's responses, in considering letting Gibraltar go and holding on to those territories which Spanish forces had actually captured, i.e., both Floridas, Honduras, and Minorca. Hence this letter of Floridablanca to Aranda.

When Aranda showed the letter to Vergennes, the French minister asked whether he could use it as a basis for negotiation and transmit its implications to Raineval and the British government, to which Aranda gave his consent. Vergennes can be censured for letting down Charles over Gibraltar, just as he himself had been let down by the Americans; but in the long term there was little for which he could be criticized unless it be charged that everyone was double-crossing everyone else. Efforts to take Gibraltar by force had failed, and flexibility in diplomacy was the only alternative. Indeed with Britain and American already arranging the terms of their separation, it was logical for France and Spain to be in on the settlement. Vergennes was only taking his cue from Aranda in giving way over Gibraltar, which in any case as a continuing bone of contention between England and Spain would prevent these two powers from combining against France.

Aranda's role is less creditable, perhaps, seeing that he was running ahead of Charles' royal instructions. But Aranda was a man of toughness and foresight, a dedicated patriot who had a difficult master; and in bowing to the inevitable deserves criticism only for a fault in which circumstances would have led to the same result. Aranda also had Floridablanca to contend with. Indeed it must have been frustrating to be continually overshadowed by the figure of the chief minister at Charles' side. On more than one occasion Aranda was shabbily treated by his rival, who

271

was not averse to negotiating behind his back, or if he was consulted, his ideas would be taken up too late to have any positive effect. He had not forgotten Floridablanca's flimsy excuses when he chided him for conducting negotiations without his knowledge in the matter of Almodóvar's mediation attempts in London on the eve of Spain's declaration of war. "Does Aranda serve this minister or the King?" he once asked himself bitterly, which aptly summed up the resentment he felt.35

Floridablanca for his part was a diplomat of highest intelligence -- if a little hesitant in making military decisions -- whose whole cast of thought was much nearer to the King's than Aranda's. It was thus easy for him to reprove Aranda from his vantage-point at Madrid and report, as was his duty, any hint of a discrepancy between Spanish and French accounts of the negotiations. Aranda was determined to mask any such differences. The reality for everyone concerned was that on the scales of power, a combination of Britain and the United States -- in the event that they acted jointly in diplomacy as it seemed at the time -- was more formidable in asserting a peace treaty than a combination of France and Spain. The two Bourbon powers thus had no option but to work together as closely as possible.

That Charles was angry with Aranda, as much as he sought to cover up his wounded pride over Gibraltar, is obvious from the letter he wrote to Louis XVI on January 2, 1783: "... We are completely agreed in bringing the benefit of peace to our peoples, but I will not trouble to burden Your Majesty with the feeling of regret at achieving this without acquiring Gibraltar, thus letting slip a chance that perhaps will never occur again ... Although my ambassador (Aranda), knowing the tender sentiments I hold towards you, has gone beyond my orders in pursuing peace negotiations without insisting on Gibraltar's return ... I will not insist on imposing such extreme vexations upon Your Majesty, either for You or your subjects ... "36

272

Final peace talks got under way within a month, Spanish interests in London being handled by Bernardo del Campo and Heredia. Charles resigned himself to losing Gibraltar, his last hopes dashed by finally giving up the idea of taking Jamaica, whose capture Aranda had been urging all along as a bargaining chip, or at least as a way of diverting British forces from Europe. What had ruined the plan was the need to reinforce New Granada to deal with the *comunero* revolt, with fever decimating the remaining troops available, while Rodney's famous victory over Comte de Grasse off Dominica in April 1782 had prevented a French juncture with the Spanish. Now it was too late.

There was much haggling in Paris before the final peace treaty was ratified at Versailles on September 3, 1783.[37] The independence of the United States was recognized. Spain recovered both Floridas, east and west, with retention of the lower Mississippi region, all of Central America (except for a small enclave in Honduras reserved for British logwood cutters extending from the bay along the Belize and Hondo rivers), as well as Minorca in Europe. Though England got back the Bahamas and Dominica, besides winning the Newfoundland fishing dispute, it was a favorable peace treaty for Spain, considerably more favorable than for France who only received trading privileges after so much effort. The Spanish nation had good cause to be satisfied, and Charles' personal sorrow over Gibraltar was immersed in the general rejoicing.

In humbling one monarchy while expanding his own, Charles had achieved the unusual feat of assisting the birth of a great new republic. Spanish victories on the Mississippi and in Florida, thus easing pressure against the Americans on the western and southern fronts respectively, besides offensives in Central America and Europe which drew enemy forces away from Virginia, had all helped to bring this about. The debt of the Americans to France is obvious. The debt of the Americans to Spain is only less obvious to the extent that, for imperial reasons of her own, she purposely fell short of actually sending troops to Washington's and Clark's armies; but in all else, from money, supplies and protection of privateers, to

frequent attacks on enemy convoys bound for the
American front, her contribution was significant.
It would be interesting to speculate, moreover, what
would have happened to the United States in its
southeastern part if Florida had remained in British
hands.

There were limitations to the treaty of course.
The fixing of the Florida boundary by Britain when
she abandoned the territory at a slightly lower latitude than formerly brought Spain into later conflict
with the United States. But the intrusion by the
latter into this region, especially West Florida, indeed the rise of Latin American independence itself,
really belong to a different age. Charles in the
meantime had won a strong position in the Americas,
eclipsing the colonial empires of both France and
England in the Hemisphere which was to outlast his
own lifetime.

Where Europe was concerned, there had been setbacks in the war. There was the futile armada of
1779 in the Channel, whose story as told through
French eyes, in putting all the blame on Spain, masked the fact that most of the blame rested with the
French themselves. Perhaps the soundest criticism
that could be made against Charles personally was his
loyalty in keeping commanders like Córdoba when he
should have been fired; but then loyalty was Charles'
special characteristic. Certainly the daring of men
like Rodney, Howe or Elliot stand out in sharp relief
against the mediocrity of their Franco-Spanish counterparts. No great sea-dog went into the attack, despite
the many ships at his disposal. Except during the
Azores battle and the capture of Minorca, Bourbon
men-of-war which were of good quality too often became
unwieldy hulks in the hands of unimaginative commanders. The crews were brave, but bravery was not
enough. Whatever may be said in Córdoba's defense --
he was in fact continually let down over money and
supplies -- it is tempting to ask whether more aggressive officers given full initiative might not have
done a better job of fighting the enemy at sea and
bringing that historic Rock nearer to capitulation.
The Duke of Crillon himself was able enough, but his
requests were often countermanded higher up.

Would the course of history in these waters have been different if Gálvez or Aranda, instead of Floridablanca, had been put in total charge of the war? Together with marine minister Castejón, who was critical enough of Floridablanca's handling of the blockade, these two might have made an aggressive team, eclipsing also the vacillating Father Eleta and the aging Múzquiz; and the reason why they did not probably lies in Charles' astuteness as much as his loyalty, for he could see perfectly well that Gálvez was scheming all the time to unseat his favored, and in so many other respects highly competent, chief minister. As for Aranda, he was a difficult man to work with in any case, and in Charles' view might well have overplayed Spain's hand by impulsive and precipitate action. Yet six thousand Spanish and French casualties had been lost in the siege, with 258,387 cannon and mortar shells fruitlessly exploded, and at a cost of 12 million pesos.[38] It was a fiasco as great as the British failure at Gallipoli during the First World war, or the failure by the Axis powers to take British-held Malta during the Second.

Despite this defeat however, there was Minorca to be satisfied with; and Spain came off extremely well in the Americas, not only against the British but against rebels of all sorts from northern Mexico to South America. In the overall context of reasserting Spanish power against the enemy, Charles came remarkably close to achieving all his objectives.

An idea of his strong armament policy can be seen in the work of men like Antonio Valdés, minister of marine after the war who continued the attempt to close the gap with Britain. Though his efforts were forlorn -- it was unfortunate for Spain in her last years of greatness to be surpassed by Britain who was rapidly emerging into a superpower -- the fact remained that the Spanish navy grew remarkably strong by the end of Charles' reign. In sheer numbers it could count on nearly eighty ships of the line and fifty frigates, catching up with the French, and having a total complement of 75,000 men. Among its achievements none was more impressive than the 120-gun flagship *San José*, or the triple-decked *Santísima Trinidad*,

in its day the largest man-of-war of any nation.
But sheer numbers of ships were running ahead of
Spain's capacity to provide for them in terms of
trained manpower, port facilities, and maintenace.
The proud *navíos* were like floating palaces of craftsmanship -- yet almost ghost-like in appearance for
there were never enough skilled crews to man them.
If Britain surpassed Spain in these respects and
could sever her communications on the high seas,
this was the only country able to do so.  The acknowledged defects of the Spanish fleet applied even
more to the fleets of other nations.  Thus not Russia,
Prussia, Sweden, Denmark or Holland (excluding the
latter's carrying trade) would equal Spain as the
second largest naval power, if we grant parity with
the French; and this increased the general respect
with which this country was viewed by the contemporary world.

Conde de Floridablanca, engraving after Goya

CHAPTER THIRTEEN

FURTHER HORIZONS

An added dimension to the international stature
achieved by Spain was the remarkable growth in industry and commerce. Many observers of the time now
grouped the country along with France, Austria, England and Prussia as among Europe's more advanced;
though whether this growth would have been sustained
if the French Revolution had never intervened, or
whether it was a burst of energy peculiar to Charles'
reign has been much disputed since. But one central
feature emerges: the stronger Spain became, the
greater her disparity in wealth and regional resources, casting in starker relief the deep divisions
of society which Charles' monarchy alone seemed to
bridge.

The obstacles were formidable from the start.
There was the backwardness of the interior compared
with provinces like Valencia or Catalonia with their
outlets to the sea. There was the monopoly of 'big
business', which as we have seen in regard to the
Indies the government had done much to curb, not to
mention the presence of foreigners in much of Spanish trade. And there was the obstructionism of craft
guilds, with all the cross-currents of jealousy and
exclusivism among Spaniards themselves. Charles
took these hurdles in his stride, and had the good
sense to listen to the advice of Floridablanca and
Campomanes, besides many others, in seeking a balance between the rival forces. The land had long
been stirred by the currents of enlightenment, which
although cannot all be attributable to him, would
never have achieved their impetus without him.

Much had been done already to promote national
industry in the bleak interior. Woolen textile and
tapestry factories were begun as early as Philip V's
reign, while Ferdinand VI authorized a big silk factory at Talavera de la Reina. After Charles came
to the throne, royal enterprises of this sort grew
rapidly. Woolen cloth mills were opened at Segovia
in 1763 and Brihuega in 1768 -- the latter place best

remembered for Charles' hunting chateau and garden with its green arbors and obelisks reminiscent of Caserta.[1] In nearby Guadalajara, a serge factory was opened in the 1770's, employing four thousand weavers with nearly eight hundred looms. There were also factories for pottery, such as the Buen Retiro's outside Madrid, as well as for glass, the one at La Granja turning out the finest mirrors in Europe. With lavish grants and tax remittances from the treasury, rentals from surrounding pasture, not to mention guaranteed markets from army officers who had to get cloth here for their uniforms, these royal textile factories seemed a big success; and indeed in a technical sense they were.

But in the end economic realities caught up with them; they were simply too large to compete in changing conditions. Their directors were more interested in excellence than utility, concentrating all phases of production in a single plant instead of dispersing skills on a 'putting-out' basis, as in Valencia or England. Reflecting a policy of vertical management, such men were no match for the seasoned entrepreneurs from Catalonia with their greater 'know-now' in organization and marketing. Competition also from imported English textiles, which the factories had been designed to thwart in the first place, doomed many of them in the long run. Much the same story applied to the royal joint-stock companies which Charles had established at Segovia (1763), Burgos (1767) and Ezcaray (1773).[2] But these enterprises provided much needed employment while they lasted, as they continually branched into new fields, with a successful cotton-velvet factory, for example, founded at Ávila in the last year of the reign.

Designed to link all this together was an elaborate scheme of canal construction. The stubborn soil aside, one of the greatest problems here was the stubbornness of Spaniards themselves. Council members knew no bounds of fatalism and procrastination, as when in the previous century they had been presented with a plan to link Madrid with Lisbon via the Manzanares and Tagus rivers. The learned bureaucrats concluded that if God had wanted these rivers to be navigable He would have made them so, but the fact that

He had not done so was sufficient reason for not making them navigable now.[3]

To Charles, at least in this context, Madrid came before God. And in the 1760's with the help of his advisers, he launched ambitious plans to make the capital more accessible to the north through Castile, and to the south through Murcia via the Guadalquivir river. A third plan was for a canal linking the coast of Aragon with the bay of Biscay. Impressive work was done with all three projects, alas unfinished, but which got as far as the great canals of Guadarrama and Manzanares with the first plan, and irrigation along the Murcia canal and at Lorca with the second. The most noteworthy achievement, perhaps, as part of the third plan was the Aragon canal to Saragossa under the direction of canon Ramón Pignatelli.[4] This scheme included an aqueduct at Tarragona besides the impressive Tortosa canal -- the latter bypassing the dangerous mouth of the Ebro river. These were great feats of engineering when taking into account the impossible terrain with huge construction costs involved, amounting to a hundred million reales for each waterway, which together completed a distance of some two hundred miles.

While maritime transport fared better because of its relative cheapness, roads were in a shocking condition. Often mere pathways for pack-animals, these were hindering the growth of industry. Feeble efforts had been made in the past, but in 1761 Charles authorized a scheme for linking Madrid radially with the surrounding provinces. Like the canals however, road-building encountered similar problems of terrain, especially with paving and grading, and involving huge costs. Indeed the best work in the north of Spain was done by private enterprise, the Basque Friends of the Nation Society being very active in repairing roads and bridges, awaiting the day when the government's plan (never finished) would link the hub of Madrid with León, the Basque provinces, and Navarre. Yet in the last decade of the reign Floridablanca as superintendent of highways had good claim to boast of nearly 400 leagues (about 1600 miles) of road being laid or repaired, especially in the south, replete with bridges, signposts, as well as inns for the weary stagecoach traveller. Noteworthy roads included the Puerto del Rey highway in Andalusia, the link between Cartagena and parts of Murcia, and that between Astorga and Málaga, revenue being raised by a series of tolls.

Aggravating the problem of transport was the decline of free pasture round the great cities. Madrid with its rising population of 150,000 was very much at fault in this respect as big landowners around it tended to enclose. This was especially harmful to the professional carters -- there were four thousand of them in Castile alone -- who relied heavily on seasonal grazing. Moreover with largely one-way traffic bringing vital supplies to the capital, it was becoming ever more difficult to keep down costs. The wealthier parts of Spain could afford to pay for luxury goods, but it was especially hard on poorer rural areas where the safe arrival of basic items such as food and clothing was essential. A greater priority given to local roads might have helped the countryside, especially in time of drought, and here the activities of local carriers often prevented starvation.[5] The effect of rising costs hindered the flow of cross-country traffic, impairing Castile's industry, in which the decline of free grazing round the cities played no small part.

But at least transport carriers were small professionals, doing a good job under difficult conditions. Landed enclosures by contrast, along with big merchant interests, often blocked economic development for the needy, and Charles with his advisers was closely watching for ways to curb their immense power. In the royal view there was nothing wrong with private capital if it worked in harmony with government objectives, but there was everything wrong with it if its monopoly tendencies stifled competition for others, dragging with it the ranks of labor as well.

Larger merchants, like those in the Indies, were organized into *consulados*. Foremost of these was the one at Seville which had loose ties with the House of Trade in this city; but there were fifteen others, many of them like the one at Cádiz responsible for running the ports, funding schools of navigation, and scheduling tariffs. Dealers and craftsmen formed

another sort of monopoly termed the *gremio*, or guild.
At the top were the big five gremios of Madrid -- a
vast conglomerate dominating trade in gold and silver
objects, silks and spices, tapestries and drugs, and
having ramifications far beyond the capital.  With
its nearly four hundred merchants controlling some
200 million reales in investment, in which its General Trading company was the most prominent, it owned
factories nationwide and had a large share in overseas monopolies as well, such as the Basque-dominated
company of Caracas.[6]

Big enterprises were tolerated at first for their
power to check foreign influence, but these were being
closely watched by Charles' government.  The aim was
to broaden competition.  Many an ambitious Spaniard
solicited royal support to secure a permit to trade,
but only after heated lawsuits with monopoly interests,
usually via the council of commerce and money, which
was growing in importance for all the disputes now
being dumped into its lap.  As time went on, the consulado at Cádiz as well as the company of Caracas began to weaken in face of competition -- the latter
through the great free trade regulation of 1778 --
and by 1785 as a further example, Charles' financial
adviser, Francisco Cabarrús, forced the General Trading company of the big five gremios to make its profits
public.

In every major city, smaller gremios existed for
local industries.  As with the consulados, grievances
against these guilds were many.  These included exclusive membership against Spaniard and foreigner
alike; the tight rules of advancement through the
usual ranks of apprentice, journeyman, and master;
the exacting standards of workmanship enforced by
frequent and over-zealous inspectors; and the general
resistance to change.  Under such circumstances the
government sought ways to breach these ramparts of
restriction and privilege.

With the royal aim to broaden the ranks of labor
at odds with guild policy, advisers led by Campomanes
drew the fire of many, including a brilliant apologist
from Catalonia, Antonio de Capmany, who was against
having foreign workers and who argued vehemently in

281

defense of guild practices.. But they were waging
a losing battle. Coming to Charles' aid, ironically,
were Catalans themselves -- businessmen flocking to
Madrid who angered the guilds by selling at retail
without government permission. By 1770 the King
stepped up the fight by directing the council of
commerce and money to remove all obstacles to industrial progress; and soon the ramparts fell one by one
in admitting all kinds of people into the guilds and
granting them better working rights. These included
foreign artisans (1772 and 1777), hidalgos (1773),
women (1779 and 1784, provided their job was proper
to their sex and strength), along with illegitimate
persons; while 'vile' tradesmen (*artesanos viles*) such
as smithies, shoemakers, wool-carders and leather
tanners, whose offensive smell had hitherto barred
them from holding various offices, were freed from
their social stigma, along with gypsies, in 1783.
This latter year marked two further assaults upon
guild privilege. The Catalans won their right to
sell at retail in Madrid, and the council of commerce
and money extended its jurisdiction in the matter of
reviewing fines imposed by guilds. Joaquín Fos,
for example, a Valencian inspector, had some silks
publicly burnt in the market place for failing to
meet tight specifications. He imposed heavy fines,
and castigated the makers.[7] A great uproar ensued
as hundreds lost their jobs. Charles reprimanded
Fos and ordered the fines returned, thus scoring a
further victory for workers' rights in general.

Labor became no longer a closed shop dominated
by exacting managers. As more young people learnt
crafts profitable to the nation, conservative restriction weakened, and with it the stigma attached to
working by hand. Artisans were allowed to sell their
labor at will, while producers over guild objections
were given new freedoms to select the width and
weight of their fabrics, or the number of looms.
Goods could now be sold reasonably anywhere on the
open market provided they bore the official stamp
and seal of origin -- a policy designed to check both
foreign competition as well as contraband. Blows
were indeed being struck at the guilds, as with the
Mesta on behalf of a freer, more mobile enterprise,
though it was not until 1813 that the Cortes of

Spain really cut the underpinnings of guild structure in industry.

The very existence of foreign influence in Spain,
meanwhile, which had been one of the guilds' objections,
was also one of Charles' dilemmas. He certainly needed
artisans from abroad, anyone in fact with skills and
capital and who were attracted by a lower cost of living, but he wanted their contributions to be develop-
mental, not exploitative, and there is sometimes a
slim margin between them. Of the thirty thousand
foreign residents in Spain, barely five thousand were
useful artisans or engineers, some of them managers
of the royal factories. Far too much trade was in
non-Spanish hands, far too many luxury goods were
flooding the nation at the expense of basic industry.
Yet neither the English or the Dutch to whom earlier
kings had given concessions in the past were really
the villains. They were more interested only in external trade, i.e., purchasing Spanish wines, raw wool,
soaps, oils or dyes, and selling finished textiles or
hardware in exchange. Embarrassingly it was the French,
if anyone, who hurt Spanish merchant pride, for having
squeezed many concessions in 1769 under the coverage
of the Family Compact (and again ten years later),
they had become strong in silk, potash holdings, and
trade in general, almost rivaling the Catalans for
enterprise, and on that account equally disliked by
the guilds.[8]

In Cádiz alone there were eight French commercial houses making a profit of nearly five million
reales a year; there were also large numbers of Italians and other nationalities. Proud city of sixty
thousand people with its wines, saltworks, and tunny-
fishing, bastion of trade across the Atlantic as well
as smuggling in the Mediterranean, Cádiz reflected
in microcosm Charles' dilemma. On the one hand immigrants with skills were welcome; on the other hand
they were blamed by patriotic reformers for penetrating native consulados, making huge profits from luxury goods and contraband, and stifling local competition. Though native agents of the big merchant houses
were doing the same thing, it was a double offence
when committed by foreigners. Many Spaniards, moreover, were riled by complicated customs and export

dues which foreign interests could circumvent. Spanish brandy and sugar may have held their own in the
Mediterranean, but it was close to the position whereby foreigners were taking out of a lucrative empire
more than they were giving back, making Spain a debtor,
instead of a creditor, nation.

The government was slow to meet these objections,
needing as it did both capital and good relations with
foreign powers, chiefly France. But it did withdraw
certain tax-exempt privileges from foreign consuls,
while Charles' ban on imported cotton goods in January
1770, which laid the basis for protecting textile manufacture, was a blow to British merchants in Cádiz.

Complicating the government's attempt to promote
national and private industry was the three-cornered
tussle going on between the producer of rawstuffs in
Spain, the manufacturer in Spain, and the colonial
producer, and Charles had to walk a tightrope between
them. Space does not permit an analysis of the bewildering array of tariff variations, depending on
the crop and season. but suffice to say whatever the
government did annoyed some sector, and the net result
was only too often an increase in smuggling. The fair
ladies of Madrid were not going to give up flaunting
their foreign shawls and capes just because of some
new regulation.[9]

Smuggling by foreigner and Spaniard alike added
a new dimension to the problem. As early as 1761
those convicted could face up to eight years in jail,
and companies of mountain musketeers were organized
to help customs patrols track down the offenders.
When even the seals marking the provenance of goods
were forged, the government lost patience and by
1783 ordered the death penalty for anyone resisting
arrest with pistols or swords. It was a state of
affairs enriching dishonest customs officials no less
than the smugglers themselves, as the latter had
breathtaking yarns to tell about how they out-fought
officials who tried to be honest. As for the merchants,
they were learning by experience just how far to go
in evading the stringency of the law. The best that
can be said is that, despite the millions of reales
lost through smuggling, Charles' policy of promoting

freer trade through the ports (as in 1765 and 1778) considerably increased the royal revenues in the long run.

The policy of protecting home industry was also beginning to pay dividends. This specially applied to the private textile industry, which began to boom as a result of the ban on imported foreign cotton goods, and on certain raw exports such as wool and silk. Thus Valencian silk looms doubled to about 3,500 in the last two decades of the reign, while looms in Catalonia, mostly of the calico type, rose threefold to nearly four thousand over the same period. This burst of activity had a significat impact on customs receipts -- up from a value of 34 million reales to an astonishing 115 million reales in the course of the reign. [10]

Reflecting this growth, real wages were rising substantially in Valencia and Catalonia, and a man earning five reales a day in Madrid could command seven or eight in Barcelona. A seven-hour day was not uncommon, and like the English Midlands, even maids were getting harder to find. Britons like Arthur Young commented that one could hear the creak of stocking-engines everywhere in the streets of Barcelona, the hammer beating on the anvil at all hours, while Joseph Townsend maintained that inventive genius was no monopoly of England, but could be found in Spain as well. [11] Certainly artisans of every kind were an increasingly common sight working in factory and cottage, as in Valencia, and using latest inventions like the improved silk-spinning machine of the French inventor Jacques de Vaucanson. [12]

It was a mini-Industrial Revolution, but its burgeoning success threw into sharper relief the backward state of the interior. Here Charles was plagued by the very unfair tax practices which had crept in over the centuries, disrupting the already imbalanced spread of labor and capital resources. Taxes largely had their origin in the Middle Ages when the Cortes voted money for the king to finance the reconquest from the Arabs. As Spain became a world power, the crown multiplied the taxes, and since Castile with León was the matrix of the new empire it was here where people fared the worst. Especially irksome were the *alcabala* and *cientos* taxes of up to fourteen per cent on the purchase and sale of transacted goods. In addition were the *millones* excise dues of about twenty-five per cent going back to Philip II's time as a military levy on items such as wine, vinegar, meat, soap and candles. Yet the more prosperous regions of Valencia, Catalonia, the Basque lands and Navarre were remitted most of the above taxes, paying a plain sales tax instead. To this inequality can be added a chaotic system of coins and measures, along with the frustrating bureaucracy that went with it, which weighed heaviest, as usual, on the poorer regions of Spain.

An example of how galling tax practices were is given by William Jacob, who visited Seville at the turn of the next century. Coming into the city, everyone, he wrote, had to get clearance from the proper office before the slightest thing could be sold, be it onions or garlic. After paying all the taxes, the same procedure had to be recorded before one could return home. Thus the whole day was wasted. When oxen were brought in for slaughter, the local matador additionally retained as his fee the hide, horns, and hoofs. By the time the alcabala and millones were paid, and the permit obtained for the meat to be sold within the city walls, the costs had risen so much that while meat was basically cheap in Spain, it ended up by being as dear in Seville as it was in London.[13]

The early Bourbons had tried to come to grips with tax-collecting problems. Some degree of standardization by the state was attempted in 1736, when a unified single tax known as the *catastro*, first tried out in Catalonia, was extended to Castile. This policy was continued by Ferdinand VI (in the form of a reassessment combining the alcabala, cientos, and millones all in one); but though things were never so bad as in Naples with its notorious *arrendamenti*, these measures were more theoretical than substantial. There was a hard core of resistance from vested groups in the interior which derived a profit from having as many separate taxes as possible. Even merchants were hit by this practice since they had to have plenty of cash on hand in advance to meet all the taxes before the goods passed down the line to the consumer. The catastro principle, on the other hand, was more of a comprehensive sales. tax varying from between eight and ten per cent and was generally preferred by consumers and middlemen of prosperous Valencia and Catalonia. It is true that here existed an additional tax called the *bolla* of fifteen per cent, but this was levied mainly on textiles.

When Charles came to the throne he established a single tax committee, but it was a long time before action was taken. In essence he was being buffeted by both sides -- Castile and Catalonia -- with the one demanding the end of the alcabala, the other demanding diminution of the bolla. At first in 1770 he gave way to Catalonia's demands; but in 1779 he gave even more to Castile by first reducing the alcabala and cientos to a mere two per cent on woolen goods, then six years later by applying this reduction to virtually everything else. The alcabala still lingered in towns and villages and whose tax rates were assigned by quota collectively, distinct from individual districts, but a big step had been taken in the right direction. The deficiency in revenue meanwhile was made up by imposing a five per cent tax on land income and a two to three per cent tax on the rental of holdings.[14]

As for money itself, this was in such a mess in 1760, with copper coins bumped about in great bags, the gold and silver ones frequently clipped or shipped illegally abroad, that a visitor, Edward Clarke, called it the money of a barbarous people.[15]  In 1771 the King ordered the Segovia mint to strike six million new vellon reales which generally held their value at par.  The real trouble was with silver coins, however, for expanded bullion production in Mexico cheapened them in Spain, while the silver shortage in Europe drained them further to help pay for increasingly expensive imports from northwestern countries of the continent.  The following year the King ordered the mints in Seville and Madrid to strike new coins, including gold ones, but surreptitiously reduced their precious metal content to keep them at home and help pay new seigniorage taxes.  In an age

287

of rising prosperity -- and inflation -- and with war
expenses mounting in 1779, the King upped the value
of the gold doubloon in relation to silver, which was
tantamount to silver devaluation.[16]   The process of
devaluation continued for both metals, however, till
the demand for cheap money led the Spanish government
in the 1780's to experiment with paper; and the founding of the royal Bank of Spain by 1783 was one important result.

Known as the Bank of San Carlos, this was indeed
a commendable success and it first opened its doors
to the general public in June of this year.  Brainchild of the French financial genius, Francisco Cabarrús who was also Charles' adviser, the bank grew
out of the need to redeem depreciated promissory notes,
or *vales reales*, which had been circulated to meet the
costs of the war with England.[17]   Now the bank served
other needs as well, such as honoring bills of exchange or letters of credit, and it handled accounts
abroad as far as Havana or Vera Cruz, besides those
of the royal Philippines company.  Despite the inflation which the war entailed, the paper notes in circulation were a reminder of the prosperity at hand,
for the bank had enough gold and silver at its disposal both to back these notes and to redeem them,
while in addition the precious metals of the Indies
were still there to draw upon.

Yet Spain was always rich in metals herself.
Many silver deposits existed, and at the valuable
mercury center at Almadén in the Sierra Morena a
school of mining was developed at Charles' initiative.
Among other mineral ores were the famed marble and
jasper lodes of Andalusia, along with the copper of
the Ríotinto mines and the lead of Linares, and there
were saltworks from Navarre to Aragon.  From here
westwards including the Basque lands were the great
wrought-iron foundries, helped by the forest resources
of the hinterland.

In this part of Spain the picture in earlier years
had been brighter.  It is interesting to recall that
in the Middle Ages nearly two-thirds of the iron used
in the Tower of London's siege machines were of Spanish origin -- a reputation that lasted well into the

seventeenth century when the British Admiralty was still giving preference to high-grade Spanish iron. But with the rise of coke-fired blast furnaces in northwest Europe and the wrought pig-iron and crucible steel produced chiefly in England, Spanish iron output began to slump. Impure charcoal smelting in open-range hearths, poor roads, and vested interests more concerned with protecting markets in England or France than with developing national ones were further reasons for the decline.

Charles' government went a long way to restoring the balance. After visits to foreign countries, the royal factory management at Guadalajara experimented with coke-fired instead of charcoal smelting, and some high-grade steel of finest quality was produced. Attention was also given to copper and brass smelting. Coal incidentally was also given a boost, when in 1780 the King granted a twenty-year tax-reduced concession to proprietors in the Oviedo region of Asturias. Spain's first charcoal-fed blast furnace, meanwhile, was finally installed at Sagardelo, Galicia, in 1796, by which date bar iron production, while vastly eclipsed by Britain's eight times over, began its long uphill climb, eventually reflecting the nation's significant iron ore reserves.[18]

With the rising pace of activity in so many fields, Charles' regime had clearly touched the roots of the nation. France may have been supreme with its Lyons silk and worsteds, but Catalonia and Valencia had their knitted textiles and lace, as well as shoe industries, and even Castile could now boast of its fine woolens and linen, its madder for dyes, its factories for gloves and hats. Luxury foods too were on the increase, while in the bay of Biscay region a beer industry developed. With all this variety, Spanish exports included wines of every hue; apparel and tapestry; leather goods; snuff, soap, and medicines; oil and mercury; pottery and glass; knives and silverware; tools and hardware; weapons of all sorts from pistol-barrels to swords; and paper products from boxes to cards.

The paper industry was enjoying a wide boom which the tax remittance on domestic books was making possible.

Indeed a reading public was growing by leaps and bounds, the royal press being busy as never before. With industry so widespread, it was not surprising that Spain became rich with economic writers, many of them moving away from the semi-mercantile ideas of Campomanes towards a more laissez-faire approach to society. To name but a few, Valentín de Foronda proposed a more liberal line of capitalism; Francisco Romá y Rosell diagnosed the phenomenon of inflation; while the young Juan Sempere y Guarinos was concerned with the problem of charity, winning an essay prize from the royal Economic Society of Madrid.[19] The spirit of enlightenment with its sharp criticism was relentlessly chipping away at the built-in remnants of feudal jurisdiction. For better or worse, the secular nation-state was dawning at last.

As for Charles, he continued to further this trend, of which the economic societies were flourishing examples. Among his many works projects not the least was the continued embellishment of Madrid -- perhaps the most intensely personal of his aspirations. His influence was felt over the land at large; and in industry, where a wider range of artisans were to be admitted in factory and guild, he had tried to forge a balance between protection and a freer trade, and to distribute financial obligations more evenly between rival regions. Despite the bewildering tax structure, revenues under the careful management of Múzquiz and Cabarrús were being diverted for investment purposes in which bullion no longer wasted away in piled-up books of account.[20] Many artisans and farmers were getting more prosperous, providing taxable sources of wealth for future use.

There were problems, of course, in view of the vast increase in goods and services which such a policy entailed. Government payrolls alone for the court and councils, armed forces, customs and mails, were rising from about one quarter of a billion reales to nearly twice this figure, which just about equalled the revenue itself; [21] for here as elsewhere in Europe, deficit spending and sheer inflation were taking their toll. But as a rapidly advancing country, the Spain of Charles III was pursuing the wise course of sacrificing immediate revenue to serve a productive end,

such as borrowing less and slowing down the public
debt, lifting a tariff, or curtailing a guild.  At
the same time generous tax-concessions were granted to
certain industrialists as a way of stimulating investment in the private sector.  The King was modifying
his centralist principles by yielding to the laissez-
faire spirit of the times; and it is plausible to
suggest that had not disasters confronted the country
on all sides after his death, Spain would have become even more properous in real growth terms than
at any other time heretofore in her history.

The Royal Palace, Madrid

# CHAPTER FOURTEEN

## THE FINAL YEARS

With peace restored and his country on a firm footing, Charles conveyed to his people a sense of pride and accomplishment. As a respected father-figure he was not only the surviving head of the Bourbon family, he was fast becoming the most senior monarch in Europe; and other governments were beginning to turn to him for advice. But personal sorrow marred these last years. Family setbacks in particular were to take a heavy toll of his time and energies, fatally impairing his health. Outwardly triumphant, he was becoming indrawn and retrospective, living out his days like a man for whom the eighteenth century had reached orderly perfection but whom the weight of power, with all its political and dynastic demands, was slowly beginning to crush. Luckily others were there to give him constructive help. Above all, there was Floridablanca.

Comte de Vaudreuil once said of the chief minister in a side remark to Comte d'Artois that he had one of the best brains in all the cabinets of Europe, not even excepting the young William Pitt.[1] Despite enemies who vilified him, Floridablanca handled the ministers of justice, the treasury, war and the marine with such consummate tact that he got them to meet together more often; and as from July 8, 1787, they attended regular sessions in a permanent cabinet, or *junta de estado*. Concerned with constitutional procedures and swifter legislative action, this junta was a remarkable achievement of Floridablanca, who as minister of State could now weld all official reports into a coherent whole. Cabinet rule in fact began to eclipse the ministerial councils, including the council of Castile, thus marking regalism's complete triumph over conciliarism. His profuse memoranda on such topics as administrative reform and foreign affairs, written in concert with the King who would add his own amendments in the margin, form illuminative reading and show that the two really worked as a team.

The climax of the minister's thought was his famous "Instrucción reservada" written in accord with

Charles' views and underscoring lines of policy for the junta de estado to follow which extended into the following reign. A monument to enlightened absolutism, it covers a wide range of topic, reflecting also many of Campomanes' ideas, and elucidates the royal right of intervention in institutions of state. It is a strong plea for rational centralism as a means of bringing about economic justice, playing down Cortes and councils alike; but it vindicates current achievements as much as it sounds prophetic warnings for the future, particularly in regard to expansionism by France.[2]

A contrasting document is the no less penetrating "Plan de gobierno" written by Aranda. Essentially it is a reply to a request from the Prince of Asturias, who needed a master-plan for action in the eventuality of his father's death.[3] Completed earlier in the 1780's the document is retrospective, in which many of Aranda's suggestions such as the redistribution of the council of the Indies' powers clearly had an influence on Floridablanca. Yet Aranda's picture of government was quite different from Floridablanca's. Less enthusiastic for cabinet domination under a single minister, Aranda placed more emphasis on the conciliar mechanism, where members would be watchdogs on the ministers instead of the other way round, thus returning government to its pristine, autonomous, and anti-centralist form. The hard fact, however, was that the team of Charles and Floridablanca was completely triumphant over that of the Prince of Asturias and Aranda; and when we consider that Charles' absolutism with justice was surely better than a broader government without it, we can sympathize with Aranda's predicament: in seeking justice himself, he had been forced to rely on the Asturias couple with all the disastrous consequences for Spain, largely from a sense of personal rejection by the King. Yet Charles in his magnanimous way had long forgiven Aranda, who since his return from Paris had settled down comfortably with a new young bride; and perhaps through all the polite formality subsisting between the two rivals, the one real bond was a secret desire to withdraw, if not from politics, then from political strife.[4]

As if to give sanction to a new era of unity
and stability, Charles and his ministers, by a decree of May 28, 1785, created Spain's first national
flag. Some fifteen designs having been submitted to
replace the traditional royal standard and the cross
of Burgundy, both of which had been in use at various
times, the flag chosen consisted of a yellow horizontal
band bordered by two red ones; and this so remained
till 1931, when the purple from the old colors of
Castile temporarily replaced the red band on the flag's
lower surface.

Where foreign affairs were concerned, Charles increasingly left their conduct to Floridablanca, but
it would be incorrect to regard the latter as dominating the formulation of a policy. It was always the
King who made policy, in which other ministers like
Gálvez could be consulted for a second opinion. It
was Charles, not the pro-French Grimaldi, who decided
the rapprochement with Choiseul in the Seven Years
war, just as the timing of Spain's declaration of war
on England in 1779 was his own and not the more moderate Floridablanca's. It was Charles, over the objections of Aranda, who had made peace with Portugal two
years before, and who then instructed Floridablanca
to ratify the peace agreements; and not even Tanucci,
perhaps his closest friend in politics, could deflect
him from his purpose, such as an alignment with France
or Austria, once his mind was made up.[5]

The King now sought to preserve peaceful stability
in Europe. Floridablanca was even proposing an entente
with England, but as this would be too much of a snub
to France, he could at least fulfill his sovereign's
instructions by offering to mediate disputes wherever
possible. One such dispute concerned the Netherlands.
With Frederick the Great gone from the scene in 1786
and with France and England drifting apart, it seemed
as if international order was breaking down, especially
in Holland and the Austrian Netherlands on the eve of
the French Revolution.[6] By an agreement of October 17,
1787, both England and France dropped their respective
support of opposite factions in Holland, promising non-
intervention in Dutch affairs, and the possibility of
a general war was averted thanks to Spanish initiative.

Elsewhere, with Russia and Denmark at odds with Sweden in the Baltic, and with Russia and Austria scheming to carve up Turkish-held Moldavia and Wallachia (the future Rumania), many powers of Europe appealed to Charles for an opinion on easing the tension, but he was not to live long enough to complete the task.

Turkey, the chief Moslem power, posed a special problem for Charles and Floridablanca. Sultan Abdul Hamid I was suzerain over the Barbary states of Algiers, Tunis, and Tripoli, but his rule was very loosely enforced, especially in regard to curbing the acts of piracy and slavery which these states committed against Spanish subjects with impunity. Yet Abdul Hamid needed Franco-Spanish support against Russia's designs; and this gave Floridablanca his chance to include in the accords signed with Turkey in 1782-3 a provision that the Sultan pressure the Barbary states to desist from piracy against Spanish nationals. Floridablanca sought the same help from the Sultan of Morocco, Mulay Sidi Mohammed, and the Barbary states thus became pressured from both sides to seek agreements with Spain on this issue.

Sidi Mohammed's motive in cooperating with Spain was to elicit support for his designs on Algiers, and thus Floridablanca had something to bargain with in his negotiations. Both Tunis and Tripoli -- the latter by November 1784 -- came to terms with Spain on the issue of piracy, but Algiers was to prove more intractable. Not only was piracy its traditional way of life, but its government in the person of the Dey saw no reason to yield to outside pressure, especially since the city had shown it could defend itself against attacks.

Floridablanca, meanwhile, was instructed to assemble a fleet jointly with Portugal, Naples and Malta for a show of force against Algiers; but in the end the ships were deemed too small for the job and the whole venture had to be abandoned. There were other reasons for the decision. The rumble of rebellion in the Sultan's own empire carried with it a clear threat that Sidi Mohammed would certainly lose face in the Islamic world if he sided with

Spanish Christians against fellow-Moslems. A
further complication was the Sultan's own pique at
the idea of Floridablanca possibly giving way to
the Algerians in the question of Oran (captured by
Spain in 1732), and whose liberalization of trade
with the rest of the country was being demanded by
Algiers as the price of peace. The Sultan took the
view that such a concession was inappropriate at a
time when Spain was still in possession of the three
garrison strongholds of Ceuta, Melilla, and Los Vélez
in Morocco itself.[7]

Relations between Charles and the Sultan, nonetheless, remained extremely friendly. The treaty of 1780
negotiated during Spain's war with England was followed
by another in the summer of 1785, which granted more
mutual tariff reductions (Morocco badly needing Spanish wheat), in the course of which, incidentally,
Charles arranged the release of some United States
prisoners captured by the Moors.[8] The Sultan also
undertook to help mediate Charles' dispute with Algiers
via appeals to Turkey, but in this they were faced with
a difficult task. A treaty of sorts was made in May
1785 by which Spain and Algiers agreed to lift their
mutual blockade and to cease taking prisoners of the
other; but Algiers, still angry over Oran, subsequently demanded blood money to the tune of three million
pesos from the Spanish treasury, so that it was not
until the following June that a final peace was made,
Oran itself being formally returned to Turkey by Floridablanca in 1792.

One of Charles' last acts in foreign affairs was
the reception given to the Turkish envoy of Sultan
Abdul Hamid in the summer of 1788. Mutual trade, unhindered passage of shipping, and religious rights for
Spanish subjects residing in the Ottoman domains of
North Africa were all negotiated, confirming earlier
treaties with the Barbary states. Piracy was ended
at last against Spanish nationals, and the coast of
Valencia southward was left free for peaceful development. Thus more had been gained by patient diplomacy
than by arms, and Spain as a Christian power had won
the lasting good will of the Sultans of both Turkey
and Morocco. With mutual respect on both sides, a

new and happier chapter in Spain's relations with
the Moslems thus began.  In the world at large, from
Turkey to Russia, from the Western Hemisphere as far
as China (with whose Emperor commercial relations at
Canton had been established via Manila), the Spanish
Empire was enjoying peace and respect, and no storm
appeared visible on the horizon to sweep it all away.

At its heart and center was the vibrant city of
Madrid.  As a smallish capital with a readership of
perhaps 50,000 persons, it may have lagged behind
London or Paris, but as a meeting-place for men and
women with ideas, for writers of all kinds, it had
become a natural focus for the lively cultural atmosphere in the Spain of the later eighteeenth century.[9]

Though Charles with his passion for planning and
design was still a bit out of step with the real
character of the people -- essentially conservative
even by his standards and secretly liking the old
ways -- there was on this account a bond of sympathy
between himself and many writers, who springing from
hidalgo or manteista stock judged society and upheld
its values by the institutions he created.  Yet it
was the people themselves with all their faults, who
provided writers with the material they needed.  There
was the famous satirist José Cadalso, young soldier
and patriot killed before Gibraltar, whose *Los eruditos
a la violeta* and *Cartas marruecas* caustically rebuked his
countrymen for their superficial attitude to learning,
for their exotic preferences in foreign manners and
dress.  There was the didactic poet and comedy writer,
Tomás de Iriarte, civil servant turned critic, who
tried to preach the new morality beneath the guise
of laughter and fable.  Drawing from the crowd especially moved the playwright Ramón de la Cruz, com-
poser of short fiery episodes about life in Madrid,
with its local color of passion and intrigue, and
where from such realism one suspects that even Nicolás
Fernández de Moratín, pro-French experimentalist and
stern critic of Calderonian drama, drew his main material for the theatre.  The works of all these writers
were being read in ever increasing numbers.  But perhaps the greatest feature were the groups of eager
citizens discussing the future of their country in

the crowded cafes, or the theatre audiences, noisy
and vituperative, yet steeped in a groundling's love
for the boards. This was also the age of the literary gathering, like the salon in France, presided
over by great ladies of society such as the Duchess
of Huéscar or the Marquesa de Santa Cruz.

Here too could be found an outstanding member
of the royal Economic Society of Madrid, Gaspar de
Jovellanos. A graduate from Alcalá de Henares,
then a lawyer in Andalusia and member of Olavide's
circle in Seville, the young thinker whose early
plays such as *El delincuente honrado* were performed
successfully in that city was destined one day to
eclipse his resplendent Peruvian friend. In 1778,
Jovellanos came to Madrid as *Alcalde de casa y corte*,
an important promotion thanks to Campomanes' help.
This brought him in contact with prominent men in
society, among them Francisco Cabarrús, financier
from France and royal adviser, and Marqués Bernardo
del Campo, a later ambassador to England. Jovellanos
studied Adam Smith and other English writers, and
held that the backward state of Spanish agriculture,
a legacy of moribund landowning practice, was one
of the country's main evils. With stinging rebuke,
he cast his barbs at estates held in mortmain, at
obstructive labor guilds, at restrictions on artistic expression.[10] But there was more to Jovellanos
than a mere polemicist who states the obvious; and
few suspected that his prolific writings on political economy and a host of other subjects would make
him the greatest figure in the later stages of the
enlightenment. Patron of writers and journalists
from his lofty position on the royal council of
Knighthood Orders, Jovellanos inspired many to follow
similar intellectual careers, among them a young
student and poet, Juan Meléndez Valdés, whom he
helped get a chair in humanities at the university
of Salamanca.

Many of these figures were painted by that supremely great master, Francisco Goya. His secret stemmed
from a rejection of accepted norms, an irrational
exultation of the bizarre, his deeper religion of
protest -- a protest as much against the international

298

brotherhood of nobles as against the bigotry and ignorance of the masses. It was the sort of gospel, given royal and Christian overtones and its earlier modesty, which even Charles might have felt at home with. As a younger artist in Saragossa and Madrid, Goya was busy absorbing the influence of traditional court painters such as Francisco Bayéu, Giovanni Tiepolo, and Anton Mengs, the latter directing his famous cartoon work for the royal tapestry factory at Santa Barbara, begun in 1775. Five years later Goya was elected a member of the royal academy of San Fernando in Madrid. Having already attracted Charles' attention, he found it a short step to the post of court painter himself in 1786, so that the King and Goya came to know each other well during these late years. A startling tapestry design of the artist, *El albañil herido* (the injured mason) reflected Charles' decree back in 1778 requiring all scaffolding for royal or public works to be safely constructed so as to prevent accidents to workers.[11] Matter-of-fact in its portrayal of suffering yet speaking a clear message, the work foreshadowed Goya's later world -- the world of the immortal *caprichos*, in which there is an affinity in color with the flesh-and-blood *sainetes* of Ramón de la Cruz, depicting dramatic, brutal, even farcical scenes from the daily life of Madrid. Though Charles was more pleased to have his Goya in a calmer mood, busily portraying his royal self as a huntsman in the familiar style of a Velázquez, it was largely this vivid spectacle of crowd scenes in the capital -- raw and untrained, yet gifted with explosive energy -- which provided a *raison d'être* for the later eighteenth-century enlightenment.

Despite the brilliant cultural atmosphere and sense of fulfillment, where Charles personally was concerned he shared less of the optimism, for he felt a deep sorrow and nostalgia at the many disappointments encountered within his own family. The death of his wife long ago at the age of thirty-six cast its shadow down the years; and about the only contact her relatives ever made with him was to beg for money.[12] But the real sting was the knowledge that the once promising union with his wife had produced a poor progeny, at least among his eldest sons.

The firstborn Felipe who was retarded, had fortuit-
ously died in 1777, while Carlos and Fernando, the
heir to the Spanish throne and the king of Naples
respectively, were both mediocre in the extreme.
Antonio Pascual, the youngest and least likely to
inherit, was quietly married off to a relative, and
it was Gabriel Antonio, a studious attentive prince
and the apple of his eye, in whom Charles placed his
hopes for the future. Of his two surviving daughters,
María Josefa was slightly deformed and never married,
while María Luisa Antonia had long left Spain to
marry Leopold of Tuscany who was destined to become
the Hapsburg Emperor in 1790.

Of Leopold's sisters, one had married Charles'
nephew the Duke of Parma, while another, Maria Carolina, was the wife of Charles' son Ferdinand. The
latter was very much the queen of Naples. Like their
ill-fated sister Marie Antoinette, these Hapsburg
princesses were strong-willed women who caused
Charles much trouble in seeming to challenge the
traditional concept of wifely propriety. Their husbands appeared in a poor light, and on frequent occasions Charles begged Ferdinand of Naples to respect
the honor and dignity of his Bourbon lineage: "Open
your eyes, my son, and recognize those who would de-
ceive you and whose purpose ... is to slight me behind your back, and after turning you into a paper
king, to force you to surrender your honor, your
concern for the well-being of your children, and
your very soul".[13]

Disgust at his son's dissipation, at his daughter-
in-law's usurping of authority, ran through all his
letters. Tanucci had brought his attention to this
sorry pass, but Tanucci's days were numbered as a new
personality had emerged to play a great part in Neo-
politan affairs. This was the Englishman John Acton,
who found it easy to work on Queen Carolina's anti-
Spanish sentiments as he insinuated himself into
cabinet politics, having been introduced thereto
through the support of Leopold. An excellent naval
captain who had once fought with Spain and Tuscany
against Algiers in 1775, Acton was soon to reorganize
the Neapolitan fleet, praising Rodney above Lángara,

300

and it was not long before the pro-Spanish minister
of state, Marchese della Sambuca was hard put to extract loyalty to Charles from the royal couple.  Indeed Charles was so angry when a visitor from Naples,
General Francesco Pignatelli, tried to explain why
Acton should not be dismissed that he turned his back
on his guest quite pointedly.  The fact was that the
Queen with her British favorite -- the future Sir John
Acton whom she was to make royal adviser -- prepared
the way for the eventual predominance of Austrian and
British influence at her court.  It was a bitter pill
for Charles to swallow after so many years of patient
diplomacy on behalf of Bourbon interests; but the
unkindest cut of all was that his own son was entirely
to blame.

Similar setbacks to his hopes occured at home.
Here Carlos his heir -- the Prince of Asturias and
the future Charles IV -- was turning out a disappointment in much the same way as Ferdinand had already
proved a disappointment in Naples.  Certainly there
was no question of the prince's mediocrity.  The many
solicitudes Charles delivered to his son fell on deaf
ears.  Fond of clocks and hunting and a bright social
life, Carlos yet lacked the political acumen of his
father or the will for serious study, preferring the
gossip of the downstairs palace staff -- a weaker
version in fact of his cousin Louis XVI.  His casual-
ness was such that he would refer to the American envoy as "Minister of the Colonies" long after the war
of Independence was over.  The future decadence of
Spain shone in his face -- benevolent but ineffectual
in the proverbial weak mouth, puffy reddish cheeks,
meaningless long nose, the jutting chin above the
strong stocky frame surmounted by a small round head.
His wife was the dominating María Luisa of Parma, and
it seemed as if the pair were deliberately heading
the so-called Aragonese faction just to provoke Charles
and oppose his policies.  What was worse, María Luisa
indulged in masquerades with which to cloak her amor-
ous intrigues, thus ushering in the latest social style,
all of which displeased her father-in-law considerably
more than her unsuspecting husband.  "What a complete
fool you are", Charles replied to his son when the
latter told him that his wife could not possibly be
unfaithful because the companions she chose were

301

necessarily inferior in rank to himself.[14] Yet
unfaithful she almost certainly was; and despite the
customary exile given to some of her more zealous
favorites, it was in this way that Manuel de Godoy
from Badajoz finally rose to power, having first
attracted her attention as a member of the royal
bodyguard when he dramatically fell from his horse.
In Godoy flowed the currents of factionalism and
corruption which were to ruin Spain after Charles'
death, as much as María Luisa herself presented to
the outside world a bewildering mixture of reckless-
ness, ruthlessness, and social charm.

Another relative who vexed Charles by his conduct was his younger brother Luis, the former Card-
inal-Archbishop of Toledo. As a music-lover, Luis
well remembered Domenico Scarlatti and often played
duets with Father Antonio Soler, besides having Luigi
Boccherini employed on his staff. Unfortunately the
prince loved pleasure a great deal more. Released
from his vows but without permission to marry, aged
nearly fifty in 1776, Luis in his state of celibate
frustration developed such a propensity for chasing
girls through forest glades, with the ulterior motive
fully realized, that his confessors had to force him
to kneel and beg forgiveness from the King. Torn between disapproval of these dark sins of the flesh and
affection for his brother, Charles would relent, and
once hit upon the idea of marrying him off to his own
daughter María Josefa, who, it was hoped, would make
of her uncle a good repentant husband. But despite
her frailty and slight physical handicap, the princess was no fool and she refused to have him. Eventually in the summer of 1776, Luis married María
Teresa Villabriga of the Torreseca family who were
minor Aragonese nobility; but not before Charles in
his desire to protect the Bourbon lineage had decreed
that no marriages of unequal rank could take place
without the royal and paternal consent. His brother,
after all, stood close to the throne; and the marriage in fact aroused Charles' deepest disgust, so
much that he insisted that Luis as the mere Conde de
Chinchón and his bride be ostracized at court for
this virtual morganatic marriage, and that their
children (unavailingly as it turned out) be denied
any other surname than that of plain Villabriga.

302

Yet Luis' death on August 7, 1785, at his residence in Arenas de San Pedro affected him deeply.[15] His brother after all had made a good hunting companion in days gone by, and this was enough to win final grace in Charles' eyes. The crowning irony greeted the King posthumously when one of Luis Chinchón's daughters married none other than Manuel de Godoy himself -- an irony softened by the beautiful portrait of the young Condesa de Chinchón which court-painter Goya has given to the world.

The early deaths of many of his grandchildren -- the future Ferdinand VII of Spain, born to María Luisa in 1784 was an exception -- also affected him deeply. Increasingly it was Gabriel Antonio in whom Charles now pinned his hopes for future progeny. For this purpose a double wedding took place in 1785 when Gabriel was married to Mariana Victoria, daughter of the Portugese sovereigns, while the heir to the Portuguese throne, John, was married to Carlota, daughter of María Luisa. Arranged through his cooperative sister María Ana, now queen mother of Portugal, and his ambassador Conde de Fernán Núñez, the marriages delighted Charles, who hoped thereby to be blest with more descendants to keep the dynasty alive. Yet it was Gabriel who was his obvious favorite, and it was no secret that in the event of the extinction of the Asturian line then Gabriel's issue would decide the future of Spain's monarchy. Under these circumstances it was not surprising that there was considerable friction between Gabriel and the heir-apparent Carlos with his scheming consort, and there was a race to beget children. If to their rivalry be added the no less scheming Maria Carolina of Naples who bullied her husband into laying plans for a joint throne of Naples and Spain under the ill-founded notion that Charles might be contemplating abdication, then we have a picture of all three branches of Bourbons jockeying for the Spanish inheritance.[16]

Saddened by the defiant attitude of his two daughters-in-law, the King looked ever more hopefully towards his third, Mariana Victoria of Portugal, by whom Gabriel was expected to produce a stalwart crop of heirs.[17] Charles' hopes were dashed when in November 1788 the princess died of smallpox, taking her newborn infant with her. But worse was to follow. A few days afterwards, the greatest blow of all was struck when

Gabriel himself died. It was as if some higher power had deliberately schemed to wipe out an entire family -- his favorite one at that. "With Gabriel gone, I hardly care to live", muttered the aging King, and it proved an apt presentiment. That same month while Gabriel's body lay in the monastery of San Lorenzo at the Escorial, Charles took to his bed with a chill for practically the first time since he had left Naples.

The monarch who once commented, apropos of hunting, that "rain breaks no bones" now felt dampness and old age creeping into them. His tragic personal loss began to undermine his frame, sapping his strength. He knew the secret motives behind his passion for the chase -- keeping up his health and spirits as a check on melancholia -- now served him little purpose, knew that Goya's portraits of him showing the once lively huntsman, gun in hand, only underscored his own mortality. Death and sorrow hung like twin shadows over the huge Escorial. With most of his friends gone -- Tanucci and Roda in 1783, Squillace and Múzquiz two years later, José de Gálvez in 1787 -- he felt his own turn could not be far away. Dutifully, with clockwork repetition, as if assured that such habits would earn him a place in heaven, Charles kept doggedly to the old routine -- the Pardo in January, the Royal Palace till approaching Easter, Aranjuez in the spring, La Granja in the summer, the Escorial in the fall. Now it was December, and it was time to go back to the capital for the winter, but on this occasion Charles did not care to move. When Floridablanca rebuked him for prolonging his stay at the Escorial, he retorted, "Have no fears, Moñino; isn't it obvious that in a few days I'll be taken on a much longer journey from these four walls"? [18]

Yet by a supreme effort he was back at the capital where he took up residence in the Palacio de Oriente, on the site of the old Alcázar where he was born. He revived a little in his confinement, but it was obvious that the chill he had caught was developing into a relentless gnawing fever. The intense cold from outside crept along the walls of the corridors, into the palatial rooms, down towards the bed on which the King lay slowly dying, strengthening his conviction that the end was near. The death on December 9 of his confessor, the mercurial Father Eleta, adviser in so many of his policies, was like a rehearsal for the royal act that was to follow.

Charles retained his composure to the last and was able to chat with a few visitors, among them the Duke of Bourgoing. As the days slipped by, the reliquary of St. Isidore was brought to the palace, the last sacrament administered, the Papal blessing given. While his will and testament were being read out, Floridablanca broke down and wept, to which Charles from his deathbed reacted with the comment, "Did you really think I was going to live for ever"? On December 14, 1788, shortly before one o'clock in the morning and close on his seventy-third year, the King died, peace and forgiveness written on his face.

By torchlight the next evening, the Spanish and Walloon Guards answered the last call of duty to their sovereign as they formed the funeral cortege, with miliary arms reversed, heading towards the Escorial. There his body was borne along the somber monastery of San Lorenzo to its last resting-place by the side of his beloved Maria Amalia, taken thither and buried with all the ceremony he had shunned. But his subjects felt that beneath all the trappings of pomp lay something precious, something beyond the death of a king, as if by instinct they recognized not merely a good and patriotic monarch but one of the greatest the nation had ever known.

# CHAPTER FIFTEEN

## VALEDICTION TO A KING

Charles' funeral on the eve of the great French Revolution gave everyone cause for reflection. His own personal view of monarchy, shared by his people, had brought on a mood of critical examination; and in high places, appropriately enough, there was some trepidation for the future.

His greatest gift was his skill in using power -- power that he well knew was limited even for absolute kings, but which he used to fullest advantage for the furtherance of his country and dynasty. These two indeed constituted his main objectives. He had not listened in vain when his father recalled the resplendent age of Louis XIV, or when his tutors spoke with equal reverence of the earlier days of Ferdinand and Philip II. To win back power for Spain, Charles eagerly absorbed the tenets of Feijóo, with his emphasis on a Catholic church marching in step with the scientific state, and he had struck up a lifelong friendship with Tanucci, that Tuscan immortal, whose ideas about curbing the power of the nobles, promoting industry, and tackling the problems of poverty all made deep impressions upon him. As a younger man he had introduced enlightened reforms in Naples and made it an important center in Italy; and along the way he had learnt how to get the best out of men and nationalities. As king of Spain he set about implementing the same kind of reforms, in which through all the complex opposition he would brook no deviation from his appointed task.

Ministers were chosen for their ability regardless of background, and in exchange for unswerving loyalty were given long tenure of office. Promotion by merit was his watchword. By subtle pressures they had been moulded into a workable team, so that rule by committee, deliberative rather than legislative outside the royal sanctum of decretal power, was brought to a higher level of efficiency than in some other countries which already had a legislature. Noble and knight, churchman and commoner, each had their say, though not in formal assembly. But in

306

the final analysis his ministers were there to advise,
not to command.  Thus he had not hesitated, for example, to dismiss Aranda, who clearly overstepped
the bounds of royal criticism, replacing him eventually by a manteista like Campomanes.  Yet it would
be a mistake to assume he preferred manteistas in
office as a class motive in itself.  When occasion
warranted he could equally employ 'Aragonese' sympathizers and nobles -- men like Múzquiz or Conde de
Ricla -- provided they fitted in with his scheme to
trim the bureaucracy of its surfeit of collegians,
dampen conciliar opposition, and expand the economy.
Within this context he was rarely prejudiced against
any individual.  Despite his excellent choice of a
manteista with Floridablanca's talents, Charles favored a cross-section of class background among his
ministers because together these could coalesce with
disparate elements in the nation at large, winning
them over to his centralist aims, if only because
too much dispersed regionalism was bad for Spain at
a time when the country was making strenuous efforts
to catch up with the rest of Europe.  Restore the
traditional councils, men of Charles' ilk might argue,
then Spain would relapse into separatist anarchy and
slip back to where she was under the later Hapsburgs.

Charles' view was essentially correct in terms
of meeting a historic need.  It was, perhaps, this
awareness of past decadence which formed a binding
link with his people, nobles included.  They may have
given him some hard knocks in the Squillace riots,
but they finally accepted his mandate to rule, and
his regime was to prove more of a unifying paternal-
ism than a harsh compelling dictatorship.  In its moderation it took Spain as it was, rather than created
a new one in its image.  The nation moreover was
ready for great things even without the presence of
Charles, for the instinct to improve had already pene-
trated the national consciousness.  Nonetheless his
special personality converted this awareness into
something of a dynamic quality, short-lived as it was,
as if Spaniards knew that this was to be the last
great chapter in Spain's imperial history and that
it needed a king to stamp it with his seal of approval,
bringing three centuries to a fitting conclusion.

The monarchy, then, shaped as well as shared in this new awakening. Economic rather than philosophical, the new enlightened mood was of French origin no doubt, but essentially Spanish and *sui generis* within its terms of reference. Spain was getting tired of theosophic tracts and in her last expanse of horizon longed for action. But the kind of action which Charles offered -- reform of dress, reform in the universities, the harnessing of the church's apparata to the needs of the state, better use of labor and land resources, the stimulus of competition -- went further than was pleasing to many of his subjects. In his insistent way he was determined to make society responsive to his own notion of change, if necessary by fiat, and by risking his popularity of which only an enlightened despotism was capable. Yet in the end he won the cooperation of most social groups, if only because there was no other alternative. To wealthy nobles aspiring to commerce, to impoverished hidalgos, to smaller merchants and artisans, even the religious orders, the regime was becoming a social revolution in the name of autocratic monarchy, a march of progress in the name of moral benevolence. Despite the fact that too few of his subjects fully understood what Charles was trying to do -- stir the national conscience to its deepest roots and help the very poor -- the contradictions strangely worked; and Spain in the last years of his reign showed a surprising degree of harmony, bringing benefits to enormous numbers of people -- and without the mass debasement of human dignity which was to characterize other revolutions shortly to follow.

It was perhaps a feeling for justice and tradition which gave this reform spirit its sense of continuum, its special vitality. As Jovellanos put it: "Without respect for custom, no state can reap permanent advantages ... Virtue should be the basis for the happiness of man as well as for the welfare of states in general ... How often have we seen wealth and sheer armed might linked to oppression ... and to the ruin of empires"?[1] The King would have agreed with Jovellanos. He did of course believe in armed might but not at the expense of virtue, which for him as for the reformers meant a moral and social appeal backed by the unifying principle of monarchy.

This meeting-point between monarchy and modernity was unusual for Spain. The reform spirit was clamoring for institutional progress, not for abstract metaphysics; and as the tide flowed, almost carrying the King along with it, it began to explore deeper confines, make deeper commitments than could be done by legislation alone. Criticism grew less self-conscious, less of a pastiche of what other countries were saying about Spain; and in response, problems began to be solved by solutions, not by bombastic rhetoric for shelving in government files. As the nation slowly opened up its resources, Charles' task became progressively easier. In a case of rare praise coming from a Frenchman, that discerning diplomat Jean-Francois Bourgoing, commented that Spain received from nature "a climate the most favorable to every kind of cultivation which will make her one of the most flourishing nations of Europe whenever she shall remedy certain errors and abuses which have hitherto proved most destructive to both her population and industry".[2]

Charles' regime had done much to remedy 'errors and abuses'. There were the experimental farms at Aranjuez, the colonizing project in the Sierra Morena, the economic societies with royal patronage of various schools. To further education, more secular subjects were introduced at secondary level, with more university chairs in public law and the sciences; and the upsurge in geology, mining, mechanical drawing, textiles, glass-making, porcelain and botany all contributed to the growth of a technical elite. Neither were the peasants neglected. The alcabala and millones taxes had been reduced in Castile, with a new tax on land instituted in their place. His government made a clean sweep wherever stagnation had fastened its hold, from the freeing of communal lands for development to the attack on the Mesta and guilds in general, thus permitting more competition among smaller farmers and artisans. In increasing labor efficiency, his government also brought private charities more under the control of the state and reduced the temporal power of the church, but without too much offending it -- a task highly delicate by any standards. The

309

effect of many funding institutions, such as the
great National Bank of San Carlos, was to release
more capital for development and create more employment.  While roads and canals still left much to be
desired, completed public works form an impressive
list, serving to make Madrid more accessible as the
hub of a great empire.  It was Charles who ordered
this capital to be cleaned and embellished, replete
with parks, avenues, and new buildings; and the city
became enriched by the flow of commerce, from fancy
goods to watches, lenses and machinery.  In the provinces the royal factories coexisted with private
industry.  The woolens and velvets of Castile, the
calico of Valencia and Catalonia, the fruits and
hides and precious stones of the south, the iron
goods of the north, all reflected the increasing respect Europe had for the products of Spanish enterprise.  From the many contradictions between planning
and regional competition, between protection and a
freer trade, Charles' regime by trial and error
managed to stimulate both alternatives, thus 'squaring
the circle' and setting a constructive course rare in
the annals of later Spanish history.

Throughout his reign, Charles sought by every
means to make his country catch up with the outside
world.  Thus he did not shirk to apply policies alien
to traditional ideas -- the study of new techniques,
attacks on monopolies, the freeing of commerce.
Neither did he begrudge the services of foreigners.
There were Italians and Irishmen in government, Frenchmen and Dutchmen in industry, while Prussian tactics
were taught in the army, English techniques studied
in the navy.  Overseas, Spanish-Americans could share
in the administration and explore new horizons on
the high seas, many of whom were raised to the rank
of nobility for their services to industry.  In the
American war, substantial aid short of actual troops
had been sent to the Patriot forces and successful
blows struck at Spain's historic English rival.  From
San Antonio to San Francisco, from Paraguay to
Patagonia, the empire expanded as never before,
and the Spanish Main became once more a fact.  With
goods and services growing by leaps and bounds, the
empire took on a new resilience, a new dimension.

Charles was like a late Roman emperor, giving it a
new lease on life; and though deeper social issues
were neglected in contrast to what he did at home,
he left Spanish America considerably larger than the
independent Spanish-speaking America which followed.
The latter has shrunk while the United States and
Brazil have expanded.

In the light of all this, it is hardly correct
to say that his foreign policy was unsuccessful. By
the close of his reign he was sought after by the
powers of Europe in many disputes, and at his death
he left Spain very much more powerful and prosperous
than when he first assumed the throne. The nation
had reached its highest pinnacle since the days of
Philip II.

Great as these achievements were, Charles did
not, indeed could not, go all the way in transforming
the country. That he herein failed was as much due
to the psyche of his subjects and the limitations of
society, as to his own. He had his peculiarities --
loving dogs and trees, perhaps, more than some human
beings, from the Jesuits to Joseph II. Yet as a prac-
ticing Catholic he sincerely wanted to help all kinds
of people. If he was unsympathetic towards Freemasons,
he would have liked to allow at least Jews the right
to re-enter the country, as he had tried to do in
Naples, but prevailing attitudes prevented such a
move. Where gypsies were concerned however, he made
short shrift of prejudice by declaring them to be in
no way an infected race, and he also supported lower
tradesmen as well as women in their struggle to work
more freely in society. Perhaps doctors as a profession aroused his displeasure too uncharitably --
there was little to please him in an age when crushed
vipers and snail-shells were still being dispensed
for a wide range of diseases -- but he did found medical buildings, and used his extensive assets in the
American quinine market, taken over from the Jesuits,
for treating the ague and other shivering fevers.
As he wrote to Louis XVI a few months before his own
death, he never had faith in new-fangled ideas like
vaccination for smallpox, it was too unreliable, but
he hoped the inoculation would work and prove harmless in the case of Louis' children.[3] He was an

unusual mixture of conservatism and innovation --
but the latter had to prove its results.

Granted his oddities he had otherwise a sympathetic nature, but his extreme caution in many respects was due to what he had come to learn by experience -- there was always the danger of riots and
revolutions. The mobs of Madrid had been won over
it was true, but other forces lurked in the background. The nobles remained the nobles -- powerful,
resentful, in some cases extremely able, especially
in the diplomatic service which Charles largely entrusted to loyal grandees; but these too could rebel.
Neither was the Inquisition wholly destroyed, nor
the Mesta, nor many monopolies, while tax reforms
certainly did not go deep enough. Enclosure landlords were getting richer, while at the other end of
the scale too many poor whom Charles had pledged to
help remained just as poor. There was a price to be
paid for development, and in having to be constantly
on his guard he could only go so far.

Perhaps the greatest problem facing him was the
inherent contradiction in reform itself. If this
was to be advanced through state direction of industry and greater freedoms in trade, then the increased ·
prosperity would only show up the inequalities further;
but if reform was pushed too far, then the resultant
reaction might be to threaten the structure of the
monarchy itself, undermining the very foundations
which the reforming forces were based. To use later
terms, progressive liberals would be at loggerheads
with Carlist conservatives (which plagued Spain in
the next century), with both appealing to regional
interests to reinforce their case. And Charles well
knew from experience how similar interest could
challenge the pivotal base upon which the Bourbons
rested. In confronting this dilemma, and to placate
in some degree noble and regional forces inherent
with the Aragonese faction, he lent government support
to widespread institutions of capitalism -- moving
away from direction by the state towards more freedom
from the state. And in the Spain of the 1780's with
all the current economic gains, the chances of a violent social upheaval overtaking the state itself as
was shortly to occur in France, seemed very unlikely.

In the light of these conditions, can Charles be regarded as a great king? Does posterity agree with those who lamented his passing? If the word 'great' means a driving lust for military expansion, the gift of a brilliant intellect, the fondness for techniques which must be taught by force to obedient subjects in the sense of a Frederick the Great who absolutely dominated his kingdom, the answer must be "no". Charles was convivial and peace-loving, he had no super-intellect beyond the shrewdest common sense, and he could not always do with Spain what he liked. But if 'great' can mean benevolent rule at a lower level of intensity, inspiring others via the arts and sciences to work towards higher goals for the nation because they understand the purpose -- making good bureaucrats of those who do not -- and all the while preventing the throne from becoming too awesome a thing, yet cleansing the nation beneath it from corruption, then Charles does certainly qualify. He was the greatest of the Spanish Bourbon kings. He had a supreme capacity for making his subjects listen -- without rhetoric or high-sounding phrases; and in the end they complied because they knew he understood their problems, because they had grown to love him. He alone was able to weld all of Spain's disparate elements into a coherent whole -- to reconcile manteista with merchant, Castile with Catalonia -- and to replace nepotism and too narrow an elitism with rationality in governing.

Though he could make immortal utterance now and then, having a keen perception with an excellent memory, perhaps there was one defect to his greatness in the very Spanish sense that the dreamer and the man of action never quite meet. His dreams were spent on hunting which he wrote too much about, his deeds buried in the obstructionism of the society he inherited. And here not even his austere piety could save him. It was a superhuman task to transform Spain into an advanced Western state, but he went a long way to bridging the gap. He was every inch a king, the first truly revolutionary one Spain ever had, who laid the groundwork for a broad social and institutional progress.[4] Of his great contemporaries, be it noted, Joseph II of Austria who had similar views, was even less successful in awakening the national conscience, while Catherine II of Russia did not dare, or deign, to awaken it at all.

"One's job", he reportedly said, "is to clarify rights, not to gloss over with compromises; I know how to pardon my own faults in this respect, and I don't expect other people to ask my pardon for theirs".[5] It was Charles with his peculiar personality -- cautious yet persistent in his achievements, stubborn yet human in his failings -- who made some mark on history as he reversed Spain's decline and left her incontestably a great European power once more, albeit for the last time. Perhaps the highest tribute that can be paid to him is one that he himself aspired to receive. When asked as a boy how he would like posterity to remember him, the prince aswered: "With the title of Charles the Wise".[6] We may grant him this wish; and this same quality is reflected in the words of advice he gave his own son: "...Carry on the work of reform as zealously as I began it ... remedy the errors so common in government, and thus you need never fear the beneficial effects of enlightenment. Kings can put things right when they make harmful but unintentional mistakes. The real harm comes from the base motives of those around you who use your authority maliciously in order to undermine it ... Avoid this very great danger ... and you will see the glow of public approval rising above the noise of passion and conflict, guiding you in safety ... This generous and loyal nation who loves her princes and crowned my father only needs such clear guidance to become the foremost nation of all. Fulfill this great commitment, and before you die you will see the inspiring example ... of thousands of subjects indebted to you for their happiness and that of future generations".[7]

A sad document indeed seeing what a failure son Charles IV turned out to be. Spain's permanent decline from the great-power status left by his father really began with the French Revolution and Napoleon, when the spiritual challenge of the one, the bloody invasion by the other, proved simply too overwhelming for the country to withstand. It was a tragedy that the reform movement of the eighteenth century came just too late to implant in the country

a strong solidifying permanence. With Spain suffering
for freedom's sake more than any other nation in the
struggle against Napoleon, the way was open for the
crumbling of her own empire. But responsibility for
these calamities can hardly be laid at the door of
Charles III. His was a precious silver age -- of
Aranda and Jorge Juan, of Campomanes and Floridablanca,
of Jovellanos and the young Goya. The French Revolution was a different age, one of violent social conflict with much physical destruction, which fortunately
for Charles he did not live to see.

Charles III, by Francisco Goya

## FOOTNOTES TO THE CHAPTERS

### ABBREVIATIONS USED IN THE FOOTNOTES

AGS            Archivo (General) de Simancas,
               Valladolid.

AHN            Archivo Histórico Nacional, Madrid.

PRO            The Public Record Office, London.

For further details, see the bibliography.

Unless otherwise stated, Charles' letters usually originate in Naples when he was king of the Two Sicilies and in Madrid when he was king of Spain.

Abbreviated titles in the footnotes refer back to their full title mentioned the first time in each chapter of footnotes. Additional works used or recommended are listed at the end of each chapter of footnotes. Full titles with their publishers can be found in the bibliography under the authors' names (with Spanish authors frequently entered under the middle name).

Currency has generally been converted to basic vellon reales where Spain is concerned, of which 9000 approximate to 100 pounds sterling, and to silver pesos where the Indies are concerned, of which one peso equals 20 reales. The term 'billion' means a thousand million, conforming to U.S. and French usage. For further details on money, see Appendix II.

Underlined words denote book titles, italics, and foreign terms.

PROLOGUE

1     For revolt in Aragon and Valencia, with their
      strong residue of pro-Hapsburg nobility see
      Henry Kamen, The War of Succession in Spain,
      1700-15, Bloomington, Ind., 1969, pp.242-308.

2     The shorter Spanish name of Isabel has been used
      throughout instead of the Italian name Isabella.

3     Whether this boy was Isabel's son by Alberoni,
      as the Jesuits were supposed to have alleged
      later according to those seeking to incriminate
      them in Charles' eyes, will never be known one
      way or the other; but the chances are that he
      was legitimate. For Charles' involvement with
      this question, see chapter 7 on the Jesuits.

David Francis, The First Peninsular War, 1702-1713,
    London, 1975.

Martin S. Hume, Spain; its Greatness and Decay
    (1479-1788), Cambridge, England, 1905, esp.
    chapter XII on Philip's involvement with the war.

Edward Armstrong, Elizabeth Farnese, "the Termagant
    of Spain", London, 1892.

Simon Harcourt-Smith, Alberoni; or the Spanish
    Conspiracy, London, 1943.

Alfred Baudrillart, "Examen des droits de Philippe V
    et de ses descendants au trône de France en dehors
    des revendications d'Utrecht", Revue d'Histoire
    diplomatique, III, 1889.

CHAPTER ONE

1     Following the Spanish form, his name would be
      'the Prince-Infante Don Carlos of Bourbon-Farnese'.

2     Charles' other maternal grandparent was Eduardo
      of Farnese-d'Este; his paternal grandparents
      were the Dauphin of France and Maria Christina
      of Bavaria.

3    María Ana, rejected as bride to Louis XV on
     account of her youth by the Duke of Bourbon's
     government, became eventually the queen of Por-
     tugal.  Felipe became Duke of Parma in 1748 by
     the treaty of Aix-la-Chapelle.  Isabel's other
     surviving children were María Teresa Rafaela
     (born 1726) who married the Dauphin in 1745;
     Luis Antonio (born 1727) who entered the church
     with the title of Cardinal-Infante, archbishop
     of Toledo; and María Antonia Fernanda (born
     1729) who became queen of Savoy-Sardinia.  These
     marriages with fellow-royalty reflect the dyn-
     astic ambition of the parents.

4    Jean Ranc as court painter was succeeded in 1737
     by Michael Louis Van Loo.

5    In fact the king's share was often reduced to
     encourage the search for minerals, reaching as
     low as one tenth in Charles' reign.

6    e.g., in January 1726, to keep specie at home,
     Philip V decreed that the gold crown (escudo de
     oro) was now worth 18 double-silver reales in-
     stead of 16, and the silver piece of eight (peso)
     was now worth 9½ double-silver reales instead of
     8, while smaller silver monies were recalled to
     the mint.  In 1728 silver pieces of eight and
     four were ordered to be rounded and milled at
     the edges.  A silver real, incidentally, equalled
     2½ vellon reales.  See also Appendix II.

7    Quoted in Ramón Otero Pedrayo, El Padre Feijóo.
     Su vida, doctrina e influencias, Orense, Spain,
     1972, p. 163.

8    Ibid., pp. 164-5.

9    Another home for British Jesuits in Spain was
     the English College at Valladolid.

10   Pro-Hapsburg nobles who had been exiled were
     allowed to return by the treaty of Vienna in 1725.
     They recovered their property in most cases.
     Nobles of both sides gradually melded and became
     a political force once more in the councils.

11    Fiscals such as Miguel de Zabala y Auñón and
      Martín de Loynaz both urged tax reforms, as
      the power of extortionate tax-farmers was only
      partially being curbed.  Zabala wrote Miscelánea
      económico-política (1732), and addressed a Mem-
      orial or Representación to Philip V, pointing
      out that sometimes barely one tenth of certain
      provincial taxes ever reached the treasury.

12    Martin S. Hume, Spain: its Greatness and Decay
      (1479-1788), Cambridge, England, 1905, p. 382.

Henry Kamen, The War of Succession in Spain, 1700-15,
      Bloomington, Ind., 1969.

Alfred Baudrillart, Philippe V et la cour de France,
      Paris, 1890-1901, esp. vols. II and III.

Enrique de Tapia Ozcariz, Carlos III y su epoca,
      Madrid, 1962.

CHAPTER TWO

1     Documents on the treaty of Seville, November 9,
      1729, Legajo 3365, AHN.  The correspondence of
      Willian Stanhope (Earl of Harrington and British
      ambassador to Spain) with his successor Benjamin
      Keene throws much light on Anglo-Spanish rela-
      tions and is found in the Spanish Papers, PRO.

2     Documents on the (second) treaty of Vienna, July
      22, 1731, with successive clauses, Legagos 3365
      and 3390, AHN.

3     One of Charles' hosts was the Prince of Campo-
      florido, commandant of Valencia, who later as
      envoy to Naples maintained strong Spanish influ-
      ence at this court.

4     Sarmiento (q.v. in bibliography) knew many sci-
      entists, besides befriending Aranda and Campo-
      manes.

5     Harold Acton, The Bourbons of Naples, 1734-1825,
      New York, 1956, pp. 13-16.

6 For Charles' travels through Florence, Parma, Colorno, and Piacenza, see his letters in French to his parents, 1731-3, Legajos 2453 and 2649, AHN.

7 Philip V's reply to Louis XV on proposals for the Family Compact (signed November 7), Bailén, May 31, 1733, Legajo 2453, AHN.

8 Philip V to Charles, Infante-Duke of Parma, San Lorenzo, October 26, 1733, Legajo 2453, AHN.

9 Supporting Montemar were the princes C. Torella and N. di Sangro, the (second) Duke of Berwick and Liria, Comte de Marsillac (who captured Aversa), Conde de Maceda (who captured Reggio), and Francesco di Eboli Duke of Castropignano (who forced Traun to withdraw to Capua and was to distinguish himself in the war of Austrian Succession). Supporting Traun were Prince Pignatelli di Monteleone and Admiral Pallavicini, the latter having hardly more than three frigates at his disposal.

10 For Charles' accounts of the invasion, see his letters to his parents from Arezzo, Perugia, and other places, March to May 1734, Legajo 2706, AHN.

11 Acton, The Bourbons of Naples ..., p. 24; Sir Charles Petrie, King Charles III of Spain, London, 1971, p. 29.

12 Isabel to Charles, San Lorenzo, October 1734, Legajo 2706, AHN.

13 See also Charles' letters to his parents, Naples and Aversa, December 1734, Legajos 2695 and 2715, AHN. Sicilian grandees included the Princes of Aragon, Pantelleria, and Poggio Reale.

14 Gaceta de Madrid, January 4, 1735.

15 Charles to his parents, Palermo, July 15, 1735, Legajo 2715, AHN.

16  Philip II of Spain gave Siena to the Duke of
    Florence in 1557, in exchange for the Presidii
    states of Tuscany, i.e., Santo Stefano, Orbe-
    tello, Porto Ercole, Talamone, Monte Argentario,
    and Porto Longone on the island of Elba. Doro-
    thea of Parma, incidentally, was asked to move
    to Naples in exchange for an annuity. See cor-
    respondence of Santisteban, fall of 1735, Legajo
    5806, AGS.

17  Diplomats included Cardinal Troiano Acquaviva
    (envoy to the Quirinal), Prince Bartolomo Cor-
    sini (the Pope's nephew), Mgr. Valenti Gonzaga,
    and Mgr. Celestino Galiani.

18  For further details, see chapter 5, footnote 7
    and text thereto.

19  The treaty of 1670 between Spain and England had
    fixed the southern-most line of English advance
    along the Altamaha river, and thus the British
    foundation of Georgia below this line was in
    violation of the treaty's terms.

20  e.g., Charles to his parents regarding naval
    stores for Spain, January 1741, Legajo 5927, AGS.

21  See Montealegre (Marqués de Salas) to Montemar
    and Castropignano, letters of January 1742, ff.,
    Legajo 5836, AGS, and Gages to Montealegre on
    his takeover of Spanish forces command from
    Montemar, September 11, 1742, Legajo 5842, AGS.

22  The half-hearted Montealegre was replaced by
    Marchese di Fogliani in 1744 when Bourbon forces
    were again threatened. Fogliani, envoy to The
    Hague and a later viceroy of Sicily, himself
    fell from power in 1755, when he was succeeded
    by Tanucci.

23  For the panic caused by earthquake tremors and
    Martin's visit, see Maria Amalia to Philip and
    Isabel, August 31, 1742, Legajo 2715, AHN, and
    Montealegre, ibid., Legajo 5927, AGS.

24  Philip V to Charles via Montealegre informing
    him of the second Family Compact between France
    and Spain, September 1743, Legajo 5841, AGS.

25  Charles to his parents on Gages' movements,
    March 20, 1744, Legajo 2711, AHN.

26  Prince Charles Stuart's father, James (the Old
    Pretender), was recognized by the Bourbons as
    titular claimant to the British throne, till
    his death in 1766, e.g., letter of 'King James
    III' to Charles III (of Spain), Rome, September
    18, 1759, Legajo 2862, AHN.

27  Charles to his parents, Velletri, August 12,
    1744, Legajo 2695, AHN.  His previous letters
    were penned mostly from Valmontone, June 30,
    July 14, July 21, and July 28, Legajo 2695, AHN.

Harold Acton, The Last Medici (Giovanni Gastone),
    London, 1932.

Gaspard Delpy, Feijóo et l'esprit européen ..., Paris,
    1936.

General Pietro Colletta, A History of the Kingdom of
    Naples, Edinburgh, Scotland, 1858, esp. vol. I.

Arthur C. Murray, An Episode in the Spanish War,
    1739-1744, London, 1952.

CHAPTER THREE

1  Santisteban (Santo Stefano in Italian), Montemar,
   Charni, Montealegre, Fogliani, Corsini, Tanucci,
   Niccolo and Placido di Sangro, Grazia Reale, and
   others, received ducat annuities for their services to the Spanish cause, funds being raised
   by setting aside two-thirds of tax proceeds from
   castles and forts in Naples.  See correspondence
   of Santisteban, 1735-6, Legajo 5806, AGS.

2  This concerned a Spanish soldier, who having de-
   serted in Tuscany after committing a crime,
   sought refuge in a church where he was arrested
   by the state, and Tanucci won his case against
   the petitioning Tuscan clergy.

3    For further details, see chapter 4, footnote 4 and text thereto.

4    See Conde de Fuenclara to the courts of Naples and Spain on the marriage question, February to April, 1737, Legajos 2561 and 2773, AHN.

5    e.g., Charles to his parents, Naples, letters of ca. January 7 and May 14, 1737, Legajo 2695 AHN.

6    Ibid., August 20, 1737.

7    Unsigned (probably Fuenclara) in response to Philip V's letter to the king of Poland regarding the marriage proposal as viewed from San Lorenzo, November 18, 1737, Legajo 2456, AHN.

8    Sebastián de la Cuadra to Fuenclara, Madrid, January 10, 1738, Legajo 2456, AHN.

9    See correspondence of Montealegre (Salas), summer of 1738, Legajo 5817, AGS.

10   Quoted in Harold Acton, The Bourbons of Naples, 1734-1825, New York, 1956, p. 73.

11   Ibid., p. 70.

12   See correspondence of Montealegre on excavations at Herculaneum, May 26 to October 31, 1739, Legajo 5826, AGS.

13   Other artists worthy of mention were: F. Chiello (an earlier painter); Francesco Solimena (portraitist); the Mengs family (portraitists); Giovanni Panini (landscape painter); Giuseppi delle Torre (painter of battle scenes); Santiago Nani (painter of flowers and animals); Nicola Sensapaura (ceramicist of allegorical figures); Sigismund Fischer (German miniaturist); and Pierre Chevalier (French jewel mounter). Many of these were associated with the Capodimonte workshops.

14   Pietro Gualtieri and Francesco Botinelli received royal grants to make white leather goods and glass mirrors respectively.

15    Caserta was a German headquarters during World
War II until it was surrendered to the British
general, Earl Harold Alexander.

E.J. Hobsbawm, *Primitive Rebels*, New York, 1959.

General Pietro Colletta, *A History of the Kingdom of
Naples*, Edinburgh, Scotland, 1858, esp. vol. I.

Enrique de Tapia Ozcariz, *Carlos III y su epoca*,
Madrid, 1962.

Sir Charles Petrie, *King Charles III of Spain*,
London, 1971.

CHAPTER FOUR

1    Charles talking to the Sardinian envoy (Monas-
terolo), quoted in Nicholas Henderson, "Charles
III of Spain: an Enlightened Despot", *History
Today*, October 1968, p. 677.

2    Giuseppe Pecchio, *L'Histoire de l'économie
politique en Italie*, Paris, 1830, pp. 414-5;
and General Pietro Colletta, *A History of the
Kingdom of Naples*, Edinburgh, Scotland, 1858,
vol. I, p. 134.

3    Pecchio, ibid., p. 414, and Colletta, ibid., pp.
25-8, 58. This total of 112,000 included 50,000
regular priests, 31,000 monks, 23,000 nuns, 116
bishops and 22 archbishops, the remainder mostly
novices.

4    Mortmain lands (see text *supra*) mean inalienable
lands vested in a corporate body, distinct from
entailed lands which are inalienably vested in
fixed heirs. The concordat itself additionally
confirmed a law of 1738 voiding the wills of
pious persons who left certain lands to the church,
the latter also losing exemption privileges in any
future expansion, with its new lands passing into
the secular category for tax purposes under the
census. Some personal tax exemptions and church
franchises were both curtailed. See also Colletta, ibid., pp. 58-61, 132; and Montealegre (Salas)
to Acquaviva re. disputes in the concordat, November 21, 1738, to May 10, 1740, Legajo 5821, AGS.

5   See correspondence of Montealegre giving reasons
    for admitting Jews, February 1740, Legajo 5829,
    AGS, and that of Fogliani giving reasons for
    expelling them, May 1747, Legajo 5849, AGS.

6   For references to measures *supra et infra* see
    Colletta, A History ... of Naples, pp. 7-137,
    *et passim*.

7   Ibid.

8   Other taxes included the *dazio* (1½ granos up-
    wards on meat, groceries, and silk cocoons);
    the *gabella* (a commune tax on the refining of
    silk and grain, the latter about 9 danari per
    Sicilian barrel); the *derrata* (about 10 carlini
    per *tomola* bushel levied on bulk products); and
    the *pedeggi* (on various items used in baking,
    pottery, etc.).  An agency known as the *real
    camara della sommaria* recorded transit and export
    taxes bearing such quaint terms as *ducato a soma,
    jus fondari, jus exiturae, due piazze* and *nuovo
    gabella*.

9   Based on a cost price of about 15 ducats per
    *salme* of olive oil at mid-century, arrendamento
    dues plus taxes to the state comprised between
    5 and 7½ ducats of this figure, which subse-
    quently raised the cost to 20 ducats.

10  The lucrative larger arrendamenti, such as those
    of the market chief and excise yielded enormous
    sums, and the treasury about tripled its gross
    revenue to make an annual net profit of 200,000
    ducats from the redemptions, though much dispute
    arose as to how to determine compensation based
    on prevailing values.

11  Total grain consumption in the city of Naples
    averaged about two million *tomola* per year during
    this period.

12  Patrick Chorley, Oil, Silk and Enlightenment:
    Economic Problems in Eighteenth-Century Naples,
    Naples, 1965, pp. 1-20, 44-55, 84-102, 137-148,
    175-7.

13    Ibid., pp. 137-148, 177-195.

14    Correspondence of Montealegre on a treaty with
      Turkey, autumn of 1740, Legajo 5830, AGS;
      Finochietti's follow-up visit, May 5, 1741,
      Legajo 5832, AGS; and the Bey of Tripoli's
      gift of animals to Charles, summer of 1741,
      Legajo 5833, AGS.

15    In the mid-1740's, conflicting money rates were
      eased; one Neapolitan carlin was fixed at half
      a Sicilian tari, with corresponding equivalents
      between Neapolitan carlini and the Sicilian scudo,
      zecchino, doppia, and oncia.  See Appendix II
      (Neapolitan values).

16    A good example of praise for Charles is given
      by Nicola Fortunato, Riflessioni intorno al
      commercio antico e moderno del regno di Napoli
      ... , Naples, 1760, p. 283, ff.

17    Though these figures are conjectural, it would
      appear from Colletta, Bianchini, and others that
      by 1760, noble revenues accounted for much more
      than the meager quarter million ducats of the
      gross in earlier years, and church revenues
      (because of the census) likewise more than the
      meager 600,000 ducats.  Both sources by 1760
      increased their yield nearly six times among
      the direct and indirect types of tax.  Redeemed
      arrendamenti also swelled the gross figure.
      But this estimate of 10 to 12 million ducats
      (about 2 million pounds sterling) cannot be
      considered a surplus because of escalating gov-
      ernment costs.

Lodovico Bianchini, Della storia delle finanze del
      regno di Napoli, Palermo, 1839, esp. vol. I.

_____, Della storia economico-civile
      di Sicilia, Palermo, 1841, esp. vol. II.

Tommaso Fornari, Delle teorie economiche nelle
      provincie napolitane dal MDCCXXXV al MDCCCXXX,
      Milan, 1888.

CHAPTER FIVE

1    Charles repeatedly expressed a wish for a son
     and heir to his parents, e.g., the letter of
     July 21, 1744, Legajo 2695, AHN. Carlos' birth
     was announced by Fogliani, November 11, 1748,
     Legajo 5850, AGS.

2    The boys' names in Italian would be Filippo
     Pasquale, Carlo, Ferdinando, Gabriele, Antonio
     Pasquale, and Francesco Xavier. Josefa Carmela
     would be Giuseppina Carmella.

3    Charles to Ferdinand VI, March 28, 1752, and
     Ferdinand to Charles, April 18, 1752, Legajo
     6080, AGS.

4    Yet Charles scotched any rumor that under French
     pressure he was thinking of proclaiming Don
     Philip as his heir; see letters of secretary
     Clemente de Aróstegui, ca. November 1754,
     Legajo 5858, AGS.

5    The acrimony can be sensed in her correspondence
     with Charles at this time, see Legajos 2755 and
     2777, AHN.

6    Enrique de Tapia Ozcariz, Carlos III y su epoca,
     Madrid, 1962. p. 160.

7    The idea of Spain buying out any renewal of the
     Asiento concession and involving the South Sea
     company's claims was discussed between the Duke
     of Sotomayor and Benjamin Keene at Lisbon in 1746,
     and again between Sotomayor and the Earl of Sand-
     wich at the Aix-la-Chapelle conference in October
     1748. Article 16 of this treaty, finalized a
     year later, extended the company's privileges
     for another four years, and laid the basis for
     the British government's abandonment of its
     slave trade dealings with the Indies in exchange
     for compensation to the company. The pro-French
     Ensenada naturally did his best to oppose com-
     pensation to the British.

8    Ensenada boosted silver mining, abolished tax-
     farming in many areas, and curtailed excise dues
     such as the *millones*. His extension of the single
     unified tax measures begun in Valencia during
     Philip V's time greatly helped the silk weaving
     industry, the number of looms increasing to over
     14,000 by 1750. At mid-century Spain's revenues
     exceeded 300 million reales, compared with about
     210 million in 1736, those from the Indies reach-
     ing 66 million, compared with about 40 million
     in 1736 (i.e., the latter up from 2 to 3 million
     pesos during this period). See also Martin S.
     Hume, Spain: its Greatness and Decay (1479-1788),
     Cambridge, England, 1905, pp. 382-8.

9    Ensenada's fall from power led to a joint effort
     by Spain and Portugal to enforce the treaty of
     1750 on the Paraguayans. Their subsequent riv-
     alry is treated in chapter 11.

10   Charles to Ferdinand, letters of September 1756
     ff., Legajo 6080, AGS.

11   Charles to Ferdinand, September 19, 1758, quoted
     in Tapia Ozcariz, Carlos III ... , p. 162.

12   Ricardo Wall to Charles via Tanucci, letters of
     September 1758, Legajo 6090, AGS.

13   Charles to the Prince of Yaci, December 19, 1758,
     quoted in Tapia, Carlos III ... , p. 164.

14   Quoted in ibid., p. 168.

15   Correspondence between Charles and Wall via
     Tanucci, letters of July 24 and August 5, 1759,
     Legajo 6090, AGS.

16   Charles to Isabel, August 22, 1759, Legajo 2714,
     AHN.

17   Proclamation of Charles as king of Spain, Sept-
     ember 11, 1759, Legajos 3028, AHN, and 6090,
     AGS.

18    Tapia, Carlos III ... , pp. 172-3. Regarding
      Tuscany and Naples (see text *infra*), Charles'
      daughter María Luisa Antonia married the Empress'
      son Archduke Leopold of Tuscany in 1764, and
      four years later her daughter Maria Josepha
      was betrothed to Ferdinand of Naples. The
      latter bride's untimely death led to her sister,
      Maria Carolina, being married to Ferdinand in-
      stead.

19    Tanucci to the government and people of Naples,
      October 5, 1759, Legajo 5866, AGS.

20    An impression of hysteria by the people is men-
      tioned by Charles on his way to Madrid through
      Catalonia in his letters to Tanucci of October
      1759, Libro 318, AGS.

Harold Acton, The Bourbons of Naples, 1734-1825,
      London and New York, 1956.

Sir Charles Petrie, King Charles III of Spain,
      London, 1971.

CHAPTER SIX

1     Squillace (Esquilache in Spanish) to Ricardo
      Wall, mutual correspondence, October to December
      1759, Legajo 2562, AHN.

2     Maria Amalia to Tanucci in Italian, commenting
      on the climate and matters of state, Aranjuez,
      May 13, 1760, Libro 317, AGS. See also Charles
      to Isabel, with post-script in French from Maria
      Amalia commenting on her failing health, Buen
      Retiro, September 13, 1760, Legajo 2777, AHN.

3     Quoted in Vicente Rodríguez Casado, La Política
      y los políticos en el reinado de Carlos III,
      Madrid, 1962, p. 77.

4     Funding for this purpose was done by raising a
      lump sum of 50 million reales, capital value
      being computed at the face amount existing in
      Philip V's time, plus a pro-rated appreciation
      factor of 10 per cent on assets and property,
      payable by the treasury.

5    Correspondence between Louis XV and Charles III
     via Grimaldi, August 15, 1761 ff., Legajo 3372,
     AHN.  Bourbon sense of family loyalty, Choiseul's
     demands on behalf of Spain (via envoy Bussy in
     London), and Charles' own demands (via Fuentes)
     on William Pitt leading to the breakdown of
     separate Anglo-French and Anglo-Spanish negoti-
     ations and to the protraction of the war, are
     described by Alfred Bourguet, "Le duc de Choiseul
     et l'Angleterre ... Le duc de Choiseul et l'ali-
     ance espagnole", Revue historique, LXXI, Sept-
     ember-October 1899, pp. 3-32.

6    Allan Christelow, "Economic Background of the
     Anglo-Spanish War of 1762", Journal of Modern
     History, XVIII, March 1946, pp. 22-36.

7    Further details of their rivalry are given in
     chapter 11.

8    For a good treatment of colegios mayores and Charles'
     manteista policy, see George M. Addy, The Enlight-
     ment in the University of Salamanca, Durham, N.C.,
     1966, pp. 56 ff., 160.

9    Sir James Harris, Diaries and Correspondence ...
     London, 1870, p. 51.

10   Situated in Calle de las Infantas near the Plaza
     del Rey, this was the residence of Prince Charles
     of England (afterwards Charles I) when he came
     over to Spain in 1623 to woo the Infanta.

11   Quoted in Enrique de Tapia Ozcariz, Carlos III
     y su epoca, Madrid, 1962, p. 225.

12   The price of bread was fixed at a maximum of 8
     cuartos (or 32 maravedis) per loaf during the
     war, which increased to 10 cuartos by 1765 when
     prices were freed; and the same trend applied
     to other basic items.  Yet a loaf of bread cost
     only 12 cuartos by 1790.

13   Sir Charles Petrie, King Charles III of Spain,
     London, 1971, p. 231.

14    Quoted in Tapia, <u>Carlos III</u> ... , p. 227.

15    Aranda to Roda, April 9, 1766, council of grace
      and justice, Legajo 1009, AGS. Aranda refers
      to a Father Yecla, while other accounts refer
      to a Father Cuenca, both of whom helped quiet
      the crowds.

16    The three favoring repressive measures were the
      Duke of Arcos, Conde de Gazola, and Conde de
      Priego. The other two favoring moderation were
      the Marqués de Sarria and Conde de Oñate.

17    Quoted in Tapia, <u>Carlos III</u> ... , p. 238.

18    Charles III to Tanucci, Aranjuez, March 26, 1766,
      Libro 330, AGS.

19    Rodríguez, <u>La Política</u> ... , p. 152; Tapia, <u>Carlos
      III</u> ... , pp. 215, 242.

20    Felipe Alvarez Requejo, <u>El Conde de Campomanes:
      su obra histórica</u>, Oviedo, 1954, pp. 31-34.

21    Rodríguez, <u>La Política</u> ... , pp. 155-161.

22    Aranda, for example was not too popular with the
      church for his benefice equalization plan of
      June 12, 1769. See the next chapter, footnote 19.

23    The big five guilds or *gremios* of Madrid were very
      strong in tapestries, cloth, silks, spices, drugs,
      jewelry, gold and silver. Having borrowed at
      2½ per cent during the Seven Years war, they then
      lent money to the government at 4¾ per cent, which
      prompted an angry Charles to comment that he had
      not borrowed from the gremios just to have them
      criticize his treasurer Squillace.

24    Political undercurrents, including Charles' in-
      dependent line from the French, and Aranda's un-
      popularity among some sections of the army, nobil-
      ity, and church are described by the Earl of Roch-
      ford and Louis Devisme to Lords Halifax and Rich-
      mond, and Henry Seymour Conway, Madrid, 1764-6,

esp. letters of June 18 and July 14, 1766,
State Papers, Series 94, piece nos. 173-5, PRO.
See also Laura Rodríguez, "The Spanish Riots of
1766", Past and Present, no. 59, May 1973, pp.
117-146, who regards factionalism as an important cause of the riots; and Pierre Vilar,
"Motín de Esquilache et crises d'ancien régime",
Historia Ibérica, I (Economía y sociedad en los
siglos XVIII y XIX), 1973, pp. 11-33, who
attributes the riots primarily to a subsistence
crisis in the cost of bread.

Edward Clarke, Letters Concerning the Spanish Nation
..., London, 1763.

O.H. Green, "On the Príncipe de Esquilache", Hispanic
Review, VII, July 1939.

Charles E. Kany, Life and Manners in Madrid, 1750-1800,
Berkeley, Calif., 1932.

Earl J. Hamilton, War and Prices in Spain, 1651-1800,
New York, 1969.

CHAPTER SEVEN

1   Also exiled were abbot Miguel de la Gándara and
    Father Isidro López.

2   Abbot Gándara, Francisco de Rávago (Ferdinand's
    confessor), and Manuel Ventura Figueroa (subse-
    quent head of the *Cruzada*, and of the council of
    Castile), were three churchmen largely responsi-
    ble for the concordat.  Father Andrés Burriel
    was also a prominent regalist of the period.

3   The Dominican general, Juan de Boxadors, and the
    Augustinian general, Francisco Vásquez, added
    to the list of complaints against the Jesuits.
    Viceroy Emmanuel Damas of Peru charged that they
    were undercutting the merchants with their many
    warehouses supplying the Indians.  Jesuits also
    had tithe exemptions on church holdings which
    ended in a successful court action against them.
    However, E.J. Burrus in reviewing The Expulsion
    of the Jesuits from Latin America (Magnus Mörner,

ed., 1965) asserts that the Jesuits' combined holdings were only a fraction of a modern university endowment, and that the Order was deeply in debt throughout the Spanish colonial world. See Burrus, _Hispanic American Historical Review_, XLVIII, November 1968, p. 761.

4   As Tanucci put it: "By education and habit I have as my spiritual director a father of the Society, but I can't understand how such a father could be spiritual director to a king". Charles, incidentally, told Tanucci he did not want his new daughter-in-law Carolina of Naples to have a Jesuit confessor in his letters of autumn 1766, Libro 331, AGS.

5   The royal assent, or _pase regio_, was accompanied by the exequatur, i.e., civil ratification by pragmatic ordinance, thus asserting crown control over papal briefs.  The exequatur was later used in Spain to prohibit the pro-Jesuit bull _In Coena Domini_, issued by Pope Clement XIII to postpone the beatification cause of Palafox (see text _infra_).

6   Felipe Alvarez Requejo, _El Conde de Campomanes: su obra histórica_, Oviedo, 1954, pp. 109-111.

7   Cayetano Alcázar Molina, _El Conde de Floridablanca_, Madrid, 1934, p. 25.

8   Rafael Olaechea, _El Conde de Aranda y el "Partido Aragonés"_, Saragossa, 1969, pp. 59, 60.

9   Antonio Ferrer del Río, _Historia del reinado de Carlos III en España_, Madrid, 1856, vol. II, pp. 126-133.

10  Ibid.

11  Moñino and Campomanes headed a tribunal of 'political faith' which condemned the works of Suárez, Mariana, and Molina on many counts, and laid the groundwork for expunging Jesuit influence from the private colleges.

12   Historians like Ferrer del Río and Manuel
     Danvila disparaged the story of the King's
     illegitimacy purported to have come to Father
     Ricci via Choiseul or Roda, but Francois Rousseau
     raised the question whether complete silence
     by Charles in his letters to Tanucci might not
     suggest some truth to the charge. In any case
     Isabel Farnese's recent death must have been a
     point of great sensitivity to the King, and his
     mother's honor as well as his own, his prime
     consideration. See François Rousseau, _Expulsion
     des Jesuits en Espagne_ ..., Paris, 1904, pp. 19-20.

13   Ibid.

14   Charles E. Chapman, _A History of Spain_, New York,
     1965, p. 451.

15   Manuel Danvila y Collado, _Reinado de Carlos III_,
     Madrid, 1888-1896, vol. III, p. 36 ff.

16   Charles III to Pope Clement XIII, Aranjuez, June 2,
     1767, Legajo 3517, AHN.

17   Charles III to Tanucci, July 14, 1767, Libro 333,
     AGS.

18   Vicente de la Fuente (ed.), _Colección de los
     artículos sobre la expulsión de los Jesuítas
     de España_, Madrid, 1867, pp. 31-3.

19   The _excusado_ (somewhat like the _Cruzada_ which col-
     lected an indulgence payment) was a subsidy levied
     on the clergy by the Spanish king, originally
     to assist him in his wars against infidels.  Aran-
     da subsequently annoyed the church with his 'bene-
     ficial plan' of June 12, 1769, which was an equali-
     zation plan designed to assess non-paying bene-
     fices along with the paying ones, for which pur-
     pose all diocesan bishops were to submit details.
     This was resented by landowner elements in the
     church, who viewed the plan as a new form of tax
     on their resources and a breach of privilege
     granted them by the concordat.

20  José de Arellano, bishop of Burgos, and others
    supported the bishop of Cuenca's letter, but
    Arellano switched to the government's side and
    became archbishop of Burgos.  In the end six ab-
    stained on the issue, thus leaving only eight
    votes, including Carvajal of Cuenca's, opposed
    to the anti-Jesuit measures.  See also Rousseau,
    Expulsion des Jesuits ..., p. 25.

21  Vicente de la Fuente, Colección de los artículos
    ..., p. 33 ff.

22  Charles III to Tanucci, San Ildefonso, August 1,
    1769, Libro 337, AGS.

23  Charles III to Tanucci, July 14, 1772, Libro 342,
    AGS.

24  Moñino was assisted by Cardinal Francisco Zelada
    in preparing much of the papal wording.  Jesuit
    writers like J.M. March and Constancio Eguía Ruiz
    argue convincingly for the innocence of the Society,
    describe the Pope's predicament, and convey their
    disgust at Moñino's ill-founded basis for negotia-
    ting the Order's suppression.

25  Charles III to Tanucci, ca. August 30, 1773,
    Libro 344, AGS.

26  Modern writers like Vicente Rodríguez Casado
    stress the conspiracy theory in explaining the
    riots.  The innocence of the Order is also upheld
    by most Spanish historians.  Vicente de la Fuente
    put the blame squarely on Aranda, Roda and Choi-
    seul, charging that Aranda's secretary, Nicolás
    Verdugo, was told to disguise the origins of var-
    ious pragmatic decrees and conceal the identity
    of those officials bribing the Jesuits to leave
    off their defense.  The great historian Antonio
    Ballesteros y Baretta affirmed that the Squillace
    riots were not wholly spontaneous but due to well-
    dressed infiltrators who lavishly paid for the
    rioters' hams and wine.  See his Historia de
    España y de su influencia en la historia universal,
    Barcelona, 1927, vol. V, p. 173.  Salvador de
    Madariaga follows J. Crétineau-Joly and others

in holding that the Duke of Alba instigated the riots in order to incriminate the Jesuits and frighten the King into action -- an attempt to embarrass the government which Alba is supposed to have confessed on his deathbed. Madariaga, The Fall of the Spanish American Empire, London, 1947, p. 227.

27  Danvila y Collado, Reinado de Carlos III, vol. III, p. 85.

28  Azara to Roda, March 31, 1768, quoted in Vicente de la Fuente, Colección do los artículos ..., p. 31. University and church reform is treated in the next chapter.

29  The lodges at Cádiz and Cartagena reveal that freemasonry existed in a small way in Spain, finally ordered to be suppressed in 1779 though the King was aware of the reluctance of Aranda and Moñino. See also his letters to Tanucci, ca. May 1776, Libro 348, and ca. May 1779, Libro 352, AGS.

30  Gaspar de Jovellanos, Diarios, Madrid, 1967, p. 72, and quoted in Laura Rodríguez, "The Spanish Riots of 1766", Past and Present, no. 59, May 1973, p. 117.

J.M. March, La Vida de beato José Pignatelli y su tiempo, Barcelona, 1944.

Constancio Eguía Ruiz, Los Jesuítas y el motín de Esquilache, Madrid, 1947.

José Francisco de Isla, Memorial en nombre de las cuatro Provincias de España de la Compañía de Jesus ..., Madrid, 1882.

Luis Sánchez Agesta, El Pensamiento político del despotismo ilustrado, Madrid, 1953.

Vicente Rodríguez Casado, La Política y los políticos en el reinado de Carlos III, Madrid, 1962.

CHAPTER EIGHT

1     Charles III to Isabel, Cuerva, April 25, 1765,
      Legajo 2777, AHN.

2     Quoted in Conde de Fernán Núñez, Vida de
      Carlos III, Madrid, 1898, vol. II, p. 52 ff.
      According to William Coxe, Charles' passion for
      the chase stemmed from his Bourbon ancestors,
      Louis XIV included, who exhorted their relatives
      to engage in this pastime to combat the hypo-
      chondria inherent in the family.  Coxe, Memoirs
      of the Kings of Spain of the House of Bourbon,
      London, 1815, vol. V, p. 216.

3     H. Swinburne, Travels through Spain in the Years
      1775 and 1776, Dublin, 1779, quoted in Coxe,
      Memoirs ..., vol. V, pp. 219-220.

4     J.F. Bourgoing, Tableau de l'Espagne moderne,
      Paris, 1807, vol. I, p. 140.

5     Other important universities were: Alcalá de
      Henares, Valladolid, Oviedo, Valencia, Seville,
      and Saragossa.  Important *colegios mayores* were
      (see text *infra*): San Ildefonso at Alcalá, Santa
      Cruz at Valladolid, San Salvador at Oviedo,
      Santiago at Cuenca, San Bartolomé and Santiago
      del Arzobispo -- the last two having links with
      Salamanca.

6     Maria Amalia to Tanucci, May 6, 1759, Legajo
      5057, AGS.

7     Pérez Bayer and Bertrán (see text *infra)* had been
      at Valencia university where the latter was
      Bayer's tutor.  Bertrán supported the Friends
      of the Nation societies, fulminated against super-
      stition, and became a 'reformist' inquisitor,
      his pastoral letters being published in 1783.
      Pérez Bayer as a classicist edited the works of
      Titus Livy for the Escorial library.  See Charles
      to Tanucci, letters of November 1763, Libro 325,
      AGS; and George M. Addy, The Enlightenment in
      the University of Salamanca, Durham, N.C.,
      1966, p. 163.

8    Addy, ibid., p. 110.

9    Regarding the Inquisition, see J.A. Llorente,
Memoria histórica ..., Madrid, 1812, republished
as La Inquisición y los españoles, Madrid, 1967.
Regarding Olavide, see Marcelin Defourneaux,
Pablo de Olavide ou L'afrancesado, Paris, 1959,
pp. 341-364; 451-470. Nearly executed during
the French Revolution, Olavide wrote the pious
and contrite best-seller El Evangelio en triunfo
before being allowed to return to his adopted
country.

10   For an explanation of mortmain, see chapter 4,
footnote 4. Despite declining numbers of clergy,
Antonio Domínguez Ortiz quotes Floridablanca as
commenting that church income rose by 50 per cent
in the late eighteenth century. See Domínguez,
La Sociedad española en el siglo XVIII, Madrid,
1955, p. 129. Yet worthy churchmen included
Pedro Quintana (bishop of Orense), Manuel Rubín
de Celis (archbishop of Cartagena), and the more
controversial Manuel Ventura Figueroa, all of
whom bequeathed large sums to charity, while
Father Pedro Sánchez of Santiago de Compostella
spoke up on behalf of oppressed lower tradesmen.

11   Measures restricting church jurisdiction include:
obligation of bishops to censure priests' gossip
during the Squillace riots; abolition of the
church's right to grant asylum to rioters (1774);
its obligation to repair buildings from the proceeds of vacant rural benefices (1780); obligation of bishops to get royal assent before appointing diocesan vicars (1781); and forfeit of
church jurisdiction in smuggling cases (1787).
But the government failed to stop the disgusting-
ly smelly practice of burials beneath the stone
slabs inside churches themselves.

12   In addition, Campomanes wrote Respuestas fiscales
sobre aboler la tasa (1764), favoring better
circulation of grain in lieu of hoarding; Juicio
imparcial (1769), a watered-down attack on mortmain practice; Discurso sobre las escuelas patri-
óticas (1775); Discurso sobre la educación

popular de los artesanos y su fomento (1775),
together with an Apéndice -- the last three
dealing with the question of technical training.
Rodríguez Casado maintains that Campomanes was
essentially a man of action and impatience, and
had his intellectual limitations. See Vicente
Rodríguez Casado, La Política y los políticos
en el reinado de Carlos III, Madrid, 1962, p. 231.

13    Juan Sempere y Guarinos, Biblioteca española
      económico-política, Madrid, 1801-1821, vol. I,
      pp. 106-133.

14    Bernardo Ward, Proyecto económico ..., Madrid,
      1782, p. 67. He also wrote Obra pía, Valencia,
      1757, and was influenced by the ideas of José
      del Campillo y Cossío.

15    Rodríguez, La Política ..., p. 85.

16    Aranda's census was probably exaggerated, but
      the population by 1787 stood at 9.3 million
      according to Domínguez Ortiz, La Sociedad
      española ..., p. 58. Populations of some larger
      cities in the early 1770's were:  Madrid,
      170,000; Barcelona, 100,000; Valencia, Seville
      and Granada, about 90,000; Cádiz, 70,000; Málaga,
      50,000; and Bilbao, 12,000.  The Canary Islands
      had about 150,000.  The provinces of Valencia
      and Catalonia each approached one million.

17  , Luis Sánchez Agesta, El Pensamiento político
      del despotismo ilustrado, Madrid, 1953, p. 142.

18    Edward Clarke, Letters Concerning the Spanish
      Nation ..., London, 1763, pp. 285-6.

19    Domínguez in his La Sociedad española ...,
      p. 62, praises the hereditary lease practice,
      enfiteusis, prevalent in Catalonia.

20    Earl J. Hamilton, War and Prices in Spain,
      1651-1800, New York, 1969, pp. 179, 268-271;
      B.H. Slicher van Bath, The Agrarian History of
      Western Europe, A.D. 500-1850, London, 1966,
      pp. 168, 226.

21  This comment by Jovellanos is quoted in Edith
    Helman, *Jovellanos y Goya*, Madrid, 1970, p.93.

22  Jean Sarrailh, *La España ilustrada de la segunda
    mitad del siglo XVIII*, Mexico City, 1957, p. 55.

23  Antonio Muñoz wrote *Discurso sobre economía-pol-
    ítica*, Madrid, 1769, quoted in Manuel Colmeiro,
    *Biblioteca de los economistas españoles* ...,
    Madrid, 1880, p. 123. Colmeiro regarded Muñoz
    as the pen-name of Enrique Ramos, as does Sánchez
    Agesta in his *El Pensamiento político* ..., p. 311.

24  Miguel de la Gándara, exiled for alleged involve-
    ment in the Squillace riots, wrote *Apuntes sobre
    el bien y mal de España*, Madrid, 1804, first
    written in 1765. Nicolás de Arriquibar, of the
    Basque Friends of the Nation Society, wrote
    *Recreación política*, Vitoria, 1779.

25  V. Vizcayno Pérez, in his *Discursos políticos
    sobre los estragos que causan los censos*, Madrid,
    1766, proposed that the nearly 3 billion reales in
    tied-up rents be invested productively to boost
    the *fanega* yield of crops, and may have influenced
    Campomanes in drafting laws from 1768 to 1773
    banning grain exports and imposing inspections
    on dealers. He condemned peasant eviction by
    landlords (lapses of rent being a time-honored
    practice), and rustling by roving shepherds (see
    text on the Mesta, *infra*).

26  *Ensayo de la Sociedad Bascongada de los Amigos
    del País* (Anonymous), Vitoria, 1762, pp. 21-92.
    Nobles predominated among the founding members
    and the women admitted later were also largely
    noble. In support of nobles engaging in trade
    was the work of abbé G.F. Coyer, *La Nobleza
    comerciante*, Madrid, 1781, translated from the
    French of this author.

27  Sempere y Guarinos, *Biblioteca española* ...,
    vol. I, pp. 130-141, vol. II, pp. 126-176;
    Rodríguez, *La Política* ..., p. 255.

28  See Defourneaux, *Pablo de Olavide* ..., pp. 175-245.

29 Memorial ajustado entre La Mesta y la provincia
de Extremadura (anonymous), San Ildenfonso, 1764,
finalized at Madrid, January 10, 1771. The
successful plaintiff representing the towns of
Extremadura was Vicente Paino y Hurtado.

30 G. Desdevises du Dézert, L'Espagne de l'ancien
régime, Paris, 1897-1904, vol. I, p. 130.

31 Quoted in Junta general de la real compañía
Guipúzcoana de Caracas, Report of June 15 to
November 24, 1772 (anonymous), Madrid, 1773,
p. 154.

Richard L. Kagan, Students and Society in Early Modern
Spain, Baltimore, Md., 1974.

William J. Callahan, "The Problem of Confinement: an
Aspect of Poor Relief in Eighteenth-Century Spain",
Hispanic American Historical Review, LI, Febru-
ary 1971.

Richard Herr, The Eighteenth Century Revolution in
Spain, Princeton, N.J., 1958.

Julius Klein, The Mesta, A Study in Spanish Economic
History, 1273-1836, Cambridge, Mass., 1920.

CHAPTER NINE

1 Quoted in William Coxe, Memoirs of the Kings of
Spain of the House of Bourbon, London, 1815,
vol. V, pp. 219, 220.

2 Ibid., p. 217.

3 Charles III to Ferdinand of Naples, September
19, 1769, Libro 337, AGS. Spanish envoys to
Naples, from Simón de las Casas to Vizconde de
la Herrería, had a difficult time maintaining
Charles' hold over this court. The Neapolitan
envoy to Spain in the 1770's, incidentally,
was the Duke of Santa Elisabetta.

4 Charles III to Ferdinand of Parma, December 24,
1776, Legajo 2646, AHN.

5　Charles III to Tanucci, letters of March 1773, Libro 343, AGS.

6　Aranda to the Prince of Asturias, recalling talks with Frederick the Great when he was envoy to Berlin in the 1750's; from his "Plan de Gobierno", Paris, April 22, 1781, Legajo 2863, AHN.

7　Charles III to Tanucci, letters of autumn 1772, Libro 342, and letters of spring 1773, Libro 343, AGS.

8　Charles III to Marqués (later Duke) de Almodóvar, March 9, 1761, Legajo 6618, AGS; and Almodóvar to Ricardo Wall (see quote *infra*), St. Petersburg, March 19, 1763, Legajo 6620, AGS.

9　Prince Masserano to Grimaldi, London, September 16, 1765, Legajo 6958, AGS.

10　Charles III to Tanucci, July 1773, Libro 344, AGS.

11　The commercial treaty was proposed in 1779 by Spanish agent Juan de Boligny and finalized three years later.

12　Following abortive disarmament proposals with England (see Charles' letters to Tanucci, May 1771, Libro 339, AGS), the King blamed this country for furthering the expansion of both Russia and Prussia, e.g., his letters to Tanucci of May-June, 1773, Libro 343, AGS.

13　J.F. Bourgoing, while praising the Spanish soldier highly, put the effective total at about 60,000 a few years later. See his Travels in Spain, London, 1789, vol. I, pp. 442-451. This figure includes 9000 crack Household Troops comprising 12 battalions from the two regiments of Foot Guards -- Spanish and Walloon -- and 9 squadrons from the three troops of Horse Guards -- Spanish, Flemish, and Italian.

14  Edward Clarke, Letters Concerning the Spanish
    Nation ..., London, 1763, pp. 211-4. A colonel's
    pay could reach 30,000 reales per year, accord-
    ing to Antonio Domínguez Ortiz, La Sociedad
    española en el siglo XVIII, Madrid, 1955, p. 380.

15  One important levy was the ordinance of May 7,
    1775. See also Juan Sempere y Guarinos, Biblio-
    teca española económico-política, Madrid,
    1801-1821, vol. I, pp. 111-128.

16  Aranda to the Prince of Asturias, commenting on
    the council of war and recalling his days as
    council of Castile president; from his "Plan de
    Gobierno", Paris, April 22, 1781, Legajo 2863,
    AHN.

17  Antonio Ferrer del Río, Historia del reinado de
    Carlos III en España, Madrid, 1856, vol. III,
    pp. 59-95.

18  Rafael Olaechea, El Conde de Aranda y el
    "Partido Aragonés", Saragossa, 1969, pp. 89-93.

19  Vicente Rodríguez Casado, Política marroquí de
    Carlos III, Madrid, 1946, pp. 118-126, 209-230.

20  Quoted in William Dalrymple, Travels through
    Spain and Portugal in 1774, London, 1777, p. 187.

21  Olaechea, El Conde de Aranda ..., pp. 98-9.

22  Ibid., p. 109.

23  Charles III to the Prince of Asturias, undated,
    prob. late summer, 1776, Legajo 2453, AHN.

24  Memorial by Grimaldi, with attached note for
    secretary of justice Roda, San Lorenzo, November
    7, 1776, Legajo 2858, AHN.

25  Olaechea, El Conde de Aranda ..., pp. 109, 110.

26  Clarke, Letters Concerning the Spanish Nation
    ..., pp. 219-226.

27     Jorge Juan y Santacilia mentions several British
        marine engineers in this work. He proposed that
        ships' linear dimensions within certain limits
        be inversely proportional in terms of length and
        beam, with maximum weight at the center, lighter
        gun-carriage, hulls made of cedar or pine instead
        of oak for better buoyancy, sturdier rigging, and
        mainsail requiring less traverse and length at
        the boom. Speed should aim to be increased from
        4 to 7 knots, especially in summer breezes around
        Cadiz. He also wrote Teoría y práctica de la
        marina.

Vera Lee Brown, "Studies in the History of Spain in
    the Second Half of the Eighteenth Century", Smith
    College Studies in History, XV, October 1929 and
    January 1930.

Cayetano Alcázar Molina, El Conde de Floridablanca,
    Madrid, 1934.

Herbert I. Priestley, José de Gálvez: Visitor-General
    of New Spain, 1765-1771, Berkeley, Calif., 1916.

CHAPTER TEN

1     Herbert I. Priestley, José de Gálvez: Visitor-
        General of New Spain, 1765-1771, Berkeley, Calif.,
        1916, pp. 16-17.

2     For further details, *supra*, see D.A. Brading, Miners
        and Merchants in Bourbon Mexico, 1763-1810,
        Cambridge, England, 1971, pp. 4-6.

3     Cayetano Alcázar Molina, El Conde de Florida-
        blanca, Madrid, 1934, p. 153.

4     the 'obedezco y no cumplo' principle meant that
        orders from the royal councils of Spain were
        honored, then suspended on the technical grounds
        that such orders were not properly endorsed by
        the appropriate officals of the council of the
        Indies. This could often take months.

5     John T. Lanning, Academic Culture in the Spanish
        Colonies, London, 1940, pp. 39-53; Alfred Barnaby
        Thomas, Latin America, a History, New York, 1956,

pp. 120, 163, the most objective and comprehensive treatment of its kind in one volume.

6   Macanaz from Murcia was a minister to Philip V before settling in The Hague after losing a fight with the Inquisition and when Italian circles round Isabel Farnese brought about his downfall. He was subsequently pardoned by Charles III. His other work, Auxilios para bien gobernar una monarquía católica, was published in Madrid, 1789. Uztáriz (infra) wrote Theórica y práctica de comercio y de marina, 1724. Campillo wrote España despierta, 1741, and Nuevo sistema de gobierno económico para la América, 1744.

7   The company board quoted Ignacio de Luzán, former president of the council of commerce and money, as praising the work of Joshua Gee, Consideraciones sobre el comercio y la navegación de la Gran Bretaña, Madrid, 1753, in which he criticized the actions of smaller merchants who were flooding a nation with foreign luxury goods as it drifted towards poverty. The company cited such references to condemn small private traders who were not serving public ends. Through prudent management, the report continued, through organizing fairs in Caracas and trading in silver and black slaves, the company had increased capital by 78 million reales, leaving a net profit of 22 million reales. The report reflected the King's decree in 1771 that no one hereafter could hold private accounts in the company or withold them from public inspection, though fired persons could appeal. This went some way to check excessive profits and peculation. See Junta general de la real compañía Guipúzcoana de Caracas, Report of June 15 to November 24, 1772 (anonymous), Madrid, 1773.

8   John Lynch, Spanish Colonial Administration, 1782-1810. The Intendant System in the Viceroyalty of Río de la Plata, London, 1958, pp. 8, 9.

9   Ibid.

345

10  Cited in Juan de la Ripia (and subsequent fiscal auditors), Práctica de la administración y cobranza de las rentas reales ..., Madrid, 1769, pp. 583-5.

11  See Charles' correspondence with Tanucci, commenting on the success of the expedition to Louisiana, from San Lorenzo, November 1769, Libro 337, AGS.

12  Lynch, Spanish Colonial Administration ..., pp. 16-17.

13  Priestley, José de Gálvez ..., p. 173.

14  Ibid., pp. 177, 201-9.

15  Ibid,, pp. 198, 362; Brading, Miners and Merchants ..., pp. 28, 114. The only limitations were that ships had to sail under Spanish colors and the goods had to bear the Spanish manufacturer's name with places of origin, though by 1784 even foreign goods could come in under certain conditions.

16  Brading, ibid., pp. 131, 140-5. After tax, the treasury dispatched all silver bar by mule-train to Mexico City. Here the royal mint cut 69 reales from every mark of silver, of which 65 reales, the legal price, was returned to the owner. The seigniorage duty on coinage required 1 real per mark of silver to go to the king, and 2 reales to the treasury. Tribute revenue from Mexico to Spain, incidentally, averaged nearly one million pesos per year, and church funds exceeded half a million. For details on revenue, see chapter 11, footnote 18.

17  Lyle N. McAlister, The "Fuero Militar" in New Spain, 1764-1800, Gainesville, Fla., 1957, pp. 2-10, 94-5.

18  Worthy of mention are Athanase de Mézières (agent in Texas), Marqués de Rubí (visitor to the frontier), Hugo Oconor (army inspector), and

Teodoro de Croix (the commandant-general, 1776-1783). Viceroys Francisco de Croix and Bucareli generally supported their actions. The chain of presidios idea originated with Rubí, and this motivated Charles' first royal order of April 25, 1770. See also Alfred Barnaby Thomas, Teodoro de Croix and the Northern Frontier of New Spain, 1776-1783, Norman, Okla., 1941, and Luis Navarro García, Don José de Gálvez y la Comandancia General de las provincias internas del norte de Nueva España, Seville, 1964, pp. xv, 218-220, 276, 504-512.

19    These imperial ideas of Gálvez were opposed by advocates of a freer commercial activity, such as Malaspina the explorer. For conflicting viewpoints about how to expand Spanish power in America, see M. Hernández Sánchez-Barba, La ultima expansión española en América, Madrid, 1957, pp. 262-293.

20    Alvaro de Navia Huemes (Vizconde de la Herrería) and Francisco Antonio (Conde de Lacy) to Grimaldi, St. Petersburg, 1767-1773, Manuscript photostats (Box 3247), Library of Congress, Washington, D.C., from Legajo 86, Document 5, Estado, Archivo General de Indias.

21    Arriaga to viceroy Francisco de Croix, January 23, 1768, in ibid. Because of Franciscan involvement displacing the Jesuits, the expedition was dubbed by critics the 'Expedición Sacra'.

22    Bucareli to Gálvez, Mexico City, November 26, 1776, conveying Father Serra's reports on San Francisco (see text *supra*); Cunningham transcripts (Box 3601), Library of Congress, Washington, D.C., from Legajo 89, Document 4, Audiencia de Mexico, Archivo General de Indias. Accompanying Anza much of the way between 1774 and 1776 were two worthy friars, Francisco Garcés (who explored the Gila and Colorado rivers), and Pedro Font (who explored much of San Francisco bay).

23    Donald C. Cutter, "California, Training Ground for Spanish Naval Heroes", California Historical

Society _Quarterly_ XL, June 1961, p. 111.

24    See Anthony H. Hull, "Spanish and Russian
       Rivalry in the North Pacific Regions of the
       New World, 1760-1812", (doctoral thesis), Ann
       Arbor, Michigan, 1966, and Warren L. Cook,
       _Flood Tide of Empire: Spain and the Pacific
       Northwest, 1543-1819_, New Haven, Conn., 1973,
       pp. 44-396.

William B. Taylor, "Landed Society in New Spain: a
       View from the South", _Hispanic American Histor-
       ical Review_, LIV, August 1974.

D.A. Brading and Harry E. Cross, "Colonial Silver
       Mining: Mexico and Peru", _Hispanic American
       Historical Review_, LII, November 1972.

Roland D. Hussey, _The Caracas Company, 1728-1784_
       ..., Cambridge, Mass., 1934.

Stuart R. Tompkins, "After Bering: Mapping the North
       Pacific", _British Columbia Historical Quarterly_,
       XIX, January 1955.

Henry R. Wagner, _Cartography of the Northwest Coast
       of America to the Year 1800_, Berkeley, Calif.,
       1937.

CHAPTER ELEVEN

1    Cayetano Alcázar Molina, _Los Virreinatos en el
      siglo XVIII_, from the _Historia de América_
      series, Barcelona, 1945, vol. XIII, pp. 433-4.

2    Cayetano Alcázar Molina, _El Conde de Florida-
      blanca_, Madrid, 1934, pp. 157-162.

3    Quoted in Conde de Fernán Núñez (Spanish am-
      bassador to Portugal in the 1780's), _Vida de
      Carlos III_, Madrid, 1898, vol. I, p. 291.

4    See John Lynch, _Spanish Colonial Administration,
      1782-1810. The Intendant System in the Vice-
      royalty of Río de la Plata_, London, 1958.

5   J.R. Fisher, Government and Society in Colonial
    Peru. The Intendant System, 1784-1814, London,
    1970, pp. 6-9, 140.

6   Ibid., pp. 17, 21.

7   Jorge Juan and Antonio de Ulloa first sent their
    report, Noticias secretas de América, to Ensenada
    in the 1730's (published in London, 1826). Ulloa's
    prologue and their secret report on conditions in
    Peru were sent in 1749. Ulloa wrote Noticias
    americanas in 1772. Consult also works by Arthur
    P. Whitaker.

8   Alcázar Molina, Los Virreinatos ..., pp. 367-373.

9   Gálvez and viceroy Croix had drawn up a plan for
    extending the intendancy system to Mexico, des-
    igned to replace hated officials like *corregidores*.
    Charles on May 20, 1768, then referred the matter
    to notables like Aranda, the Duke of Alba, Jaime
    Masones de Lima, Grimaldi, Wall, Múzquiz and
    Muniain, all of whom favored the proposed reform;
    and by royal order of August 10, 1769, Croix was
    authorized to set up intendancies in Sonora,
    Sinaloa, and Vera Cruz. But the office lacked
    legislative powers by ordinance -- an omission
    the viceroys took full advantage of to defend
    their position. See also Herbert I. Priestley,
    José de Gálvez: Visitor-General of New Spain,
    1765-1771, Berkeley, Calif., 1916, p. 292.

10  See Lynch, Spanish Colonial Administration ...,
    pp. 53-74, 196-8; Fisher, Government and Society
    ..., pp. 33, 78, 88, 236; and Alfred Barnaby
    Thomas, Latin America, a History, New York, 1956,
    p. 164.

11  Alcázar Molina, Los Virreinatos ..., pp. 369,
    378, 409.

12  Ibid., pp. 278-286.

13  D.A. Brading, Miners and Merchants in Bourbon
    Mexico, 1763-1810, Cambridge, England, 1971,
    p. 36.

14    Jacques A. Barbier, "Elite and Cadres in Bourbon
      Chile", <u>Hispanic</u> <u>American</u> <u>Historical</u> <u>Review</u>, LII,
      August 1972, pp. 416-435.

15    Brading, <u>Miners</u> <u>and</u> <u>Merchants</u> ..., p. 170.

16    Thus reverting to creole predominance before
      Galvez had intervened. See also Mark A. Burk-
      holder, "From Creole to Peninsular: the Transfor-
      mation of the Audiencia of Lima", <u>Hispanic</u> <u>Amer-</u>
      <u>ican</u> <u>Historical</u> <u>Review</u> LII, August 1972, pp. 400-9,
      and Leon G. Campbell, "A Colonial Establishment:
      Creole Domination of the Audiencia of Lima during
      the Late Eighteenth Century", <u>Hispanic</u> <u>American</u>
      <u>Historical</u> <u>Review</u>, LII, February 1972, pp. 1-25.

17    Quoted in Vicente Rodríguez Casado, <u>La</u> <u>Política</u>
      <u>y</u> <u>los</u> <u>políticos</u> <u>en</u> <u>el</u> <u>reinado</u> <u>de</u> <u>Carlos</u> <u>III</u>,
      Madrid, 1962, p. 248.

18    Authorities differ as to how much increase from
      the Indies revenue went into the treasury. In
      terms of gold and silver minted in the late 1780's
      (to the nearest round figure in pesos), Mexico
      produced nearly 20 million annually, Peru with
      Chile about 7 million, La Plata about 4.2 million,
      and New Granada 2.6 million. This 34 million
      total was nearly double what it was twenty years
      before, though only about 20 million actually
      reached Spain for specie circulation, the rest
      being diverted for trade purchases. In terms of
      direct royal revenue from mining (the <i>quinto</i> <i>real</i>,
      mintage receipts, seigniorage duties. mercury sales
      etc.), the figures in the late 1780's were 4.6
      million for Mexico, and nearly 8 million for all
      four viceroyalties. In terms of total royal re-
      venue from all four viceroyalties (mining, monop-
      olies, excise, tribute, church taxes etc.), the
      figures approached about 14 million for Mexico and
      22 million in all. But with so many expenses in-
      curred by running the army and bureaucracy in the
      Indies where government costs alone absorbed 4
      million, the net annual income to the treasury
      barely exceeded 8 million pesos (or 160 million
      reales), though this was double what it was in
      the early 1760's. Some authorities regard even

this figure as nominal because of escalating colonial expenditures. Yet the domestic treasury itself often confronted a deficit, despite its half a billion reales raised from taxes, excise, etc. in the peninsula, and it relied heavily on its American revenue to finance administration and defense. Nonetheless, the proportion of the net American revenue to the whole jumped from about one sixth the total in the 1760's to one third the total by the end of Charles' reign (i.e., from about 80 million to 160 million reales), thanks largely to Gálvez' efforts. For further details, see Edward Clarke, Letters Concerning the Spanish Nation ..., London, 1763, p. 250; William Coxe, Memoirs of the Kings of Spain of the House of Bourbon, London, 1815, vol. V, Appendix II, p. 386; Priestley, José de Gálvez ..., pp. 34, 318-320, 381-3; Fisher, Government and Society ..., p. 254; and Brading, Mining and Merchants ..., pp. 29, 53, 131, 145.

19    Aranda to the Prince of Asturias concerning the council of the Indies, from his "Plan de Gobierno", Paris, April 22, 1781, Legajo 2863, AHN.

20    Rodríguez, La Política ..., p. 249; Fisher, Government and Society ..., p. 60. Also discarded was Gálvez' fleeting attempt to get the accounts department to keep to a double-entry method of bookkeeping.

21    Alfred B. Thomas points out that exports from Spain increased by 300 per cent between 1765 and 1778, with annual revenues nearly doubling by the turn of the century. See his Latin America ..., p. 172.

22    These figures conform to an anonymous statement of commerce between Spain and Spanish America in 1788, which put the value of Spanish cargo exported to the Americas (in nearest round figures) at 158 million reales; the value of foreign cargo exported to the Americas (presumably via Spanish ports) at 142.5 million reales; and the value of

cargo from the Americas to Spain at nearly 805
million reales. Travels through Spain (anonymous),
Boston, Mass., 1808, p. 211.

Francisco Cervera, Jorge Juan y la colonización española en América, Madrid 1927.

J.P. Moore, The Cabildo in Peru under the Bourbons,
Durham, N.C., 1966.

Richard Herr, The Eighteenth Century Revolution in
Spain, Princeton, N.J., 1958.

Jaime Vicens Vives, An Economic History of Spain,
Princeton, N.J., 1969.

Salvador de Madariaga, The Fall of the Spanish American
Empire, London, 1947.

CHAPTER TWELVE

1    Catherine the Great's hold on Alaska enabled the
     Russians to work up resentment among King George
     III's British subjects in Canada who might be ex-
     cluded from the operations of the Hudson's Bay
     company.  Spanish envoy Conde de Lacy claimed to
     have received this information from a confidant
     in Russia.  Lacy to Grimaldi, St. Petersburg,
     April 23, 1773, Manuscript photostats (Box 3247),
     Library of Congress, Washington, D.C., from
     Legajo 86, Document 5, Estado, Archivo General
     de Indias.

2    Floridablanca to the King at a cabinet meeting,
     February 3, 1777, Legajo 2630, AHN.  The region
     of 'Campeche' guarded the Yucatán peninsula and
     the approaches to Honduras.

3    Enrique de Tapia Ozcariz, Carlos III y su epoca,
     Madrid, 1962, p. 318.

4    Ibid.,pp. 318-321.  Gardoqui became Spain's first
     representative to the United States, while two
     Spanish agents in this country at the time were
     Miralles and Rendón.

5  Floridablanca to the King, February 3, 1777
   with a subsequent memorandum in March, Legajo
   2630, AHN.

6  Floridablanca to the King, San Ildefonso, September 24, 1778, Legajo 2453, AHN.

7  Lord Grantham to Lord Weymouth, Madrid, November
   1778 ff., State Papers, Series 94, piece no. 207,
   PRO. A copy of the final Spanish mediation offer
   (see text *infra*) was sent by Grantham to Weymouth
   on April 1, 1779.

8  Lord Weymouth to Lord Grantham, quoting Almodóvar's
   withdrawal of Charles' mediation offer, Court
   of St. James, May 28, 1779, State Papers, Series
   94, piece no. 298, PRO.

9  Charles and Floridablanca to José de Gálvez and
   other ministers, May 15, 1779, Legajo 4224, AHN.

10 Sir Charles Petrie, King Charles III of Spain,
   London, 1971, p. 205.

11 Thomas Lloyd to Bernardo de Gálvez, May 4, 1777,
   State Papers, Series 94, piece no. 207, PRO.

12 Alfred Barnaby Thomas, Latin America, a History,
   New York, 1956, p. 180.

13 For the Anglo-Spanish conflict in Honduras and
   the rest of Guatemala, see the Memorial presented to Lord Frederick North by British subjects expelled from Yucatán and the bay of Honduras in 1779; and the proclamation by President
   Matías de Gálvez on behalf of "the free and independent nation of Indians inhabiting the Mosquito shore" of July 23, 1782. Foreign Office
   Papers, Series 72, piece no. 1, pp. 399-403, PRO.

14 Charles to Tanucci, Aranjuez, May 23, 1780,
   Libro 353, AGS.

15 Charles to Tanucci, El Pardo, January 30, 1781,
   Libro 354, AGS.

16 Conde de Fernán Núñez, Vida de Carlos III, Madrid,
   1898, vol. I, pp. 333, 349.

17    Charles to Tanucci, San Ildefonso, July 17 and
      August 28, 1781, Libro 354, AGS.

18    Charles to Tanucci, December 4, 1781, Libro 354,
      AGS.

19    In ratifying the accords of the previous year,
      Morocco allowed Spanish ships to be provisioned
      at her ports while banning British ships from
      Tangiers and Tetuán. Free trade was allowed at
      ports such as Barcelona. The Sultan needed
      Spanish wheat and also Spanish help in his designs
      on Algiers. The full terms of this treaty signed
      at Tetuán, January 4, 1781 are given in Legajo
      4323, AHN.

20    For data on ships of both sides, see Gálvez to
      Floridablanca and Castejón, 1778-9, esp. docu-
      ments 148-160, Legajos 2453 and 2630, AHN; and
      Lord Grantham to Weymouth, ca. May 27, 1779,
      State Papers, Series 94, piece no.208, PRO.

21    See Vergennes to Floridablanca via Aranda, Paris,
      June 14, 1779, Legajo 2841, AHN.

22    Fernán Núñez, Vida de Carlos III, vol. I, pp.
      305-332.

23    Quoted in Tapia, Carlos III ..., p. 336.

24    The commandant's report, Cádiz to Madrid, relay-
      ing Córdoba's victory, August 16, 1780, Libro 353,
      AGS; Gaceta de Madrid, August 29, 1780, p. 634;
      and Fernán Núñez, Vida de Carlos III, vol. I, pp.
      366-8. Captured British troops included four
      companies bound for Bombay to reinforce the East
      India company, 860 men bound for Jamaica, one
      company of Hessians bound for America, besides
      the family of General Dilling.

25    Richard Cumberland to Lord Hillsborough, near
      San Roque, December 12, 1780, State Papers,
      Series 94, piece no. 209, PRO.

26    The declaration did ban certain articles of contr-
      band aboard neutral ships, while belligerents had
      to impose an effective blockade to assert their
      claims, not just a paper blockade. For Spanish-
      Russian relations at this time, see Floridablanca

to Zinoviev and Normande, April to December, 1780, Legajos 2630 and 4226, AHN, and José Sánchez-Diana, "Relacciones diplomáticas entre Rusia y España en el siglo XVIII, 1780-1783", Hispania, XII, May 1952.

27    Charles to Marqués de la Torre, Instrucción, Madrid, January 23, 1781, Legajo 6618, AGS. Torre was posted to Vienna where he fell ill and was replaced by Aguilar; see also Floridablanca to Torre, September 30, 1781 ff., Legajo 6646, AGS.

28    The planned attack on Minorca was a rare example of secret confidence between Floridablanca and Aranda, as reflected in Aranda's letters from Paris, December 9, 1781 ff., Legajo 2850, AHN. Assisting Crillon were Marqués de Peñafiel (who took Fornell) and Marqués de Avilés (who took Ciudadela).

29    Floridablanca to Marqués de la Torre, El Pardo, February 16, 1782, Legajo 6648, AGS.

30    Charles to Tanucci, San Ildefonso, promising victory at Gibraltar as with Minorca, July 9, 1782, and relating Prince Masserano's report of the siege's preparations, August 27, 1782, Libro 355, AGS.

31    Rafael Olaechea, El Conde de Aranda y el "Partido Aragonés", Saragossa, 1969, p. 185. Aranda's final request to the Prince of Asturias was dated March 13, 1782.

32    Juan del Alamo, Gibraltar antes de la historia de España, Madrid, 1964, pp. 276-298.

33    If Charles chose the option of keeping Puerto Rico, then Santo Domingo was to go to France to compensate her for having to give to England the two West Indian islands of Guadeloupe and Dominica (the latter temporarily captured by France in 1778). See Floridablanca to Aranda, November 1782 ff., Legajos 2841 and 2862, AHN.

In retrospect, this was a better option than
it seemed, for Charles could have at least re-
gained Gibraltar and West Florida.

34  Quoted in Tapia, Carlos III ..., p. 360.

35  Quoted in Olaechea, El Conde de Aranda ..., p. 121.

36  Quoted in Alamo, Gibraltar ..., pp. 303.

37  See Aranda's correspondence with Floridablanca via
    Bernardo del Campo, following the latter's contacts
    with the Duke of Manchester and Charles James Fox,
    March to September, 1783, Legajos 2841 and 2862,
    AHN.  British envoys to Spain (till 1788) are given
    in Foreign Office Papers, Series 72, piece no. 1 ff.,
    and Series 185, piece nos. 1-5, PRO.

38  Alamo, Gibraltar ..., p. 309.

Troy Floyd, The Anglo-Spanish Struggle for Mosquitía,
    Albuquerque, N.M., 1967.

Isabel de Madariaga, Britain, Russia, and the Armed
    Neutrality of 1780, New Haven, Conn., 1962.

Stetson Conn, Gibraltar in British Diplomacy in the
    Eighteenth Century, London, 1942.

Jack Russell, Gibraltar Besieged, 1779-1783, London,
    1965.

CHAPTER THIRTEEN

1  Sacheverell Sitwell, Spain, London, 1950, p. 80.

2  James C. LaForce, The Development of the Spanish
   Textile Industry, 1750-1800, Berkeley, Calif.,
   1965, pp. 28-67, 152; Jaime Vicens Vives, An
   Economic History of Spain, Princeton, N.J., 1969,
   pp. 526-7.

3  Edward Clarke, Letters Concerning the Spanish
   Nation ..., London, 1763, p. 284.

4   See Luis Sánchez Belda *et al.* (ed.), Exposi-
    ción de la administración en la epoca de
    Carlos III, Alcalá de Henares, 1962, pp. 65-7.

5   David R. Ringrose, "Transportation and Economic
    Stagnation in Eighteenth-Century Castile",
    Journal of Economic History, XXVIII, March 1968,
    pp. 51-79.

6   Vicente Rodríguez Casado, La Política y los
    políticos en el reinado de Carlos III, Madrid,
    1962, pp. 120-2; Vicens Vives, An Economic
    History ..., pp. 555, 575.

7   J. LaForce, The ... Spanish Textile Industry,
    p. 94. Such specifications imposed a standard
    width or *vara* and a certain required weight.

8   Rodríguez, La Política ..., pp. 100-3; Vicens,
    An Economic History ..., p. 487.

9   To protect home cotton producers, Charles in 1760
    and 1771 taxed imported raw cotton 20%, imposing
    similar tariffs on silk, linen, hemp, madder and
    wool; but this angered home manufacturers, so in
    1766, 1772, and 1782, raw textile tariffs were re-
    laxed. Foreign muslins, moreover, banned in 1770,
    and certain apparel, banned in 1779, were allowed
    in during the 1780's, provided the fabrics met
    standards in vara and weight. Yet Charles gen-
    erally pleased manufacturers with his protection
    policy, at various times banning exports of raw
    silk (as in 1774), as well as cork, hides, rags,
    esparto, grain, and wool, unless bumper crops or
    over-production brought the price too low.

10  J. LaForce, The ... Spanish Textile Industry,
    pp. 136-147.

11  Arthur Young, Travels during the Years 1787,
    1788, and 1789, Dublin, 1793, vol. I, p. 635,
    and Joseph Townsend, A Journey through Spain in
    the Years 1786 and 1787, London, 1791, vol. I,
    pp. 138-146, quoted in Richard Herr, The Eight-
    eenth Century Revolution in Spain, Princeton,
    N.J., 1958, pp. 142-3.

12    See Francisco Ortells y Gombau, Disertación
      descriptiva de la hilaza de la seda, según
      ... Vocanson, Valencia, 1783, pp. 8-21.

13    Quoted in William Coxe, Memoirs of the Kings
      of Spain of the House of Bourbon, London, 1815,
      vol. V, Appendix II, pp. 380-1. For more on
      taxes, see footnote 20, infra.

14    Martin S. Hume, Spain: its Greatness and Decay
      (1479-1788), Cambridge, England, 1905, p. 409.

15    A royal cedula against extracting gold and silver
      and distributing or exporting same was issued on
      August 5, 1768. See Juan de la Ripia (and sub-
      sequent fiscal auditors), Práctica de la admin-
      instración y cobranza de las rentas reales ...,
      Madrid, 1769, pp. 593-7.

16    Earl J. Hamilton, War and Prices in Spain,
      1651-1800, New York, 1969, p. 65; Vicens, An
      Economic History ..., p. 584.

17    Vales reales were essentially interest-bearing
      paper notes backed by a syndicate of interna-
      tional bankers. As the need for money increased,
      so did the number of vales, till by 1782 they
      totalled nearly 85,000 to the value of 450 million
      reales, and in the process had depreciated. The
      bank accepted them at par, paying in gold or in-
      creasingly with its own bankbills. Its subscribed
      capital of 30 million reales rose tenfold by the
      issue of further shares, contributed by the king,
      nobles, brotherhoods, merchants and municipali-
      ties.

18    Ronald H. Chilcote, Spain's Iron and Steel Industry,
      Austin, Texas, 1968, pp. 13-16.

19    Sempere y Guarinos wrote Ensayo de una biblio-
      teca española de los mejores escritores del
      reinado de Carlos III, 6 vols., 1785-9, and
      Biblioteca española económico-política, 4 vols.,
      Madrid, 1801-1821.

20    General and royal revenues included customs re-
      ceipts, together with the 5% almojarifazgo export
      duty; profits from mines; seigniorage dues from

the mint; silver exports; taxes on lead, salt,
and brandy; royal factory receipts and those
from royal monopolies in tobacco, mercury, gunpowder, and cards; the mails; stamped paper; the
lottery; sales of certain offices; taxes on pro-
fessions; licenses and fines; right of chancery
payments; fees from the military orders; the
*lanzas* or feudal commutation tax on the nobility;
and the *media anata*, or half the first year's salary on public offices. These accounted for about
two-thirds of the total. Provincial and other
types of revenue included the *alcabala* and *cientos*
transaction taxes; the *milliones* excise taxes on
certain items; other local excise; the *catastro*
and *bolla* sales taxes in Catalonia; the 5% tax on
land income and the 2 to 3% tax on the rental of
holdings; municipal taxes on land and property
(*propios* and *arbitrios*); municipal duties (the *sisa*);
lodgement dues and effects of Castile and other
provinces. Various ordinary and extraordinary
*servicios* levied on the commonality by the Cortes
to help the crown, taxes on the Mesta, wool,
weights, and measures, as well as the *lanzas* feudal
commutation tax on the militia were also originally included in this category. All these accounted for over one quarter of the total. Revenues
from the church included the *Cruzada*; the *excusado*;
the *subsidio* tax on property; various charity levies;
income from vacant benefices; the two-ninths income from church tithes (distinct from the church's
own one-tenth tithe and first-fruits levy on crops
and pasture); and the *media anata*, or half the first
year's salary on church offices. These accounted
for about 7% of the total. The Indies revenue
was separate, including the *quinto real*, or one-
tenth royal tax on bullion, precious stones etc.,
coming from the Americas; see chapter 11, footnote
18.

21  This figure of half a billion reales is conjectural.
Authorities vary as to exact government revenues
and expenses. To the nearest round figure in
vellon reales, Edward Clarke put annual revenues
in 1761 at about 486 million; William Coxe put
the figure in 1789 at 467 million (quoting the
British ambassador) and at 610 million (quoting
Spanish treasurer Pedro de Lerena). This does
not include revenues from the Indies. Regarding

expenditures, Clarke put these in 1761 at about 270 million; William Coxe put the figure between 1784 and 1787 at about 476 million (quoting the British ambassador) and at 685 million (quoting Lerena). Charles E. Chapman, while noting that receipts exceeded expenditures in the 1760's, underscored the deficit in the 1780's and Spain's overall trade imbalance (as often happens with a fast developing nation), citing an import value in 1789 of 717 million as against an export value of 290 million, while the growing volume of internal commerce approached 2.5 billion. This deficit in face of Spain's rising prosperity can partly be explained by heavy state investments, armaments and wars, the public debt (though actually diminished under Charles III) high cost of imports (e.g. corn and textiles), foreign wool competition, purchases from an expanding American market, colonial administrative expenses, and the outflow of silver. The inflationary cost of living for many commodities (as well as land, equipment, and transport expenses) was rising by at least 50% between 1770 and 1789. For above figures see Clarke, _Letters Concerning the Spanish Nation_ ..., London, 1763, p. 247; Coxe, _Memoirs of the Kings of Spain of the House of Bourbon_, London, 1815, vol. V, Appendix II, pp. 383-6 and reproduced in the present work as Appendix IV; Chapman, _A History of Spain_, New York, 1965, pp. 436, 469; and Earl J. Hamilton, _War and Prices in Spain, 1651-1800_, New York, 1969, Appendix I, pp. 229-257.

David Felix, "Profit, Inflation, and Industrial Development, 1750-1800", _Quarterly Journal of Economics_, LXX, August 1956.

CHAPTER FOURTEEN

1   Quoted in Rafael Olaechea, _El Conde de Aranda y el "Partido Aragonés"_, Saragossa, 1969, p. 115.

2   See Cayetano Alcázar Molina, _El Conde de Floridablanca_, Madrid, 1934.

3   Olaechea, _El Conde de Aranda_ ..., p. 125.

360

4   See Aranda's letter to Floridablanca, Paris,
    January 2, 1787, Legajo 2850, AHN.

5   Vicente Palacio Atard, "Dos palabras sobre un
    catálogo y sobre Tanucci", from the Catálogo
    XXI del archivo de Simancas (Secretaría de
    Estado, Reino de las Dos Sicilias, siglo
    XVIII), R. Magdaleno Redondo (ed.), Valladolid,
    1956, introducción, p. viii.

6   In Holland the Stadholder was supported by Eng-
    land and Prussia, while a rival group was sup-
    ported by France. In the Austrian Netherlands
    resistance was mounting against Joseph II's
    reformist attacks on privilege. Events in
    Vienna, incidentally, were relayed to Madrid
    by an experienced Spanish diplomat, Marqués de
    Llano.

7   For a study of these facets, also the threat to
    the Sultan's position posed by Mulay Eliacit,
    see Vicente Rodríguez Casado, Política marroquí
    de Carlos III, Madrid, 1946, pp. 340-367.

8   Ibid., p. 346.

9   Prominent periodicals included El Censor, Correo
    de Madrid, Diario de Madrid, Semanario erudito,
    Mercurio histórico, Memorial literario, and
    the long-standing Gaceta de Madrid. In 1780 and
    1786 there appeared briefly the government weekly,
    Correo literario de la Europa, largely devoted
    to foreign scientific knowledge.

10  Apart from his early plays, Jovellanos wrote
    works on public banks (1782), on muslins (1784),
    on the navy (1784), and on the freedom of the
    arts (1785). Also worthy of note are his Elogio
    de Carlos III (1789), and his great Informe
    sobre la ley agraria (1795). Colmeiro held that
    Jovellanos, while supporting the ideas of Adam
    Smith in theory, vacillated between ancient and
    modern systems, yet praised him for his censure
    of trade guilds which hampered industry and for
    exposing the faults in agriculture. See Manuel
    Colmeiro, Biblioteca de los economistas españ-
    oles ..., Madrid, 1880, p. 102.

11    Edith Helman, Jovellanos y Goya, Madrid, 1970,
      p. 248.

12    The requests were mostly refused. See Charles'
      letter to relatives Clement and Elizabeth of
      Saxony residing at Ehrenbreitstein, near Cob-
      lenz, March 26, 1775, Legajo 2630, AHN.

13    Charles III to Ferdinand, prob. San Ildefonso,
      July 20, 1784, Legajo 6084, AGS. Maria Carolina
      was the go-between in Charles' disputes with his
      son, as seen in her letters to Charles of October
      1785, Legajo 5893, AGS.

14    María Luisa's defense was that the slightest im-
      propriety at masquerades led to everyone suspect-
      ing her of infidelity. For her alleged miscon-
      duct with guardsman Pérez de Guzmán y Gallo and
      other trivia, see her letters to Charles (via
      Floridablanca) of April 1782 ff., Legajo 2850,
      AHN.

15    Enrique de Tapia Ozcariz, Carlos III y su epoca,
      Madrid, 1962, pp. 396-9.

16    This tension was observed by the Duke of Vauguyon,
      French ambassador to Spain, and is reflected in
      Charles' correspondence with Louis XVI, 1787-8,
      Legajo 2850, AHN.

17    Charles to Mariana Victoria, Aranjuez, May 19,
      1785, Legajo 2626, AHN. He was overjoyed by the
      birth of the (unsurviving) child by this marriage;
      see his letter to Louis XVI, San Lorenzo, October
      28, 1788, Legajo 2734, AHN. Charles' comment *infra*
      is quoted in Tapia, Carlos III ..., p. 408.

18    Quoted, with comment *infra*, in Tapia, Carlos III
      ..., pp. 410-1.

Charles E. Kany, Life and Manners in Madrid, 1750-
      1800, Berkeley, Calif., 1932.

Nigel Glendenning, A Literary History of Spain: the
      Eighteenth Century, London, 1972.

José Gudiol, The Arts of Spain, London, 1964.

CHAPTER FIFTEEN

1   Quoted in Vicente Rodríguez Casado, La Polí-
    tica y los políticos en el reinado de Carlos
    III, Madrid, 1962, p.260

2   J.F. Bourgoing, Travels in Spain, London, 1789,
    vol. III, p. 421.

3   Charles III to Louis XVI, Aranjuez, April 29,
    1788, Legajo 2734, AHN.

4   Manuel Danvila y Collado, Reinado de Carlos
    III, Madrid, 1888-1896, vol. II, p. 173.

5   Quoted by Francisco Cabarrús, Elogio de Carlos
    III ... (addressed to the royal Economic Society
    of Madrid on July 25, 1789), Madrid, 1789, p. 37.

6   Recounted by Feijóo in his dedication to Prince
    Charles of vol. IV of his Teatro crítico univer-
    sal, Madrid, in 1730.

7   Quoted by Cabarrús, Elogio de Carlos III ...,
    pp. 48-9.

Joseph Addison, Charles III of Spain, Oxford, England,
    1900.

# BIBLIOGRAPHY

## ARCHIVAL SOURCES

### ARCHIVO GENERAL DE SIMANCAS (AGS)

The following legajos from the Secretary of State (Secretaria de Estado) were used and footnoted: 5057, 5806, 5817, 5821, 5826, 5829, 5830, 5832, 5833, 5836, 5841, 5842, 5849, 5850, 5858, 5866, 5893, 5927, 6080, 6084, 6090, 6618, 6620, 6646, 6648, 6958. All but the last five contain correspondence mainly to or from the government of Naples (Reino de las Dos Sicilias). Legajo 1009 was taken from the Secretaryship of Grace and Justice. The following libros from Estado (Reino de las Dos Sicilias) were used and footnoted: 317, 318, 325, 330, 331, 333, 337, 339, 342, 343, 344, 348, 352, 353, 354, 355.

### ARCHIVO HISTÓRICO NACIONAL (AHN)

The following legajos from the Secretaryship of State (Estado) were used and footnoted: 2453, 2456, 2561, 2562, 2626, 2630, 2646, 2649, 2695, 2706, 2711, 2714, 2715, 2734, 2755, 2773, 2777, 2841, 2850, 2858, 2862, 2863, 3028, 3365, 3372, 3390, 3517, 4224, 4226, 4323. The periodical Gaceta de Madrid, properly located in the Biblioteca Nacional, Madrid, exists in scattered fragments among the legajos of the AHN.

### LIBRARY OF CONGRESS, WASHINGTON, D.C.

Division of Manuscripts.
Box no. 3247 (Photostats). Correspondence of Spanish envoys at St. Petersburg, Russia, 1761-1773; from Legajo 86, Document 5, Estado, Archivo General de Indias, Seville.

Box no. 3601 (Cunningham and Dunn transcripts). Correspondence on the Spanish expeditions to Upper California, 1774-1776; from Legajo 89, Document 4, Audiencia de Mexico, Archivo General de Indias.

364

PUBLIC RECORD OFFICE, LONDON (PRO)

State Papers to 1780. British envoys and consuls in Spain to London, Series 94, piece nos.
ranging from 172 to 209.

Foreign Office Papers, 1780-1788. London to
British envoys in Spain, Series 72, piece no.
1 ff.

Foreign Office Papers, 1781-1787. British envoys in Spain to London, Series 185, piece nos.
1 to 5.

WORKS IN GENERAL

ACTON, Harold M. The Last Medici. London, Faber &
Faber, 1932.

_____ The Bourbons of Naples, 1734-1825.
London, Methuen; New York, St. Martin's, 1956.

ADDISON, Joseph. Charles III of Spain (the Stanhope
Essay). Oxford, England, 1900.

ADDY, George M. The Enlightenment in the University
of Salamanca. Durham, N.C., Duke University
Press, 1966.

ALAMO, Juan del. Gibraltar antes de la historia de
España. Madrid, Instituto de estudios políticos,
1964.

ALCÁZAR MOLINA, Cayetano. El Conde de Floridablanca.
Madrid, Aguilar, 1934.

_____ Los Virreinatos en el
siglo XVIII (from the Historia de América
series). Barcelona, Salvat, 1945.

ALTAMIRA Y CREVEA, Rafael. See CHAPMAN, *infra*.

ALVAREZ REQUEJO, Felipe. El Conde de Campomanes:
su obra histórica. Oviedo, Instituto de
Estudios Asturianos, 1954.

AMAT Y JUNIET, Manuel de. Memoria de gobierno.
Written ca. 1780. Published, Seville, Escuela
de Estudios Hispano-Americanos de Sevilla, 1947.

ARANDA, Conde de. "Plan de gobierno". (addressed
to the Prince of Asturias). Paris, 1781.

ARMSTRONG, Edward. Elizabeth Farnese, "the Termagant of Spain". London, 1892.

ARRIQUIBAR, N. de. Recreación política. Vitoria, 1779.

BALLESTEROS Y BERETTA, Antonio. Historia de España
y de su influencia en la historia universal.
9 vols., Barcelona, Salvat, 1918-1941.

BARBIER, Jacques A. "Elite and Cadres in Bourbon
Chile". Hispanic American Historical Review,
Baltimore, Md., LII, August 1972.

BAUDRILLART, Alfred. "Examen des droits de Philippe
V et de ses descendants au trône de France en
dehors des revendications d'Utrecht". Revue
d'Histoire diplomatique, Paris, III, 1889.

_____ Philippe V et la cour la France.
5 vols., Paris, 1890-1901.

BECATTINI, Francesco. Storia del regno di Carlo III.
2 vols., Turin, 1790.

BERGAMINI, John D. The Spanish Bourbons. Toronto,
Longman Canada, 1974.

BERTRAN, Felipe. Colección de las cartas pastorales.
2 vols., Madrid, 1783.

BÉTHENCOURT MASSIEU, Antonio. Patiño en la política
internacional de Felipe V. Valladolid, pubs.
de Universidad de Valladolid, 1954.

BIANCHINI, Lodovico. Della storia delle finanze
del regno di Napoli. 3 vols., Palermo, 1839.

_____ Della storia economico-civile
di Sicilia. 2 vols., Palermo, 1841.

BOLTON, Herbert Eugene. _Outpost of Empire: the Story of the Founding of San Francisco._ New York, A. Knopf, 1939.

BOURGOING, J.F. _Nouveau voyage en Espagne._ 3 vols., Paris, 1789. Translated in English as _Travels in Spain._ 3 vols., London, 1789.

_____ _Tableau de l'Espagne moderne._ 3 vols., Paris, 1797-1807.

BOURGUET, Alfred. "Le duc de Choiseul et l'Angleterre, mission de Bussy à Londres. Le duc de Choiseul et l'aliance espagnole". _Revue historique,_ Paris, LXXI, September-October 1899.

BRADING, D.A. _Miners and Merchants in Bourbon Mexico, 1763-1810._ Cambridge, England, Cambridge University Press, 1971.

_____ and Harry E. CROSS. "Colonial Silver Mining: Mexico and Peru". _Hispanic American Historical Review,_ LII, November 1972.

BROWN, Vera Lee. "Studies in the History of Spain in the Second Half of the Eighteenth Century". _Smith College Studies in History,_ Northampton, Mass., XV, October 1929 and January 1930.

BURKHOLDER, Mark A. "From Creole to Peninsular: the Transformation of the Audiencia of Lima". _Hispanic American Historical Review,_ LII, August 1972.

BURRUS, Ernest, S.J. Review of M. Mörner, _The Expulsion of the Jesuits_ q.v...., _Hispanic American Historical Review,_ XLVIII, November 1968.

CABARRÚS, Francisco. _Elogio de Carlos III, rey de España y de las Indias._ Madrid, 1789.

CADALSO, José. _Los eruditos a la violeta_ ... Madrid, 1772.

_____ _Cartas marruecas._ Madrid, 1789.

CALLAHAN, William J. "The Problem of Confinement: an Aspect of Poor Relief in Eighteenth-Century Spain". Hispanic American Historical Review, LI, February 1971.

_____ Honor, Commerce, and Industry in Eighteenth-Century Spain. Boston, Mass., Harvard Graduate School of Business Administration, 1972.

CAMPBELL, Leon G. "A Colonial Establishment: Creole Domination of the Audiencia of Lima during the Late Eighteenth Century". Hispanic American Historical Review, LII, February 1972.

CAMPILLO Y COSSÍO, José del. España despierta. Madrid, 1741.

CAMPOMANES, Rodríguez de. Discurso sobre el formento de la industria popular. Madrid, 1774.

_____ Discurso sobre la educación popular de los artesanos y su fomento. Madrid, 1775.

_____ Apéndice a la educación popular. 4 vols., Madrid, 1776.

CARRIÓN, Pascual. Los latifundios en España ... Madrid, Gráficas Reunidas, 1932.

CAUGHEY, John W. Bernardo de Gálvez in Louisiana, 1776-1783. Berkeley, University of California Press, 1934.

CERVERA, Francisco. Jorge Juan y la colonización española en América. Madrid, Editorial Voluntad, 1927.

CHAPMAN, Charles E. A History of Spain (founded on the Historia de España y de la civilización española of Rafael Altamira, pub. Barcelona, 1911). London, Collier-Macmillan, 1965; New York, Free Press, 1965.

CHILCOTE, Ronald H. Spain's Iron and Steel Industry. Austin, University of Texas Press, 1968.

CHORLEY, Patrick. Oil, Silk, and Enlightenment: Economic Problems in Eighteenth-Century Naples. Naples, Nella sede dell' Istituto, 1965.

CHRISTELOW, Allan. "Economic Background of the Anglo-Spanish War of 1762". Journal of Modern History, Chicago, Ill., XVIII, March 1946.

CLARKE, Edward. Letters Concerning the Spanish Nation: Written at Madrid during the Years 1760 and 1761. London, 1763.

COLLETTA, General Pietro. A History of the Kingdom of Naples. Susan Horner (trans.), 2 vols., Edinburgh, Scotland, 1858.

COLMEIRO, Manuel. Biblioteca de los economistas españoles de los siglos xvi, xvii, y xviii. Madrid, 1880.

CONN, Stetson. Gibraltar in British Diplomacy in the Eighteenth Century. London, Oxford University Press, 1942.

COOK, Warren L. Flood Tide of Empire: Spain and the Pacific Northwest, 1543-1819. New Haven, Conn., Yale University Press, 1973.

COXE, William. Memoirs of the Kings of Spain of the House of Bourbon. 5 vols., London, 1815.

COYER, G.F. La nobleza comerciante. Jacobo María de Espinosa (ed. and trans. from French). Madrid, 1781.

CUTTER, Donald C. "California, Training Ground for Spanish Naval Heroes". California Historical Society Quarterly, San Francisco, Calif., XL, June, 1961.

DALRYMPLE, William. Travels through Spain and Portugal in 1774. London, 1777.

369

DANVILA Y COLLADO, Manuel. Reinado de Carlos III
   (from the Historia general de España, Real Acade-
   mia de la Historia). 6 vols., Madrid, 1888-1896.

DEFOURNEAUX Marcelin. Pablo de Olavide ou
   L'afrancesado. Paris, Presses Universitaires
   de France, 1959.

DELPY, Gaspard. Feijóo et l'esprit européen ...
   Paris, Hachette, 1936.

DESDEVISES DU DÉZERT, G. L'Espagne de l'ancien
   régime. 3 vols., Paris, 1897-1904.

DÍAZ-PLAJA, Fernando. La Vida española en el siglo
   XVIII. Barcelona, A. Martín, 1946.

DOMÍNGUEZ ORTIZ, Antonio. La Sociedad española en
   el siglo XVIII. Madrid, Instituto Balmes de
   sociología, 1955.

EGUÍA RUIZ, Constancio. Los Jesuítas y el motín
   de Esquilache. Madrid, Instituto Jerónimo de
   Zurita, 1947.

Ensayo de la Sociedad Bascongada de los Amigos del
   País (anonymous, prob. based on Peñaflorida's
   contribution). Vitoria, 1768.

FEIJÓO, Benito Jerónimo. Teatro crítico universal.
   9 vols., Madrid, 1726-1740, 1778.

─────────────────────────── Cartas eruditas y curiosas
   ... Madrid, 1751-3.

FELIX, David. "Profit, Inflation, and Industrial
   Development, 1750-1800". Quarterly Journal
   of Economics, Cambridge, Mass., LXX, August 1956.

FERNÁN NÚÑEZ, Conde de. Vida de Carlos III. 2 vols.,
   Madrid, 1898.

FERRER DEL RÍO, Antonio. Historia del reinado de
   Carlos III en España. 4 vols., Madrid, 1856.

FILANGIERI, Gaetano. La scienza della legislazione.
   Naples, 1780.

FISHER, John R. Government and Society in Colonial Peru: the Intendant System, 1784-1814. London, Athlone Press, 1970.

FLORIDABLANCA, Conde de. "Instrucción reservada para dirección de la Junta de Estado". (Addressed to Charles III, with a subsequent Memorial.) Madrid, 1787-8.

FLOYD, Troy. The Anglo-Spanish Struggle for Mosquitía. Albuquerque, University of New Mexico Press, 1967.

FORNARI, Tomasso. Delle teorie economiche nelle provincie napolitane dal MDCCXXXV al MDCCCXXX (Largely based on works by Carlo Broggia, F. Galiani, A. Genovesi, and Troiano Spinelli). Milan, 1888.

FORTUNATO, Nicola. Riflessioni intorno al commercio antico e moderno del regno di Napoli ... Naples, 1760.

FRANCIS, David. The First Peninsular War, 1702-1713. London, Ernest Benn, 1975.

FUENTE. See VICENTE DE LA FUENTE, infra.

GAETANI, Honorato. Elogio storico di Carlo III ... Naples, 1789.

GALIANI, Ferdinando. Della Moneta ... Naples, 1750.

GÁLVEZ, Bernardo de. Instrucciones ... Mexico City, 1786. Republished as Instructions for Governing the Interior Provinces of New Spain. Donald E. Worcester (ed.). Berkeley, University of California Press, 1951.

GÁNDARA, Miguel Antonio de la. Apuntes sobre el bien y mal de España. Madrid, 1804.

GEE, Joshua. Consideraciones sobre el comercio y la navegación de la Gran Bretaña. Benito de Noboa (trans. from French). First published London, 1729. Madrid, 1753.

GENOVESI, Antonio.  See FORNARI, *supra*.

GIANNONE, Pietro.  Istoria civile del regno di Napoli.  Naples, 1723.

GLENDINNING, Nigel.  A Literary History of Spain: the Eighteenth Century.  London, Ernest Benn, 1972.

GONZÁLEZ-BLANCO, Edmundo.  Jovellanos: su vida y sus obras.  Madrid, 1911.

GOODWIN, Albert (ed.).  The European Nobility in the Eighteenth Century.  London, A. & C. Black, 1953; New York, Harper & Row, 1967.

GREEN, O.H.  "On the Príncipe de Esquilache".  Hispanic Review, Philadelphia, Penn., VII, July 1939.

GUDIOL, José.  The Arts of Spain.  London, Thames and Hudson, 1964.

HAMILTON, Earl J.  War and Prices in Spain, 1651-1800.  New York, Russell & Russell, 1969.

HARCOURT-SMITH, Simon.  Alberoni; or the Spanish Conspiracy.  London, Faber & Faber, 1943.

HARGREAVES-MAWDSLEY, W. Norman.  Spain under the Bourbons, 1700-1733.  London, Macmillan, 1973.

_____  Eighteenth-Century Spain, 1700-1788.  London, Macmillan, 1978.

HARING, Clarence H.  The Spanish Empire in America.  New York, Oxford University Press, 1947.

HARRIS, Sir James (First Earl of Malmesbury).  Diaries and Correspondence ...  London, 1845, 1870.

HELMAN, Edith.  Jovellanos y Goya.  Madrid, Taurus, 1970.

HENDERSON, Sir Nicholas.  "Charles III of Spain: an Enlightened Despot".  History Today, London (Bracken House), October 1968.

HERR, Richard.  The Eighteenth-Century Revolution
in Spain.  Princeton, N.J., Princeton University
Press, 1958.

HOBSBAWM, E.J.  Primitive Rebels.  New York, Norton,
1959.

HULL, Anthony H.  "Spanish and Russian Rivalry in
the North Pacific Regions of the New World,
1760-1812".  Microfilmed thesis, Ann Arbor,
Michigan, 1966.

HUME, Martin S.  Spain: its Greatness and Decay
(1479-1788).  Cambridge Historical Series,
G.W. Prothero (ed.).  Cambridge, England, 1905.

HUSSEY, Roland D.  The Caracas Company, 1728-1784 ...
Cambridge, Mass., Harvard University Press, 1934.

ISLA, José Francisco de.  Memorial en nombre de las
cuatro provincias de España de la Compañía de
Jesus ...  Madrid, 1882.

JOVELLANOS, Gaspar Melchor de.  Elogio de Carlos III.
Madrid, 1795.

_____  Informe sobre la ley
agraria. Madrid, 1795.

_____  Diarios.  Madrid,
Alianza Editorial, 1967.

JUAN, Jorge.  Examen Marítimo teórico y práctico,
o tratado de mecánica ...  Madrid, 1771.

_____  and Antonio de ULLOA.  Noticias
secretas de América.  London, 1826.

Junta general de la real compañía Guipúzcoana de
Caracas.  Report of June 15 to November 24,
1772 (anonymous).  Madrid, 1773.

KAGAN, Richard L.  Students and Society in Early Modern
Spain.  Baltimore, Md., Johns Hopkins University
Press, 1974.

373

KAMEN, Henry. The War of Succession in Spain, 1700-1715. Bloomington, Indiana University Press, 1969.

KANY, Charles E. Life and Manners in Madrid, 1750-1800. Berkeley, University of California Press, 1932.

KINNAIRD, Lawrence (ed.). Spain in the Mississippi Valley, 1765-1794. Annual Report of the American Historical Association for the Year 1945. Vols. II, III, IV, Washington, D.C., 1949.

KLEIN, Julius. The Mesta, A Study in Spanish Economic History, 1273-1836. Cambridge, Mass., Harvard University Press, 1920.

KREBS WILCKENS, Ricardo. El Pensamiento histórico, político, y económico del Conde de Campomanes. Santiago de Chile, pubs. de Universidad de Chile, 1960.

LA FORCE, James C. The Development of the Spanish Textile Industry, 1750-1800. Berkeley, University of California Press, 1965.

LA SOUCHÈRE, Eléna de. An Explanation of Spain. Eleanor R. Levieux (trans.). New York, Random House, 1965.

LANNING, John Tate. Academic Culture in the Spanish Colonies. London, Oxford University Press, 1940.

LLORENTE, Juan Antonio. Memoria histórica ... Madrid, 1812. Republished as La Inquisición y los españoles. Madrid, Editorial Ciencia Nueva, 1967.

LUNA, José Carlos de. Historia de Gibraltar. Madrid, Gráficas Uguina, 1944.

LYNCH, John. Spanish Colonial Administration, 1782-1810: the Intendant System in the Viceroyalty of Río de la Plata. London, Athlone Press, 1958.

MACANAZ, Melcho de. Testamento de España. The
    Hague, 1740.

MADARIAGA, Isabel de. Britain, Russia, and the Armed
    Neutrality of 1780. New Haven, Conn., Yale
    University Press, 1962.

MADARIAGA, Salvador de. The Fall of the Spanish Amer-
    ican Empire. London, Hollis and Carter, 1947.

MARCH, J.M. La Vida de beato José Pignatelli y su
    tiempo. 2 vols., Barcelona, Ibérica, 1935 and
    1944.

McALISTER, Lyle N. The "Fuero Militar" in New Spain,
    1764-1800. Gainesville, University of Florida
    Press, 1957.

Memorial ajustado entre la Mesta y la provincia de
    Extremadura (anonymous). San Ildefonso, 1764;
    completed, Madrid, 1771.

MIGUÉLEZ, P. El jansenismo y regalismo en España.
    Valladolid, 1895.

MOORE, J.P. The Cabildo in Peru under the Bourbons.
    Durham, N.C., Duke University Press, 1966.

MORCILLO Y VALERO, Jesualdo. Los estadistas de
    Carlos III. Cáceres, 1894.

MORET Y PRENDERGAST, Segismundo. El Conde de Aranda.
    Madrid, 1878.

MÖRNER, Magnus (ed.). The Expulsion of the Jesuits
    from Latin America. New York, Knopf, 1965.

MORTON, H.V. A Stranger in Spain. London, Methuen,
    1965.

MUÑOZ, Antonio. Discurso sobre economía-política.
    Madrid, 1769.

MURRAY, Arthur C. (Viscount Elibank). An Episode in
    the Spanish War, 1739-1744, London, Seeley,
    Service & Co., 1952.

375

NAVARRO GARCÍA, Luis. Don José de Gálvez y la Comandancia General de las provincias internas del norte de Nueva España. Seville, Escuela de Estudios Hispano-Americanos de Sevilla, 1964.

OLAECHEA, Rafael. El Conde de Aranda y el "Partido Aragonés". Saragossa, Universidad de Zaragosa, 1969.

OLAVIDE, Pablo de. El Evangelio en triunfo, ó historia de un filósofo desengañado. (Published anonymously.) 4 vols., Valencia, 1797-8.

ORTELLS Y GOMBAU, Francisco. Disertación descriptiva de la hilaza de la seda, según el antiguo modo de hilar y el nuevo llamado de Vocanson. Valencia, 1783.

OTERO PEDRAYO, Ramón. El Padre Feijóo. Su Vida, doctrina e influencias. Orense, Instituto de Estudios Orensanos 'Padre Feijóo', 1972.

OTS CAPEDQUÍ, José María. Instituciones de gobierno del Nuevo Reino de Granada durante el siglo XVIII. Bogotá, pubs. de Universidad Nacional de Colombia, 1950.

PALACIO ATARD, Vicente. Areche y Guirior: Observaciones sobre el fracaso de una visita al Perú. Seville, Escuela de Estudios Hispano-Americanos de Sevilla, 1946.

——————————— "Dos palabras sobre un catálogo y sobre Tanucci". Catálogo XXI del archivo de Simancas (Secretaría de Estado, Reino de las dos Sicilias, siglo XVIII). R. Magdaleno Redondo (ed.). Valladolid, Archivo de Simancas, 1956.

PASTORE, Miguel. Saggio filosofico sopra la vita di Carlo III di Spagna. Naples, 1789.

PECCHIO, Giuseppe. L'Histoire de l'économie politique en Italie. Léonard Gallois (trans.). Paris, 1830.

376

PEERS, E. Allison. The Church in Spain, 1737-1937.
London, Burns Oates and Washbourne, 1938.

PÉREZ, Vicente V. See VIZCAYNO PÉREZ, *infra*.

PÉREZ BAYER, Francisco. "Por la libertad de la literatura española". Madrid, 1769.

PETRIE, Sir Charles. King Charles III of Spain.
London, Constable, 1971.

PIQUER, Andrés. Lógica moderna, o Arte de hallar la verdad y perfeccionar la razón. Valencia, 1747.

PLÁ, José Cárceles. El alma en pena de Gibraltar.
D. Round (trans.), and published as Gibraltar.
London, Hollis and Carter, 1955.

PRIESTLEY, Herbert I. José de Gálvez: Visitor-General of New Spain, 1765-1771. Berkeley, University of California Press, 1916.

RAMOS, Enrique. See MUÑOZ, *supra*.

RINGROSE, David R. "Transportation and Economic Stagnation in Eighteenth-Century Castile". Journal of Economic History, New York, XXVIII, March 1969.

RIPIA, Juan de la, *et al*. Práctica de la administración y cobranza de las rentas reales y visita de los ministros que se ocupan en ellas. Madrid, 1676-1769.

RODRÍGUEZ, Laura. "The Spanish Riots of 1766".
Past and Present, Oxford, England, No. 59,
May 1973.

RODRÍGUEZ CASADO, Vicente. Política marroquí de Carlos III. Madrid, Instituto Jerónimo de Zurita, 1946.

_____ La Política y los políticos en el reinado de Carlos III. Madrid, Rialp, 1962.

ROUSSEAU, François. Expulsion des Jesuits en
    Espagne: démarches de Charles III pour leur
    secularisation. Extracted from Revue des
    questions historiques, January 1904. Paris, 1904.

_____ Règne de Charles III d'Espagne
    (1759-1788). 2 vols., Paris, 1907.

RUSSELL, Jack. Gibraltar Besieged, 1779-1783.
    London, Heinemann, 1965.

SÁNCHEZ AGESTA, Luis. El Pensami to político del
    despotismo ilustrado. Madrid, Instituto de
    estudios políticos. 1953.

SÁNCHEZ BELDA, Luis, et al.(ed.). Exposición de la
    administración en la epoca de Carlos III
    (catalogue). Alcalá de Henares, Universidad, 1962.

SÁNCHEZ-BARBA, Mario Hernández. La ultima expansión
    española en América. Madrid, Instituto de
    estudios políticos, 1957.

SÁNCHEZ-DIANA, José. "Relaciones diplomáticas entre
    Rusia y España en el siglo XVIII, 1780-1783".
    Hispania, Madrid, XII, May 1952.

SARMIENTO, Martín. Demostración crítico-apologética
    en el Theatro Crítico Universal que dío a luz
    el Fr. Benito Jerónimo Feijóo. Madrid, 1732.

SARRAILH, Jean. La España ilustrada de la segunda
    mitad del siglo XVIII. Antonio Alatorre (trans.).
    Mexico City, Fondo de Cultura Económica, 1957.

SEMPERE Y GUARINOS, Juan. Ensayo de una biblioteca
    española de los mejores escritores del reinado
    de Carlos III. 6 vols., Madrid, 1785-9.

_____ Biblioteca española
    económico-política. 4 vols., Madrid, 1801-1821.

SHAFER, Robert J. Economic Societies in the Spanish
    World, 1763-1821. Syracuse, N.Y., Syracuse
    University Press, 1958.

SITWELL, Sacheverell. _Spain_. London, Batsford, 1950.

SPELL, Jefferson Rea. _Rousseau in the Spanish World before 1833_. Austin, University of Texas Press, 1938.

STEIN, S.J. & B.H. _Colonial Heritage of Latin America_. London, New York, Oxford University Press, 1979.

SWINBURNE, Henry. _Travels through Spain in the Years 1775 and 1776_. Dublin, 1779.

TAPIA OZCARIZ, Enrique de. _Carlos III Y su epoca_. Madrid, Aguilar, 1962.

TARANTO, Gonzalo di. _L'Infante di Spagna Carlo III di Borbone in Italia, prima della conquista del Regno_. Naples, 1905.

TAYLOR, William B. "Landed Society in New Spain: a View from the South". _Hispanic American Historical Review_, LIV, August 1974.

THOMAS, Alfred Barnaby. _Teodoro de Croix and the Northern Frontier of New Spain, 1776-1783_. Norman, University of Oklahoma Press, 1941.

_____ _Latin America, a History_. New York, Macmillan, 1956.

TOMKINS, Stuart R. "After Bering: Mapping the North Pacific". _British Columbia Historical Quarterly_, Victoria, XIX, January 1955.

TOWNSEND, Joseph. _A Journey through Spain in the Years 1786 and 1787_ ... 3 vols., London, 1791.

_Travels through Spain_ (anonymous). Boston, Mass., 1808.

ULLOA, Antonio de. _Noticias americanas_. Madrid, 1772. See also Jorge JUAN, _supra_.

UZTÁRIZ, Jerónimo de. _Theórica y práctica de comercio y de marina_. Madrid, 1724, 1742.

VAN BATH, B.H. Slicher. The Agrarian History of
    Western Europe, A.D. 500-1850. London, Edward
    Arnold, 1966.

VICENS VIVES, Jaime. An Economic History of Spain.
    Frances M. López-Morillas (trans.). Princeton,
    N.J., Princeton University Press, 1969.

VICENTE DE LA FUENTE (ed.). Colección de los artí-
    culos sobre la expulsión de los Jesuítas de
    España. Extracted from the weekly review La
    Cruzada. Madrid, 1867.

VILAR, Pierre. "Motín de Esquilache et crises de
    l'ancien régime". Historia Ibérica, New York
    (Long Island City), I, 1973.

VIZCAYNO PÉREZ, Vicente. Discursos políticos sobre
    los estragos que causan los censos ... Madrid,
    1766.

VOLTES BOU, Pedro. Carlos III y su tiempo. Barce-
    lona, Editorial Juventud, 1964.

WAGNER, Henry R. Cartography of the Northwest Coast
    of America to the Year 1800. Berkeley, Univer-
    sity of California Press, 1937.

WALKER, G.J. Spanish Politics and Imperial Trade,
    1700-1789. Bloomington, Indiana University
    Press, 1979.

WARD, Bernardo. Proyecto económico ... Written, 1762;
    published, Madrid, 1779 and 1782.

YOUNG, Arthur. Travels during the Years 1787, 1788,
    and 1789 ... 2 vols., Dublin 1793.

ZABALA Y AUÑÓN, Miguel de. Representación al Rey
    Nuestro Señor D. Felipe V. Madrid, 1732-4.

Publishers names are given for works appearing only
    after 1914.

The Hispanic American Historical Review is published
    at Durham, N.C. by Duke University Press.

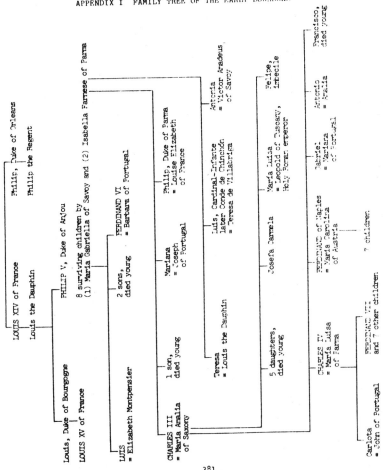

# APPENDIX II

## SOME SPANISH AND NEAPOLITAN VALUES, CA. 1760

SPANISH

| | |
|---|---|
| 1 real (vellon money) | = 34 maravedis, or 12 granos |
| 1 real (silver) | = 2½ vellon reales |
| 1 piaster (silver) | = approx. 15 vellon reales, or 3.33 English shillings |
| 1 peso duro (silver dollar) | = 20 vellon reales or 8 silver reales |
| 1 Castilian mark of silver | = 8½ pesos (cut therefrom) |
| 1 escudo (gold) | = approx. 37½ vellon reales |
| 1 pistole or doubloon (gold) | = 2 escudos |
| 9 escudos (vellon) <br> 90 reales (vellon) | = approx. one pound sterling |
| 9 ducados (vellon) <br> (copper ducats) | = approx. 1.1 pound sterling |
| 9 pesos duros (silver dollars) <br> 9 reales de a ocho (silver pieces of eight) <br> 72 silver reales, or <br> 180 vellon reales | = approx. two pounds sterling |
| 1 doblón de a ocho <br> (gold piece of eight) | = approx. 301 vellon reales, or 3.3 pounds sterling |
| 1 vara or Castilian yard | = approx. 33 inches or .835 meters |
| 1 Spanish league | = approx. 4.125 miles or 6.6 kilometers (with variations in each kingdom) |
| 1 fanega (area and measure) | = approx. 1.59 acres, 1.5 bushels, or 53 liters |

| | |
|---|---|
| 1 arroba (weight) | = approx. 25 pounds, 11.34 kilograms, and approx. one half of a fanega in weight |
| 1 quintal | = 4 arrobas, or 101.5 pounds |

NEAPOLITAN (including Sicily)

| | |
|---|---|
| 1 ducat (silver) | = 5 tari, 10 carlini, 100 granos, or approx. 3.8 English shillings |
| 1 scudo (silver) | = 12 carlini |
| 1 zecchino (gold) | = 20 carlini |
| 1 doppia (gold) | = 40 carlini |
| 1 oncia (gold) | = 60 carlini |
| 1 salme | = approx. 300 liters |
| 1 tomola, or corn bushel | = one third of a septier, or approx. 80 French livres in weight |

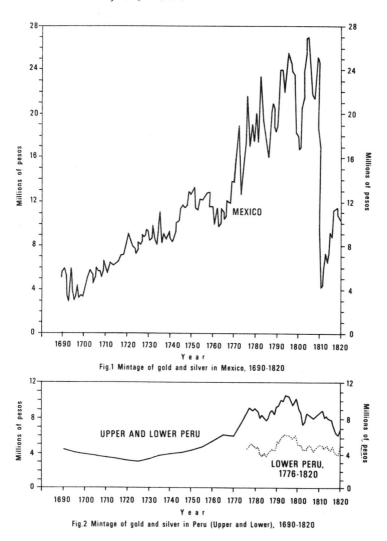

Fig.1 Mintage of gold and silver in Mexico, 1690-1820

Fig.2 Mintage of gold and silver in Peru (Upper and Lower), 1690-1820

384

# APPENDIX IV

## THE REVENUE, 1789

The grand total below represents the annual average over approximately the period 1784-1789, in vellon reales. The figures are based on estimates by the British ambassador in Madrid. Spanish treasurer Pedro de Lerena gives a more liberal total estimate of 609,624,198 reales.

| | |
|---|---:|
| General revenues | 151,000,000 |
| Provincial revenues | 91,000,000 |
| Tobacco | 95,000,000 |
| Salt | 20,000,000 |
| Wool | 22,000,000 |
| Brandy | 2,500,000 |
| Propios and arbitrios | 6,000,000 |
| Posts and couriers | 14,000,000 |
| Cards | 8,500,000 |
| Stamped paper | 4,500,000 |
| Arrendamiento of Madrid & Customs | 8,000,000 |
| Royal fabric of crystal, & fabric of San Fernando | 2,500,000 |
| Effects of Castile | 1,000,000 |
| Royal lottery | 6,000,000 |
| Cruzada | 14,000,000 |
| Lanzas and medias anatas | 3,000,000 |
| Masterships of the Military Orders | 2,000,000 |
| Medias anatas of ecclesiastics | 3,000,000 |
| Excusado and subsidio | 12,000,000 |
| Rights of Lodgment | 800,000 |
| Pasture of the Serena (Mesta) | 140,000 |
| Grand total | 466,940,000 |

The above figures are taken from William Coxe, Memoirs of the Kings of Spain of the House of Bourbon, 5 vols., London, 1815, vol. V, Appendix II, p. 385.

MAP OF SPAIN

MAP OF NAPLES AND SICILY

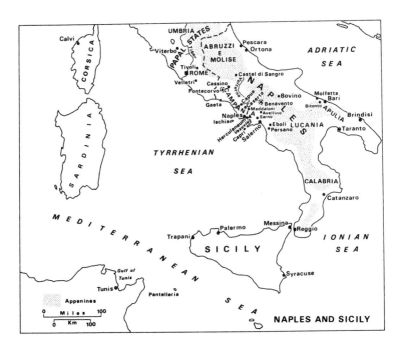

# MAP OF SPANISH NORTH AMERICA, ca. 1780

SPANISH NORTH AMERICA ca.1780

SPANISH SOUTH AMERICA ca. 1780

# INDEX

Acquaviva, Cardinal T. 29, 39-46

Aix-la-Chapelle, treaty of 46, 84

Alba & Huéscar, Duke of 89, 117, 133-5, 143, 161-5, 189, 298

Alberoni, Cardinal G. 4, 19, 135

Alcázar & Oriente palaces see Royal Palace

Algiers 187, 295

Almansa, battle of 2, 24

Almodóvar, Duke of 155-6, 180, 250, 272

Amat, Manuel de 226-8

America
See Indies, West Indies, Guatemala, United States, and each viceroyalty

Andalusia and south Spain 161-5, 206, 280, 288

Anza, Juan Bautista de 218

Aragon 2, 18, 95, 121, 161-3, 279, 288

Aragonese faction 121, 173-6, 185-192, 301-7

Aranda, Conde de
early career: 102, 116, 156

Aranda, Conde de (continued)
chief of Castile council: 119-124, 149, 163
re: Jesuits & church: 121, 132-4
& Prince of Asturias: 175, 185, 240, 268, 293
heads Aragonese: 132, 173, 185-7
Falkland Islands & fall: 184-7
envoy to France: 187-9, 246, 268-273
pro-creole: 240
hawkish views v. England: 246, 273-5

Aranjuez 8, 113, 159, 304-9
treaty of: 84-8, 93

Areche, Antonio de 226-9, 237

Arriaga, Julián de 99, 173, 187-197, 204, 212-7

Asiento 2, 23, 36, 86

audiencias 18, 119, 201, 232, 240

Augustus III of Poland 27, 55-7, 180

Austria 1, 5, 27-55, 83-4, 93, 140, 177, 195, 213

Austrian Succession, war of: 38-46, 84

Azara, José de 132, 140-5, 152

Azores , battle of 263, 274

Bahama Islands 257, 268, 273

Bank of San Carlos 288, 310

Barbara of Spain  15-7, 83-
    90

Barceló, Antonio de  258-9
    264-6

Barcelona  22, 94, 207

Basques & Navarre  18, 143,
    157, 163, 204, 211-3,
    286-8

Beaumarchais, Caron de  247

Bernis, Cardinal F.  140

Bertrán, Felipe  153

Berwick y Liria, Dukes of
    21-4, 30

Bitonto, battle of  31

blacks & mulattos  36, 86,
    199, 209, 224-9

Bodega y Quadra, Juan  218

Bourgoing, Duke of  149,
    305-9

Bucareli y Ursúa, Antonio
    201, 212-5, 226-8

Buen Retiro palace  8-9, 14,
    92-8, 109, 277

Caballero y Góngora, Arch-
    bishop  234

Cabarrús, Francisco  281-8,
    298

cabildos  18, 120, 161, 201,
    212, 242

Cadalso, José  267, 297

Cádiz  194, 205, 213
    261-6, 280-4

California & no. Pacific
    215-220

Campillo, José del  51, 203

Campo, Bernardo del  192,
    273, 298

Campo Villar, Marqués de
    132

Campomanes, Pedro de
    pro regalism & golillas:
    130, 157, 293, 307
    as fiscal v. Jesuits:
    132-8
    re. education & labor:
    154-8, 171, 281-290
    re. Moreno colonies &
    Mesta:  158, 167-8
    Indies policy:  212, 236

Canada  218, 245

captaincies-general  18, 200

Carlos, see Charles IV

Carvajal y Lancaster, José
    86, 101

Caserta, palace of  63-7, 85
    106, 278

Castejón, Pedro de  193, 275

Castile & León  18, 107, 160-
    7, 280-9

Castile, council of  18, 90-5,
    104-7, 117-9, 124, 130-158,
    180, 212, 292

Castropignano, Duke of  30,
    39-45, 94

391

Catalonia 2, 18, 22, 94-8, 121, 163, 279-289

Catherine the Great 142, 180, 217, 264, 314

Cavanilles, Antonio 150

Cevallos, Pedro de 222-4

Charles IV (Prince of Asturias) 83, 94, 108, 149, 173-5, 185-191, 268, 293, 300-1, 314

Charles VI, Emperor 1, 13, 21, 34, 54

Charles Edward Stuart 24, 43

Charles Emmanuel & family 27, 39, 46, 84, 93, 176

Chile 231-6

China 297

Choiseul, Duke of 100-5, 132-5, 186, 208-9, 245

Church
    & Indies: 202, 211-8, 241-2
    & Inquisition: 70, 126, 134, 145, 155, 166, 197, 232
    & Naples 29, 35-9, 45, 52, 68-70, 93
    & Popes: 34, 45, 52, 68, 124-143, 153, 171, 185, 192
    & Spain: 116, 124-143, 157-9, 171, 308
    see also Jesuits

Clarke, Edward 162, 287

Colonia do Sacramento 102-103, 221

Commerce & Money, council of: 118, 281

comunero revolt
    see New Granada

consulados 211, 243, 281

Córdoba, Juan de 261-9, 274

corregidores 202, 227-231, 241

creoles 198, 201, 210-4, 225-7, 235-8, 242

Crillon, Duke of 266-9, 274

Croix, Francisco de 210
    Teodoro de 232-9

Cuba 38, 102, 206-7, 246, 257

Diderot & encyclopedists 116, 132, 155

Diplomatic Revolution 88

Dorothea of Parma 22-7

Duras, Duke of 85

economic societies 166, 290

Ecuador 229

Eleta, Father Joaquín de 94, 130, 140, 153, 173, 185, 236, 275, 305

Elizabeth sisters of
   Orleans  10, 54

Elliot, Sir George  259,
   269, 274

England
      & Italy: 5, 20-4, 38-
      46, 80, 258
      & Indies: 2, 23, 36-8,
      86-8, 136, 182-6, 204-8,
      215-9, 253, 270-3
      Jenkins' Ear & Austrian
      wars: 37-46
      Seven Years' War: 88,
      99-103, 260
      Charles' fear of: 40,
      89, 182, 196, 216-7,
      246, 283
      war with Spain, 1779:
      227, 234, 245-275
      see also Gibraltar

Ensenada, Marqués de 87,
   99,104, 122-4, 194-5,
   259

Escorial  8, 159, 304

Eslava, Sebastián de  38,
   233

factories, royal  18, 277,
   289

Falkland Islands  185-7,
   195, 216

Family Compact  28, 35, 41,
   100-5, 179, 249-251

Feijóo  16-7, 23-7, 95, 125,
   203, 306

Ferdinand VI of Spain  8,
   83-95, 127, 221, 260

Ferdinand IV of  Naples 83,
   94, 177, 256, 300-3

Ferdinand, Duke of Parma
   140, 178

Fernán Núñez, Conde de  113,
   303

Figueroa, Manuel Ventura  187

Fleet system  10, 205-7, 253

Flores, Manuel A.  233

Florida  37, 103, 248, 256,
   273-4

Floridablanca, Conde de
      general picture: 131,
      192, 272, 292
      & Charles  131, 192, 223,
      246-275, 292-5, 304-5
      work v. Jesuits: 141, 185,
      192
      pro golilla: 158, 185-
      192, 212
      role in trade: 169, 279
      & Indies: 199, 224,
      236, 240
      & war with England, 1779:
      245-275
      rivalry with Aranda:
      185, 192, 240-8, 268-
      271, 293

Foronda, Valentín de  290

France
      & Naples: 54, 77-85
      & Spain: 1-28, 35-8,
      46, 86, 99-103, 122,
      178, 185, 193, 205-9,
      246- 276, 283
      cultural influence: 17,
      23, 105, 116, 125, 132,
      155-6, 165-7, 297-8, 306-8

France (continued)
Charles' independence
of: 84, 100-4, 122,
167, 179, 185, 208,
246-9, 252, 266, 294
French Revolution: 120,
277, 315

Francis of Lorraine, Emper-
or 34-8, 46, 177

Frederick the Great 38, 43-
46, 88, 142, 167, 179,
313

Freemasons 70, 131, 146,
152, 311

Friends of the Nation societies
see economic societies

Fuenclara, Conde de 54-8

Fuentes, Conde de 99, 141,
189

Gabriel Antonio 84, 94-7,
167, 175, 300-4

Gages, Conde de 39-45

Galicia & Asturias 164,
194, 289

Gálvez, Bernardo de 238,
252-7
José de 193, 209-217,
226, 230, 238-248, 251-
257, 275, 304

Gándara, Miguel de la 165

Genovesi, Antonio 68, 81

George III 102, 182-6,
249, 267-9

Gibraltar 2, 20, 89, 248,
258-275

Godoy, Manuel de 302-3

Goya, Francisco 298-9, 304

Grantham, Lord 250, 267

gremios 122, 207, 281-3

Grimaldi, Marchese di
general traits: 105,
192
& Charles: 149, 166,
173-6, 192, 247, 294
& Seven Years war: 100,
216, 294
re. Squillace & Jesuits:
112-6, 132-8
re. golillas & Galvez:
173, 185-193, 209, 212
rivalry with Aranda:
173, 185-9
foreign policy & fall:
105, 176, 187-192, 248

Guatemala & Honduras 36, 87,
99, 103, 216, 233, 254-6,
273

The Hague, treaty of 5, 10-4

Harris, Sir James 105, 186,
264-5

Heredia, Ignacio de 269, 273

Herrería, Vizconde de la 217

Hussey, Father Thomas 262

Indians 195-9, 211, 227-233,
241

Indies
commerce & revenue: 19,
204-214, 222-9, 233-4,
242-3, 285
council of: 95, 118-9,
150, 200-7, 212, 229, 241

defenses: 37, 196, 209, 214-9
Indies in general: 36, 196-210, 242-4, 275, 310
mining: see under same
reglamento of 1778: 213, 238, 281
universities: 202-3

Intendants 18, 163, 220, 230-9, 244

Isabel Farnese
early years: 3-5, 12, 135
Italian aims: 5, 14, 20-7, 39, 46, 84, 258
influence on Charles: 6, 9, 17, 32-8, 42-8, 53-6, 85, 92, 121
treatment by Ferdinand: 8, 85, 91
re. Squillace & Jesuits: 113, 129, 133

Isla, José F. de, S.J. 139

Italy, north 2, 5, 34-9, 84, 93, 176

Jamaica 36, 253, 273

Jansenism 71, 126-9

Jáuregui, Agustín de 227-230

Jesuits 71, 104, 123-146, 152-4, 179, 185-221, 311

Jews 69, 311

John Gaston 14, 22-5, 34

Joseph I of Portugal 14, 222

Joseph II, Emperor 93, 179, 311-3

Jovellanos, Gaspar de 298, 308

Juan, Jorge 187, 195, 203, 229

Keene, Sir Benjamin 23, 86-9

Lacy, Conde de 217, 265

Lángara, Juan de 262-4

Lee, Arthur 247, 251

Leopold of Tuscany 60, 93, 177, 300

Liani, Francesco 59, 65

Lobkowitz, Count 33-45

Losada, Duke of 50, 94-9, 113, 148

Lottery of Spain 158

Louis XIV 1, 4, 11, 94, 125, 178

Louis XV 4, 11, 22-7, 84-8, 99-103, 134, 141, 178, 185

Louis XVI & Marie Antoinette 178, 246, 251-2, 266, 272, 300, 311

Louisiana 103, 208, 242-5, 252-4, 273

Luis I of Spain 8, 12

Luis, Cardinal-Infante 35, 85, 135, 149, 302

Luzán, Ignacio de 165

Macanaz, Melchor de 18, 203

Madrid
    cleaning of: 106, 121,
    149, 158, 290, 310
    life in: 107-9, 148-9,
    158, 284-7, 297-9
    routes around: 278-280
    royal economic society
    of: 167, 290-8

Malaspina, Alessandro 204

Malta 85, 139

manteistas & golillas 99,
    103-4, 116, 122, 130,
    173-5, 185, 190-2,
    210-2, 307

Maria Amalia 39, 55-63, 83,
    91-8, 148, 152, 175,
    299, 305

María Ana of Portugal 8-15,
    56, 176, 223, 303

María Antonia Fernanda 84-
    85, 176

Maria Carolina of Naples
    177, 300-3

María Josefa Carmela 60,
    94-7, 300-2

María Luisa Antonia 60,
    93-4, 177, 300

María Luisa, wife of
    Carlos 108, 174,
    189, 301-3

Maria Theresa, Empress 13,
    21, 34, 38-46, 88, 93
    177-9

Masserano, Prince 181-6

medicine 60, 90, 150-4,
    199, 202, 311

Medinaceli, Duke of 94, 111,
    161

Meléndez Valdés, Juan 298

Mengs, Anton 98, 299

Mesta 158, 168

mestizos 198-9, 242

Mexico 128, 136, 143, 158,
    197-219, 231-2, 236-242

mining & gold 10, 36, 107,
    198, 207, 213, 226, 234,
    242, 288

Minorca 2, 89, 248, 258, 266,
    273-5

Miranda, Francisco de 257

Mita 198, 228, 231

money & wages 72, 80, 107,
    121, 160-4, 285-8
    see also Commerce &
    money, council of; &
    mining

Montealegre, José de 40,
    51, 69

Montemar, Conde de 28-35,
    39

Montesquieu 125, 155, 165

Montmorin, Comte de 249,
    251

Moreno, Ventura 266-7

Morocco & Sp. bases  187,
    258, 295

Mourelle, Francisco  218

Muniain, Gregorio  116,
    173-4, 184

Muñoz, Antonio  165, 203

Múzquiz, Miguel  116, 173,
    183-7, 193, 212, 275,
    290, 304-7

Naples  28-96, 100-1, 120-9,
    139-140, 162-3, 177,
    180, 255-6, 286, 300-6

Nelson, Horatio  255

Netherlands  1, 5, 21, 80,
    205-7, 265, 276, 294

Newfoundland  100-3, 263,
    273

New Granada  36, 199-200,
    2336, 273

New Mexico  215-8, 232

Nicaragua  255

Normande, Pedro de  264

North, Lord  186, 249, 267

O'Higgins, Ambrosio  201-4,
    235

Olavide, Pablo de  155, 298

Oran  19, 87, 296

O'Reilly, Alejandro  188, 208

Orleans, Philip Duke of  4,
    10

Ossun, Marquis d'  94, 101,
    141

Palafox, bishop of Puebla
    130-3, 140-2, 193

Panama
    see Asiento & New Granada

Paraguay  87, 127, 143, 198,
    221-4

Pardo palace  14, 109, 159,
    304
    treaties: 37, 224

Paris, treaty of, 1763  103,
    216, 222, 254

Parma & Piacenza  6, 14, 20-8,
    34, 84, 93, 100, 139,
    176

Patiño, José  19, 22-9, 259

peninsulares  198, 201, 235-
    237

Peñafiel, Marqués de  166

Peñaflorida, Conde de  166

Peñaranda, Francisco  155

Pérez, Juan, navigator  218

Pérez Bayer, Francisco  153

Peru & Bolivia  128, 198-
    207, 220, 225-237, 242

Philip II  286, 311

Philip V  1-19, 22-35, 44-55,
    81-3, 135, 153, 258,
    370

397

Philip (Don) of Parma  8,
  38-9, 45-6, 84-8, 93,
  108

Philippines & Manila galleon
  102, 136-9, 202-7, 216,
  288

Pignatelli, Ramón  157, 189,
  279

Piquer, Andrés  89, 203

Pitt the Elder  89, 100-1,
  186, 216, 249

Polish Succession, war of
  27-35

Pombal, Marquês de  128, 222

Portugal & Brazil  1, 15, 87,
  102-3, 128, 140, 189,
  221-4, 258, 303

Prado, the  150

Puerto Rico  167, 270

Raineval, Gerard de  269-270

regalism  71, 126, 156, 171,
  292, 306-314

repartimientos  227, 231, 241

Revilla Gigedo family  113,
  239, 241, 258

Ricla, Conde de  184-9, 307

Río de la Plata  200, 221-
  224, 238

Ripperdá, Baron J.W.  13,
  51-4

Rochford, Earl of  122

Roda, Manuel de  131-5, 152,
  173, 185-9, 304

Rodney, Admiral George  256,
  262, 273-4

Romá y Rosell, Francisco  290

Rousseau, Jean Jacques  155

Royal Palace  8-10, 32, 98,
  112-9, 153, 304

Russia & Alaska  27, 80, 145,
  177, 180, 216-9, 264-5,
  295

Sabbatini, Francesco  64, 106,
  268

Salamanca, university of
  151-4, 202

San Fernando, royal academy
  of  150, 189, 299

San Francisco, California
  218

San Ildefonso  8, 14, 86,
  159, 304
  treaty of  223

Santisteban, Duke of  24-8,
  35, 51-8

Santo Domingo  270

Sarmiento, Martín  23, 203

Sempere y Guarinos, Juan
  290

Serra, Junípero  218

Seven Years war  88, 99-103, 183, 208, 216, 222, 260

Seville (& treaty of) 20, 165, 263, 280-7

Shelburne, Lord  267, 270

Sicily  32, 49, 51, 67-81

Sierra Morena colonies  156, 167, 215

smuggling  37, 79, 101, 206, 210-3, 284

Solano, José  257, 262

Sotomayor family  189, 258, 265-7

Spain
    army & navy: 19, 24-46, 87, 101-8, 116, 161, 182-195, 214, 244-276
    arts & literature: 98, 139, 297-9
    commerce & industry: 18, 101, 122, 161-6, 189, 213, 242, 277-290, 310
    economy & taxes: 18-9, 87, 106-8, 120-2, 160, 170, 285-291
    education & enlighten-ment: 16-7, 23, 104, 125-9, 134, 145, 151-166, 171-2, 290-1, 307-309
    foreign relations: see by country
    general state of: 1-3, 19, 95, 104-9, 121, 133, 159-165, 277, 290-7, 312

Spain (continued)
    government & laws: 18, 99, 106-121, 133-140, 150-176, 185-196, 206-213, 231, 240-1, 278-299
    noble orders & society: 17-8, 94-8, 104, 118-123, 129-133, 145-6, 152, 161-6, 170-5, 183-189, 282, 297-9, 306-312
    peasants & population: 103-8, 121-2, 158-171, 235, 278-288, 309, 312
    places in: 95-7, 115, 164-9, 277-9, 287-9, 299
    public works & welfare: 150, 157-9, 171, 278-9, 309

Spanish Succession, war of: 1-2, 13, 94

Squillace, Marchese di, & riots  94-9, 106-124, 133, 142-6, 153-8, 192, 216, 304-7

Sweden  80, 180

Tanucci, Bernado
    career in Naples: 51-53, 66-75, 82, 91-3, 306
    & Charles: 52-8, 66-71, 91-5, 106, 115, 137-8, 145, 178-181, 255-7, 268, 294, 304-6
    re. church & Jesuits: 68-71, 129, 137, 145

Texas  208, 215, 253

Tiepolo, Giovanni  98, 299

Torre, Marqués de la 265-7

Townsend, Joseph 173, 285

Trade, House or Board of
19, 205, 241

Traun, Marshal Otto 29-31

Túpac Amaru 229-233

Turkey & Barbary states
80, 181, 295

Tuscany, see John Gaston &
Leopold

Ulloa, Antonio de 195, 203-
208, 226-9

United States (& the Revolution) 219, 232-8, 245-
257, 270-3, 310

universities 81, 104, 129,
151-5, 202

Ursinos, Princesa de los
3, 85

Uruguay 221-4

Utrecht, treaty of 2-3,
36, 86, 199, 258

Uztáriz, Jerónimo de 203

Valdecebro, Father Andrés de
170

Valdés, Antonio 241, 275

Valencia (with city & university of) 2, 18, 95,
121, 154, 163, 278,
285-9, 296

Valle, Gen. José del 230

Velletri, battle of 43-6,
83, 184

Venezuela 204-7, 213, 281

Vergennes, Charles 245-8,
270-1

Versailles, treaty of 273

Vértiz, Juan José de 224,
235

viceroys & residencias 200,
210-7, 224-7, 231-9

Vienna, treaties of 13,
21-3, 34, 84

Villahermosa, Duke of 145,
189

Villalba, Juan de 210-4

Villaviciosa de Odón 2, 90

Vizcayno Pérez, Vicente 165

Voltaire 23, 125, 131, 155,
165

Wall, Ricardo 87-90, 99-105,
131, 156, 174

Walloon Guards 108-112,
121, 183, 305

Walpole, Sir Robert 20, 37,
119, 259

Ward, Bernardo 158, 203

Washington, George 37, 257,
273

West Indies  36, 206-7, 252, 270-3

Weymouth, Lord  186, 250

Winkelmann, Johann  62

women  49, 109, 166-7, 191, 282-5, 298, 311

Yaci, Prince & Princess of 90-4

Yorktown, battle of  257, 266

Zahn, Johann  16

Note:  Some place names and all commercial companies are given under their respective countries.  Thus Buenos Aires is under Río de la Plata, Cartagena under New Granada, company of Caracas under Venezuela.

ANTHONY H. HULL, Professor of History at Boston State College, Boston, Massachusetts, since 1966, is a graduate of Magdalen College, Oxford. After World War II service, he taught at schools in a number of countries ranging from England to Mexico and the Middle East. In the latter region he was appointed British government representative to the International Labor Office, a U.N. agency in Geneva, Switzerland. Coming to America, he subsequently took his Ph. D. in History at the University of Alabama. In the early 1960's he served as Hispanic manuscript specialist at American University, Washington, D.C. before joining Boston State College. He has contributed to a production on Hispanic manuscripts in the Library of Congress, and his other publications include a Teacher's T.V. Guide (2 vols., Montgomery, Ala., 1960), besides articles in periodicals such as the Sunday Times of London (November 22, 1959), and in journals such as the Hispanic American Historical Review (August, 1968).

Mr. Hull takes the view that the Hispanic world has been rather neglected in commercial books on History, and that students taking similar basic courses are being short-changed about Hispanic contributions to civilization or not being informed at all. To use his own words, "Spain alone, not to mention Mexico and a host of Spanish-speaking countries, offer a treasure mine of historical interest, the vein of which has been barely tapped. We have all heard of George III, but how many know sufficently about his greater contemporary, Charles III? The latter achieved much more with relatively less power at his disposal, and he gave his empire a final spurt of glory during his reign". Hull seeks to put the record straight with the present work.

In addition to history, he writes poetry and here his productions include two volumes -- From a Foreign Shore (Scrivener Press, Oxford, England, 1956), and Weather in Spectrum (Cambridge Circle Press, Cambridge, Mass., 1969). His works have appeared in Best Poems of 1962 (of Dryden, Va.,), and in the Shenandoah, Prairie Poet, and American Poet. He lives with his family in Sherborn, Massachusetts.